0°
20°E
40°E
60°E
80°E
100°E
120°E
140°E
160°E
180°
Arctic Ocean
80°N
ARCTIC CIRCLE
60°N
40°N
20°N
0°
20°S
40°S
60°S
80°S
TROPIC OF CANCER
TROPIC OF CAPRICORN
ANTARCTIC CIRCLE
NORWAY
SWEDEN
FINLAND
ESTONIA
LATVIA
LITHUANIA
(Rus.)
DENMARK
NETH.
GERMANY
POLAND
BELARUS
BEL.
LUX.
CZECH REP.
SLOVAKIA
UKRAINE
FRANCE
AUS.
HUNG.
MOLDOVA
ROMANIA
SWITZERLAND
ITALY
BULGARIA
GEORGIA
Naples, Italy
TURKEY
ARMENIA
AZERBAIJAN
GREECE
Instanbul, Turkey
TUNISIA
CYPRUS
LEBANON
ISRAEL
SYRIA
IRAQ
JORDAN
IRAN
KUWAIT
ALGERIA
LIBYA
EGYPT
Musha, Egypt
BAHRAIN
QATAR
U.A.E.
SAUDI ARABIA
OMAN
NIGER
Wodabe
CHAD
SUDAN
ERITREA
YEMEN
DJIBOUTI
NIGERIA
BENIN
TOGO
CAMEROON
CENTRAL AFRICAN REP.
Nuer, Dinka
ETHIOPIA
SOMALIA
Mbuti
UGANDA
KENYA
GUINEA
GABON
CONGO
SAO TOME & PRINCIPE
RWANDA
BURUNDI
DEMOCRATIC REPUBLIC OF THE CONGO
Maasai, Kikuyu
Hutu, Tutsi
CABINDA (Angola)
TANZANIA
SEYCHELLES
COMOROS IS.
ANGOLA
MALAWI
ZAMBIA
ZIMBABWE
MOZAMBIQUE
MADAGASCAR
MAURITIUS
NAMIBIA
BOTSWANA
SWAZILAND
WALVIS BAY (Status to be determined)
SOUTH AFRICA
LESOTHO
RUSSIA
Europe-Asia Boundary
KAZAKHSTAN
UZBEKISTAN
KYRGYZSTAN
TURKMENISTAN
TAJIKISTAN
AFGHANISTAN
PAKISTAN
Yarahmadzai
MONGOLIA
Bejing, China
CHINA
NORTH KOREA
SOUTH KOREA
JAPAN
Shanghai, China
Na
NEPAL
BHUTAN
Hijra
BANGLADESH
INDIA
TAIWAN
HONG KONG (U.K.)
MACAU (Port.)
MYANMAR (BURMA)
LAOS
Lua
THAILAND
VIETNAM
CAMBODIA
PHILIPPINES
SRI LANKA
MALDIVES
Agata
BRUNEI
MALAYSIA
Borneo
Sumatra
SINGAPORE
INDONESIA
Pacific Ocean
NORTHERN MARIANA ISLANDS (U.S.)
REPUBLIC OF THE MARSHALL ISLANDS
FEDERATED STATES OF MICRONESIA
Arapesh, Mundugamor, and Tchambuli
PAPUA NEW GUINEA
SOLOMON ISLANDS
Trobriand Islanders
TUVALU
Indian Ocean
FIJI
VANUATU
NEW CALEDONIA (Fr.)
Aborigines
AUSTRALIA
NEW ZEALAND
Maori
ANTARCTICA
1. SLOVENIA
2. CROATIA
3. BOSNIA AND HERZEGOVINA
4. ALBANIA
5. MACEDONIA

CULTURE COUNTS

A Concise Introduction to Cultural Anthropology

Serena Nanda
John Jay College of Criminal Justice
City University of New York

Richard L. Warms
Texas State University–San Marcos

WADSWORTH
CENGAGE Learning™

Australia • Brazil • Japan • Korea • Mexico • Singapore • Spain • United Kingdom • United States

Culture Counts: A Concise Introduction to Cultural Anthropology

Serena Nanda
Richard L. Warms

Anthropology Editor: Lin Gaylord

Assistant Editor: Liana Monari

Editorial Assistant: Arwen Petty

Marketing Manager: Meghan Pease

Marketing Communications Manager: Tami Strang

Project Manager, Editorial Production: Jerilyn Emori

Creative Director: Rob Hugel

Art Director: Caryl Gorska

Print Buyer: Judy Inouye

Permissions Editor: Roberta Broyer

Production Service: Dan Fitzgerald, Graphic World Publishing Services

Text Designer: Norman Baugher

Photo Researcher: Billie Porter

Cover Designer: Yvo Riezebos

Cover Image: Anthropologist Stacy Surla interviews a woman in the village of Akum, Northwest Province, Cameroon. Image © Adam Koons/Anthro-Photo

Compositor: Graphic World Inc.

Library of Congress Control Number: 2008927768
Student Edition:
ISBN-13: 978-0-495-00787-6
ISBN-10: 0-495-00787-0

Wadsworth
10 Davis Drive
Belmont, CA 94002-3098
USA

Cengage Learning is a leading provider of customized learning solutions with office locations around the globe, including Singapore, the United Kingdom, Australia, Mexico, Brazil, and Japan. Locate your local office at international.cengage.com/region.

Cengage Learning products are represented in Canada by Nelson Education, Ltd.

For your course and learning solutions, visit **academic.cengage.com.** Purchase any of our products at your local college store or at our preferred online store www.ichapters.com.

Printed in Canada
1 2 3 4 5 6 7 12 11 10 09 08

Dedication

To the grandchildren: Alexander, Adriana, Charlotte, Kai, and Waverly. —SN—

To the students of Texas State University whose questions, comments, and occasional howls of outrage have, for 20 years, made being an anthropology professor the best job I can imagine. —RW—

BRIEF CONTENTS

CHAPTER 1
What Is Anthropology and Why Should I Care? 1

CHAPTER 2
Culture Counts 21

CHAPTER 3
Doing Cultural Anthropology 43

CHAPTER 4
Communication 69

CHAPTER 5
Making a Living 93

CHAPTER 6
Economics 115

CHAPTER 7
Marriage, Family, and Kinship 141

CHAPTER 8
Sex and Gender 169

CHAPTER 9
Political Organization 193

CHAPTER 10
Inequalities: Class and Caste 217

CHAPTER 11
Inequalities: Race and Ethnicity 239

CHAPTER 12
Religion 263

CHAPTER 13
Power, Conquest, and a World System 287

CHAPTER 14
Globalization and Change 311

Glossary 337

References 345

Photo Credits 363

Index 364

FEATURES CONTENTS

FROM THE FIELD

The Nacirema 2

Autism and Culture 22

Arriving at Fontana del Re 44

Inner City Ebonics 70

Where Have All the Icebergs Gone? 94

Ultimate Dictator 116

A Society without Marriage: The Na of China 142

Neither Man nor Woman: The Hijras of India 170

Wealth and Power in the Asante State 194

The American Dream 218

Trouble in Paradise 240

Cargo Cults 264

Veterans of Colonial Armies 288

Global Poverty 312

BRINGING IT BACK HOME

Anthropology and Homelessness 17

Does the Idea of Culture Belong to Anthropology? Should It? 40

Anthropologists and Human Rights 64

English Only 90

You Are What You Eat: Culture and Food Choices 112

Product Anthropology 137

Polygamy in the United States 164

Female Genital Operations and International Human Rights 189

Do Good Fences Make Good Neighbors? 212

Government Responsibility versus the Gospel of Wealth 235

Class, Ethnicity, Race, and Educational Achievement 260

Religion, Art, and Censorship 282

Celebrating Ghana's 50th Anniversary 308

How Flat Is Your World? 334

DETAILED CONTENTS

CHAPTER 1

WHAT IS ANTHROPOLOGY AND WHY SHOULD I CARE? 1

The Nacirema 2

Specialization in Anthropology 7

- Cultural Anthropology 7
- Anthropological Linguistics 8
- Archaeology 9
- Physical or Biological Anthropology 10
- Applied Anthropology 11

Anthropology and "Race" 12

Why Study Anthropology? 13

Bringing It Back Home: Anthropology and Homelessness 17

- You Decide 18
- Chapter Summary 18
- Key Terms 19

CHAPTER 2

CULTURE COUNTS 21

Autism and Culture 22

Culture Is Made Up of Learned Behaviors 24

Culture Is the Way Humans Use Symbols to Organize and Give Meaning to the World 27

Culture Is an Integrated System—Or Is It? 30

Culture Is a Shared System of Norms and Values—Or Is It? 32

Culture Is the Way Human Beings Adapt to the World 35

Culture Is Constantly Changing 36

Culture Counts 39

Bringing It Back Home: Does the Idea of Culture Belong to Anthropology? Should It? 40
- You Decide 41
- Chapter Summary 41
- Key Terms 42

CHAPTER 3

DOING CULTURAL ANTHROPOLOGY 43

Arriving at Fontana del Re 44

A Little History 46
- Franz Boas and American Anthropology 47
- From Haddon to Malinowski in England and the Commonwealth 49

Anthropological Techniques 50
- Ethnographic Data and Cross-Cultural Comparisons 54

Changing Directions and Critical Issues in Ethnography 55
- Feminist Anthropology 55
- Postmodernism 56
- Engaged and Collaborative Ethnography 57
- Studying One's Own Society 58

Ethical Considerations in Fieldwork 60

New Roles for the Ethnographer 62

Bringing It Back Home: Anthropologists and Human Rights 64
- You Decide 65
- Chapter Summary 65
- Key Terms 67

CHAPTER 4

COMMUNICATION 69

Inner City Ebonics 70

The Origins and Characteristics of Human Language 73

The Structure of Language 75

Language and Culture 78
- Language and Social Stratification 80
- The Sapir-Whorf Hypothesis 82

Nonverbal Communication 83

Language Change 86
- Language and Culture Contact 87
- Tracing Relationships Among Languages 88

Bringing It Back Home: English Only 90
- You Decide 90
- Chapter Summary 91
- Key Terms 92

CHAPTER 5

MAKING A LIVING 93

Where Have All the Icebergs Gone? 94

Human Adaptation and the Environment 96

Major Types of Subsistence Strategies 98
- Foraging 99
- Pastoralism 100
- Horticulture 102
- Agriculture 105
- Industrialism 108
- The Global Marketplace 111

Bringing It Back Home: You Are What You Eat: Culture and Food Choices 112
- You Decide 113
- Chapter Summary 113
- Key Terms 114

CHAPTER 6

ECONOMICS 115

Ultimate Dictator 116

Economic Behavior 118

Allocating Resources 119

Organizing Labor 122
- Specialization in Complex Societies 123

Distribution: Systems of Exchange and Consumption 125
- Reciprocity 125
- Redistribution 127
- Market Exchange 130
- Capitalism 131
- Resistance to Capitalism 134

Bringing It Back Home: Product Anthropology 137
- You Decide 138
- Chapter Summary 138
- Key Terms 139

CHAPTER 7

MARRIAGE, FAMILY, AND KINSHIP 141

A Society without Marriage: The Na of China 142

Forms and Functions of Marriage 143

Marriage Rules 145
- Incest Taboos 145
- Exogamy 146
- Endogamy 147
- Preferential Marriages 147
- Number of Spouses 148
- Choosing a Mate 150

The Exchange of Goods and Rights in Marriage 151
- Bride Service and Bridewealth 152
- Dowry 153

Family Structures, Households, and Rules of Residence 154
- Nuclear Families 154
- Composite Families 156
- Extended Families 156

Kinship Systems: Relationships through Blood and Marriage 157
- Rules of Descent and the Formation of Descent Groups 158
- Types of Unilineal Descent Groups 158
- Bilateral Kinship Systems 162

The Classification of Kin 163
- Principles for the Classification of Kin 163

Bringing It Back Home: Polygamy in the United States 164
- You Decide 165
- Chapter Summary 166
- Key Terms 167

CHAPTER 8

SEX AND GENDER 169

Neither Man nor Woman: The Hijras of India 170

Sex and Gender as Cultural Constructions 172

Cultural Variation in Sexual Behavior 173

Male and Female Rites of Passage 177
- Male Rites of Passage 178
- Female Rites of Passage 179

Power and Prestige: Gender Stratification 180

Gender Relations: Complex and Variable 181
- Gender Relations in Foraging Societies 182
- Gender Relations in Horticultural Societies 183
- Gender Relations in Pastoral and Agricultural Societies 185
- Gender Relations in the Global Economy 187

Bringing It Back Home: Female Genital Operations and International Human Rights 189
- You Decide 191
- Chapter Summary 191
- Key Terms 192

CHAPTER 9

POLITICAL ORGANIZATION 193

Wealth and Power in the Asante State 194

Political Organization 195
- Power and Authority 195
- The Political Process 196
- Political Organization and Social Complexity 197

Social Control and Conflict Management 199

Types of Political Organization 200
- Band Societies 200
- Tribal Societies 201
- Chiefdoms 206
- State Societies 208

Bringing It Back Home: Do Good Fences Make Good Neighbors? 212
- You Decide 213
- Chapter Summary 213
- Key Terms 214

CHAPTER 10

INEQUALITIES: CLASS AND CASTE 217

The American Dream 218

Explaining Social Stratification 220

Criteria of Stratification: Power, Wealth, and Prestige 221

Ascription and Achievement 223

Class Systems 223
- The American Class System 224
- Class Stratification in China 229

Caste 230
- The Caste System in India 231

Bringing It Back Home: Government Responsibility versus the Gospel of Wealth 235
- You Decide 236
- Chapter Summary 236
- Key Terms 237

CHAPTER 11

INEQUALITIES: RACE AND ETHNICITY 239

Trouble in Paradise 240

The Cultural Construction of Race 242

Racial Stratification Systems 243
- Cultural Construction of Race in the United States 243
- Racial Classification in Brazil 245

Ethnicity and Ethnic Stratification 248

Ethnicity and the Nation State 249
- Ethnic Conflict 252
- Ethnic Stratification and Indigenous Peoples 253
- Ethnicity and Immigration in the United States 256

Bringing It Back Home: Class, Ethnicity, Race, and Educational Achievement 260
- You Decide 261
- Chapter Summary 261
- Key Terms 262

CHAPTER 12

RELIGION 263

Cargo Cults 264

Defining Religion 265

Some Functions of Religion 266
- The Search for Order and Meaning 266
- Reducing Anxiety and Increasing Control 266
- Reinforcing or Challenging the Social Order 267

Characteristics of Religion 267
- Sacred Narratives 267
- Symbols and Symbolism 268
- Supernatural Beings, Powers, States, and Qualities 269
- Rituals and Ways of Addressing the Supernatural 270
- Religious Practitioners 275

Religion and Change 278
- Varieties of Religious Prophecies: Revitalization Movements 279

Bringing It Back Home: Religion, Art, and Censorship 282
- You Decide 283
- Chapter Summary 284
- Key Terms 284

CHAPTER 13

POWER, CONQUEST, AND A WORLD SYSTEM 287

Veterans of Colonial Armies 288

Making the Modern World 290

European Expansion: Motives and Methods 291
- Pillage 292
- Forced Labor 293
- Joint Stock Companies 294

The Era of Colonialism 297
- Colonization 1500 to 1800 297
- Colonizing in the 19th Century 299
- Colonialism and Anthropology 304

Decolonization 305

Bringing It Back Home: Celebrating Ghana's 50th Anniversary 308
- You Decide 309
- Chapter Summary 309
- Key Terms 310

CHAPTER 14

GLOBALIZATION AND CHANGE 311

Global Poverty 312

Development 315
- Modernization Theory 315
- Human Needs Approaches 316
- Structural Adjustment 317

Multinational Corporations 319

Urbanization 322

Population Pressure 324
- China's One Child Policy 325

Environmental Changes 327
- Pollution 327
- Global Warming 329

Political Instability 330

Migration 331

Looking to the Future 332

Bringing It Back Home: How Flat Is Your World? 334
- You Decide 335
- Chapter Summary 335
- Key Terms 336

Glossary 337

References 345

Photo Credits 363

Index 364

PREFACE

ANTHROPOLOGY is the study of all people, in all places and at all times. Students and scholars alike are drawn to anthropology as part of the realization that our lives and experiences are limited, but human possibilities are virtually endless. We are drawn to anthropology by the almost incredible variability of human society and our desire to experience and understand it. We are drawn by the beauty of other lives and sometimes by the horror as well. We write *Cultural Counts* to transmit some of our sense of wonder at the endless variety of the world and to show how anthropologists have come to understand and analyze human culture and society.

Culture Counts is a brief introduction to anthropology written particularly for students in their first 2 years of college but is accessible to and appropriate for other audiences as well. Our goal has been to write in a clean, crisp, jargon-free style that speaks to readers without speaking down to them. Each chapter is relatively brief but is packed with ethnographic examples and discussions that keep readers involved and focused. Although it is written in an extremely accessible style, *Culture Counts* sacrifices none of the intellectual rigor or sophistication of our longer work, *Cultural Anthropology,* now in its ninth edition. Each chapter of *Culture Counts* opens with an ethnographic situation, circumstance, history, or survey designed to engage the readers' interest and focus their attention on the central issues of the chapter. These chapter opening essays raise questions about the anthropological experience, the nature of culture, and the ways in which anthropologists understand society. Passages later in each chapter refer readers back to the opening examples to show the ways in which they are illuminated by anthropological thinking.

Each chapter concludes with a feature entitled "Bringing It Back Home," which contains a relatively brief example of a current controversy, issue, or debate. Each example is followed by a series of three critical thinking questions entitled "You Decide." The questions encourage students to apply anthropological understandings as well as their own life experiences and studies to the issue under discussion. Through these exercises, students learn to use anthropological ideas to grapple with important issues facing our own and other cultures. They learn to apply anthropology to the realities of the world.

Design is an important feature of *Culture Counts.* One of our goals is to present students with a clear, easy-to-follow text that is uncluttered and that highlights the main source of anthropology—ethnographic data.

To address the visual orientation of contemporary students, we have taken considerable care to choose visually compelling photographs and to include high-quality maps and charts that provide visual cues for content and help students remember what they have read. Each image is linked to a specific passage in the text. Each photo has an explanatory caption identifying its source and importance. Extended ethnographic examples are accompanied by maps that provide the specific geographical location of the group under discussion.

PERSPECTIVE AND THEMES

As with *Cultural Anthropology,* our main perspective in this book is ethnographic and our theoretical approach eclectic. Ethnography is the fundamental source of the data of anthropology, and the desire to hear about and read ethnography is one of the principal reasons students take anthropology courses. Ethnographic examples have the power to engage students and encourage them to analyze and question their own culture. Ethnographic examples chosen to illuminate cultures, situations, and histories, both past and present, are used extensively in every chapter of *Culture Counts. Culture Counts* describes the major issues and theoretical approaches in anthropology in a balanced manner, drawing analysis, information, and insight from many different perspectives. It takes a broad, optimistic, enthusiastic approach and promotes the idea that debates within the field are signs of anthropology's continued relevance rather than problems it must overcome.

Additionally, we believe that issues of power, stratification, gender, and ethnicity are central to understanding contemporary cultures. These topics are given chapters of their own as well as integrated in appropriate places throughout the text.

Culture Counts continues the collaboration between Serena Nanda and Richard Warms. Warms's specialties in West Africa, anthropological theory, and social anthropology complement Nanda's in India, gender, law, and cultural anthropology. The results have been synergistic. Our experiences, readings, discussions, and debates, as well as feedback from reviewers and professors who have adopted our other books, have led to the production of a book that reflects the energy and passion of anthropology.

Both Nanda and Warms have extensive experience in writing textbooks for university audiences. In addition to *Cultural Anthropology,* now in its ninth edition, Nanda writes *American Cultural Pluralism and Law,* now in its third edition, with Jill Norgren. Warms, with R. Jon McGee, is author of *Anthropological Theory: An Introductory History,* now in its fourth edition, and of *Sacred Realms: Readings in the Anthropology of Religion,* second edition, with James Garber and R. Jon McGee. Collaborative writing continues to be an exciting intellectual adventure for us, and we believe that the ethnographic storytelling approach of this book will promote students' growth as well.

CHAPTER OVERVIEWS

Each chapter is organized so that the main ideas, secondary ideas, important terms and definitions, and ethnographic material stand out clearly. Although we have a deep appreciation for classic ethnography and cite it frequently, each chapter also presents current work in anthropology and includes many references to books and essays published in the past 5 years.

Chapter 1, "What Is Anthropology and Why Should I Care?" introduces the major perspectives of anthropology and the subfields of the discipline. It highlights race as a social construction and the many ways anthropology contributes to a sensitive understanding of human differences. The chapter explains the importance of anthropology as a university discipline and the reasons that understanding anthropology is critical in the world today. The chapter opens with the classic essay on the Nacirema, and the Bringing It Back Home feature is about homelessness.

Chapter 2, "Culture Counts," exposes students to a range of theoretical positions in anthropology by examining the ways different anthropologists have understood the idea of culture. It demonstrates that different theoretical positions lead anthropologists to ask different sorts of questions and do different sorts of research. The chapter concludes with a discussion of the cultural change mechanisms of innovation and diffusion. A full discussion of culture change and the expansion of capitalism is found in Chapters 13 and 14. The chapter opening essay explores the relationship between culture and autism, and Bringing It Back Home is about the uses of the idea of culture within anthropology and outside of it.

Chapter 3, "Doing Cultural Anthropology," considers the history and practice of fieldwork in anthropology. The chapter opens with historical background, describing the contributions of Boas, Malinowski, and others. It provides a brief analysis of the different techniques anthropologists use in the field, including participant observation, survey techniques, mapping, photography, and cross-cultural analysis. Issues in anthropological methodology and theory, including feminist anthropology, postmodernism, collaborative anthropology, and the problems of studying one's own culture, are discussed. The chapter concludes with an extended discussion of anthropological ethics. The chapter opening essay recounts the story of an anthropologist arriving at his fieldwork site, and Bringing It Back Home raises critical issues about human rights.

Chapter 4, "Communication," provides a solid background for anthropological linguistics. Phonology, morphology, and other elements of linguistics are briefly discussed. Much of the chapter focuses on sociolinguistics, particularly the performance of language and the complex interrelationships among culture, language, and social hierarchies. The chapter also explores nonverbal communication and the relationship of language change to political and technological changes. The chapter opens with a dialogue from African American English Vernacular, or Ebonics, and Bringing It Back Home concerns the English Only movement.

Chapter 5, "Making a Living," brings cultural adaptation into focus. It examines subsistence strategies, including foraging, pastoralism, horticulture, agriculture, and the industrial food industry, using extended ethnographic examples from the Maasai of East Africa, the Lua' of Thailand, Egyptian villagers, and the American meatpacking industry. The chapter opening essay focuses on the effects of global warming in the Arctic, and the Bringing It Back Home essay is about the cultural and environmental implications of consumer food preferences.

Chapter 6, "Economics," explores the nature of economic behavior and economic systems in cross-cultural perspective. Special attention is paid to issues of access to resources, the organization of labor, systems of distribution and exchange (including classic examples such as the potlatch and the kula ring), and reactions to the spread of capitalism. The chapter opening essay explores the results of experiments in which people from very different cultures play economic simulation games. Bringing It Back Home is about the use of anthropology by large corporations.

Chapter 7, "Marriage, Family, and Kinship," focuses on types of family systems, emphasizing the diversity of forms and functions of families. It includes sections on marriage rules, the exchange of goods at marriage, and family composition and residence rules, using extended examples from the Na of China, the contemporary American family, and the Hopi of the southwestern United States, among others. A section on kinship introduces the major kinship ideologies and the kinds of social groups formed by kinship. The chapter opening essay discusses the Na of China, a culture that seems to have no marriage practices, and Bringing It Back Home discusses polygamy in the United States.

Chapter 8, "Sex and Gender," begins with an explanation of the cultural construction of gender, using ethnographic data from cultures with more than two genders. It explores initiation rites for men and women and the relationship among gender, power and prestige, and the complex and variable nature of gender roles in foraging, pastoralist, horticulturalist, agricultural, and industrial societies. Key ethnographic examples come from India, New Guinea, Spain, Polynesia, and China. The chapter opening essay examines Nanda's work with the hijra, a third gender group in India, and Bringing It Back Home discusses the issues raised by female genital operations.

Chapter 9, "Political Organization," begins with a description of social differentiation in egalitarian, rank, and stratified societies. It goes on to explore the issue of power and social control before turning to a systematic discussion of leadership, social control, and conflict resolution in bands, tribes, chiefdoms, and states. The chapter opening essay describes the Asante State, a historic kingdom in West Africa, and the Bringing It Back Home exercise discusses illegal immigration and the construction of a barrier along the Mexico–United States border.

Chapter 10, "Inequalities: Class and Caste," begins by introducing functionalist and conflict perspectives on social stratification and continues with an exploration of the relationship among power, wealth, and prestige. It then describes achieved and ascribed status with extended examples of each. The chapter explores class in the United States and the increasing social differentiation in China. The section on caste focuses on India. The chapter opening essay describes the attempts of different Americans to achieve their social and economic dreams. The Bringing It Back Home essay explores the debate between those who favor and those who oppose strong government intervention to help the poor.

Chapter 11, "Inequalities: Race and Ethnicity," begins by exploring theoretical perspectives on race and then turns to a comparison of the racial stratification systems of Brazil and the United States. Following an examination of the concept of ethnicity from several theoretical perspectives, the chapter moves to an examination of the relationships between ethnicity and the nation-state. Using examples from Yugoslavia, indigenous peoples, and the immigration debate in the United States, the chapter shows the ways in which ethnicity is historically situated. The chapter opening essay describes how history, politics, and race intersected in a court case in Hawaii in the 1930s, and Bringing It Back Home is about race, class, ethnicity, and educational achievement in the United States.

Chapter 12, "Religion," moves from a brief consideration of the functions of religion to a definition of religion that includes stories and myths, symbolism, supernatural beings and powers, rituals, practitioners, and change. It then looks at each of these aspects of religion using examples from different cultures. This is followed by an exploration of the ways in which religion changes and the relationship between social change and religious change. The chapter opening essay about cargo cults raises questions about religion and materialism, and the Bringing It Back Home exercise raises questions about religion and the censorship of art in the United States.

Chapter 13, "Power, Conquest, and a World System," takes a historical perspective, exploring the ways in which the expansion of the power of today's wealthy nations fundamentally changed cultures throughout the world. It begins with an exploration of the motives and means for European expansion and discusses the effects of this expansion on people in the 15th through 18th centuries. This is followed by an analysis of the colonialism of the 19th and early 20th centuries and its effect on patterns of wealth and poverty in the world today. The chapter concludes with the decolonization movement of the mid-20th century. The chapter opening essay describes Warms's work with veterans of an African colonial army. The Bringing It Back Home essay describes the controversy over Ghana's 50th anniversary celebrations.

Chapter 14, "Globalization and Change," examines the challenges and prospects faced by peoples and cultures in the globalized contemporary world. It begins with a historical overview of development efforts and continues with an exploration of some of the key issues facing people in poor nations today. They include the presence of powerful multinational corporations, urbanization, population pressure, environmental degradation, social and political instability, and migration. The chapter concludes by emphasizing the importance of anthropological understandings as we face these issues. The chapter opening essay describes wealth and poverty in several locations around the world. The Bringing It Back Home essay explores whether or not advances in technology are creating a world of increasing opportunity and equity.

TEACHING FEATURES AND STUDY AIDS

Each chapter includes outstanding pedagogical features to help students identify, learn, and remember key concepts and data. Several learning aids help students better understand and retain the chapter's information, as follows:

- Full-color opening photos with captions are placed at the beginning of each chapter.
- An outline at the beginning of each chapter clearly shows the organization of the chapter and the major topics covered.

- Each chapter opens with an essay that focuses on an ethnographic situation, circumstance, or history designed to capture students' interest and launch them into the chapter.
- Each chapter concludes with a brief essay and questions that encourage the application of anthropological thinking to a current controversy, issue, or debate. The questions can be used as assignments or to promote classroom discussion.
- Summaries, arranged as numbered points at the end of each chapter, recap critical ideas and aid study and review.
- Key terms are listed alphabetically at the end of each chapter, for quick review.
- A glossary at the end of the book defines the major terms and concepts, in alphabetical order for quick access.
- References for every source cited within the text are listed alphabetically at the end of the book.

SUPPLEMENTS

Instructor Resources

- **Annotated Instructor's Edition.** To help you prep in record time for the course and to better enhance your students' learning experience, the authors have written almost 100 instructor's annotations under the following categories: Teaching Tip, Discussion Tip, Writing Assignment, Classroom Challenge, and Active Learning. Using their years of teaching experience, they have provided from 5 to 10 ideas for assignment and active student engagement for each chapter.
- **Online Instructor's Manual and Test Bank.** This instructor resource provides detailed chapter outlines, lecture suggestions, key terms, student activities such as exercises from the Anthropology Resource Center, PowerPoint slides, and test questions that include multiple choice, true/false, fill in the blank, short answer, and essay.
- **ExamView Computerized Test Bank.** Create, deliver, and customize tests in minutes with this easy-to-use assessment and tutorial system. ExamView offers both a Quick Test Wizard and an Online Test Wizard that guide you step by step through the process of creating tests, while its unique "WYSIWYG" capability allows you to see the test you are creating on screen exactly as it will print or display online. You can build tests of up to 250 questions using up to 12 question types. Using ExamView's complete word processing capabilities, you can enter an unlimited number of new questions or edit existing questions.

- **PowerLecture Multimedia Manager for Anthropology.** This new CD-ROM contains digital images and Microsoft PowerPoint presentations for all of Wadsworth's © 2009 introductory texts, placing images, lectures, and video clips at your fingertips. The CD includes preassembled Microsoft PowerPoint presentations and charts, graphs, maps, line art, and photos with a ZOOM feature from all Wadsworth © 2009 anthropology books. You can add your own lecture notes and images to create a customized lecture presentation.
- **Instructor Resources on the Anthropology Resource Center (ARC).** Supplement your resources with a community share-bank of digital images organized by key course concepts and a syllabus integrating the ARC with the first edition of *Culture Counts: A Concise Introduction to Cultural Anthropology.*
- **Wadsworth Anthropology Video Library.** Qualified adopters can select full-length videos from an extensive library of offerings drawn from such excellent educational video sources as *Films for the Humanities and Sciences.*
- **AIDS in Africa DVD.** Expand your students' global perspective of human immunodeficiency virus (HIV)/acquired immunodeficiency syndrome (AIDS) with this award-winning documentary series that focuses on controlling HIV/AIDS in southern Africa. Films focus on caregivers in the faith community; how young people share messages of hope through song and dance; the relationship of HIV/AIDS to gender, poverty, stigma, education, and justice; and the story of two HIV-positive women helping others.
- **Visual Anthropology Video (ISBN 0-534-56651-0).** Bring engaging anthropology concepts to life with this dynamic 60-minute video from Documentary Educational Resources and Wadsworth Publishing. Video clips highlight key scenes from more than 30 new and classic anthropological films that serve as effective lecture launchers.
- **Interactive Map CD-ROM with Workbook for Cultural Anthropology (ISBN 0-534-49560-5).** Bring concepts to life with this CD-ROM, which offers 10 interactive full-color maps covering contemporary topics such as global population, life expectancy, global income disparity, the global water supply, and global Internet usage. The accompanying booklet includes critical thinking questions that students can complete as homework or for extra credit.

Student Resources

- **Book-specific Companion Website** that includes interactive exercises, video exercises, flash cards, and quiz questions for each chapter.

- **Discipline-specific Anthropology Resource Center,** with interactive exercises, video clip exercises, Meet the Scientist interviews, a Case Study Forum with critical thinking questions, and more.
- **Additional Student Resources.** For a complete listing of our case studies and modules, go to http://www.academic.cengage.com/anthropology.
- ***Case Studies in Cultural Anthropology,*** edited by George Spindler and Janice E. Stockard, offer a diverse array of case studies that emphasize culture change and the factors influencing change in the peoples depicted. New topics include *Challenging Gender Norms: Five Genders Among the Bugis in Indonesia* by Sharyn Graham Davies (ISBN 0-495-09280-0) and *Hawaiian Fisherman* by Edward W. Glazier (ISBN 0-495-00785-4), which looks at the social, political, and economic aspects of fishing in Hawaii.
- ***Case Studies on Contemporary Social Issues,*** edited by John A. Young, offer a variety of case studies that explore how anthropology is used today in understanding and addressing problems faced by human societies around the world. Barry S. Hewlett and Bonnie L. Hewlett explore the cultural practices and politics affecting the spread of disease in their new case study entitled *Ebola, Culture and Politics: The Anthropology of an Emerging Disease* (ISBN 0-495-00918-0), while James F. Eder explores livelihood and resource management as a result of global changes in the Philippines in his new case study, *Migrants to the Coasts: Livelihood, Resource Management, and Global Change in the Philippines* (ISBN 0-495-09524-9), and Michael Ennis-McMillan explores water resource management in *A Precious Liquid: Drinking Water and Culture in the Valley of Mexico* (ISBN 0-534-61285-7).
- ***Classic Readings in Cultural Anthropology,*** Second Edition (ISBN 0-495-50736-9). Practical and insightful, this concise and accessible reader by Gary Ferraro presents a core selection of historical and contemporary works that have been instrumental in shaping anthropological thought and research over the past decades. Readings are organized around eight topics that closely mirror most introductory textbooks and are selected from scholarly works on the basis of their enduring themes and contributions to the discipline.
- ***Current Perspectives: Readings from InfoTrac® College Edition: Cultural Anthropology and Globalization* (ISBN 0-495-00810-9).** Ideal for supplementing your cultural anthropology textbook, this new reader will evoke lively classroom discussions about real-world challenges and opportunities of globalization. Selected articles about globalization are drawn from InfoTrac College Edition's vast database of full-length, peer-reviewed articles from more than 5000 top academic journals, newsletters, and periodicals.

- **Modules for cultural anthropology** include new modules entitled *Medical Anthropology in Applied Perspective* by Lynn Sikkink (ISBN 0-495-10017-X) and *Human Environment Interactions: New Directions in Human Ecology* by Cathy Galvin (ISBN 0-534-62071-X). Each free-standing module is actually a complete text chapter, featuring the same quality of pedagogy and illustration that are contained in Wadsworth/Cengage Learning anthropology texts.

ACKNOWLEDGMENTS

It gives us great pleasure to thank the many people who have been associated with this book. We are most appreciative of the helpful comments made by our reviewers: Augustine Agwuele, Texas State University; Stephanie W. Alemán, Iowa State University; Diane Baxter, University of Oregon; Frances Berdan, California State University, San Bernardino; Kira Blaisdell-Sloan, Louisiana State University; Margaret Bruchez, Blinn College; Catherine Cameron, Cedar Crest College; Haley Duschinski, Ohio University; James G. Flanagan, University of Southern Mississippi; Michael Freedman, Syracuse University; David A. Kideckel, Central Connecticut State University; Ian Lindsay, University of California, Santa Barbara; Heather McIlvaine-Newsad, Western Illinois University; Kenna Noone-Kirkpatrick, Seminole Community College; Kerry Josef Pataki, Portland Community College; Joycelyn Ramos, University of Akron; Alison Rukeyser, California State University, Sacramento; Kathleen Saunders, Western Washington University; Mary Jo Schneider, University of Arkansas; Henry W. Schulz, City College of San Francisco; Michael Spivey, University of North Carolina, Pembroke; Hal Starratt, Western Nevada Community College; Phillips Stevens, Jr., SUNY at Buffalo; Gerry Tierney, Webster University; and Sam Weitz, Michigan Technological University.

For their support and assistance, we thank Raksha Chopra, Kojo Dei, Stanley Freed, and Joan Gregg. For the use of photographs, we thank Soo Choi, Ronald Coley, Kojo Dei, Chander Dembla, Joan Gregg, James Hamilton, Jane Hoffer, Ray Kennedy, Jerry Melbye, Judith Pearson, and Jean Zorn.

We gratefully acknowledge the support of our universities and the help of the staffs of our departments at John Jay College of Criminal Justice and Texas State University–San Marcos. In addition, many of our students have contributed ideas, reflections, and labor to this project.

Our families continue to form an important cheering section for our work, and we thank them for their patience and endurance and for just plain putting up with us.

We are deeply grateful to the people at Wadsworth, particularly our Development Project Manager, Lin Marshall Gaylord, for their support, their encouragement, and their insight. In addition, we thank Paige Leeds, Editorial Assistant; Liana Monari, Assistant Editor; Alexandra Brady, Technology Project Manager; and Jerilyn Emori, Content Production Manager.

Finally, we thank Dan Fitzgerald of Graphic World Publishing Services, who shepherded us through the production process, and Billie Porter, who did the photo research.

The knowledge, editing skills, and superb suggestions made by the many people involved in the production of this book have greatly contributed to it.

ABOUT THE AUTHORS

Serena Nanda is professor emeritus of anthropology at John Jay College of Criminal Justice, City University of New York. In addition to *Cultural Anthropology,* ninth edition, her published works include *Neither Man nor Woman: The Hijras of India,* winner of the 1990 Ruth Benedict Prize; *American Cultural Pluralism and Law;* and *Gender Diversity: Cross-Cultural Variations.* She is also the author of *New York More Than Ever: 40 Perfect Days in and Around the City* and is currently writing an anthropological murder mystery set in the Indian immigrant community of New York City. She has always been captivated by the stories people tell and by the tapestry of human diversity. Anthropology was the perfect way for her to immerse herself in these passions and, through teaching, to spread the word about the importance of understanding both human differences and human similarities.

Richard L. Warms is professor of anthropology at Texas State University–San Marcos. In addition to *Cultural Anthropology,* ninth edition, his published works include *Anthropological Theory: An Introductory History* and *Sacred Realms: Essays in Religion, Belief, and Society* as well as journal articles on commerce, religion, and ethnic identity in West Africa; African exploration and romanticism; and African veterans of French colonial armed forces. Warms's interests in anthropology were kindled by college courses and by his experiences as a Peace Corps Volunteer in West Africa. He has traveled extensively in Africa, Europe, and, most recently, Japan. He continues to teach Introduction to Cultural Anthropology every year but also teaches classes in anthropological theory, the anthropology of religion, economic anthropology, and film at both the undergraduate and graduate levels. Students and faculty are invited to contact him with their comments, suggestions, and questions at r.warms@txstate.edu.

© Jean Pierre Dutilleux

Anthropologists study cultural practices such as widowhood all over the world. In all societies widows have special status, but there is great variability in cultural practices. During their mourning period, these widows in Papua New Guinea wear 40-pound necklaces. Thus, they are unable to bend and can drink from a spring only with the help of a bamboo rod.

CHAPTER 1

WHAT IS ANTHROPOLOGY AND WHY SHOULD I CARE?

CHAPTER OUTLINE

The Nacirema

Specialization in Anthropology

- Cultural Anthropology
- Anthropological Linguistics
- Archaeology
- Physical or Biological Anthropology
- Applied Anthropology

Anthropology and "Race"

Why Study Anthropology?

Bringing It Back Home: Anthropology and Homelessness

- You Decide

THE NACIREMA

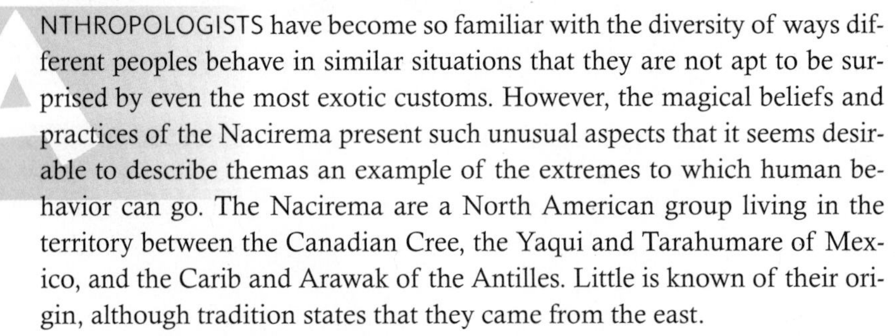

ANTHROPOLOGISTS have become so familiar with the diversity of ways different peoples behave in similar situations that they are not apt to be surprised by even the most exotic customs. However, the magical beliefs and practices of the Nacirema present such unusual aspects that it seems desirable to describe themas an example of the extremes to which human behavior can go. The Nacirema are a North American group living in the territory between the Canadian Cree, the Yaqui and Tarahumare of Mexico, and the Carib and Arawak of the Antilles. Little is known of their origin, although tradition states that they came from the east.

Nacirema culture is characterized by a highly developed market economy, but Naciremans spend a considerable portion of the day in ritual activity. The focus of this activity is the human body, the appearance and health of which loom as a dominant concern in the ethos of the people.

The fundamental belief underlying the whole system appears to be that the human body is ugly and has a natural tendency to debility and disease. People's only hope is to avert these through the use of ritual and ceremony, and every household has one or more shrines devoted to this purpose. The rituals associated with the shrine are secret and are discussed with children only when they are being initiated into these mysteries. I was able, however, to establish sufficient rapport with the natives to examine these shrines and to have the rituals described to me.

The focal point of the shrine is a box or chest built into the wall in which are kept the many charms and magical potions no native believes he could live without. Beneath the charm-box is a small font. Each day every member of the family, in succession, enters the shrine room, bows his head before the charm-box, mingles different sorts of holy water in the font, and proceeds with a brief rite of purification. The holy waters are secured from the Water Temple of the community, where the priests conduct elaborate ceremonies to make the liquid ritually pure.

The Nacirema have an almost pathological horror of and fascination with the mouth, the condition of which is believed to have a supernatural influence on all social relationships. Each day, Naciremans perform a complex set of rituals devoted to the mouth. Were it not for these rituals, they believe that their teeth would fall out, their gums bleed, their jaws shrink, their friends desert them, and their lovers reject them.

In addition to daily mouth-rites, the people seek out a holy-mouth-man once or twice a year. These practitioners have an impressive set of paraphernalia, consisting of a variety of augers, awls, probes, and prods. The use of these objects in the exorcism of the evils of the mouth involves almost unbelievable ritual torture of the client. The holy-mouth-man uses these tools to scrape, prod, and cut particularly sensitive areas of the mouth.

Magical materials believed to arrest decay and draw friends are inserted in the mouth. The extremely sacred and traditional character of the rite is evident in the fact that the natives return to the holy-mouth-men year after year, despite the fact that their teeth continue to decay. One has but to watch the gleam in the eye of a holy-mouth-man, as he jabs an awl into an exposed nerve, to suspect that a certain amount of sadism is involved in these practices. And indeed much of the population shows definite masochistic tendencies. For example, a portion of the daily body ritual performed only by men involves scraping and lacerating the surface of the face with a sharp instrument.

Nacirema medicine men have an imposing temple, or latipsoh, in every community of any size. The more elaborate ceremonies required to treat very sick patients can be performed only at this temple. These ceremonies involve not only the priests who perform miracles but also a permanent group of vestal maidens who move sedately about the temple chambers in distinctive costume.

The latipsoh ceremonies are so harsh that it is surprising that sick adults are not only willing but eager to undergo the protracted ritual purification, if they can afford to do so. No matter how ill the supplicant or how grave the emergency, the guardians of the temple will not admit a client if he cannot give a rich gift to the custodian. Even after one has gained admission and survived the ceremonies, the guardians continue to demand gifts, sometimes pursuing clients to their homes and businesses.

Supplicants entering the temple are first stripped of all their clothes. Psychological shock results from the fact that body secrecy is suddenly lost. A man whose own wife has never seen him in an excretory act suddenly finds himself naked and assisted by a vestal maiden while he performs his natural functions into a sacred vessel. Female clients find their naked bodies are subjected to the scrutiny, manipulation, and prodding of the medicine men. The fact that these temple ceremonies may not cure, and may even kill, in no way decreases the people's faith in the medicine men.

In conclusion, mention must be made of certain practices that have their base in native esthetics but depend upon the pervasive aversion to the natural body and its functions. There are ritual fasts to make fat people thin and ceremonial feasts to make thin people fat. Still other rites are used to make women's breasts larger if they are small, and smaller if they are large. General dissatisfaction with breast shape is symbolized by the fact that the ideal form is virtually outside the range of human variation. A few women afflicted with almost inhuman hypermammary development are so idolized that they make a handsome living by simply going from village to village and permitting the natives to stare at them for a fee.

Our review of the ritual life of the Nacirema has shown them to be a magic-ridden people. It is hard to understand how they have managed to exist so long under the burdens they have imposed upon themselves. But even exotic customs such as these take on real meaning when they are viewed with the insight provided by Malinowski when he wrote: "Looking from far and above, from our high places of safety in civilization, it is easy to see all the crudity and irrelevance of magic. But without its power and guidance early man could not have mastered his practical difficulties as he has done, nor could man have advanced to the higher stages of civilization."

The essay you've just read is adapted from a classic piece of American anthropology by Horace Miner. Despite being half a century old, it has lost none of its bite. The essay is good because it plays upon two critical themes that continue to draw people to anthropology: our quest to gain knowledge and understanding of people who are vastly different from ourselves and our desire to know ourselves and our own culture better.

Miner's essay draws you in as you read about the strange and bizarre customs of people who at first appear utterly different from yourself. You're titillated by the details of exotic customs of the other but also comforted by the scientific writing style that seems to assure you that somehow these odd practices make sense. At some point in your reading, you may have realized that Miner is, in fact, describing American customs as they may be seen from the point of view of an unknowing but perhaps quite perceptive observer. Your first reaction might be to chuckle at the narrator's misunderstandings and treat the essay as an example of just how deeply an outside observer might misunderstand a culture. But if you're a reflective person, you might have also wondered if the narrator hadn't turned up some fairly penetrating insights about the nature of our society. Clearly the narrator has misunderstood how Americans think about bathrooms, dentists, and hospitals. But is the narrator so far off in describing the American attitude toward disease, decay, and death? Finally, if you caught the joke early enough, you might have pondered the meaning of the quote that ends the essay: Have we really "advanced to the higher stages of civilization?" What does that mean anyway?

Miner's essay deals with some of the critical questions and desires at the heart of anthropology: How do we understand other people and actions that seem different, odd, or strange? Why do people do what they do? And, perhaps more profoundly, how do we go about describing other people's cultural worlds, and how do we know if these descriptions are accurate? We will return to these issues in many places in this book. But first, a brief definition and description of anthropology: **Anthropology** is the scientific and humanistic study of human beings. It encompasses the evolutionary history of humanity, physical variation among humans, the study of past societies, and the comparative study of current-day human societies and cultures.

A **society** is a group of people who depend on one another for survival or well-being. **Culture** is the way members of a society adapt to their environment and give meaning to their lives.

A critical goal of anthropology is to describe, analyze, and explain different cultures, to show how groups live in different physical, economic, and social environments, and to show how their members give meaning to their lives. Anthropology attempts to comprehend the entire human experience. Through human paleontology it describes the evolutionary development of our species. Through archaeology it reaches from current-day societies to those of the distant past. Through primatology it extends beyond humans to encompass the animals most closely related to us.

Human beings almost everywhere are **ethnocentric.** That is, they consider their own behavior not only right but natural. We often want other people to behave just like we do, and we feel troubled, insulted, or outraged when they do not. Indeed, part of our reaction to the Nacirema essay stems from the fact that the Nacerimans seem to do things that are neither right nor natural. However, as the essay suggests to us, the range of human behavior is truly enormous. For example, should you give your infant bottled formula, or should you breast-feed not only your own child but, like the Efe of Zaire, those of your friends and neighbors as well (Peacock 1991:352)? Is it right that emotional love should precede sexual relations? Or should sexual relations precede love, as is normal for the Mangaian of the Pacific (Marshall 1971)? If a child dies, should we bury it, or, as Wari' elders say was proper, should it be eaten (Conklin 1995)? And what about sex? Are boys naturally made into men through receipt of semen from older men, as the Sambia claim (Herdt 1987)? For anthropologists, these examples suggest that what is right or natural is not easily determined and that attempts to understand human nature and theories of human behavior cannot be based simply on our own cultural understandings. To accurately reflect humanity, they also must be based on studies of human groups whose goals, values, views of reality, and environmental adaptations are very different from our own. We can achieve an accurate understanding of humanity only by realizing that other groups of people who behave very differently from us and have very different understandings also consider the way they do things and understand the world to be normal and natural. One job of anthropology is to understand what actions and ideas mean within their contexts and to place these within the broader framework of human society, environment, and history. Anthropologists refer to the practice of attempting to understand cultures within their contexts as **cultural relativism.** It is important to understand that practicing cultural relativism does not mean that anthropologists believe all cultural traditions to be good or

Ethnocentrism is the belief that one's own culture is superior to any other.

© Margaret Bourke-White/Time & Life Pictures/Getty Images

to be of equal worth. People around the world, and indeed in our own society, do terrible things. Slavery, human sacrifice, and torture are all cultural practices. Anthropologists do not defend such customs on the basis of cultural relativism. However, anthropologists do try to understand how all cultural practices, even those that horrify us, developed, how they work in society, and how they are experienced by the people who live them. Both ethnocentrism and cultural relativism are examined in greater detail in Chapter 3.

Anthropologists bring a holistic approach to understanding and explaining. To say anthropology is **holistic** means that it combines the study of human biology, history, and the learned and shared patterns of human behavior and thought we call *culture* in order to analyze human groups. Holism separates anthropology from other academic disciplines, which generally focus on one factor—biology, psychology, physiology, or society—as the explanation for human behavior.

Because anthropologists use this holistic approach, they are interested in the total range of human activity. Most anthropologists specialize in a single field and a single problem, but together they study the small dramas of daily living as well as spectacular social events. They study the ways in which mothers hold their babies or sons address their fathers. They want to know not only how a group gets its food but also the rules for eating it. Anthropologists are interested in how people in human societies think about time and space and how they see colors and name them. They are interested in health and illness and the significance of physical variation as well as many other things. Anthropologists maintain that culture, social organization, history, and human biology are tightly interrelated. Although we can never know absolutely everything about any group of people, the more we know about the many different facets of a society, the clearer picture we are able to draw and the greater the depth of our understanding.

SPECIALIZATION IN ANTHROPOLOGY

In the United States, anthropology has traditionally included four separate subdisciplines: cultural anthropology, anthropological linguistics, archaeology, and biological or physical anthropology. In this section we briefly describe each of them.

Cultural Anthropology

Cultural anthropology is the study of human society and culture. As we have said, a society is a group of people who depend upon one another for survival or well-being. Anthropologists also understand society as a set of social relationships among people—their statuses and roles. Societies are often thought of as occupying specific geographic locations, but due to rapid transportation and electronic communication societies are increasingly global. Culture is the way members of a society adapt to their environment and give meaning to their lives. It includes behavior and ideas that are learned rather than genetically transmitted as well as the material objects produced by a group of people. Cultural anthropologists attempt to understand culture through the study of its origins, development, and diversity.

Change is one of the most basic attributes of all cultures and is clearly evident in any examination of recent society. Cultural anthropologists are particularly interested in documenting and understanding it. Understanding the underlying dynamics of change is critical for individuals, governments, and corporations. Many anthropologists study topics that have strong implications for this. For example, Scott Atran (2003, 2007) studies the origins and development of suicide terrorism in the Middle East, Caitlin Zaloom (2006) studies the ways in which technology affects the dynamics of stock and commodity trading in Chicago and London, and Michael Wesch (2007) studies the development of social networks on Facebook. Thus, cultural anthropology contributes to public understanding and debate about our promotion of and reaction to change.

Although most cultural anthropologists focus on current-day cultures, studying the ways in which societies change demands a knowledge of their past. As a result, many cultural anthropologists are drawn to historical ethnography: description of the cultural past based on written records, interviews, and archaeology.

Ethnography and ethnology are two important aspects of cultural anthropology. Ethnography is the description of society or culture. An ethnographer attempts to describe an entire society or a particular set of cultural institutions or practices. Ethnographies may be either emic or etic, or they may combine the two. An **emic** ethnography attempts to capture what ideas and practices mean to members of a culture. It attempts to give the reader a sense of what it feels like to be a member of the culture it describes. An **etic** ethnography describes and analyzes culture according to principles and theories drawn from Western scientific tradition, such as ecology, economy, or psychology. For example, the Nacirema essay is an etic analysis drawn from a psychological perspective. **Ethnology** is the attempt to find general principles or laws that govern cultural phenomena. Ethnologists compare and contrast practices in different cultures to find regularities.

Anthropological Linguistics

Anthropological linguistics is the study of language and its relation to culture. The human ability to use language is one of our most fascinating attributes. Other animals make noise too: birds chirp and elephants trumpet, but human noise differs from animal noise in important ways. First, humans have a huge number of words and complex patterns that we use to put them together. As far as we know, no other animal has as large a language. Second, we form communities of speech. Different groups of humans speak different languages, and each has culturally based customs for determining what kinds of speech are appropriate for different social situations. Finally, although researchers have been able to teach other animals to use very limited humanlike vocabularies and language structures, the use of complex language is central to being a human being. There are no groups of humans who don't use complex language. And, as far as we know, there are no other animals that, in their natural setting, do.

Anthropological linguists try to understand how words work in human communities. Sometimes they are interested in the histories of language. Sometimes they focus on the structure of language. More often they are concerned with discerning the patterns of speech and rules of verbal interaction that guide communication in different groups and in different social settings within a group. They focus on the social learning that enables people to know when it is appropriate to speak and what is appropriate to say.

Archaeology

A friend of ours once had a tee-shirt with the logo "All that remains is archaeology," a pun that gets close to explaining what **archaeology** is about. Human beings in every culture make physical changes to their environment and leave traces of their activities behind them. In some cases these changes are large and easily visible . . . like New York City. In other cases, the changes are very small: only a fire circle, small objects of stone, remains of meals, and, perhaps, places where wooden poles were stuck in the ground.

One of the fundamental insights of anthropology is that, although surprising things may happen, our lives are not random. The things we do form some sort of pattern. Consider two simple examples. Every day most professors leave their homes and go to their offices. The vast majority of their possessions are in one of these places with little scattered between the two. If you were to make a guess at professorial behavior based on the distribution of professors' belongings, you'd guess correctly that professors spent most of their time at their home or at their office. Similarly, if you were to look at professors' homes, you would find that in most cases pots and pans are located in the kitchen and the books are located in the den. You might occasionally find a book in the kitchen or a pot in the den, but that would be rare. From this distribution, you probably would conclude that, in general, professors cooked in the kitchen and read in the den. These simple examples get at a central insight: the patterns of our lives impress themselves on our material belongings.

The key focus of archaeology is to look at the material remains people leave behind and to try to infer their cultural patterns from it. Understanding this is important for at least two reasons. First, most people probably have an "Indiana Jones" conception of archaeology. In the movies, archaeology is about collecting exciting or beautiful objects for museums and personal collections. Although it is perhaps true that every researcher likes finding a really beautiful artifact, archaeology is not really about finding objects; it is about interpreting their patterns to provide insights into the lives and cultural ways of other people in other times. Second, a focus on pattern provides a small moral reminder. Archaeological sites are a highly limited resource. Once they are destroyed, they are gone for good. Looters and amateur collectors disturb sites to take artifacts. The loss of the artifacts themselves is bad, but these objects rarely have scientific importance in themselves. The loss of the patterns is far worse. A site that has been looted or otherwise disturbed cannot tell us much about the lives and culture that went on there.

Physical or Biological Anthropology

The fourth subdiscipline of anthropology is **physical** or **biological anthropology.** Physical and biological anthropologists study humans as physical and biological entities. Understanding human biology is critical to anthropology because all human culture rests on a biological base. For example, we have highly accurate depth perception, hands with opposable thumbs, and the ability to manipulate objects with great precision. These features are fundamental to the making of tools, and without them human culture would be vastly different, if it existed at all. Anthropologists are engaged in an often fierce debate about the biological origins of specific behaviors, but no one doubts that our evolutionary history, patterns of health and sickness, hereditary transmission of diseases such as sickle-cell anemia and cystic fibrosis, and many other biological factors both shape and are shaped by culture.

There are numerous foci within physical and biological anthropology, some of which are very well known. When we think about humans as biological organisms, one of the first things we'd like to understand is where we came from, our evolutionary history. **Human paleontology** is a focus within biological anthropology that tries to answer this question. Human paleontologists search for fossils to discover and reconstruct the evolutionary history of our species. They extract biological and chemical data from ancient bones or from living humans to help discover the biological histories of humanity and the relationships among different human groups.

Primatology is a second well-known focus in biological anthropology. Humans are primates, and other primates, such as apes, Old World and New World monkeys, and prosimians, are biologically very close to us. We share about 98 percent of our genes with our closest ape relations. Studying these relatives may give us important insights into the behavior of our evolutionary ancestors. It is useful to keep in mind that although the 2 percent genetic difference between us and our nearest ape relations sounds like a small amount, it is clearly extraordinarily important. It is that 2 percent that, in some critical way, makes us who we are. We learn more about what it means to be not-an-ape, to be human, by studying our nonhuman relations.

Forensic anthropology, a third major focus, is concerned with using the tools of physical anthropology to aid in the identification of skeletal or badly decomposed human remains. Forensic anthropologists identify the victims of crimes, warfare, and genocide. Their work often is critical in bringing those guilty of crimes against individuals or crimes against humanity to justice. In recent years, several books, including Mary Manheim's *The Bone Lady* and William Maples and Michael

Browning's *Dead Men Do Tell Tales,* and television shows, such as *Bones* and *Forensic Files,* have brought forensic anthropology to the public's attention.

There are numerous other fields within physical and biological anthropology. These include the study of human variation, population genetics, and anthropometry: the measurement of human bodies.

Applied Anthropology

From the start, anthropologists have been interested in the application of their studies. Anthropologists such as Franz Boas contributed to debates on race and foreign policy at the turn of the 20th century. Margaret Mead, Ruth Benedict, and others did studies aimed at helping America's war effort during World War II. However, in the first half of the 20th century, almost all anthropologists worked in universities. In the past 50 years, anthropology has increasingly become a full-time profession for people outside of academe. **Applied anthropology** is the use of cultural anthropology, linguistics, archaeology, and biological anthropology to solve practical problems in business, politics, delivery of services, and land management. There are anthropologists who analyze factory floors and decision-making structures for large corporations. There are those who try to determine the best ways to sell products or deliver services. There are anthropologists who work for hospitals and health care organizations, improving the ability of these agencies to serve their patients. Some anthropologists work in politics, performing foreign and domestic policy analysis for governmental agencies. Some are employed in trying to find effective ways to deliver aid to people in poor nations. There are anthropologists who work in museums and those who work on public lands, uncovering our archaeological heritage and both preserving it and making it available to the public.

In all of these cases and many others besides, anthropologists take the knowledge and the methodological skills they have learned in the classroom and through fieldwork and apply them to the real-world tasks of making money, providing better services to people, and, we would like to think, making the world a bit better.

Jerry Melbye

Forensic anthropologist Jerry Melbye and graduate students conduct a body recovery in San Saba, Texas.

ANTHROPOLOGY AND "RACE"

One thing that anthropology can help us understand is "race." In the United States, most people see humanity as composed of biological "races." Census forms, applications, and other documents ask us to indicate our "race." Although "race" is clearly an important social and historical fact in America, most anthropologists believe that "race" is not a scientifically valid system of classification. Despite more than a century of attempts, no agreed-on, consistent system of "racial" classification has ever been developed. We have put the word "race" in quotation marks in this paragraph to begin to focus your attention on these problems. To make reading easier, we dispense with the quotation marks for the remainder of the book.

There are many problems in developing a scientifically valid racial classification scheme. First, most Americans understand race as a bundle of traits: light skin, light hair, light eyes, and so on. But, if this is so, the races you create are the result of the traits you choose. For example, races based on blood type would be very different than races based on skin color. However, there is no biological reason to think that skin color is more important than blood type. Almost all traits we use to assign people to a race are facial traits. It is hard to imagine a biological reason why the shape of one's eye or nose should be more important than the characteristics of one's gallbladder or liver. It is easy to find a social reason: traits easily visible on the face enable us to rapidly assign individuals to a racial group. This is a good clue that race is about society, not biology.

There are many other problems with racial classifications. For example, if race is biological, members of one race should be genetically closer to each other than to members of different races. But, measurement reveals that people are as different from others classified in their same race as they are from those in different races. Or consider people from Central Africa, Melanesia (islands in the Western Pacific), and France. Most Central Africans and most Melanesians have dark-colored skin. Most French are light. However, Africans are more closely related to the French than either is to Melanesians. This isn't surprising considering the geographical distances involved, but it suggests that traits like skin color have arisen at many times and many places in the past. Furthermore, although the characteristics of our species, *Homo sapiens,* were fully present 35,000 to 40,000 years ago, a recent study argues that all current-day humans have common ancestors who lived only 2000 to 5000 years ago. At a time depth of more than 5000 years, all people alive today have exactly the same ancestors (Rohde, Olson, and Chang 2004). Thus, differences among people are very recent and unlikely to be of great biological importance.

Anthropology teaches us that the big differences among human groups result from culture, not biology. Adaptation through culture, the potential for cultural richness, and creativity are universal. They override physical variation among human groups. We explore issues surrounding race and ethnicity many places in this book, particularly in Chapter 11.

WHY STUDY ANTHROPOLOGY?

Let's be honest. If you're reading this book for a course at a college or university, what happened when you told your friends you were taking anthropology? Some certainly thought it was cool, but others no doubt said something like "Why would you do that? What's that good for?" If you're a traditional student (age 18–23) and you told your parents that you're planning on majoring in anthropology, they might have told you it was a great idea, but more likely they threw up their hands and conjured up visions of you moving back into their house in your mid-20s. So what did you tell them? Why should you major in anthropology or even take a course in it? Well, you might have told them that you want to work in some aspect of applied anthropology or you want to become a college professor, but we think there are other good answers as well.

Anthropology, in most colleges, is part of a liberal arts curriculum. The liberal arts generally also include English, geography, history, modern languages, philosophy, political science, psychology, and sociology. They may include many other departments and programs as well. Some liberal arts departments have teacher training programs. If you want to teach middle school English, in most places you probably need a degree in English. Some liberal arts programs involve training in highly technical skills that are directly applicable to jobs. For example, geography departments may offer training in remote sensing, acquisition and analysis of aerial photography, or multispectral and infrared imagery and radar imagery for use by government and business, highly complex skills with very specific job applications. However, the vast majority of liberal arts programs produce generalists. An undergraduate degree in psychology does not generally get you a job as a psychologist. Most people who study political science do not go on to be politicians, and few who study sociology go on to work as sociologists. In fact, survey data show that there often is little connection between people's undergraduate major and their eventual career. For example, in a survey of 3000 alumni from the University of Virginia School of Arts and Sciences, 70 percent reported that there was little such connection. This survey included many who had majored in subjects that required specific technical skills (University of Virginia 2006; Tang 2007).

In fact, both job prospects and the careers that people eventually pursue are about the same for students who study anthropology and for those who major in other liberal arts disciplines. Like the others, anthropology graduates go on to government, business, and the professions. Some are executives at large corporations, some are restauranteurs, some are lawyers, some are doctors, some are social service workers, some sell insurance, some are government officials, some are diplomats, and yes, no doubt, some still live with their parents. Any you could say the same of every other liberal arts program.

To refocus the question we might ask: What are the particular ways of thought that anthropology courses develop and that are applicable to the very broad range of occupations that anthropologists follow? How is anthropology different from other social science disciplines? Although there certainly are many ways to answer these questions, it seems to us that three are of particular importance.

First, anthropology is the university discipline that focuses on understanding other groups of people. This focus on culture is one of the most valuable contributions anthropology can make to our ability to understand our world, to analyze and solve problems.

Although America has always been an ethnically and culturally diverse place, for most of the 20th century, the reins of wealth and power were held by a dominant group: white Protestant men of northern European ancestry. Members of other groups sometimes did become rich, and many white Protestants certainly were poor. However, wealthy white Protestants held the majority of positions of influence and power in American society, including executive positions at most large corporations, high political offices at both state and national levels, and seats on the judiciary. As a result, if you happened to be born white, Protestant, and male, you had an advantage. Of course, you might inherit great wealth. But, even if (as was more likely) you were the son of a factory hand or a shopkeeper, you were a representative of the dominant culture. The ways of the powerful were, more or less, your ways. If members of other cultural groups wanted to speak with you, do business with you, or participate in public and civic affairs with you, they had to learn to do so on your terms . . . not you on theirs. They had to learn to speak your style of English, the customs of your religion, the forms of address, body language, clothing, manners, and so on, appropriate to their role in your culture. Because it was others who had to do the work of changing their behavior, you yourself probably were almost completely unaware of this; you simply accepted it as the way things were. Miami Herald columnist Leonard Pitts (2007) has pointed out that "if affirmative action is defined as giving preferential treatment on the basis of gender or race, then no one in this country has received more than white men."

Although the white, Protestant, northern European male is hardly an extinct species in America (such people today still control most of the nation's wealth), by the late 20th century, their virtual monopoly on power began to break up. In America, members of minority groups have moved to stronger economic and political positions. Moreover, America increasingly exists in a world filled with other powerful nations with very different histories and traditions. It is less and less a world where everyone wants to do business with America and is willing to do so on American terms. Instead, it is a rapidly globalizing world characterized by corporations with headquarters and workforces spread across the world, by international institutions such as the World Bank, the International Monetary Fund, and the World Trade Organization, and by capital and information flows that cross cultural boundaries in milliseconds. Americans who wish to understand and operate effectively in such a world must learn other cultures and other ways; failure to do so puts them at a distinct disadvantage.

At home, America once again is a nation of immigrants. Until the late 20th century, most immigrants were cut off from their homelands by politics and by the expense and difficulty of communication. In this condition, assimilation to the dominant American culture was essential. Although politics will always be an issue, today's immigrants can, in most cases, communicate freely and inexpensively with family and friends in their homelands and may be able to travel back and forth on a regular basis. Thus, complete assimilation is far less necessary or desirable.

Some people may applaud multiculturalism; others may bemoan what they feel is the passing of the "American" way of life. What no one can really dispute is that the world of today is vastly different from the world of 1950. Given the increasing integration of economic systems, the declining costs of communication and transportation, and the rising economic power of China and other nations, we can be sure that people of different ethnic, racial, and cultural backgrounds will meet more and more frequently in arenas where none has clear economic and cultural dominance. Thus, an understanding of the nature of culture and a knowledge of the basic tools scholars have devised to analyze it is essential, and anthropology is the place to get it.

In addition to this first, very practical application, there is a second, more philosophical concern of anthropologists. Like scholars in many other disciplines, anthropologists grapple with the question of what it means to be a human being. However, anthropologists bring some unique tools to bear upon this issue. Within anthropology we can look for the answer to this question in two seemingly mutually exclusive ways. We can look at culture as simply the sum total of everything that humans have done, thought, created, and believed. In a sense, as individual humans, we are heirs to the vast array of cultural practices and experiences humans have ever had. Anthropology is the discipline that attempts to observe, collect, record, and understand the full range of human cultural experience. Through anthropology we know the great variety of forms that cultures can take. We know the huge variation in social organization, belief system, production, and family structure that is found in human society. This gives us insight into the plasticity of human society as well as the limits to that plasticity.

Alternatively, we can answer the question by ignoring the variability of human culture and focusing on the characteristics that all cultures share. In the 1940s, George Murdock listed 77 characteristics that he believed were common to all cultures. These included such things as dream interpretation, incest taboos, inheritance rules, and religious ritual. More recent authors (Brown 1991; Cleaveland, Craven, and Danfelser 1979) have developed other lists and analyses. Brown (1991:143) notes that human universals are very diverse, and there likely is no single explanation for them. However, thinking about such commonalities among cultures may guide us in our attempt to understand human nature.

Finally, anthropology presents many useful ways of thinking about culture. One particularly effective way of understanding culture is to think of it as a set of answers to a particular problem: How does a group of human beings survive together in the world? In other words, culture is a set of behaviors, beliefs, understandings, objects, and ways of interacting that enable a group to survive with greater or lesser success and greater or lesser longevity. At some level, all human societies must answer this critical question, and to some degree each culture is a different answer to it.

In the world today and in our own society, we face extraordinary problems: problems of hunger, poverty, inequality, violence between groups, violence within families, drug addiction, pollution, crime. . . . The list is long. However, we are not the only people in the world ever to have faced problems. At some level, all of these problems are the result of our attempt to live together as a group on this planet. Learning how other peoples in other places, and perhaps other times as well, solved their problems may give us the insight to solve our own; we might learn lessons, both positive and negative, from their cultural experiences.

In some ways the cultures of today are unique. Societies have never been as large and interconnected as many are today. They have never had the wealth that many societies have today. They have never had the levels of technology, abilities to communicate, and abilities to destroy that our current society has. These characteristics make it naive to imagine that we could simply observe a different culture, adopt their ways as our own, and live happily ever after. We can no more re-create tribal culture or ancient culture or even the culture of industrialized nations of 50 years ago than we can walk through walls. But it does not follow that the answers of others are useless to us.

In Greek drama, the notion of hubris is critical. Hubris probably is best understood as excessive pride or confidence that leads to both arrogance and insolence toward others. In Greek tragedy, the hubris of characters is often their fatal flaw and leads to their downfall. Heroes such as Oedipus and Creon are doomed by their hubris.

We surely won't find that the members of other cultures have provided ready-made answers to all the problems that confront us. But to imagine ourselves as totally unique, to imagine that the experiences of other peoples and other cultures have nothing to teach us, is a form of hubris and, as in tragedy, could well lead to our downfall.

The ancient Greeks contrasted hubris with arete. Arete implies a humble striving for perfection along with the realization that such perfection can not be reached. With this notion in mind, we approach the study of anthropology cheerfully and with a degree of optimism. From anthropology we hope to learn new ways of analyzing, understanding, celebrating, and coming to terms with the enormous variations in human cultural behavior. We hope to be able to think creatively about what it means to be human beings and to use what we learn to provide insight into the issues, problems, and possibilities of our own culture. We hope that, with the help of such understanding, we will leave the world a better place than we found it.

BRINGING IT BACK HOME: ANTHROPOLOGY AND HOMELESSNESS

Most anthropologists would like their work to further a deep understanding of the human condition. But they also want to provide practical help that enables people to live their lives and do their jobs more effectively. They want to help find meaningful solutions for problems in our own society. The work of Vincent Lyon-Callo, an anthropologist who studies social services for homeless people, is a good example. Lyon-Callo hopes to understand homelessness but also to move attention on its causes to the center of American culture and politics.

Lyon-Callo believes that most homelessness in the United States results from a cultural and political philosophy that embraces the free markets and private initiative as the solution to social problems. He argues that most Americans believe the problem of homelessness can be solved through charity or services aimed at reforming homeless people, who are seen as deviant or disabled. This understanding undercuts attempts to see homelessness as a result of systemic inequalities, such as increasing unemployment, declining relative wages, and exploitation of workers. Lyon-Callo argues that by distracting action from these issues, the social services orientation helps to maintain homelessness.

Working in collaboration with community members and homeless people in Northampton, Massachusetts, Lyon-Callo promoted new understandings of homelessness. His emphasis on structural causes of homelessness, such as lack of jobs and lack of housing, led to the creation of a winter-cot program in community churches, a living-wage campaign, and new job opportunities for the homeless.

Lyon-Callo suggests that anthropological analysis can challenge routine understandings, raise new questions, and get people to think in new ways. He argues that in the absence of political efforts to transform the economy, caring and helping cannot themselves end homelessness. Anthropologists must work in public political forums to expose the connections between social problems, political ideologies, and inequality. However, promoting profound change is slow and discouraging work. Even those who basically agree with Lyon-Callo note that the current social service approach at least offers a degree of immediate hope for homeless people.

YOU DECIDE

1. Lyon-Callo promotes a politically engaged anthropology in which the researchers become advocates for their subjects. What are the advantages and disadvantages of such an approach?
2. Lyon-Callo's research focuses on a critique of American society, and the critical problems he identifies are very difficult to correct. Have you ever had a problem that seemed impossible to solve? Did you wish the problem would go away, or did you enjoy "digging in" and finding a solution? Is it fair to be critical of your society? Are you?
3. What are some specific American cultural values that underlie both the causes and the treatment of homelessness in the United States? How might an understanding of those cultural values help provide solutions to the problem of homelessness? Have you ever spent the night outside? Was it because you wanted to, or was it beyond your control? Was it fun? Were you scared? What did others think? Would you do it again? Could you live like that?

CHAPTER SUMMARY

1. The essay on "Body Ritual Among the Nacirema" by Horace Miner illustrates two critical themes that continue to draw people to anthropology: our quest to gain knowledge and understanding of people who are vastly different from ourselves and our desire to know ourselves and our own culture better.

2. Anthropology is a comparative study of humankind. Anthropologists study human beings in the past and in the present and in every corner of the world.
3. Anthropology is holistic. Anthropologists study the entire range of human social, political, economic, and religious behavior as well as the relationships among the different aspects of human behavior.
4. Anthropology is divided into subfields: cultural anthropology, anthropological linguistics, archaeology, biological or physical anthropology, and applied anthropology.
5. Anthropology stresses the importance of culture in human adaptation. It asserts that critical differences among individuals are cultural rather than biological.
6. Anthropology demonstrates that race is not a valid scientific category but rather is a social and cultural construct.
7. Anthropology is part of the liberal arts curriculum. Both the job prospects and the careers of those who study anthropology are similar to those who study other liberal arts disciplines.
8. Anthropology courses develop three important ways of thought that are applicable to the broad range of occupations followed by anthropologists. (1) Anthropology focuses on understanding other groups of people. (2) Anthropologists grapple with the question of what it means to be a human being. Anthropology is the discipline that attempts to observe, collect, record, and understand the full range of human cultural experience. (3) Anthropology presents many useful ways of thinking about culture.
9. Learning how other peoples in other places solved their problems may give us insight into solving our own problems. In addition, we can learn lessons, both positive and negative, from their cultural experience.

KEY TERMS

Anthropological linguistics
Anthropology
Applied anthropology
Archaeology
Biological (or physical) anthropology
Cultural anthropology
Cultural relativism
Culture
Emic

Ethnocentrism
Ethnography
Ethnology
Etic
Forensic anthropology
Holism
Human paleontology
Primatology
Society

© adrian arbib/Alamy

Many dimensions of culture are expressed in the ritual dress of these Masaai men participating in an initiation ritual. They are dressed in styles and patterns that have been used by the Masaai for many years, but each wears a wristwatch as well.

CHAPTER 2

CULTURE COUNTS

CHAPTER OUTLINE

Autism and Culture

Culture Is Made Up of Learned Behaviors

Culture Is the Way Humans Use Symbols to Organize and Give Meaning to the World

Culture Is an Integrated System—Or Is It?

Culture Is a Shared System of Norms and Values—Or Is It?

Culture Is the Way Human Beings Adapt to the World

Culture Is Constantly Changing

Culture Counts

Bringing It Back Home: Does the Idea of Culture Belong to Anthropology? Should It?

- You Decide

AUTISM AND CULTURE

AUTISM is a developmental disorder characterized by difficulties in both verbal and nonverbal communication, impairment of social interaction, and a host of other symptoms. It is generally diagnosed in children between the ages of 18 and 36 months. The incidence of autism is increasing rapidly in the United States, and a government report issued in early 2007 states that autism may affect as many as one in 150 children. Given that statistic, you likely either know or know of someone with autism.

Autism can occur at many different levels of severity. Some individuals with profound autism are silent and profoundly withdrawn. However, many others have a mild-to-moderate form of autism called *Asperger's syndrome.* People with Asperger's syndrome can master language and learn to participate in society.

Some individuals with autism or Asperger's have exceptional intellectual skills. Dr. Temple Grandin is among the best known of such people. Dr. Grandin is an associate professor of animal science at Colorado State University. As a researcher, Grandin is best known for her work on the humane slaughter of cattle. However, Grandin has also written extensively on her experience with autism and the ways in which she has learned to interact with other people and navigate her social world.

As Grandin and psychologist Oliver Sacks explain it, autistics think in extremely concrete terms and have profound difficulty understanding social conventions and cultural presuppositions of every sort. Some researchers say that autistics lack a "theory of mind." That is, autistics find it very hard to attribute mental states, such as intention, desire, deceit, and belief, to others or perhaps even to themselves. Although Grandin does not agree with this analysis, her work shows that she has learned to relate to others in ways that are fundamentally different from the ways of most people. Writing about Grandin, Sacks (1995:270) says, "The implicit knowledge, which every normal person accumulates and generates throughout life on the basis of experience and encounters with others, Temple seems to be largely devoid of. Lacking it, she has instead to 'compute' others' intentions and states of mind, to try to make algorithmic and explicit, what for the rest of us is second nature." Members of another, highly functioning autistic family interviewed by Sacks (1995:276) said, "We know the rules and conventions of the 'normal' but there is no actual transit. You act normal, you learn the rules and obey them. . . . You learn to ape human behavior . . . [but] don't understand what is behind the social conventions."

Grandin has often described herself as an "anthropologist on Mars." To her, being in human society is like being on a different planet. She is an outsider confronted with a wholly different way of life. She can observe what people do, but their actions make no sense. She has no intuitive feel for the things going on around her. In other words, for Grandin, other people have this thing we call "culture." Either she lacks culture, or her culture is enormously different from what other people have. Grandin has been very successful because she has learned to imitate normality. That is, through observation and analysis (and with the help of mentors) she has learned many of the rules of cultural behavior. She has learned when she needs to say certain things and to perform certain actions. But, despite her success, Sacks reports that Grandin does not think she understands others. She feels that there is something mechanical about her mind and that "the emotion circuit is not hooked up" (Sacks 1995:286). For example, when Sacks and Grandin visit the Rocky Mountains, Grandin tells Sacks, "you look at the brook, at the flowers. I see what great pleasure you get out of it. I'm denied that. . . . You get such joy out of the sunset. . . . I wish I did too. I know it's beautiful, but I don't 'get' it" (Sacks 1995:293–294). The classical music critic Tim Page (2007:36), who has Asperger's syndrome, recently wrote: "I am left with the melancholy sensation that my life has been spent in a perpetual state of parallel play, alongside, but distinctly apart from, the rest of humanity."

Accounts of autistic individuals such as Grandin and Page show that it is extremely difficult for them to become functioning members of society. Grandin's experiences as well as her notion of herself as an anthropologist on Mars strongly suggest that she does not participate in culture in the way that most people do. Such cases make it clear that, without the constraints, assumptions, and patterns imposed by culture, it is extraordinarily difficult to express our human qualities and abilities. But what is culture?

Although it is difficult to come up with a useful brief definition of culture, an anthropologist from Mars observing the many different human cultures might come up with six characteristics shared by all cultures.

1. Cultures are made up of learned behaviors. People are not born knowing their culture. They learn it through a process called **enculturation.**
2. Cultures all involve classification systems and symbols. A **symbol** is simply something that stands for something else. People use cultural symbols to create meaning.
3. Cultures are patterned and integrated. Thus, changes in one aspect of culture affect other aspects. However, elements of culture do not necessarily work smoothly with one another.
4. Cultures are shared. Although there may be disagreement about many aspects of a culture, there must be considerable consensus as well.

5. Cultures are adaptive and include information about how to survive in the world. Cultures also contain much that is maladaptive.
6. Cultures are subject to change. Whether propelled by their internal dynamics or acted upon by outside forces, cultures are always in flux.

Based on this list, we might define culture as the learned, symbolic, at least partially adaptive, and ever-changing patterns of behavior and meaning shared by members of a group. Although anthropologists agree on the basic characteristics of culture, they disagree on their relative importance, how to study them, and indeed the goal of anthropology itself. For example, some anthropologists are deeply concerned with observable behavior. For these scholars, what people actually do is far more important than what they say or how they understand the world. Other anthropologists take precisely the opposite view. Their primary goal is to comprehend the ways in which other people understand their world. Some anthropologists hope to find general laws of human cultural behavior. Others are more concerned with describing cultures or describing specific aspects of culture. These disagreements reflect different theoretical positions within anthropology. For our purposes, an anthropological theory is a set of propositions about which aspects of culture are critical, how they should be studied, and what the goal of studying them should be. Although those who hold different theoretical perspectives may insist that there is a right way and a wrong way to do anthropology, we suggest that theoretical perspectives are more like different windows through which one may view culture. Just as the view changes as one moves from one window of a building to another, so does the anthropologist's understanding of society change as he or she changes focus from one aspect of culture to another. Just as two windows may have views that overlap or views that show totally different scenes, perspectives on culture may overlap or reveal totally different aspects. In this chapter, we examine each element of our definition of culture. Each is a common characteristic of all human groups. However, each also raises questions, problems, and contradictions. Through examining these elements we come to a keener appreciation of the nature of culture and, ultimately, what it means to be human.

CULTURE IS MADE UP OF LEARNED BEHAVIORS

Just about everything that is animate learns. Your dog, your cat, even your fish show some learned behavior. But, as far as we know, no other creature has as much learned behavior as human beings. Almost every aspect of our lives is layered with learning. Our heart beats, our eyes blink, and our knees respond reflexively to the doctor's rubber mallet, but to get much beyond that, we need learning. Food is a good example. Humans must eat; that much is determined biologically. However, we don't just eat; our culture teaches us what is edible and what is not. Many things that are perfectly nutritious we decline as not-food. Many insects, for example, are perfectly edible. The philosopher Aristotle was particularly fond of eating cicadas, and Northern Europeans ate some species of beetles well into the 19th century. Yet most Americans have learned that insects are not-food, and they will go hungry, to the point of starvation, before eating them. Further, we eat particular things at particular times, in particular places, and with particular people. For example, although it is perfectly acceptable to eat popcorn at the movies, you would be unlikely to have lamb chops and asparagus there, or a nice stir-fry.

We sometimes think of learning as an aspect of childhood, but in every society, human beings learn their culture continuously. We are socialized from the moment of our births to the time of our deaths. Although in many societies large demands for labor and responsible behavior may be placed on children, all humans remain physically, emotionally, and intellectually immature well into their teen years and perhaps into their early 20s. This lengthy period of immaturity has profound implications. First, it allows time for an enormous amount of childhood learning. This means that very few specific behaviors need be under direct genetic or biological control. Second, it demands that human cultures be designed to provide relatively stable environments that protect the young for long periods of time.

Human infants become adults in a particular human society. Thus, the infant grows into a child and later into an adult not simply as a human but as a particular kind of human: a Kwakiutl, Trobriand Islander, Briton, or Tahitian. Child-rearing practices in all cultures are designed to produce adults who know the skills, norms, and behavior patterns of their society—the cultural content. But the transmission of culture involves more than just knowing these things. It also involves patterning children's attitudes, motivations, values, perceptions, and beliefs so that they can function in their society (which itself adapts to external requirements of the physical and social environment). The process of learning to be a member of a particular cultural group is called enculturation.

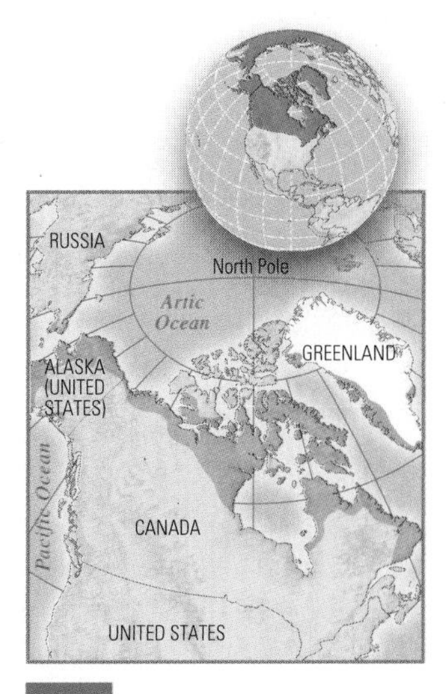

The Inuit.

As an example, we can consider child rearing among the Inuit, a hunting people of the Arctic. The Inuit teach their children to deal with a world that is a dangerously problematic place, in which making wrong decisions might well mean death (Briggs 1991). To survive in this harsh environment, Inuit must learn to maintain a "constant state of alertness" and an "experimental way of living." Therefore, developing skills for solving problems quickly and spontaneously is central to Inuit child rearing. Children are brought up to constantly test their physical skills in order to extend them and to learn their own capacity for pain and endurance (Stern 1999).

Inuit children learn largely through observing their elders. Children are discouraged from asking questions. Rather, when confronted with a problem situation, they are expected to observe closely, to reason, and to find solutions independently. They watch, practice, and then are tested, frequently by adults asking them questions. For example, when traveling on the featureless, snow-covered tundra, an adult may ask a child, "Where are we?" "Have you ever been here before?"

Play is a critical part of Inuit child rearing. Inuit games prepare children for the rigors of the arctic environment by stressing hand–eye coordination, problem solving, and physical strength and endurance. Some games involve learning by taking objects apart and trying to put them back together. This process develops careful attention to details and relationships, to patient trial and error, and to a mental recording of results for future reference. Many games stress the body and test the limits of the individual's psychological and physical endurance (Nelson 1983). For example, in the ear pull game, a thin loop of leather is positioned behind the ears of each of two competitors, who then pull away from each other until one gives up in pain (Canadian Broadcasting Company 1982).

The emphasis on experiential learning means that Inuit children are less physically restrained or verbally reprimanded than children in many other cultures. Inuit mothers are willing to permit a child to experiment with potentially harmful behavior so that the child learns not to repeat it.

The Inuit ear pull game is a harsh test of physical endurance. Contestants pull against each other until one can no longer endure the pain.

In addition to being physically adept and independent, Inuit children must learn to be cooperative and emotionally restrained. Under the conditions of their closely knit and often isolated camp life, expressions of anger or aggression are avoided. The Inuit prize reason, judgment, and emotional control, and these characteristics are thought to grow naturally as children grow.

The Inuit believe that children have both the ability and the wish to learn. Thus, educating a child consists of providing the necessary information, which sooner or later the child will remember. Scolding is seen as futile. Children will learn when they are ready; there is no point in forcing a child to learn something before he or she is ready to remember it. Inuit elders believe that frequent scolding makes children hostile, rebellious, and impervious to the opinions of others.

The study of enculturation has a central place in the history of anthropology and gave rise to some of its classic works. Margaret Mead's 1928 book, *Coming of Age in Samoa,* was a popular bestseller and a landmark work that changed how Americans looked at childhood and culture (Mead 1971/1928). Mead and others who studied childhood learning are known as **culture and personality** theorists. Culture and personality theorists held that cultures could best be understood by examining the patterns of child rearing and considering their effect on adult lives and social institutions. Culture and personality theory was extremely influential from the 1920s to the 1950s. Although few anthropologists today would call themselves culture and personality theorists, enculturation remains an important topic of anthropological research.

CULTURE IS THE WAY HUMANS USE SYMBOLS TO ORGANIZE AND GIVE MEANING TO THE WORLD

Consider this: Can you really see your environment? For example, when you walk into a classroom, you notice friends and other students, the professor, the video equipment, and so on. You might spend an entire semester without ever seeing the cracks in the ceiling, the pattern of the carpeting, or the color of the walls. Yet these things are as physically present as the chairs and your friends.

You see certain things in the classroom and overlook others because you mentally organize the contents of the classroom with respect to your role as a student. It is virtually impossible to see things without organizing and evaluating them in some manner. If you paid as much attention to the cracks in the wall, the patterns on the floor, and the humming of the ventilation system as you did to the professor's lecture, not only would you likely fail the class, but you would live in a world that was overwhelming and impossibly confusing. Only through fitting our perceptions and experiences into systems of organization and classification can we comprehend our lives and act in the world. A human without this ability would be paralyzed, frozen by an overwhelming bombardment of sensations. Indeed, this is one of the problems that autistic people such as Temple Grandin often experience.

Methods of organizing and classifying are products of a group. You are not the only one who thinks that the students and professors in a classroom are more important than the ceiling tiles; that perception is probably shared by all students and professors.

Anthropologists have long proposed that culture is a shared mental model that people use to organize, to classify, and ultimately to understand their world. A key way in which this model is expressed is through language, a symbolic system.

Different cultures have different models for understanding and speaking about the world. For instance, in English, the verb *smoke* describes the action of ingesting a cigarette and the verb *drink* describes the action of consuming a liquid. However, in the Bamana language, spoken by the Bambara of Mali, the verb *min* is used both for smoking and for drinking. Americans classify rainbows as objects of beauty and frequently point them out to each other. However, Lacondon Maya in Southern Mexico classify rainbows as dangerous and frightening, and pointing them out to other people is highly inappropriate.

Anthropologists who are particularly interested in describing the systems of organization and classification used by individual cultures often use a theoretical perspective called **ethnoscience.** Generally these anthropologists are interested in capturing the understanding of members of a culture. Ethnoscience is one position or technique within a broader perspective called **cognitive anthropology,** which focuses on the relationship between the mind and society. Understanding classification systems is also extremely important for scholars interested in ethnobotany and ethnomedine. **Ethnobotany** focuses on the relationship between humans and plants in different cultures. **Ethnomedicine** examines the ways in which people in different cultures understand health and sicknesses as well as the ways they attempt to cure disease. In each case, discovering how people classify and organize their world is a critical element in this process.

Human beings not only classify the world, but they also fill it with meaning. A key way that they do this is through the use of symbols. The simplest definition of a symbol is something that stands for something else. Words, both spoken and written, objects, and ideas can all be symbols. Symbols enable us to store information. For example, the book you are currently holding contains a huge amount of information all stored symbolically. Nonhuman animals must learn through experience or imitation. Because humans can store information symbolically, as stories and teachings passed from generation to generation or as written words, their learning is not so limited. Human cultures can be endlessly large.

Symbols also have the ability to condense meaning. People may take a single symbol and make it stand for an entire constellation of ideas and emotions. Religious symbols and national symbols often have this characteristic. The meaning of a national flag or a religious symbol cannot be summed up in a word or two. These symbols stand for vast complexes of history, ideas, and emotions. People are often literally willing to fight and die for them.

Symbolic anthropologists try to understand a culture by discovering and analyzing the symbols that are most important to its members. These often reflect the deep concerns of the culture's members in ways that may be difficult for them to articulate. For example, according to Victor Turner (1967), among the Ndembu of East Africa the mudyi tree is a central symbol and plays an important role in girls' puberty rites. The tree has a white, milky sap that symbolizes breast-feeding, the relationship between mother and child, the inheritance through the mother's family line, and, at the most abstract level, the unity and continuity of Ndembu society itself. It is unlikely that all Ndembu think deeply about all of these meanings during the puberty rites of their girls. However, Turner argues that this complex symbolism helps hold Ndembu society together by reaffirming its central tenants. For anthropologists, understanding the meaning of the mudyi tree and the role it plays in Ndembu society is to have penetrated deeply into the Ndembu view of the world.

Culture can also be analyzed using the tools of literature, and this is the job of **interpretive anthropology.** Clifford Geertz, one of the best known interpretive anthropologists, said that, in a sense, culture is like a novel. It is an "ensemble of texts . . . which the anthropologist strains to read over the shoulders of those to whom they properly belong" (Geertz 2008, orig 1973: 531). He meant that culture is a story people tell themselves about themselves. Like all good stories, culture engrosses us and helps us understand the nature and meaning of life. It comments on who we are and how we should act in the world. Interpretive anthropologists often find these cultural texts in public events, celebrations, and rituals. Analyzing them gives us clues and insights into the meaning of culture for its participants.

Consider the American fascination with football. American football has little appeal outside the United States, but here it draws more fans than any other sport. Football has lots of excitement and action, but so do many less popular sports. Some anthropologists argue that football's popularity is related to its symbolic meanings, that is, the unique ways in which it presents and manipulates important American cultural themes. Football attracts us because, more than other sports, it displays and manipulates ideas about topics such as the violence and sexuality underlying competition between men, the social role of women, the relationship of the individual to the group, rules and their infringement, gaining and surrendering territory, and racial character (Oriard 1993:18). Football is just a game, but so is checkers. Millions watch football because it is meaningful in ways that checkers is not. For interpretive anthropologists, its meaning derives from the ways in which it explores and comments on critical themes in American culture. Those who wish to understand American culture would do well to consider the meanings of football.

Interpretive and symbolic anthropologists use methods drawn from the humanities rather than from the sciences to uncover and interpret the deep emotional and psychological structure of societies. Their goal is to understand the experience of being a member of a culture and to make that experience available to their readers (Marcus and Fischer 1986).

CULTURE IS AN INTEGRATED SYSTEM—OR IS IT?

Consider a biological organism. The heart pumps blood, the lungs supply the blood with oxygen, the liver purifies the blood, and so on. The various organs work together to create a properly functioning whole. An early insight in anthropology was the usefulness of comparing societies to organisms. The subsistence system provides food, the economic and political systems determine how the food is distributed, religion provides the justification for the distribution system, and so on. Societies, like bodies, are integrated systems.

This **organic analogy** has strengths and weaknesses. It allows us to think about society as composed of different elements (such as kinship, religion, and subsistence), and it implies that anthropologists should describe the shape and role of such elements as well as the ways in which changes in one affect the others. For example, subsistence and social structure are two identifiable social elements and are related to each other. Foraging is an activity that is most often done in small groups and requires little direction or coordination. People who forage for their food will probably have relatively loosely defined social groups with changing membership. Farming requires more coordination than foraging; therefore, people who farm will likely have a society with a more rigid structure and a more stable membership. If a group was to move from foraging to farming, we would expect it to develop an increasingly well-defined social structure.

However, the organic analogy also implies that properly functioning societies should be stable and conflict free. The parts of a biological organism work together to keep the entire being alive and well. The lungs do not declare war on the liver. The result of conflict between the parts of a living thing is sickness or death. If such conflict occurs (an autoimmune disease for example), we understand that the organism is not functioning properly, and steps should be taken to restore the system. Thinking of cultures as systems may similarly suggest that their parts should work in harmony and that conflict and struggle are deviations from normality. But are cultures really like that? Do their elements really fit well together?

Consider, for example, whether the American family system fits well with the demands made by most American jobs. Most Americans want to maintain long-term marriage commitments, raise families, and live middle-class lifestyles. Most jobs in the United States provide inadequate income for this purpose. Many jobs require mobility, long hours, and flexibility, which come at the expense of the family. Americans must negotiate the contradictions between the lifestyle they desire, the demands of their families, and the requirements of their jobs.

Consider that, in socially stratified societies, different groups have different interests, and this creates conflict. For example, in capitalist societies, both workers and owners want their company to do well, but within this context, the owners hope to maximize their profit and the workers want to maximize their pay. However, increases in workers' pay come at some expense to owners' profits. Therefore, there is a structural conflict between the owners and the workers. This conflict does not occur because society is not working properly. Rather, it is a fundamental condition of a capitalist society.

There is nothing uniquely American or modern about contradiction and conflict within culture. People in nonindustrialized societies must also handle conflicting commitments to their families and other social groups, such as secret societies or religious associations. Even in societies that lack social groups beyond the family, the interests of men and women, or those of the old and the young, may differ. Thus, in all societies, social life may be characterized by conflict as well as concord. Although culture certainly is patterned and surely is a system, often the parts may rub, chafe, and grind against each other.

Anthropologists who are drawn to the study of the relationships among different aspects of culture have often sought to find laws of cultural behavior. In the first half of the 20th century, **functionalists** such as A.R. Radcliffe-Brown and Bronislaw Malinowski searched for such laws in the mutually supportive relationships among kinship, religion, and politics. For example, Radcliffe-Brown (1965/1952:176) argued that religion supports social structure by giving individuals a sense of dependence on their society.

More recently, **ecological functionalists** have focused on the relationship between environment and society. Rather than seeing cultures as being like organisms, these anthropologists view social institutions and practices as elements in broader ecological systems. They are particularly concerned with ways in which cultural practices both altered and were altered by the ecosystem in which they occurred. For example, Marvin Harris's (1966) classic explanation of the Hindu taboo on eating beef focused on the effect of cattle in the Indian environment rather than on the Hindu belief system. Harris noted that despite widespread poverty and periodic famine in India, Hindus refuse to eat their cattle. Although superficially this seems unreasonable, it makes good ecological sense. Cows are important in India because they provide dung for fertilizer and cooking fuel, and they give birth to bullocks, the draft animals that pull the plows and carts essential to agriculture. If a family ate its cows during a famine, it would deprive itself of the source of bullocks and could not continue farming. Thus, the Hindu religious taboo on eating beef is part of a larger ecological pattern that includes the subsistence system.

Many anthropologists today, although they accept that culture is a patterned system, choose to focus on conflicts within the system. This often reflects the deep influence of the work of Karl Marx and the early 20th-century sociologist Max Weber. Both Marx and Weber saw conflict in society as a key factor driving social change. For example, Marx understood society to be made up of different social groups, such as factory owners and workers, who had opposing interests. Marx believed that, over time, these opposing interests inevitably would lead to both conflict and social change.

CULTURE IS A SHARED SYSTEM OF NORMS AND VALUES—OR IS IT?

What would a person with their own private culture be like? Perhaps they would be like Temple Grandin, Tim Page, or other high functioning autistics: able to exist in the social world but unable to "get it." Alternatively, such a person might live in a world in which everything has one set of meanings to them but different meanings to everyone else. People with certain forms of schizophrenia seem to have just this problem; they live in worlds filled with symbols that are of meaning only to themselves. In either case, it would be very difficult for such people to interact with others; they would probably be isolated and, in some cases, clearly insane. It is clear, then, that at some level members of a culture must share ways of thinking and behaving. Often, we refer to these as *norms* and *values.*

Norms are shared ideas about the way things ought to be done—rules of behavior that reflect and enforce culture. **Values** are shared ideas about what is true, right, and beautiful. For example, the notion that advances in technology are good is an American value; most Americans agree that humans can and should transform nature to meet human ends. Shaking hands rather than bowing when introduced to a stranger is an American norm.

© Adam G. Sylvester/Photo Researchers, Inc.

Cultures do share ideas about the correct way to behave, but members of a single culture often show great variability in knowledge, beliefs, and styles.

Human behavior is not always consistent with cultural norms or values. People do not necessarily do what they say they should do. Norms may be contradictory and manipulated for personal and group ends. For example, in India people believe that women should stay in their homes rather than go out with their friends. They also believe that women should spend a lot of time in religious activities. Modern Indian women use the second of these ideals to get around the first. By forming clubs whose activities are religious, they have an excuse to get out of the house, to which their elders cannot object too strongly.

This example raises important questions about norms and values. How do we determine the norms and values of a society? Do all people in society agree on these things? How many people must agree on something before it is considered a norm or a value? Research shows that, even in small societies, norms are not always followed and values are not universal. Individuals differ in their knowledge, understanding, and beliefs. For example, one might expect that in a small fishing society all members would agree on the proper names for different kinds of fish, but on Pukapuka, the small Pacific atoll studied by Robert Borofsky (1994), even experienced fishermen disagreed much of the time.

The degree to which people do not simply share a single culture is even more obvious in large societies. Sometimes the term **subculture** is used to designate groups within a single society that share norms and values significantly different from those of the **dominant culture.** The terms *dominant culture* and *subculture* do not refer to superior and inferior but rather to the idea that the dominant culture, because it controls greater wealth and power, is more able to impose its understanding of the world on subcultures than the reverse.

Dominant cultures retain their power partly through control of institutions, like the legal system, criminalizing practices that conflict with their own (Norgren and Nanda 1996). In contemporary society, public schools help maintain the values of the dominant culture, and the media plays an important role in encouraging people to perceive subcultures in stereotypical (and usually negative) ways. For example, in a study that focused on television news and reality shows, Oliver (2003) found that images of race and crime systematically overrepresented African Americans as criminal. Furthermore, such shows tended to portray black men as particularly dangerous and presented information about black suspects that assumed their guilt.

Although in some situations domination of one group by another is extreme, rarely is it complete. People contest their subjugation and protect their subcultures through political, economic, and military means. Sometimes, when domination is intense, minorities can protect themselves only through religious faith or by building cultural tales in which they hold positions of power and their oppressors are weak (Scott 1992).

The result of struggles between groups in society is that norms and values, ideas we sometimes think of as timeless and consensual, are constantly changing and being renegotiated. This involves conflict and subjugation as well as consensus. Which norms and values are promoted and which are rejected is particularly important because such cultural ideas influence and are influenced by wealth, power, and status.

For example, what are American norms and values about using drugs to alter one's state of consciousness? Should the use of such drugs be legal? Clearly these are difficult questions. In the past, Americans considered alcohol a dangerous mind-altering substance. Its manufacture, sale, and transport were prohibited in the United States between 1920 and 1933. Even today, substantial numbers of Americans oppose alcohol. In 2006 the Southern Baptist Convention, which represents about 16 million church members, passed a resolution expressing "total opposition to the manufacturing, advertising, distributing, and consuming of alcoholic beverages" (Southern Baptist Convention 2006). Marijuana, on the other hand, has been illegal in the United States since 1937, but currently, about one third of Americans say they favor its legalization (Carroll 2005).

Believing that people should consume or not consume either alcohol or marijuana clearly does not make one more or less "American." However, which of these notions is held by those in power is critical. It influences the laws and social policies that shape our lives and history.

The focus on culture as a shared set of norms and values is often associated with the American anthropologists of the first half of the 20th century, a school of thought referred to as **historical particularism.** These anthropologists were interested in presenting objective descriptions of cultures within their historical and environmental context. Their emphasis on norms and values was designed to show that although other cultures were very different from our own, they were coherent, rational, and indeed often beautiful. In contrast to the logical coherence seen by the historical particularists, some contemporary anthropologists, particularly **postmodernists,** hold that culture is a context in which norms and values are contested and negotiated. Rather than assuming a cultural core of shared beliefs and values, these anthropologists see culture and society as battlegrounds where individuals and groups fight for power and the right to determine what is accepted as true.

CULTURE IS THE WAY HUMAN BEINGS ADAPT TO THE WORLD

All animals, including human beings, have biologically based needs. All need habitat and food, and each species must reproduce. All creatures are adapted to meet these needs. **Adaptation** is a change in the biological structure or lifeways of an individual or population by which it becomes better fitted to survive and reproduce in its environment. Nonhuman animals fill their needs primarily through biological adaptation. Lions, for example, have a series of biologically based adaptations that are superbly designed to enable them to feed themselves (and their mates). They have large muscles for speed as well as sharp teeth and claws to capture and eat their prey.

Humans are different. We lack offensive biological weaponry, and, if left to get our food like the lion, we would surely starve. There is little evidence that we have an instinct to hunt or consume any particular kind of food, to build any particular sort of structure, or to have a single fixed social arrangement. Instead, human beings, in groups, develop forms of knowledge and technologies that enable them to feed themselves and to survive in their environments. They pass this knowledge from generation to generation and from group to group. In other words, human beings develop and use culture to adapt to the world.

Most of a lion's adaptation to the world is set biologically. The growth of its teeth and claws, its instinct to hunt, and the social arrangement of a pride are largely expressions of the lion's genetic code. Humans also have a biological adaptation to the world: learning culture. All humans automatically learn the culture of their social group. The only exceptions are people with profound biologically based difficulties (such as autism) and, sometimes, victims of extreme abuse. The fact that humans universally learn and use culture strongly suggests that such learning is a manifestation of our genetic code. Although our biology compels us to learn culture, it does not compel us to learn a particular culture. The range of human beliefs and practices is enormous (although perhaps not limitless). However, people everywhere learn to fill their basic needs, such as food and shelter, through cultural practices. Culture everywhere must, to some extent, be adaptive.

Cultural adaptation has some distinct advantages over biological adaptation. Because humans adapt through learned behavior, they can change their approach to solving problems quickly and more easily than creatures whose adaptations are primarily biological. Lions hunt and eat today in much the same way as they have for tens of thousands of years. The vast majority of human beings today do not live like humans of even three or four generations ago, let alone like our distant ancestors. Our means of feeding ourselves, our culture, have changed. **Plasticity**—the ability to change behavior—has allowed human beings to thrive under a wide variety of social and ecological conditions.

Cultural adaptation has some disadvantages too. Misinformation, leading to cultural practices that hinder rather than aid survival, may creep into human behavior. Cultural practices, such as unrestrained logging, mining, or fishing that encourage destruction of the environment, may lead to short-term success but long-term disaster. Furthermore, it is clear that many human practices are not adaptive, even in the short run. Political policies of ethnic cleansing and genocide that urge people to murder their neighbors may benefit their leaders, but it is hard to see any meaningful way in which these practices are adaptive. A normal lion will always inherit the muscle, tooth, and claw that let it survive. Normal humans, on the other hand, may inherit a great deal of cultural misinformation that hinders their survival.

Historically, a focus on the adaptive aspect of culture is associated with a theoretical position called **cultural ecology,** first proposed in the 1930s. Although many of our ideas have changed since then, investigating the adaptive (and maladaptive) aspects of culture continues to be an important aspect of anthropology. Anthropologists who view culture as an adaptation tend to be concerned with people's behavior, particularly as it relates to their physical well-being or the relationship of cultural practices to ecosystems. They investigate the ways in which cultures adapt to specific environments and the ways in which cultures have changed in response to new physical and social conditions.

CULTURE IS CONSTANTLY CHANGING

Did you ever want to visit a culture where people were untouched by the outside world, living just the same way they have been living for thousands of years? Well, you are out of luck. One of the most romantic notions of anthropology presented in the media is that there are "stone-age" cultures waiting to be discovered. But this is false. No culture has ever been stuck in time or isolated from others for very long. Cultures are constantly changing. They change because of conflict among different elements within them. They change because of contact with outsiders. Population growth, disease, climate change, and natural disaster all drive culture change. However, cultures do not always change at the same speed. Cultural change may happen in small increments, or it may happen in revolutionary bursts. Historically, in most places and at most times, culture change has been a relatively slow process. However, the pace of change has been increasing for the past several hundred years and has become extremely rapid in the past century.

Since the 16th century the most important source of culture change has been the development of a world economic system based primarily in the wealthy nations of Europe and Asia. This has involved invasions, revolutions, and epidemic diseases. These historic processes and the resultant global economic system are the primary foci of Chapters 13 and 14. Here, we focus on some of the more traditional ways in which anthropologists have examined culture change.

Anthropologists usually have discussed cultural change in terms of innovation and diffusion. An **innovation** is an object, a way of thinking, or a way of behaving that is new because it is qualitatively different from existing forms (Barnett 1953:7). Although we often think of innovations as technological, they are not limited to the material aspects of culture. New art forms and new ideas are also innovations.

New practices, tools, or principles may emerge from within a society and gain wide acceptance. Anthropologists sometimes call these *primary innovations*, and they are frequently chance discoveries and accidents. In our own society, some examples of accidental discovery include penicillin, discovered when British researcher Alexander Fleming noticed that bacteria samples he had left by a window were contaminated by mold spores, and Teflon, discovered by Roy Plunkett, who was trying to find new substances to use in refrigeration. All such innovations are based on building blocks provided by culture. For example, although Fleming is justly famous for the discovery of penicillin, this innovation also illustrates the importance of context and incremental discovery. Fleming was not a random person who woke up one morning thinking about mold and bacteria. He was a trained bacteriologist who had been looking for a substance to fight infection for more

Innovation often involves crafting familiar things from new materials. In Niger, a craftsman fashions sandals from old tires.

than a decade. He was very aware of the work of other scientists studying the problem of infection. It does not diminish his achievement to point out that he, like every other inventor or discoverer, did not create something totally new. He realized the critical importance of new combinations of things that already existed. His culture provided him with the training, tools, and context in which his discovery could be made.

Innovations tend to move from one culture to another, a process known as **diffusion.** Diffusion can happen in many ways; trade, travel, and warfare all promote it. Direct contact among cultures generally results in the most far-reaching changes, and cultures located on major trade routes tend to change more rapidly than do those in more isolated places. However, because no human society has ever been isolated for a long time, diffusion has always been an important factor in culture. This implies that "pure" cultures, free from outside influences, have never existed.

Innovation and diffusion are not simple processes. People do not "naturally" realize that one way of doing things is better than another or that one style of dress, religion, or behavior is superior. In order for innovation and diffusion to occur, new ideas must be accepted, and even when the desirability of an innovation seems clear, gaining acceptance is a very complex process. Again, the discovery of penicillin provides a good example. Although Fleming understood some of the importance of his discovery in 1928, human trials did not take place until World War II, and the drug was not widely prescribed until the mid to late 1950s (Sheehan 1982; Williams 1984).

People may not accept an idea because they do not fully understand it, but other factors are usually involved as well. For psychological reasons, individuals may vary in their willingness to adopt change. Far more importantly, changes rarely provide equal benefits to everyone. For example, new agricultural techniques were introduced in Latin America and Asia from the 1940s to the 1960s (an era known as the "Green Revolution"). The new techniques did radically improve crop yields, but large landowners received the greater part of the benefit. Laborers, many of whom were landless, were often impoverished by the change and, as a result, were very resistant to it (Das 1998).

Change is often promoted or resisted by powerful interests. Innovations that have strong political, economic, or moral forces behind them may be rapidly accepted. But, when those forces are arrayed against an innovation, it can be delayed. New technologies may face resistance from those who have invested heavily in older ones. For example, FM radio broadcasting is clearly superior to AM broadcasting; it has greater fidelity and is much less susceptible to static and interference. Although it was invented in 1933, the opposition of CBS, NBC, and RCA, powerful corporations heavily invested in AM technology, prevented FM from gaining popularity until the late 1960s (Lewis 1991).

Like innovation, diffusion is often accompanied by conflict. People who are colonized or captured by others are often forced to assume new cultural practices. New rulers may require that older traditions be abandoned. Economic demands by governments or creditors often compel the adoption of new technologies and practices. Although these processes happen in most places where cultures confront one another, they have been particularly important in the past 500 years. During this time, cultures have been increasingly tied together in an economic system controlled largely in Northern Europe, North America, and Japan, a process we explore further in Chapters 13 and 14.

The rapid pace of cultural change and diffusion, particularly in the past 100 years, raises the question of cultural homogenization. Are cultural differences being erased? Are we all being submerged in a single global culture? There are no simple answers to these questions. On the one hand, modern technological culture now penetrates virtually every place on earth. On the other hand, this penetration is uneven. The wealthy have far greater access to technology than the poor. People in rural African villages may have radios, but they are unlikely to be connected to the Internet any time soon.

The world dominance of industrialized nations has affected cultures everywhere, but rather than annihilating local culture, the result may be the creation of new cultures. Cultural traits are transformed as they are adopted, and new cultural forms result. Radio, television, and video recording are good examples. Developed by industrialized societies, these technologies have spread around the world. However, they do not necessarily promote the values and practices of the societies that created them. Recently, Osama bin Laden as well as insurgents and jihadists in Iraq and elsewhere have made extensive use of television, cell phones, and the Internet in their campaign against Western secular society.

Anthropologists have traditionally worked in tribal and peasant societies. Because such cultures have been profoundly affected by their contact with industrial societies, most anthropologists today, whatever their theoretical orientations, are interested in change. The study of cultural change has special interest for applied anthropologists, particularly those who investigate issues related to the economic development of poor nations.

CULTURE COUNTS

Culture is many different things. It is learning, symbolism and meaning, patterns of thought and behavior, the things we share with those around us, the ways in which we survive in our world, and dynamism and change. It is both consensus and conflict. Culture makes us human and ties us to others everywhere. Ultimately, because all societies are based around fundamental patterns of culture, no society can be utterly incomprehensible to members of another. On the other hand, enormous variability is built into these patterns. The fact that human lifeways are shared, learned, and symbolic, the fact that we don't simply adapt to our environment but fill it with meaning, results in extraordinary differences in human cultures.

Naked mole rats are a highly social species found in the horn of Africa. Their behavior is extremely complex, but they lack culture in a human sense. Each colony is more or less identical to every other. Imaginary mole rat explorers visiting each colony would understand everything they saw or heard. But the history of human exploration is one of miscomprehension. Because cultures are so different and count for so much in human life, we need tools to help us understand them. One job of anthropology is to provide these tools. In Chapter 3 we examine the methods anthropologists have used to investigate culture.

BRINGING IT BACK HOME: DOES THE IDEA OF CULTURE BELONG TO ANTHROPOLOGY? SHOULD IT?

In an essay titled "Who Stole Culture From Anthropology," Tony Waters (2006) notes that, 50 years ago, anthropology was the only university subject that dealt routinely with culture. Today, however, "on university campuses around the world, few students hear about 'culture' from anthropologists anymore. Instead, they hear about it in education, business, genetics, political science, psychology, history, or sociology classes."

Some quick numbers reveal the increased prevalence of culture as a critical idea in American society. In July 1967, the word "culture" was mentioned in 82 articles in *The New York Times.* Twenty years later, in July 1987, culture was mentioned in 192 articles in *The New York Times.* In July 2007, culture was mentioned in 348 articles in *The New York Times.* Thus, over the past 40 years, the number of articles mentioning culture increased more than fourfold. But what about anthropology? There, the increase is not as striking. In July 1967, the word "anthropology" appeared in 11 articles in *The New York Times.* In July 1987, it appeared in 19 articles. Whereas use of the word "culture" in July 2007 was almost double that of its use in July 1987, use of "anthropology" only rose from 19 to 22 articles.

Clearly, although Americans are writing and thinking more and more about culture, they may be doing so from nonanthropological perspectives. Waters (2006) writes that "Geneticists teach that culture is the product of selfish genes, in business courses culture is described as a series of logical utilitarian choices, and in education culture is reduced to a unit of study for a public school curriculum." As this chapter has shown, anthropologists think of culture as both complex and problematic. Anthropologists' ideas about culture are formed by their personal long-term detailed fieldwork and informed by more than a century of theoretical writing and ethnographic data. This means that anthropological understandings undoubtedly are more sophisticated than most of those coming from other disciplines. Yet, the role of anthropology in presenting the idea of culture to the public is not as great as many anthropologists think it should be.

YOU DECIDE

1. Based on your reading and your class thus far, formulate a way to tell your sociology, psychology, or history professor how anthropology is different from what he or she teaches.
2. What is one thing about what you have learned about culture from anthropology that you would hesitate to say in a sociology, psychology, or history class?
3. Why do you think knowledge of anthropology is not more widespread? What can and should anthropologists (and students of anthropology) do to increase the presence of anthropology in the public sphere?

CHAPTER SUMMARY

1. Culture is the learned, symbolic, at least partially adaptive, and ever-changing patterns of behavior and meaning shared by members of a group. Humans are vitally dependent on culture for their existence.
2. Almost all human behavior is learned. Humans learn throughout their entire life span. The example of the Inuit shows how children are taught to survive in a harsh environment.
3. Humans understand the world by classifying it and using symbols to give it meaning. Different cultures use different systems of classification. People use symbols to give meaning to their lives. Anthropologists analyze and interpret symbols and rituals to understand cultural meanings.
4. Culture is a system of related elements working together. However, cultural systems include contradictions that lead to conflict.

5. Members of a culture must share many things in common, including norms and values. However, there are substantial group and individual differences in understanding.
6. Culture is the way that humans adapt to their world. Unlike other species, adaptation by humans is primarily learned, which enables people to rapidly adapt to change.
7. All cultures change. Innovation and diffusion are two sources of change. Many factors determine the acceptance or rejection of a culture change.
8. Culture makes humans unique. The vast differences between human cultures make cultural understanding a challenge. Anthropology supplies tools to meet that challenge.

KEY TERMS

Adaptation
Cognitive anthropology
Cultural ecology
Culture and personality
Diffusion
Dominant culture
Ecological functionalism
Enculturation
Ethnobotany
Ethnomedicine
Ethnoscience
Functionalism
Historical particularism
Innovation
Interpretive anthropology
Norms
Organic analogy
Plasticity
Postmodernism
Subculture
Symbol
Symbolic anthropology
Values

Anthropologists do their fieldwork in many different locations. They often work in small isolated communities, but sometimes they work in cities as well. This picture shows a neighborhood in Naples, Italy perhaps similar to the one described in the opening paragraphs of this chapter.

CHAPTER 3

DOING CULTURAL ANTHROPOLOGY

CHAPTER OUTLINE

Arriving at Fontana del Re

A Little History

- Franz Boas and American Anthropology
- From Haddon to Malinowski in England and the Commonwealth

Anthropological Techniques

- Ethnographic Data and Cross-Cultural Comparisons

Changing Directions and Critical Issues in Ethnography

- Feminist Anthropology
- Postmodernism
- Engaged and Collaborative Ethnography
- Studying One's Own Society

Ethical Considerations in Fieldwork

New Roles for the Ethnographer

Bringing It Back Home: Anthropologists and Human Rights

- You Decide

ARRIVING AT FONTANA DEL RE

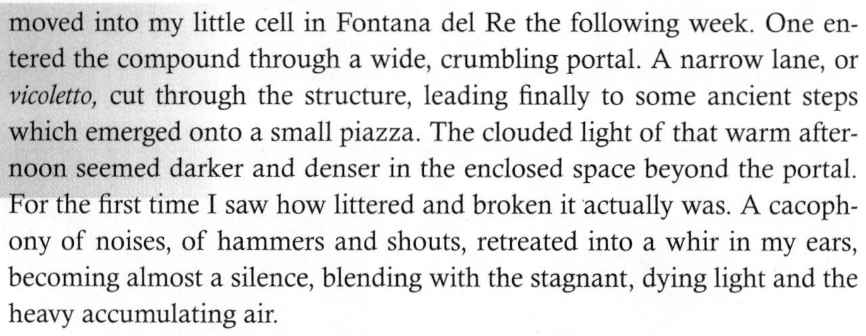

I moved into my little cell in Fontana del Re the following week. One entered the compound through a wide, crumbling portal. A narrow lane, or *vicoletto,* cut through the structure, leading finally to some ancient steps which emerged onto a small piazza. The clouded light of that warm afternoon seemed darker and denser in the enclosed space beyond the portal. For the first time I saw how littered and broken it actually was. A cacophony of noises, of hammers and shouts, retreated into a whir in my ears, becoming almost a silence, blending with the stagnant, dying light and the heavy accumulating air.

All the faces in all of the windows, from first floor to sixth, stared down at me intently. People murmured from balcony to balcony, "l'americano, l'americano." Their looks were questioning and puzzled, but not hostile. . . .

As I walked toward my apartment, with Carlo at my side, I became aware of a commotion behind us. The space of the courtyard flooded with the sounds of the Neapolitan language. A small crowd had gathered in front of an old woman, standing in a second-floor balcony. An old man from a window above, his skin furrowed and brown, caught my eye and began to shout at me his version of what was going on. One of his eyes was pure white, tinged with blue, frozen and unmoving. The other eye darted about as if it were dancing a pantomime, vividly displaying every nuance of his changing meanings. I understood nothing.

The old woman beneath whom the crowd had gathered was heavy and bowed, with white thinning hair and a soiled apronlike garment. Her face was fat and large, with deep fissures and crevices for wrinkles, and massive, jowled cheeks. Her eyes told of her plight. They were limpid and tender, infected, and wet with pain, and floated in the terrible red pools which were her sockets. Her arms were outstretched to the noisy arguing crowd below in a proclamation of helplessness. One arm was crudely bandaged with a filthy cloth. She trembled like a shivering animal. An ambulance arrived. The attendants led her down the stairway.

Her balcony window remained open. A torn black sweater was cast aside on a broken stool, and a tattered piece of nylon had been nailed to the frame as a curtain. I approached closer, but young Pepe pulled me back, warning me of the smell which issued from her room. The small crowd dispersed as people returned to their daily labors. Then I was told why the old woman's arm had been bandaged up. Her arm had been bitten by the rats, they said, which infested her squalid room. She would never be back. They knew it as a certainty. Some were glad to see her go, referring to the stench hanging about her room. And there was talk of blocking up her windows to seal in the rats, and the smell.

This was what happened on my first day at *Fontana del Re.* That night, alone and apprehensive in my strange new home, I thought about her wretched end, and wondered about her life, and tried in vain to know, what awful conspiracy of forces had led the infant to this.

In this passage, Thomas Belmonte describes his arrival at Fontana del Re, the housing complex in Naples, Italy, where he lived as an anthropologist documenting the lives of some of the city's poorest citizens. Belmonte's writing captures some of the feeling of fieldwork. He is bombarded by almost overwhelming sights, sounds, and smells. People are engaged in actions he does not understand and shouting in a language he does not fully comprehend. Confronted with all of this strangeness, Belmonte feels alone and alienated and is drawn to reflect on the nature of human life itself.

Although Belmonte's particular experiences are unique, almost all anthropologists must face the confusion and disorientation of immersion in a different culture and the intense learning and reflection that ensue.

If you have any picture of anthropologists at all, you probably think of men and women who share the lives of people who are different than themselves. Indeed, one of the fundamental ways in which anthropologists work is by spending time in other cultures. Psychologists or sociologists may be able to do research without leaving the college campus. They conduct surveys using the telephone, the Internet, or the postal service, or they may bring students into a laboratory and ask them questions or observe their reactions. Philosophers or scholars of literature may work by reading, observing, and pondering. But anthropologists must go into the field.

Although anthropologists spend a great deal of time reading, pondering, and writing, fieldwork is an essential component of the anthropological experience. For more than 100 years, anthropologists have gone into other cultures. They have lived among small isolated groups that forage for their food, have joined with societies that travel with their herds, and have spent time in agricultural villages and in bustling modern cities. They have lived among farmers, craftsmen, thieves, and crack cocaine dealers. If you are attracted to anthropology as a discipline, fieldwork is probably one of the key reasons. There is something profoundly romantic about the idea of living with members of another culture, learning their way of life, and attempting to understand the world in a new and different manner. However, as Belmonte's description of his first experiences at Fontana del Re shows, there is also confusion, strangeness, alienation, and a host of challenges and dilemmas. Fieldwork is a wonderful experience. It is essential to the ways in which anthropology is done. However, it can also be intensely lonely and disturbing. In this chapter, we explore some of the history and practice of fieldwork. We examine fieldwork techniques and different trends in anthropological data collection and discuss some of the ethical issues raised by the practice of anthropology.

A LITTLE HISTORY

Anthropology was not always based around fieldwork. The first scholars who called themselves anthropologists worked in the second half of the 19th century. Among the most famous of them were Sir Edward Burnett Tylor and Louis Henry Morgan. Both were brilliant men who had traveled widely (Tylor in Mexico and Morgan in the western United States), but they saw themselves as compilers and analysts of ethnographic accounts rather than as field researchers. For their data they relied largely upon the writings of amateurs—travelers, explorers, missionaries, and colonial officers—who had recorded their experiences in remote areas of the world. Because of this method, critics of Tylor and Morgan sometimes referred to them as "armchair anthropologists."

Morgan and Tylor were deeply influenced by the evolutionary theories of Charles Darwin and Herbert Spencer. They assumed that such theories could be applied to human society, and they used data from archaeological finds and colonial accounts of current-day peoples to produce evolutionary histories of human society. Thus, as they analyzed societies, they used type of technology and social institutions, such as family and religion, to place each society on an evolutionary scale of increasing complexity. Their scale began with simple, small-scale societies (classified as "savages"), passed through various chiefdoms (usually classified as "barbarians"), and ended with societies such as their own (classified as "civilization"). Although Morgan and Tylor were deeply critical of many aspects of their own societies, they were also convinced that they lived in the most highly evolved society that had ever existed.

There were numerous problems with Morgan and Tylor's evolutionary anthropology. Explorers, colonial officials, and missionaries had particular interests in playing up the most exotic aspects of the societies they described. Doing so increased the fame of explorers (and the number of books they were able to sell). It made the native more in need of good government or salvation for the colonial official and missionary. Perhaps more importantly, the evolutionists were so sure that they had properly formulated the general evolutionary history of society that they twisted and contorted their data to fit their theories. For example, Tylor (2008, orig 1871: 33) wrote that his theoretical perspective was so well established that he could ignore any data that did not fit with the surety that such data were inaccurate.

Franz Boas and American Anthropology

Problems such as these led to a radical reappraisal of evolutionary anthropology at the end of the 19th century. The most important critic of evolutionism was Franz Boas. Born in Minden, Germany, Boas came to the United States after completing his doctorate in geography and living among the Inuit on Baffin Island. In the late 1890s he became the first professor of anthropology at Columbia University in New York City. From there, he was critically involved in the training of many students who became the leading anthropologists of the first half of the 20th century. As a result, Boas' ideas had a profound impact on the development of anthropology in the United States.

Boas' studies and his experiences among the Inuit convinced him that evolutionary anthropology was both intellectually flawed and, because it treated other people and other societies as inferior to Europeans, morally defective. He was deeply critical of the data gathering techniques and the reasoning of Morgan, Tylor, and others. Boas argued that anthropologists should not be collectors of tales and spinners of theories but should devote themselves to fieldwork, to objective data collection. Anthropologists must live among the people they are studying, both observing their culture and, where possible, participating in it. They should record the cultural patterns of the group and their language, their material goods, and their religion. Anthropologists should investigate the group past using archaeology and collect statistical measures of their bodies. Boas' style of fieldwork became known as **participant observation** and has been the hallmark of American anthropology. Although few anthropologists today would investigate society in precisely the same way as Boas (today, for example, archaeology and body measurements are left to archaeologists and biological anthropologists), almost all anthropologists do fieldwork in which they both observe members of a culture and participate with them to the greatest extent possible.

One of Boas' core beliefs was that cultures are the products of their own histories. He argued that a culture's standards of beauty and morality as well as many other aspects of behavior could be understood only in light of that culture's historical development. Since our own ideas were also the products of history, it was inappropriate to use our standards to judge other cultures. Evolutionists failed in part because they made just this mistake. They assumed, incorrectly, that the more a culture's values approached those of Europeans, the more evolved it was. In other words, the evolutionists failed because of their own ethnocentrism. In one sense, **ethnocentrism** is simply the belief that one's own culture is better than any other. In a deeper sense, it is precisely the application of the historical standards of beauty, worth, and morality developed in one culture to all other cultures.

The American tourist who, presented with a handful of Mexican pesos, asks, "How much is this in real money?," is being ethnocentric—but there is nothing uniquely American or Western about ethnocentrism. People all over the world tend to see things from their own culturally patterned point of view. For example, when the people living in Highland New Guinea first saw European outsiders in the 1930s, they believed them to be the ghosts of their ancestors. It was the only way they could initially make sense of what they were seeing (Connolly and Anderson 1987).

Although most people are ethnocentric, the ethnocentrism of Western societies has had greater consequences than that of smaller, less technologically advanced, and more geographically isolated peoples. Wealth and military technology have given Westerners the ability to impose their beliefs and practices on others. It may matter little, for example, to the average Frenchman if the Dogon (an ethnic group in Mali) believe their way of life to be superior. The Dogon have little ability to affect events in France. However, French ethnocentrism mattered a great deal to the Dogon. The French colonized Mali and imposed their beliefs and institutions on its people.

Some ethnocentrism seems necessary. A group's belief in the superiority of its own way of life binds its members together and helps them to perpetuate their values. To the extent that ethnocentrism prevents building bridges between cultures and leads members of one culture to force their ways of life on another, it is maladaptive. It is but a short step from this kind of ethnocentrism to **racism**—beliefs, actions, and patterns of social organization that exclude individuals and groups from the equal exercise of human rights and fundamental freedoms. The transformation from ethnocentrism to racism underlies much of the structural inequality that characterizes modern history.

Boas insisted that anthropologists free themselves, as much as possible, from ethnocentrism and approach each culture on its own terms, in light of its own notions of worth and value. This position came to be known as **cultural relativism** and is one of the hallmarks of anthropology. Boas and his followers maintained that anthropologists must suspend judgment in order to understand the logic and dynamics of other cultures. Researchers who view the actions of other people simply in terms of the degree to which they correspond to their own notions of the ways people should behave systematically distort the cultures they study.

Boas was a tireless campaigner for human rights and justice. He argued that all human beings have equal capacities for culture and that although human actions might be considered morally right or wrong, no culture was more evolved or of greater value than another. He was an unwavering supporter of racial equality. His work and that of his students, notably Ruth Benedict and Margaret Mead, were widely used by Americans who argued for the equality of men and women and for the rights of African Americans, immigrants, and Native Americans. Today, virtually all anthropologists rely on Boas' basic insights.

From Haddon to Malinowski in England and the Commonwealth

While Boas was forming his ideas in America, a separate fieldwork tradition was developing in Britain. In the late 19th century, Alfred Cort Haddon mounted two expeditions to the Torres Straits (between New Guinea and Australia). Haddon originally was a biologist, but his travels turned his interest to **ethnography,** the gathering and interpretation of information based on intensive firsthand study. Haddon's second expedition included scholars from several different fields. Haddon and his colleagues became professors at Cambridge and the London School of Economics, where they trained the next generation of British Commonwealth anthropologists. Like Boas, their understandings were based in fieldwork, and they made it a basic part of their students' training.

Bronislaw Malinowski was one of the most prominent students of the Torres Straits scholars. Malinowski grew up in Krakow, then part of the Austro-Hungarian Empire (now in Poland). He came to England to study ethnography, and his mentor, Charles Seligman, sent him to do fieldwork on the Trobriand Islands (in the Torres Straits). Malinowski arrived in the Trobriands in 1914, as World War I broke out. Since the Trobriands were governed by Australia and Malinowski was a subject of the Austro-Hungarian Empire, he was considered an enemy national. As a result, he was unable to leave the islands until the end of the war. Thus, what he had intended as a relatively short fieldwork expedition became an extremely long one.

Malinowski's time on the Trobriands was a signal moment in British Commonwealth anthropology. A diary he kept during those years shows he was frequently lonely, frustrated, and angry. Despite his problems, he revolutionized fieldwork. The Torres Straits scholars had studied culture at a distance, observing and describing it for a short time. Malinowski spent years with native Trobrianders, learning their language, their patterns of thought, and their cultural ways. He developed a form of ethnography centered on empathic understandings of native lifeways and on analyzing culture by describing social institutions and showing the cultural and psychological functions they performed. Malinowski also stressed the interrelations among the elements of culture.

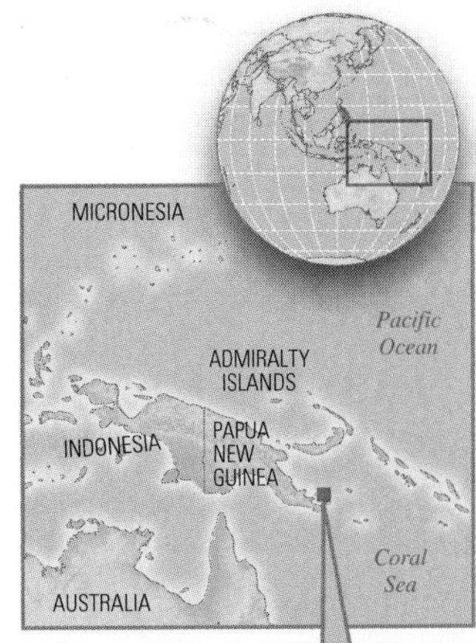

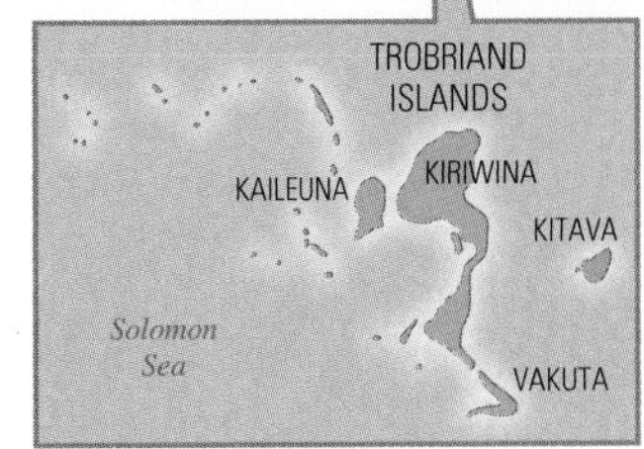

The Trobriand Islands.

In an era when non-Europeans were often considered incomprehensible and illogical, Malinowski forcefully promoted the idea that native cul-

London School of Economics Archives, Malinowski/3/18/2

Bronislaw Malinowski, one of the pioneers of participant observation, worked in the Trobriand Islands between 1915 and 1918.

tural ways were logical and rational. For example, in a famous essay on science and magic, he argued that natives used magic only for goals they were unable to attain by more rational means (such as controlling the weather). Furthermore, he argued that magic was like science in that it had "a definite aim intimately associated with human instincts, needs, and pursuits." Like science, magic was "governed by a theory, by a system of principles which dictate the manner in which the act has to be performed in order to be effective" (Malinowski 1948).

The anthropologies of Malinowski and Boas were quite different. Boas and his students focused on understanding cultures with respect to their context and histories. Malinowski and his students emphasized the notion of function: the contribution made by social practices and institutions to the maintenance and stability of society. However, both developed traditions of fieldwork and participant observation. Both traditions have strong histories of opposition to racism. Both see other cultures as fully rational and as neither superior nor inferior to their own. Despite the great many new approaches in anthropology since the days of Boas and Malinowski, their fundamental insights and principles remain basic to current-day anthropology.

ANTHROPOLOGICAL TECHNIQUES

Today anthropologists work in a wide variety of settings. They work for universities, for businesses, and for government. You find them investigating shopping behavior and the ways in which people relate to their computers. Because of the multiplicity of anthropologies, it would be impossible to describe all of the different ways that anthropologists go about their work. Anthropologists began by studying small communities, and the techniques they develop in so doing form the framework for other techniques. Therefore, we will focus on the ways in which fieldwork is done in such communities.

Most anthropologists begin to do fieldwork as part of their graduate training and continue fieldwork as a basic element of their careers. Fieldwork is often funded by grants given by universities, government agencies, and nonprofit organizations that promote social science research. Sometimes anthropologists pay for their research themselves, but doing so is fairly expensive because research frequently involves extended stays in distant places.

Decisions about which communities anthropologists investigate are based on a large number of factors. Some of these include personal history, geographical preferences, political stability, cost, physical danger, and connections their professors and other mentors may have. However, the most critical aspect of choosing a location has to do with the particular research questions that the anthropologist wishes to answer.

In the early 20th century, anthropologists studying relatively small groups often attempted to write complete descriptions of societies. Their books, with titles such as *The Tiwi of Northern Australia* (Hart and Pilling 1960), *The Sebei* (Goldschmidt 1986), and *The Cheyennes* (Hoebel 1960), had chapters on subjects such as family, religion, farming, and legal affairs. In a sense, it did not matter much where anthropologists chose to work; any small-scale community or society could be described.

Today, few anthropologists attempt to write such descriptions. This is partly because most feel that societies are so complex that they cannot be adequately described in a single work. But, more importantly, although societies never were really isolated, today they are so interconnected and so changed by these connections that they must be seen in regional and global contexts. Current ethnographies focus on specific situations, individuals, events, and, frequently, on culture change. Some examples describe Native Americans and casino gambling (Darian-Smith 2004), the relationship between indigenous peoples and national parks (Igoe 2004), and the ways in which immigrant communities cope with new customs and values (Stepick 1998). As research has narrowed, both the questions anthropologists ask and the conditions and locations where they can be answered have become more specific.

After they have identified an area of general interest, anthropologists spend a great deal of time reading the existing research on their subject. It is no exaggeration to say that most researchers spend several hours reading for each hour they spend actually doing active field research. From their studies, they gain an understanding of the geography, history, and culture of their chosen area. They find out what is known and what remains to be learned about the subjects of their interest. They then try to design projects that help to close the gaps in existing knowledge. It is a bit like filling in pieces of a jigsaw puzzle, with one important exception: You can finish a puzzle, but good research leads to the posing of interesting questions and, thus, more research.

Arriving at a field location can be a difficult and disorienting experience. Often anthropologists will have made a brief trip to their field location to arrange logistics such as obtaining the necessary research clearances and finding a place to stay. Despite this and a great deal of other preparation, for most people, living in another culture and trying to learn its ways is a difficult experience. Culture is learned behavior, and we have been learning our culture since the moment of our births. When we move to a radically different culture, much of that learning is no longer relevant.

Anthropologists arriving in new cultures are in many ways like children. Their language skills are often weak, and their speech is sometimes babyish. Their social skills are undeveloped. They are ignorant of many aspects of their environment and their new culture. One common result of this situation is the syndrome often called **culture shock**—the feelings of alienation, loneliness, and isolation common to one who has been placed in a new culture. Thomas Belmonte's experience arriving at Fontana del Re, recounted at the opening of the chapter, is a good example. Almost all researchers experience some degree of culture shock. For graduate students, sometimes the journey stops there. You can be an outstanding scholar—well versed in literature and able to think and write creatively—yet be unable to do fieldwork.

Getting past culture shock is a process of learning—learning language, customs, and social organization—and gaining the fundamental grounding knowledge that it takes to be an adult in a different culture. It probably is accurate to say most anthropologists never feel like they are truly members of the cultures they study. We are separated from our subjects by our backgrounds, by our education, and sometimes by the color of our skin. Perhaps most importantly, we're separated by the knowledge that our time in the field is temporary and that we will leave to rejoin our other lives. However, in our best moments, anthropologists do come close to acting and feeling like members of the cultures we study.

In most cases, as anthropologists begin to adapt to new cultures, they develop networks of friends and contacts. Often these are the people who both guide them in their new surroundings and offer insights into the culture. Traditionally in anthropology these people are called **informants,** although the word has fallen somewhat out of use (to some, it sounds too much like spying). More modern words are **respondents,** interlocutors, and **consultants.** These terms emphasize the collaborative nature of fieldwork and suggest that the people who work with the anthropologist are active and empowered. Much of what anthropologists know they learn from such people, who frequently become enduring friends. In some cases, anthropologists work with a few individuals whom they believe to be well informed and eager to talk with them (sometimes called "key informants"). Alternatively, they may construct statistical models and use techniques such as random sampling to choose their consultants. Sometimes, they are able to interview all members of a community.

In fieldwork, anthropologists both observe culture and participate in it, as with this anthropologist living with the Mentawai in Sumatra, Indonesia. The tattoos usually are incised with needles and vegetable dye, but these are being done with washable pigments.

Working with consultants is often informal, but anthropologists also use an arsenal of more formal tools depending on their theoretical interests. Much of anthropology is done by interviewing, and many different interview techniques are available. Some anthropologists prepare exhaustive inventories and questionnaires; however, more frequently they design a series of open-ended questions that allow their subjects to talk freely and extensively on a topic. Occasionally, they use a structured interview, a technique designed to help identify the objects and ideas that their consultant thinks are important. Because kinship structures are important elements of many societies, anthropologists become adept at gathering genealogical information.

In addition to interviewing, anthropological data gathering includes mapping, photography, careful silent observation of a wide range of activities, measurements of various kinds of production, and, in some cases, serving apprenticeships. It all depends on the nature of the problem the anthropologist is investigating.

As with the techniques used, analysis of data also depends on the questions being asked and the theoretical perspective of the researcher. Anthropological data generally come in the form of extensive field notes, tape recordings, and photographs. In most cases, organizing data presents substantial challenges. Notes have to be indexed, recordings transcribed, and data entered in spreadsheets. Aspiring anthropologists should keep in mind that, as with background research, successful anthropologists often spend more time working with their data than they did collecting it in the first place. Recording an interview may take only an hour or two. Transcribing and indexing that recording may take several days.

Ethnographic Data and Cross-Cultural Comparisons

Boas and his students were interested in describing cultures in their contexts. Because they understood each culture as the product of its unique history, they did not attempt systematic comparison of one culture to another, and they were not very interested in discovering laws or principles of cultural behavior. However, some level of comparison has always been implicit in anthropology. For example, one goal of the Boasians was to use their research to cause Europeans and Americans to think about their own societies in a new light.

British and European anthropologists were more explicitly interested in **ethnology,** the attempt to find general principles or laws that govern cultural phenomena. They compared societies in the hope of deriving general principles of social organization and behavior. Starting in the 1860s, Herbert Spencer began to develop a systematic way of organizing, tabulating, and correlating information on a large number of societies, a project he called *Descriptive Sociology.* The American scholar William Graham Sumner, his student Albert Keller, and Keller's student George Murdock brought Spencer's ideas about cross-cultural comparison to the United States. In the late 1930s, Murdock and Keller created a large, indexed ethnographic database at Yale University. First called the *Cross Cultural Survey,* in the late 1940s the project was expanded to include other universities, and its name was changed to the ***Human Relations Area Files*** (HRAF).

The HRAF is an attempt to facilitate cross-cultural analysis. It provides a single index to ethnographic reports and other sources on 710 numbered subject categories. Some examples of categories are 294 (techniques of clothing manufacture) and 628 (traditional friendships and rivalries within communities). Using the HRAF, a researcher can find information on these and many other topics for a wide range of current and historic societies.

The HRAF frequently comes under fire as critics charge that the project takes cultural data out of context and therefore corrupts it. They say that the works indexed in the HRAF were written from different perspectives, for different purposes, and in different eras. Because of this process, indexing often is inconsistent or inappropriate, so analyses based on the HRAF are suspect. Despite these problems, work based on the HRAF is often both interesting and insightful. For example, back in the 1950s, the rising divorce rate in the United States was causing alarm. Was divorce truly something new and different, a product of modernity? Murdock used the HRAF to show that almost all societies had some form of divorce and that the divorce rate in America (in the 1950s) was lower than average. Thus, his use of the HRAF allowed people to think about divorce in a comparative context. In recent years, the HRAF, now available online and in computer searchable formats, has been used to consider a wide variety of issues. They include family violence (Levinson 1989), corporal punishment of children (Ember and Ember 2005), patterns of cultural evolution (Peregrine, Ember, and Ember 2004), and adolescent gender and sexuality (Schlegel and Barry 1991).

CHANGING DIRECTIONS AND CRITICAL ISSUES IN ETHNOGRAPHY

Feminist Anthropology

By the 1960s, the role of fieldwork in anthropology was extremely well established. Additionally, the position of women within academic anthropology was relatively good, particularly in comparison to other areas of the university. Franz Boas had trained several female anthropologists who had gone on to become well known within the discipline. One, Margaret Mead, had become a household name outside of anthropology as well. Despite this (or perhaps because of it), the political movements of the 1960s, particularly the civil rights movement and the feminist movement, caused anthropologists to begin thinking about gender and their discipline in new ways.

Feminists soon discovered that the presence of some very-high-profile women within anthropology did little to counteract the fact that the overwhelming majority of anthropologists were men and that their areas of interest tended to focus on the social roles, activities, and beliefs of men in the societies they studied. There were several reasons why anthropologists had focused on men. First, in many societies, men and women live quite segregated lives. Because they were men, most anthropologists had little access to the lives of women. Second, anthropologists tended to assume that men's activities were political and therefore important, whereas women's activities were domestic and therefore of less importance. Third, in most societies, men's activities were far more public than women's activities. Anthropologists tended to assume that what was public and visible was more important than what was more behind the scenes and less visible. However, this clearly is not always (or even often) the case.

The result of taking men more seriously than women was a systematic bias in anthropological data and understandings. Anthropologists had often reported with great detail and accuracy about men's social and cultural worlds, but they had barely scratched the surface of women's worlds. Furthermore, the assumption that men spoke for all of society that is frequently implicit in ethnographies often made cultures appear more harmonious and homogeneous than they actually were.

Starting in the 1970s, increasing numbers of women joined university anthropology faculties. By the late 1990s, more than 50 percent of new anthropology PhDs and more than 40 percent of all anthropology professors were women (Levine and Wright 1999). They began paying greater attention to women's lives in the societies they studied and to the nature of sexuality and gender. We will address these issues more fully in Chapter 8.

Postmodernism

Ultimately, the issue of women in anthropology focused on ways of knowing. Feminists argued persuasively that male anthropologists had missed vital dimensions of society because their gender and their academic interests predisposed them to see certain things and not others. These ideas dovetailed well with **postmodernism,** a critique of both natural and social sciences that gained prominence in the 1980s. Postmodernists hold that all knowledge is influenced by the observer's culture and social position. They claim fieldworkers cannot discover and describe an objective reality because such a thing does not exist (or exists but cannot be discovered or comprehended by human beings). Instead, postmodernists propose that there are many partial truths or cultural constructions, which depend on frame of reference, power, and history.

Postmodernists urged anthropologists to examine the ways they understood both fieldwork and writing. They demanded that anthropology become sensitive to issues of history and power. Some postmodernists challenged the ethnographer's role in interpreting culture, claiming that anthropological ethnographies were just one story about experienced reality and the ethnographer's voice was only one of many possible representations.

The publication of Edward Said's *Orientalism* in 1978 was a critical moment in opening anthropology to postmodern ideas. The "orient" of Said's title refers to the colonial British name for what is now called the Middle East. Said argued that European art and drama as well as anthropology and other social sciences gave a simplified, distorted, and romanticized view of Middle Eastern cultures, portraying them as timeless societies full of savagery and exotic wonder. Said believed that this portrayal was politically and culturally motivated, demonstrating western European superiority and justifying military conquest and colonization. However, it also drew attention from the area's actual history, economics, and politics. It particularly ignored the roles the British and other colonizers had played in shaping Middle Eastern politics and culture. One area of Western fascination was gender and sexuality. Because they focused on multiple wives, the harem, and the role of Islam, Western observers almost entirely misunderstood the actual lives of Middle Eastern women.

During the 1990s, reflection on the nature of fieldwork and the anthropological enterprise became a central focus of writing in anthropology. Work such as Said's encouraged anthropologists to think about the ways in which their own status, personality, and culture shape their view of others and how ethnographers interact with members of other cultures to produce data. In many cases, anthropologists turned from writing about culture to writing about anthropology itself, and critical analyses of earlier anthropological literature became common. In other cases, rather than trying to describe culture or to find principles underlying cultural practices, anthropologists wrote about their own experience of living in other cultures.

The claims of postmodernists have been a subject of intense debate in anthropology. Few anthropologists accept the postmodern critique in its entirety. To do so would be to understand anthropology as a rather peculiar sort of travel writing or a school of literary criticism. However, some of the ideas of postmodernism have become part of the mainstream. For example, almost all anthropologists today agree that ethnographers need to reflect critically on their positions as observers and be aware of the moral and political consequences of their work. Most ethnographies now include information about the conditions under which the fieldwork was carried out and the nature of the relationships between the anthropologist and his or her consultants. Most are sensitive to issues of voice and power and the ways anthropology is written.

Engaged and Collaborative Ethnography

Engaged and **collaborative ethnography** reflect some of the concerns just noted. Collaboration is the process of working closely with other people and in a sense describes all anthropological research. Collaborative anthropologists highlight this aspect of their work. They consult with their subjects about shaping their studies and writing their reports. They attempt to displace the anthropologist as the sole author representing a group, turning research into a joint process between researcher and subject. The work of James Spradley (1933–1982) is an important contribution to collaborative, engaged anthropology. His classic ethnography, *You Owe Yourself a Drunk* (Spradley 1970), was aimed at getting the public to understand and help the homeless alcoholics who were the subject of the book.

Erik Lassiter, an anthropologist inspired by Spradley, has done collaborative work with the Kiowa Indians in Oklahoma. The Kiowa were particularly interested in an ethnography of Kiowa song. They stipulated that it be written so that it could be read and understood by the Kiowa people themselves and that they would be acknowledged for their contributions. Lassiter emphasizes that a critical aspect of his collaboration with the Kiowa was to give the highest priority to representing the Kiowa cultural consultants as they wished to be represented, even if this meant adding or changing information or changing his interpretations. For Lassiter (2004), collaborative ethnography is not just eliciting the comments of the cultural consultants but, even more importantly, integrating these comments back into the text.

Although many anthropologists practice some elements of collaborative anthropology, there are deep problems with the notion that an anthropologist's primary job is to write and say what his or her consultants want. First, most probably would agree that anthropologists have an obligation to accurately report what people say and do to the best of their ability. They may have an additional obligation to not knowingly falsify information. Furthermore, communities are rarely so homogeneous that they speak with a single voice. Collaborative anthropology may give voice and legitimacy to one element of a community over another. Often, writing what consultants want really means choosing their side in a political contest.

Studying One's Own Society

When most people think of anthropologists, they imagine researchers who study others in exotic locations, but, since the early 20th century anthropologists have also studied their own societies. W. Lloyd Warner, Solon T. Kimball, Margaret Mead (1942), Zora Neale Hurston, and Hortense Powdermaker (1936) were all American anthropologists who wrote about American culture. Kenyan anthropologist (as well as freedom fighter and first president of Kenya) Jomo Kenyatta wrote about the Gikuyu of Kenya in 1936, and Chinese anthropologist Francis Hsu wrote extensively on Chinese society. In recent years, writing about one's own culture has become even more common. This trend is driven by many factors, including the training of more anthropologists from more different cultures, the increasing total number of anthropologists, the rise of interest in ethnicity in America and Europe, as well as the dangers of violence in some areas where anthropologists have studied in the past.

The emphasis on more reflective fieldwork and ethnography affects all anthropologists but particularly those who study their own societies. Traditionally, anthropologists doing fieldwork try hard to learn the culture of the people with whom they are working. In a sense, anthropologists working in their own culture have the opposite problem: They must attempt to see their culture as an outsider might. This is challenging since it is easy to take cultural knowledge for granted. In addition, it may be as difficult to maintain a neutral stand in one's own culture as it is in a different one. As Margaret Mead once noted, it may be easier to remain culturally relativistic when we confront patterns, such as cannibalism or infanticide, in other cultures than when we confront problematic situations such as child neglect, corporate greed, or armed conflict in our own.

© Doranne Jacobson

Contemporary anthropologists work in a wide range of communities and use many different methods. Many anthropologists do fieldwork in their own societies.

Some of the problems and the rewards of studying one's own culture can be seen in Barbara Myerhoff's books and films. Myerhoff contrasted her work with the Huichol of northern Mexico (1974) with her work among elderly Jewish people in California (1978). She notes that, in the first case, doing anthropology was "an act of imagination, a means for discovering what one is not and will never be." In the second case, fieldwork was a glimpse into her possible future, as she knew that someday she would be a "little old Jewish lady." Her work was a personal way to understand that condition and to contemplate her own future. Tragically, it was a future that never arrived. Myerhoff died of cancer when she was only 49.

Another dilemma experienced by many anthropologists, but particularly poignant for native anthropologists, is whether one should be a disinterested researcher or an advocate for the people one studies. Can the two be combined? Delmos Jones, an African-American anthropologist who worked in the United States, was deeply concerned with improving the position of African Americans. He studied voluntary organizations whose goal was to create political and social change in African-American urban communities (Jones 1995). He was able to get access to such organizations both because he was an African American and because he shared their goals. One of his important findings was that, for a variety of reasons, there was considerable dissent between the leadership and the rank and file in the groups he studied. Furthermore, he found that leaders used a variety of means to stifle this dissent. Jones' findings left him with a variety of unpleasant choices. If he publicized problems within the organizations, he risked both alienating the leaders who had befriended him and potentially damaging causes in which he believed deeply. On the other hand, if he failed to publicize such problems, he would be omitting an important aspect of his findings and supporting leadership practices he considered troubling.

Reflecting on his research experience, Jones concluded that although being a cultural insider offers certain advantages, such as access to the community, it also poses special dilemmas, particularly when the group being studied has been oppressed by the larger society. Indeed, he noted that the very concept of a native anthropologist is itself problematic. An individual has many identities, including race, culture, gender, and social class. Being a native in one identity does not make one a native in all one's identities (Cerroni-Long 1995; Narayan 1993).

ETHICAL CONSIDERATIONS IN FIELDWORK

Jones' position as a native anthropologist involved him in a delicate ethical situation. This is not at all unusual. Ethical issues frequently arise in anthropological research. Anthropologists have obligations to the standards of their discipline, to their sponsors, to their own and their host governments, and to the public. However, their first ethical obligations are to the people they study and to the people with whom they work. These obligations can supersede the goal of seeking new knowledge. According to the American Anthropological Association Statement on Ethics (1998), "Anthropological researchers must do everything in their power to ensure that their research does not harm the safety, dignity, or privacy of the people with whom they work. . . ." This includes safeguarding the rights, interests, and sensitivities of those studied, explaining the aims of the investigation as clearly as possible to the persons involved, respecting the anonymity of informants, not exploiting individual informants for personal gain, and giving "fair return" for all services. It also includes the responsibility to communicate the results of the research to the individuals and groups likely to be affected as well as to the general public.

Informed consent is a critical aspect of anthropological ethics. Generally, obtaining the informed consent of study participants requires anthropologists to take part in ongoing and dynamic discussion with their consultants about the nature of the study as well as the risks and benefits of participation in it (Clark and Kingsolver n.d.). In particular, informed consent means that study participants should understand the ways in which release of the research data are likely to affect them. Further, individuals must be free to decide whether or not they will participate in the study.

Numerous projects have tested the boundaries of ethics in anthropology. One of the best known of these was "Project Camelot," a mid-1960s attempt by the Army and Department of Defense to enlist anthropologists and other social scientists in achieving American foreign policy goals. The goal of Project Camelot was to create a model for predicting civil wars, but the project also was implicated in using military and cultural means to counter insurgency movements and to prop up friendly governments (Horowitz 1967). When Project Camelot was made public in 1965, the United States had recently invaded the Dominican Republic and was escalating the war in Vietnam.

Project Camelot created controversy both inside and outside of anthropology. In countries where anthropologists worked, people began to see them as spies whose presence presaged an American invasion. At the American Anthropological Association, Project Camelot led to vitriolic debate, where members raised concerns for the integrity of research, the safety of anthropologists in the field, and the purposes to which anthropological knowledge might be put. These concerns eventually led to the issuing of the first official statement on anthropological ethics in 1971.

Similar concerns have been raised recently over the use of anthropologists by the military in operations in Afghanistan and Iraq. Starting in early 2007, the Pentagon has employed teams of anthropologists and other social scientists to help its combat brigades. According to some, this program has been very successful. For example, *The New York Times* reported that Col. Martin Schweitzer, commander of the 82nd Airborne Division, credited anthropologists with helping reduce combat operations by 60 percent (Rohde 2007). However, the use of anthropologists in such circumstances continues to be extremely problematic. A recent American Anthropological Association report notes that engagement with the military raises concerns about obligations to those whom anthropologists study, perils for the discipline and one's colleagues, perils for the broader academic community; as well as issues of secrecy and transparency (Peacock et al. 2007).

It is difficult to see how many of anthropology's ethical requirements can be met under conditions of warfare. How, for example, are participants to give coercion-free consent while they are subject to military occupation? How can anthropologists assure, within reason, that the information they supply will not harm the safety, dignity, or privacy of the people with whom they work? When anthropologists supply information directly to military officers in the field, do they become legitimate targets of war? On the other hand, do these problems mean that anthropologists have no place in the military? The answer is far from clear. Surely, a military force that is informed about the cultures among which it operates will be more effective than one that is not. Soldiers of all ranks who understand the dynamics of culture, the importance of critical meanings and symbols, and the structure and distribution of power within a society are liable to be more successful and less destructive than are those who do not. Where are they to get this knowledge if not from anthropology? One possible solution to the dilemma is for anthropologists to play a role in military training but not in military operations. However, this answer is not likely to satisfy all anthropologists.

Ultimately, ethical behavior is the responsibility of each individual anthropologist. The American Anthropological Association issues statements about ethics to which its members are supposed to subscribe. Universities and some research organizations have institutional review boards that examine all research involving human subjects for ethical violations. However, not all anthropologists are subject to the American Anthropological Association or to institutional review boards. Lawyers who behave unethically can be disbarred—legally forbidden to practice law. Doctors can have their medical licenses revoked. There is no comparable sanction for anthropologists (and, indeed, for members of most disciplines). Therefore, there will always be a great diversity of anthropological practice.

NEW ROLES FOR THE ETHNOGRAPHER

Although there have been native anthropologists for a long time, until the 1970s the prevailing model of fieldwork was a European or North American ethnographer visiting a relatively isolated and bounded society who reported on that society to other Europeans and North Americans. In the past several decades this model has become unrealistic. Immigration, inexpensive communication, and relatively cheap airfare have altered the world and the nature of the anthropologist's job.

Whether working in cities or villages or with tribal groups, almost all ethnographers must take into account the interaction of these local units with larger social structures, economies, and cultures. Such connections may extend from the region to the entire world. Thus, research may mean following consultants from villages to their workplaces in cities or collecting genealogies that spread over countries or even continents. In addition to expanding the research site, contemporary ethnographers must often use techniques such as questionnaires, social surveys, archival material, government documents, and court records in addition to participant observation. The deep connections among cultures and the global movement of individuals means that we must constantly reevaluate the nature of the cultures we are studying, their geographical spread, their economic and political position, and their relation to each other.

Today, not only are native anthropologists much more common, but the people anthropologists study generally have far greater knowledge of the world than they did in earlier times. Often they understand what anthropology is and what anthropologists do, something not true in the past.

In some cases, this has led to difficulties as people struggle over the question of who has the right to speak for a group. In other cases, people from the groups that anthropologists have described have publicly taken issue with their analysis. For example, in the early 2000s, a fierce controversy broke out over anthropological descriptions of the Yanomamo, an often studied Amazonian group. Had their primary ethnographer, Napoleon Chagnon, portrayed them accurately? Was the research team that he was part of responsible for spreading disease and decimating Yanomamo villages? Anthropologists, journalists, and Yanomamo tribe members debated these questions at meetings and in the popular press (for a review of the debate see Borofsky 2005).

Despite controversies, for the most part natives' increased knowledge of the outside has resulted in closer relations among anthropologists and the people they study as well as more accurate ethnography. Ethnographic data are often useful to a society. Sometimes they serve as the basis for the revitalization of cultural identities that have been nearly effaced by Western impact (Feinberg 1994). Sometimes they play important roles in establishing group claims to "authenticity" and are useful in local political and economic contexts. For example, when Kathleen Adams (1995) carried out her fieldwork among the Toraja of Sulawesi, Indonesia, she became a featured event on tourist itineraries in the region. Toraja tour guides led their groups to the home of her host, both validating his importance in the village and bolstering the tourists' experience of the Toraja as a group sufficiently "authentic" and important to be studied by anthropologists.

In the past, anthropologists sometimes worried about their subject disappearing. They argued that the main thing anthropology was designed to study was small-scale, relatively isolated "primitive" societies. They worried that as economic development spread around the world, such societies would go out of existence and anthropology would essentially be done. In a small sense they were right, but in the larger sense they were wrong. Any anthropologist today looking to study a society untouched by the outside world would be out of luck. No such societies have existed for a long time. On the other hand, the forces of globalization have been as productive of diversity as they have been of homogeneity. Economic, political, and social forces bring groups of people together in new ways, in conflict and in cooperation. New cultural forms are created and old ones modified. Human cultural diversity, imagination, and adaptability show no signs of dying out, so anthropologists will always have material to study. Wherever human cultures exist and however they change, anthropologists will be there, devising means to study, understand, and think about them.

BRINGING IT BACK HOME: ANTHROPOLOGISTS AND HUMAN RIGHTS

What could be more obvious than that anthropologists should support human rights and be actively engaged in their promotion? Doubting the value of human rights is like arguing against freedom of speech or claiming that children are not important. Yet, human rights pose ethical dilemmas for anthropologists. Almost all anthropologists believe firmly in their duty to promote human rights in our own society. Many also believe that they have an obligation to promote the interests of those they study. For example, Laura R. Graham (2006:5) writes that "Our privileged position, specialized training, and unique skills . . . carry with them specific ethical obligations to promote the well-being of the people who are collaborators in our anthropological research and in the production of anthropological knowledge." Ida Nicolaisen points out that standing for human rights is often a matter of life and death. For example, she notes that in the Philippines between 2005 and late summer 2006, at least 73 indigenous people were "subjected to extra-judicial killings" and concludes that "We owe it to indigenous peoples and other marginalized groups to stand up for their basic human rights when needed" (Nicolaisen 2006:6).

But there often are difficulties determining what rights are and whether or not we should stand up for them. Laura Nader (2006:6) writes that ideas about human rights were developed in a largely western European context and are often conceived of as "something Euro-Americans take to others." Promoting Western notions of human rights may mean denying people in other societies what they consider to be their rights to pursue individual and cultural choices. Female genital mutilation is a good example and is covered in more detail in Chapter 8, but there are many others. Consider Islamic hadd ("to the limit") punishments, such as stoning for adultery, amputation of limbs for theft, and flogging for moral offenses. Hadd punishments deeply offend many people (including many Muslims), yet they form a core component of ethical belief and practice for many people in some Islamic nations. The organization Human Rights Watch reports that courts in Saudi Arabia continue to impose punishments such as amputations of hands and feet for robbery and floggings for lesser crimes such as "sexual deviance" and drunkenness (Human Rights Watch 2001:14). In northern Nigeria, between 2000 and 2004, courts passed more than 60 amputation sentences (Human Rights Watch 2004:38). Anthropologist Carolyn Fluehr-Lobban (2005) interviewed attorneys, judges, social scientists, and journalists in Sudan, a country that has practiced hadd punishments. She notes that most Sudanese Muslims oppose the use of hadd, and see it as an abuse of religion by the state. However, they also think that Western interest in eliminating such punishment is unwarranted interference in their right to determine their own culture. They point to a double standard: Westerners, particularly Americans, see hadd punishments as "barbaric" while they ignore their own abuses of human rights, such as the death penalty, waterboarding, Abu Ghraib, and Guantanamo.

YOU DECIDE

1. Given the diversity of culture and the anthropological importance of cultural relativism, can there be such a thing as universal human rights?
2. If anthropologists have moral obligations to the people with whom they work, should they ever work with people whose beliefs and practices they disapprove of? If yes, then what obligations do they have to such people? If no, how are we to accurately represent such people?
3. What sorts of things do you consider to be universal human rights? How good is our society at assuring the rights you have identified? Do you think there is a core set of universal rights upon which most people could or should agree?

CHAPTER SUMMARY

1. Anthropology began in the 19th century. In that era, anthropologists were compilers of data rather than fieldworkers. Their goal was to describe and document the evolutionary history of human society. There were numerous problems with their data and methods.
2. In the United States, Franz Boas established a style of anthropology that rejected evolutionism. Boas insisted that anthropologists collect data through participant observation. He argued that cultures were the result of their own history and could not be compared to one another, a position now called *cultural relativism.*
3. In Britain, Bronislaw Malinowski and others also developed a tradition of fieldwork. Although their focus was different than Boas', they also saw members of other cultures as fully rational and worthy of respect.
4. Almost all anthropologists today do fieldwork, and many continue to work in small communities. Most focus on answering specific questions rather than describing entire societies. Anthropological techniques include participant observation, interviews, questionnaires, and mapping.

5. Cross-cultural comparison has always been an aspect of anthropology. The Human Relations Area File (HRAF) is a large database that facilitates cross-cultural research.
6. Despite the presence of important women in early 20th-century anthropology, women were historically underrepresented in anthropological writing. This situation began to be redressed in the late 1960s.
7. In the 1980s, postmodernists urged anthropologists to become more sensitive to issues of voice, history, and power. Postmodernists' insistence that the objective world was unknowable and the anthropologist's voice uncertain created intense debate but ultimately enriched ethnography.
8. One response to postmodernism was collaborative anthropology. Some anthropologists placed special emphasis on the political dimensions of their work. They often took great pains to involve members of the group being studied in the production of ethnographic knowledge.
9. Anthropologists who study their own society have become more numerous. Although native anthropologists may have advantages of access and rapport in some cases, they also experience special burdens more intensely, such as whether to expose aspects of the culture that may be received unfavorably by outsiders.
10. Doing anthropology often raises ethical questions. Anthropological ethics require protecting the dignity, privacy, and anonymity of the people one studies. However, anthropological ethics are rarely simple. The use of anthropologists in pursuit of foreign relations goals is sometimes extremely problematic.
11. Anthropologists are increasingly enmeshed in a global society. Those they study are rarely isolated and are often quite knowledgeable about anthropology. Anthropological knowledge is often important in the ways people understand their identity and, as such, is increasingly political.

KEY TERMS

Collaborative ethnography
Consultant
Cultural relativism
Culture shock
Ethnocentrism
Ethnography
Ethnology
Human Relations Area Files
Informant
Participant observation
Postmodernism
Racism
Respondents

Serena Nanda

Human language consists of words and gestures, as illustrated in this interaction between Israeli Bedouin in a marketplace.

CHAPTER 4

COMMUNICATION

CHAPTER OUTLINE

Inner City Ebonics

The Origins and Characteristics of Human Language

The Structure of Language

Language and Culture

- Language and Social Stratification
- The Sapir-Whorf Hypothesis

Nonverbal Communication

Language Change

- Language and Culture Contact
- Tracing Relationships Among Languages

Bringing It Back Home: English Only

- You Decide

INNER CITY EBONICS

LARRY H., a fifteen-year-old core member of the Jets [a teenage gang in Philadelphia] is one of their loudest and roughest members. He gives the least recognition to conventional rules of politeness. Most of you meeting Larry for the first time probably wouldn't like him any more than his teachers do, and the dislike would be mutual. Larry causes trouble in and out of school. He was put back from the eleventh grade to the ninth and has been threatened with further action by the school authorities. In the dialogues that follow, John Lewis (JL) interviews Larry:

JL: What happens to you after you die? Do you know?

Larry: Yeah, I know. (What?) After they put you in the ground, your body turns into—ah—bones an' shit.

JL: What happens to your spirit?

Larry: Your spirit—soon as you die, your spirit leaves you. (And where does the spirit go?) Well, it all depends. . . . (On what?) You know, like some people say if you're good an' shit, your spirit goin' t'heaven. . . . 'n' if you bad, your spirit goin' to hell. Well, bullshit. Your spirit goin' to hell anyway, good or bad.

JL: Why?

Larry: Why? I'll tell you why. 'Cause, you see, doesn' nobody really know that it's a God, y'know, 'cause I mean I have seen black gods, pink gods, white gods, all color gods, and don't nobody know it's really a God. An' when they be sayin' if you good, you goin' t'heaven, tha's bullshit, 'cause you ain't goin' to no heaven, 'cause it ain't no heaven for you to go to.

Larry is a paradigmatic speaker of African-American English Vernacular (AAEV) as opposed to Standard English. His grammar shows a high concentration of such characteristic AAEV forms as negative inversion ("don't nobody know"), negative concord ("you ain't goin' to no heaven"), invariant *be* ("when they be sayin'"), dummy *it* for standard *there* ("it ain't no heaven"), optional copula deletion ("if you're good . . . if you bad") and full forms of auxiliaries ("I have seen"). . . .

Our particular interest here is on the logical form of this passage. Larry presents a complex set of interdependent propositions which can be explained by setting out the Standard English equivalents in linear order: Everyone has a different idea of God, therefore no one knows if God exists. A God that doesn't exist couldn't have made a heaven, therefore you can't go there. Thus you are going to hell.

This hypothetical argument is not carried on at a high level of seriousness. It is a game played with ideas as counters in which opponents use a wide variety of verbal devices to win. The interviewer, John Lewis, challenges Larry's logic:

> **JL:** Well, if there's no heaven, how could there be a hell?
>
> **Larry:** I mean—ye-eah. Well, let me tell you, it ain't no hell, 'cause this is hell right here, y'know. (This is hell?) Yeah, this is hell right here.

. . . Despite the fact that Larry does not believe in God and has just denied all knowledge of him, John Lewis advances the following hypothetical question:

> **JL:** . . . but, just say that there is a God, what color is he? White or black?
>
> **Larry:** Well, if it is a God . . . I wouldn' know what color, I couldn' say,—couldn' nobody say what color he is or really would be.
>
> **JL:** But now, jus' suppose there was a God—
>
> **Larry:** Unless'n they say . . .
>
> **JL:** No, I was jus' saying jus' suppose there is a God, would he be white or black?
>
> **Larry:** . . . He'd be white, man.
>
> **JL:** Why?
>
> **Larry:** Why? I'll tell you why. 'Cause the average whitey out here got everything, you dig? And the nigger ain't got shit, y'know? Y'unnerstan'? So—um—for—in order for that to happen, you know it ain't no black God that's doin' that bullshit.

No one can hear Larry's answer to this question without being convinced that they are in the presence of a skilled speaker with great "verbal presence of mind," who can use the English language expertly for many purposes. Larry's answer to John Lewis is a complex argument. The formulation is not in Standard English, but it is clear and effective, even for those not familiar with the vernacular.

In these passages from *Language in the Inner City,* linguist William Labov (1972) analyzes African-American English Vernacular (AAEV), which today is sometimes called *Ebonics.* AAEV has deep roots in the African-American community, particularly among rural and urban working-class blacks. Although not all Americans of African origin speak it, in the minds of many Americans AAEV has become emblematic of black speech. There are lots of different ways of speaking English in the United States, but few have been as widely criticized as AAEV.

From the 1950s to the 1970s, a group of linguists, psychologists, and educators called *cultural deficit theorists* argued that African-American children did poorly in school because of general cognitive deficiencies, in which language played a key role. They argued that the poor speech of these children, which they characterized as coarse, simple, and irrational, was due to a culturally deprived home environment (Ammon 1971). They proposed that if people could be taught to speak Standard English they would be able to think more logically, and this would help lift them from poverty (Bereiter and Engelmann 1966; Engelmann and Engelmann 1966).

The work of William Labov and others was central to countering the arguments of the deficit theorists. Through analysis of dialogues such as those with Larry, Labov showed that inner-city black speech, particularly the speech of children of poverty, was no more or less complex, rational, or orderly than that of other English speakers. It simply followed different rules, many of which were also found in other languages. Labov demonstrated that AAEV was just a different way of speaking and, from a linguistic point of view, neither better nor worse than any other.

So, what is good English? Consider the example of the double negative. Almost everyone reading this book has heard someone (perhaps a teacher) claim that a double negative is really a positive. Thus, saying "I don't want no" is really saying I want some. This is simply incorrect. When Mick Jagger sings, "I can't get no satisfaction," no native English speaker believes he is saying how satisfied he is. And no one imagines that the kids singing in Pink Floyd's "The Wall" are telling us how much they want to go to school.

But sometimes two negatives do make a positive, as when a child who refuses to do her homework says: "I won't not do my homework if you buy me some ice cream." And two or more positives can sometimes make a negative, as in:

Speaker A: "Yes, I will do it."

Speaker B: "Yeah, yeah, yeah, sure you will."

The point is that, from a linguistic perspective, one way of speaking is as good as the next. There is no reason to prefer "I don't have any money" to "I ain't got no money," and there is no reason that saying "I'm about to go get lunch" is better than saying "I'm fixin to get me some lunch." All the statements are fully logical, comprehensible, and communicate the information the speaker desires.

So why does society act as if one statement is good and the other bad? Because speech often identifies the speaker's ethnic background, social class, geographical location, and other aspects of their life. Our judgments are really about people, based on their speech, not on the comprehensibility of the speech itself.

Although all humans who are physically able to do so communicate through language, speech is not just biology. The language we speak, the style of our speaking, who we speak to, and how we speak to them are all aspects of culture.

THE ORIGINS AND CHARACTERISTICS OF HUMAN LANGUAGE

Although passing information is critical to the survival of most living things, members of other species communicate very differently than humans. Extensive research shows that no member of any other species can make up a story and tell it to another, understand a piece of poetry, or discuss what it would like to eat tomorrow, yet these are things that people in all human cultures do regularly.

Animal vocalizations are referred to as *calls,* and animal **call systems** may have up to 60 sounds. However, even large call systems are restricted to a fixed number of signals generally uttered in response to specific events. Human language, on the other hand, is capable of recreating complex thought patterns and experiences in words.

So, when did humans first begin to speak? Anthropologists offer several answers to this question. Certainly our most distant ancestors communicated, but they probably used call systems similar to modern-day primates. Some believe that language might have begun as early as two million years ago, at the time of the emergence of the genus *Homo* (Schepartz 1993:119), but most anthropologists think that language like our own has been limited to members of our own species. The earliest *Homo sapiens* date from about 200,000 years ago, so language may well have emerged at that time. A third position (Bickerton 1998) holds that modern human language emerged about 50,000 years ago, in connection with a big jump in the sophistication of human toolmaking and symbolic expression.

Colorado University

Some nonhuman animals show surprising linguistic abilities. Here a chimpanzee signs "double apple" to his trainer. However, human language is uniquely complex, sophisticated, and abstract.

Whichever date is correct, anthropologists generally agree that language is part of our biological adaptation. Although in any culture some people talk with greater or lesser artistry than others, all physiologically normal individuals in every culture develop adequate language skills.

Language is more than simply a human capacity or ability. For example, people have the capacity to learn algebra or ice skating. They may do it or not as their culture and their individual choices dictate. Language is different. Unless prevented by total social isolation or physical incapacity, all humans learn a first language as part of the developmental process of childhood. All go through the same stages of language learning in the same sequence and at roughly the same speed regardless of the language being learned. Language is an innate property of the mind.

Humans have what Steven Pinker (1994) calls a "language instinct." Pinker points out that the language "instinct" in humans is very different from instinctive communication in other animals. Among animals the instinct for communication means that dogs do not *learn* to wag their tails when they are content and growl when they are angry: They do these things as an expression of their underlying genetic code. Dog behavior is specieswide. A growl means the same thing to a dog in Vladivostok as it does to a dog in Manhattan. But language is not instinctual in this way. The human "instinct" is to learn the language of the group into which the individual is socialized. There is no biological basis for learning one language over another. For example, an infant born to French-speaking parents but raised in an English-speaking family has no predisposition to speak French.

The universality of the process of learning a first language as well as the underlying similarities that unite all human languages led Noam Chomsky (1975) and many others to propose that there is a **universal grammar**—a basic set of principles, conditions, and rules that form the foundation of all languages. Children learn language by applying this unconscious universal grammar to the sounds they hear.

The social element of language learning is critical. To learn language, we must be able to interact verbally with others. There is a particularly important period from our birth until about 6 years of age. Children deprived of contact during these years never learn to speak like other members of their community. This is illustrated by the case of Genie, a child discovered in the 1970s by social workers in California. Genie had been locked in an attic for the first 12 years of her life. With training and good living conditions, she rapidly acquired a large vocabulary, but she was never able to master English syntax; she created sentences like "Genie have momma have baby grow up" (Pinker 1994:292). Children like Genie demonstrate that although language is a biological capacity of humanity, it can only be activated within a social group. Thus, language provides an outstanding example of the interrelation of biology and culture.

Human language is first and foremost a system of symbols. A **symbol** is just something that stands for something else. Words are symbols, and they stand for things, actions, and ideas because speakers of a language agree that they do, a feature of human language called **conventionality.** An animal is no more a dog than it is a *chien* (French), a *perro* (Spanish), or a *kutta* (Hindi).

This seemingly trivial fact is critical for two reasons. First, because the relationship between a series of sounds (a word) and their meaning is symbolic, relatively few sounds can be used to refer to an infinitely large number of meanings. For nonhuman animals there is a direct connection between a sound and its meaning; 60 sounds equals 60 meanings. Most human languages have only 30 to 40 sounds. However, used in combination, these sounds can produce an endless variety of words and meanings. There is no maximum number of words or sentences in any human language. People constantly create new ones, a characteristic known as **productivity.**

Second, symbols enable humans to transmit and store information, a capacity that makes our cultures possible. If humans had to learn everything they know by trial and error, by reward and punishment, or by watching someone else do it, our lives would be vastly different and much simpler than they are. Human beings do learn by these methods, but they also learn by talking. We tell each other our experiences and the stories passed down to us. We discuss the past and plan for the future using words. This human ability to speak about different times and places is called **displacement.**

The ability of humans to use symbols allows us to store information. In cultures with writing, such stored information is vast. Consider, for example, that no one individual could possibly know everything written in the books in even a relatively small university library. However, because we can store our knowledge symbolically as words, we can have access to everything that is there. And with the Internet . . . well, you get the point!

THE STRUCTURE OF LANGUAGE

Although there are enormous differences among languages, there are also some compelling similarities. Every language has a structure: an internal logic and a particular relationship among its parts. Descriptive, or structural, linguistics is the study of the internal workings of language. A basic insight of structural linguistics is that all languages are composed of four subsystems: **phonology** (a system of sounds), **morphology** (a system for creating words from sounds), **semantics** (a system that relates words to meanings), and **syntax** (a system of rules for combining words into meaningful sentences).

At a very basic level, all language is made up of sounds. Humans use a vast array of sounds in their languages. For example, the International Phonetic Alphabet (IPA), a system designed to represent the sounds of all human languages in writing, has more than 100 base symbols, which can be altered by about 55 modifiers. The total set of sounds found in human language is referred to as the **phones** of language. No individual language uses more than a small subset of this huge set. The sounds that are used in any individual language are called the **phonemes** of that language. Thus, humanity as a whole has a single set of phones. Individual languages, such as English, each have a set of phonemes.

Phonemes distinguish meaning within a given language. For example, the English words *den* and *then* have different meanings, and this difference is indicated by the sounds that are made when we produce the consonants /d/ or /th/ at the beginning of the word. In other languages, such as Spanish, both of these sounds exist, but they are not used to convey different meanings. Rather, their usage depends on whether their phoneme is found in the middle or at the beginning of a word. Thus, they are **allophones;** that is, both phones indicate only one phoneme.

At some level, almost everyone is aware of the phonemic differences among languages. For example, the "rolled r" common in Spanish is not found in most varieties of English, and many English speakers find the sound difficult to make. On the other hand, the /th/ sound (as in the word *the*) is common in most varieties of English but does not exist in French or Japanese (as well as many other languages). Attempting to speak one language using the phonemes of another results in an accent.

At a more profound level, phonemes are probably the first aspect of language that an infant learns. This is partially a process of learning which sounds affect the meanings of words and which sounds do not. Every child has the biological capacity to acceptably make all the sounds of all human language. However, they learn the breathing and the tongue and lip positions associated only with the sounds of their own language. Learning as an adult to hear and make new sounds can be very difficult.

All languages are made up of units that have meaning. We refer to these as **morphemes.** Morphemes can be composed of any number of phonemes. Some are as simple as a single phoneme (the English morphemes "A" and –s for example), and most are relatively brief. Words are composed of morphemes. Again, some are extremely simple. "A" is a phoneme, a morpheme, and a word.

Morphemes that can be used as words are called **free morphemes.** However, not all morphemes are free. Consider the morpheme –s, previously noted. In English –s, as in "dogs," is a morpheme that means "make what comes before this sound plural." Similarly un–, as in "undo," means "make what comes after this negative." For these morphemes to make sense in speech, they must be attached, or bound, to other morphemes. In consequence, they are called **bound morphemes.**

Words can be composed of any number of morphemes. For example, the word "teacher" has two: "teach" and "–er" (here –er refers to someone who does what came before it). Long words, for example, antidisestablishmentarianism are simply strings of morphemes.

Languages differ in the way morphemes and words are related. **Isolating languages** such as English and Chinese tend to have few morphemes per word and fairly simple rules for combining them. **Agglutinating languages** have a great number of morphemes per word. In languages such as Mohawk or Inuktitut (an Arctic Canadian language), translating a single word may require an entire English sentence. For example, the Inuktitut word qasuirrsarvigssarsingitluinarnarpuq contains 10 morphemes and is best translated as "someone did not find a completely suitable resting place" (Bonvillain 1997:19).

The total stock of words in a language is known as its **lexicon.** A lexicon often provides clues to culture because it tends to reflect the objects and ideas that members of that culture consider important. For example, the average American can name 50 to 100 types of plants, but members of foraging societies can often name 500 to 1000 types (Harris 1989:72). Germans in Munich have a vocabulary of more than 70 words to describe the strength, color, fizziness, clarity, and age of beer because beer is so central to their culture (Hage 1972, cited in Salzmann 1993:256). Americans have large numbers of words to describe cars or money but have far fewer to describe bicycles.

Anthropologists can sometimes use vocabulary as a clue to understanding experience and reality in different cultures. For example, the words people use for their kin tells us something of the nature of their families. In English, a woman uses the term brother-in-law to speak about her sister's husband, her husband's brother, and the husbands of all her husband's sisters. The use of a single term for all of these relations reflects the similarity of a woman's behavior toward the men in these kinship statuses. In Hindi, a language of North India, a woman uses separate terms for her sister's husband (behnoi), her husband's elder brother (jait), her husband's younger brother (deva), and her husband's sisters' husbands (nandoya). The variety of words in Hindi reflects the fact that a woman treats the members of each of these categories differently.

Languages build vocabularies around ideas and things important to their speakers. Germans in Munich have more than 70 words to describe beer.

Sounds and words alone, however, do not make up a language. In order to convey meaning, every language has syntax, rules that structure the combination of words into meaningful utterances. Languages differ in their syntactic structures. In English, word order is a basic element of syntax, so statements such as "The dog bit the man" and "The man bit the dog" have very different meanings. Word order is not equally important in all languages. In Japanese, for example, the subject and object of a sentence are indicated by word endings, and order is less important. In Japanese, John gave Mary the book is translated *John-san ga Mary-san ni hon o ageta.* The same word order, with the word endings *ga* and *ni* reversed *(John-san ni Mary-san ga hon o ageta)* would be Mary gave John the book.

Parts of speech (nouns, verbs, and so on) are a critical aspect of syntax. All languages have a word class of nouns, but different languages have different subclasses of nouns, frequently referred to as *genders.* (In linguistics the word *gender* does not refer to masculine and feminine traits but rather to the category or "class" of a word.) For example, Papago, a Native-American language, divides all the features of the world into two genders: "living things" and "growing things." Living things include all animated objects; growing things refer to inanimate objects. Spanish, French, Italian, and many other languages divide nouns into masculine and feminine subclasses. German and Latin have masculine, feminine, and neuter subclasses. Some languages have many more subclasses. Kivunjo, a language spoken in East Africa, has 16 of them (Pinker 1994:27).

Applying the rules of grammar turns meaningless sequences of words into meaningful utterances, but we can recognize a sentence as grammatical even if it makes no sense. To use a now classic example (Chomsky 1965), consider the following sentences: "Colorless green ideas sleep furiously," and "Furiously sleep ideas green colorless." Both sentences are meaningless in English, but the first is easily recognized as grammatical by an English speaker, whereas the second is both meaningless and ungrammatical.

LANGUAGE AND CULTURE

Phonemes, morphemes, syntax . . . these are essentially elements of the biology of language, but language is much more than just its structure. Consider the following exchange:

Scene: It's a clear, hot evening in July. J and K have finished their meal. The children are sitting nearby. There is a knock at the door. J rises, answers the knock, and finds L standing outside.

J: Hello, my friend! How're you doing? How are you feeling, L? You feeling good? *(J now turns in the direction of K and addresses her.)*

J: Look who here, everybody! Look who just come in. Sure, it's my Indian friend, L. Pretty good, all right. *(J slaps L on the shoulder and, looking him directly in the eyes, seizes his hand and pumps it wildly up and down.)*

The Western Apache.

J: Come right in, my friend! Don't stay outside in the rain. Better you come in right now. *(J now drapes his arm around L's shoulder and moves him in the direction of a chair.)*

J: Sit down! Sit right down! Take your loads off you ass. You hungry? You want crackers? Maybe you want some beer? You want some wine? Bread? You want some sandwich? How about it? You hungry? I don't know. Maybe you sick. Maybe you don't eat again long time. *(K has now stopped what she is doing and is looking on with amusement. L has seated himself and has a look of bemused resignation on his face.)*

J: You sure looking good to me, L. You looking pretty fat! Pretty good all right! You got new boots? Where you buy them? Sure pretty good boots! I glad . . . *(At this point, J breaks into laughter. K joins in. L shakes his head and smiles. The joke is over).*

The joke is over . . . So what was the joke? This joke, from the Western Apache, recorded by Keith Basso (1979), is about how the Apache see white people as communicating with them and with each other. In the joke, *J* pretends he is a white man. The joke is that white speech, as *J* presents it, is highly inappropriate and offensive. For starters, you do not publicly call someone a friend or ask how he or she is feeling. For the Western Apache, these are very personal statements and questions. To use them in a highly public way as *J* does here conveys insincerity. The Apache believe that one should enter and leave a room as unobtrusively as possible, so *J* making a big to-do about *L* coming into the room is inappropriate as well. Actions such as putting an arm around another man's shoulder or asking repeatedly if he wants something to eat are understood as both violations of individual dignity and overwhelming bossiness. To the Apache, such actions suggest that the speaker thinks the person he or she is talking to is of no account and that his wishes can be safely ignored. Perhaps worst of all is suggesting that another might be sick. Not only is this a violation of privacy; the Apache fear that talking about misfortune may well bring it on.

Knowing only the technical grammatical aspects of language would not help much in understanding *J* and *L's* speech. Their speech embeds critical cultural concepts and values. Without understanding their culture, an observer cannot possibly get the joke. Language is so heavily freighted with culture that understanding one is almost always a key to understanding the other. One way anthropologists analyze this relationship is to think in terms of speech performance. Such performance includes what people are saying as well as what they are communicating beyond the actual words. **Sociolinguistics** is the study of the relationship between language and culture. Sociolinguists study speech performances and attempt to identify, describe, and understand the ways in which language is used in different social contexts.

The ways in which people actually speak are highly dependent on the context of their speech as well as issues such as class, ethnicity, and geography. For example, a public political speech has different purposes and is limited by different norms than a political discussion among friends. And different cultures have different norms regarding political speeches: who can participate as speaker and audience, the appropriate topics and cultural themes for such a speech, where such speeches can take place, the relationship between the speaker and hearer, the language used in a multilingual community, and so forth.

In some cultures, different speech forms are used depending on whether the speaker and hearer are intimate friends, acquaintances on equal footing, or people of distinctly different social statuses. French, German, and Yoruba, among many other languages, have formal and informal pronouns that are not found in English. The rules for their use vary among cultures. In France, parents use the informal term to address their children, but children use the formal term to address their parents. In the Spanish spoken in Costa Rica, many people use three forms: the informal *tú* is used by an adult speaking to a child (or lover), the formal *usted* is used among strangers, and the intermediate term *vos* can be used among friends. In India, the status of a husband is higher than that of a wife, and among most Hindi speakers a wife never addresses her husband by his name (certainly not in public) but uses a roundabout expression that would translate into English as something like "I am speaking to you, sir."

In many speech communities, the ordinary person knows and uses more than one language. Sociolinguists are interested in the different contexts in which one or the other language is used and what this language choice indicates. For example, does it serve to solidify ethnic or familial identity, or is it a means to distance oneself from another person or group?

Language and Social Stratification

From a linguistic perspective, all languages are equally sophisticated and serve the needs of their speakers equally well, and every human being speaks with equal grammatical sophistication. Despite this, in complex stratified societies such as the United States, some speech is considered "correct" and other speech is judged inferior (see the example that opens this chapter).

In hierarchical societies, the most powerful group generally determines what is "proper" in language. Indeed, the grammatical constructions used by the social elites are considered *language,* whereas deviations from them are often called *dialects.* Because the power of the speaker rather than any inherent qualities of a speech form determines its acceptability, linguist Max Weinreich has defined a language as "a dialect with an army and a navy" (quoted in Pinker 1994:28).

The relation of language usage to social class and power is reflected in the speech of different social classes in the United States. In a classic study, sociolinguist William Labov (1972) noted that elites and working-class people have different vocabularies and pronounce words differently. The forms associated with higher socioeconomic status are considered "proper," whereas forms spoken by those in lower socioeconomic statuses are considered incorrect and stigmatized.

Labov found that speakers often vary their vocabulary and pronunciation in different contexts and that the degree of such variation is related to their social class. At the bottom and top of the social hierarchy there is little variation. Elites use privileged forms of speech and the poor use stigmatized forms. However, members of the lower–middle class often use stigmatized forms in casual speech but privileged forms in careful speech. One interpretation is that people at the bottom and top of the social hierarchy do not vary their speech because their social position is stable. The very poor do not believe they have much chance to rise, and the wealthy are secure in their positions. Members of the lower–middle class, however, are concerned with raising their social position and in consequence copy the speech patterns of the wealthy in some social situations. However, they are also concerned with maintaining connections to family and friends and therefore use stigmatized speech with them. Labov's study makes clear what many of us know but do not like to admit: We do judge a person's social status by the way he or she speaks. What we say and how we say it are ways of telling people who we are socially or, perhaps, who we would like to be.

Although there are many stigmatized variants of American English, including Appalachian English, Dutchified Pennsylvania English, Hawaiian Creole, Gullah, and emergent Hispanic Englishes, the most stigmatized is African-American Vernacular English (AAVE), also called *Ebonics.* As we noted earlier, AAVE is simply a variant of Standard English, neither better nor worse than any other. Further, from Mark Twain and William Faulkner to Toni Morrison and Maya Angelou, from George Gershwin to Public Enemy and Run DMC, Ebonics has had deep influences on American art, speech, fiction, and music.

Since the 1970s, controversy over Ebonics has frequently been politicized. For example, in the mid-1990s, the Oakland School Board in California encouraged its teachers to *make use of* Ebonics in teaching Standard English (Monaghan 1997). Many Americans misunderstood the Oakland School Board as encouraging the teaching of Ebonics, and this misunderstanding ignited a national furor. A North Carolina legislator denounced Ebonics as "absurd," an *Atlanta Constitution* editorial referred to "the Ebonic plague," and laws banning the teaching of Ebonics were introduced in several state legislatures (Matthews 1997; Sanchez 1997).

Individuals who speak only Ebonics are at a disadvantage in the larger society, and most realize that AAVE is stigmatized as symbolizing ignorance while Standard Spoken American English (SSAE) is considered "normal" and symbolizes intelligence. Most AAVE speakers, however, through school, exposure to mass media, and their job situations, do become effective speakers of several varieties of English. AAVE and SSAE have similar capacities to deliver both "formal and informal knowledge as well as local knowledge and wisdom" (Morgan 2004), but speakers of AAVE, like others who are bilingual, must learn to code switch, to move seamlessly between two languages, which requires an acute awareness of the politics of language.

The Sapir-Whorf Hypothesis

The close relationship between culture and language raises interesting questions about the connections between language and thought. At the opening of the chapter, we pointed out that in the 1950s and 1960s some social scientists believed, incorrectly, that AAVE was less logical than SSAE and that, as a result, AAVE speakers thought illogically. In so doing, they assumed a strong relationship between speaking and thinking. The existence of such a relationship is an old and controversial idea in anthropology. It is often associated with the work of Edward Sapir and his student Benjamin Lee Whorf.

In the early 20th century, Sapir and Whorf argued that since language played a critical role in determining the way people understand the world, people who spoke different languages must understand the world in different ways. They proposed that the ability to think about things such as time, space, and matter are conditioned by the structure of the languages people speak. They argued that we perceive the world in certain ways because we talk about the world in certain ways. This idea has come to be known as the **Sapir-Whorf hypothesis.**

We clearly choose our words to guide and direct the thoughts of others. Politicians, for example, routinely search for derogatory words and phrases to characterize their opponents. Or consider the term *side effect.* A side effect is an unwanted consequence of something such as a drug. However, the phrase *side effect* encourages us to think of it as off to the side and therefore less important than the *"central" effect* of the drug. But is it less important? In the late 1950s and early 1960s, thalidomide was prescribed to calm the stomachs of pregnant mothers. The drug was effective but had the horrible side effect of causing severe malformities in babies born to those mothers. Calling the deformities *side effects* did not prevent people from thinking that they were more important than the drug's effect. In fact, the thalidomide case led to special testing of drugs prescribed during pregnancy. This makes an important point: Word choice can encourage people to think certain ways. However, words cannot force people to think in one way or another. Even a government that controlled all the words people used could not control their thoughts. People merely invent new words or give the old ones new and ironic meanings.

Sapir and Whorf also argued that the grammatical structure of languages compelled their speakers to think and behave in certain ways. For example, Whorf (1941) claimed that because tenses in the Hopi language were very different from tenses in English, Hopi speakers necessarily understood time in ways very different from English speakers. This position is sometimes called "strong determinism," and it has some deep problems. For example, consider the differences in the way we speak about missing a person in English and in French. In English, we say "I miss you." "I," the person doing the missing, is the subject; "you," the person being missed, is the object. In French, however, the order is reversed: You say "Tu me manques." The person being missed is the subject and the person doing the missing the object. Literally translated, the French sentence appears to mean "you miss me." A strong determinist would expect this structural difference to indicate that speakers of French and English have different understandings of missing a person. However, no evidence suggests that this is so.

This is not to say that language structure and thought are completely unrelated. Bowerman (1996) argues that space is understood differently in English and Korean, and Gordon (2004) reports that members of the Brazilian tribe he studied have difficulty understanding and recalling numbers for which they have no words. However, the relationship between language and thought seems fairly weak and related primarily to the vocabulary rather than the structure of language.

NONVERBAL COMMUNICATION

Before returning to our discussion of spoken language, it is important to note that anthropologists also study the nonverbal ways in which humans communicate. Our use of our bodies, interpersonal space, physical objects, and even time can communicate worlds of information: "Time talks" and "space speaks" (Hall 1959). Nonverbal communication includes artifacts, haptics, chronemics, proxemics, and kinesics.

In the context of nonverbal communication, **artifacts** such as clothing, jewelry, tattoos, piercings, and other visible body modifications send messages. For example, among the Tuareg, a people of the Sahara, men often wear veils and use their position as an important part of nonverbal communication (Murphy 1964). A Tuareg man lowers his veil only among intimates and people of lower social status. He raises it high when he wishes to appear noncommittal. The use of artifacts to send messages is familiar to every American. Tattoos, piercings, and jewelry all provide information about those who wear them.

Haptics refers to the study and analysis of touch. Handshakes, pats on the back or head, kisses, and hugs are all ways we communicate by touch. Many American males, for example, believe that the quality of a handshake communicates important information. Strong, firm handshakes are taken to indicate power, self-confidence, and strength of character, whereas limp handshakes may be interpreted as suggesting lack of interest, indecisiveness, or effeminacy.

Some anthropologists suggest that societies can be divided into "contact" cultures, where people tend to interact at close distances and touch one another frequently, and "noncontact" cultures, where people tend to interact at greater distance and avoid touching (Hall 1966; Montagu 1978). Contact cultures are common in the Middle East, India, the Mediterranean, and Latin America. Noncontact cultures include those of northern Europe, North America, and Japan. But this dichotomy is too simplistic. India, for example, may be a contact culture between equals, but it is very much a noncontact culture between persons regarded as socially unequal. In the United States, in public social relationships, the person who touches another is likely to have more power than the person who is touched. Bosses touch their subordinates, but these rarely touch their bosses (Leathers 1997:126).

Chronemics refers to the study of cultural understandings of time. For example, in North American culture, what does it say when a person shows up for an appointment 40 minutes late? Does it mean something different if he or she shows up 10 minutes early? Is a Latin American who shows up late for an appointment saying the same thing?

In addition to speaking, people use hands and facial expressions as well as interpersonal space to communicate.

Edward Hall (1983) divided cultures into those with monochronic time (M-time), such as the United States and northern European countries, and those with polychronic time (P-time). Hall argued that in M-time cultures, time is perceived as inflexible and people organize their lives according to schedules. In P-time cultures, time is understood as fluid. The emphasis is on social interaction, and activities are not expected to proceed like clockwork. Thus, being late for an appointment in P-time cultures does not convey the unspoken messages that it conveys in an M-time culture (Victor 1992).

Like the contact/noncontact dichotomy, M-time and P-time seem to capture a basic truth about cultural variation but fail to account for the enormous variability within cultures. How long an individual is kept waiting for an appointment may have more to do with power than with cultural perceptions of time. People are more likely to be on time for their superiors but may keep their subordinates waiting.

Proxemics is the social use of space. Hall (1968) identified three different ranges of personal communicative space. *Intimate distance,* from 1 to 18 inches, is typical for lovers and very intimate friends. *Personal distance,* from 18 inches to 4 feet, characterizes relationships among friends. *Social distance,* from 4 to 12 feet, is common among relative strangers. These distances are also affected by circumstances, culture, gender, and aspects of individual personality. We speak to strangers at a much closer distance in a movie or a classroom than we would in an unconfined space. In the United States, women and mixed-gender pairs talk to each other at closer distances than do men. In Turkey, on the other hand, men and women talk at close distances with members of their own sex but at very large distances with members of the opposite sex (Leathers 1997).

Finally, **kinesics** refers to body position, movement, facial expressions, and gaze. We use our posture, visual expression, eye contact, and other body movements to communicate interest, boredom, and much else. Smiling and some other facial expressions likely are biologically based human universals. There are no societies in which people do not smile. In fact, smiling is also found in chimpanzees and gorillas, our nearest nonhuman relations. Moreover, some aspects of smiling seem to transcend cultural variation. In any society, social interactions are more likely to have a positive outcome if people are smiling than if they are frowning or scowling.

But smiling also shows the powerful effects of culture on biology. A smile does not mean the same thing in all cultures. Americans generally equate smiling with happiness, but people in many cultures smile when they experience surprise, wonder, or embarrassment (Ferraro 1994). A guidebook on international business advises American managers that the Japanese often smile to make their guests feel comfortable rather than because they are happy (Lewis 1996:267). Despite this, Japanese and Americans agree that smiling faces are more sociable than neutral faces (Matsumoto and Kudoh 1993), and most often interpret smiles in the same way (Nagashima and Schellenberg 1997).

LANGUAGE CHANGE

Fæder ure þu þe eart on heofonum
Si þin nama gehalgod
to becume þin rice
gewurþe ðin willa
on eorðan swa swa on heofonum.
urne gedæghwamlican hlaf syle us todæg
and forgyf us ure gyltas
swa swa we forgyfað urum gyltendum
and ne gelæd þu us on costnunge
ac alys us of yfele soþlice

This 11th-century version of the Lord's Prayer shows how much English has changed in the past thousand years. All language is constantly changing on many levels, including sound, structure, and vocabulary, and some of the change happens in patterned ways.

Consider sound. When we imagine people speaking English hundreds of years ago, we often think of them using different words than we do but otherwise sounding pretty much like us. But this is incorrect. English spoken in the 14th century sounded very different from the English of today. Between 1400 and 1600 there was a change in sound of English that is called the **great vowel shift.** A correct reading aloud of the Lord's Prayer above would involve more than just trying to speak the words. They would have to be spoken with the sounds of 11th-century English. For example, the fifth word of the last line, yfele, gives us the modern English word "evil." The medieval pronunciation is close to "oo-vah-la." Shifting sounds are not just something out of the past. Language sounds are constantly changing. For example, since about 1950, some vowel sounds in U.S. cities around the Great Lakes have been changing, a process linguists call the *northern city shift* (Labov 2005).

The grammatical structures of a language (its syntax) also change. For example, as we have seen, meaning in modern English is tightly tied to word order. But in Old English, as in Latin, the endings of nouns indicated whether they were subjects or objects, making word order within sentences less important. Thus, in Old English, the two sentences "The dog bit the child" and "The dog the child bit" would have the same meaning and be equally grammatical.

Vocabulary is the most noticeable aspect of language change, particularly slang. Consider slang terms from the 1950s and 1960s, such as "boss" to mean great (as in "The new Little Richard album is really boss") or "bag" to mean something that an individual likes (as in "What's your bag" or "Reading anthropology is really my bag"). Many of us still understand the slang expressions of the 1960s, but terms from the 19th century and early 20th century are almost entirely lost: Would you know what "ramstuginous" or "kafooster" mean?

New words are constantly added to language. In the past 10 to 20 years, for example, an entire vocabulary has grown up around computers and the Internet. Words such as software, dot-com, disk drive, gigabyte, and e-mail would have been unintelligible to most people in 1980. WiFi, spyware, domain name, text message, and many others would have been meaningless to people in the mid-1990s.

Language and Culture Contact

The meeting of cultures through travel, trade, war, and conquest is a fundamental force in linguistic change. Languages thus reflect the histories of their speakers. Current-day English has French words such as "reason," "joy," "mutton," and "liberty," which came into the language after the Norman Conquest of England in the 11th century. Other words speak of more recent political events. For example, "cot," "pajamas," and "jungle" come from Hindi and reflect the British colonization of India. "Gumbo," "funky," and "zebra" come from Kongo and reflect the slave trade. Nahuatl, a language spoken in Mexico and Central America, gives us "tomato," "coyote," "shack," and "avocado." Most Americans in 1970 probably did not know the meanings of words such as "sunni," "muhajadin," or "fatwa." Today, we do.

When societies where different languages are spoken meet, they often develop a new language that combines features of each of the original ones. Such languages are called *pidgins.* No one speaks a pidgin as a first language, and the vocabulary of pidgins is often limited to the words appropriate to the sorts of interactions engaged in by the people speaking it.

As culture contact deepens and time passes, pidgins are sometimes lost, and people speak only the language of the dominant power. Or pidgin languages may become creoles. A *creole* is a language composed

Pidgins develop when people who speak different languages come together. This church banner in Papua New Guinea, where people speak more than 750 different languages, means "Jesus is Lord."

of elements of two or more different languages. But, unlike a pidgin, people do speak creoles as their first languages, and the vocabulary of these languages is as complex and rich as any others.

Many creoles were formed as Europeans expanded into Asia and the Americas. Often, in countries that were colonized, upper classes speak the language of the colonizing power, while the lower classes speak creoles. For example, in Haiti, 70 to 90 percent of the population speaks only Creole, but almost all governmental and administrative functions are performed in French, the language of the elite.

Tracing Relationships Among Languages

Comparative linguistics is a field of study that traces the relationships of different languages by searching for similarities among them. When such similarities are numerous, regular, and basic, it is likely that the languages are derived from the same ancestral language.

Linguists have identified a **core vocabulary** of 100 or 200 words, such as I, you, man, woman, blood, skin, red, and green, which designate things, actions, and activities likely to be named in all the world's languages. Many believe that core vocabularies change at a predictable rate (about 14 percent per 1000 years). **Glottochronology** is a statistical technique that uses this idea to estimate the date of separation of related languages. Linguists use glottochronology to discover historic relationships among languages and to group languages into families. However, the accuracy of the technique has long been controversial, and many modifications have been used to improve it (Renfrew, McMahon, and Trask 2000).

Considering the history of language raises two interesting questions. First, at any point was there a single original human language? Second, in the future will there be a world with one language? Neither of these questions is fully answerable, but we can speculate about each of them.

We do not know if there was a single original human language. However, the development of language almost certainly involved specific genetic changes. Such changes probably happened in a single small group. If this is the case, an original language probably did exist. What might it have been like? Well, again, we cannot say with any confidence. There are no established techniques for discovering the patterns and content of language that can reach back tens of thousands of years.

The question of whether a single world language is emerging is provocative. We are clearly moving toward a world of linguistic homogenization. The number of languages in the world has clearly declined. About 10,000 years ago there may have been as many as 15,000 different languages. Today there are only about 6500, and half of these are under threat of extinction in the next 50 to 100 years (Krauss 1992). Today, 95 percent of the world's languages are spoken by only 5 percent of the world's population. Almost one third of the world's languages have fewer than 1000 people who speak them. At the same time, more than half of the world's population speaks one of the 20 most common languages (Gibbs 2002).

Languages may disappear for various reasons: All their speakers may be killed by disease or genocide. Government policies may deliberately seek to eliminate certain languages. For example, in 1885 the American government explicitly forbade the use of Indian languages in Bureau of Indian Affairs schools. Children were beaten and otherwise punished for speaking their tribal languages (Coleman 1999).

Nation states often try to suppress linguistic diversity within their borders, insisting that government, the court system, and other aspects of public life be conducted in the language of the most numerous and politically powerful groups. Global trade favors people who speak the languages of the wealthiest and most populous nations. Similarly, the vast majority of television and radio broadcasts, as well as the Internet, are in a very few languages. In the face of such forces, people who are members of linguistic minorities often abandon their languages because they find it more convenient, prestigious, or profitable to speak the languages of wealth and power.

In some senses, linguistic homogenization is a positive development. Today, more people are able to speak to each other than ever before. In the future, this may be true to an even greater extent. However, the global movement toward fewer languages is troubling. There is generally a strong connection between language and ethnic identity. Language often is rooted in culture and is entwined with it. As language is lost, so are important elements of cultural identity. Additionally, the disappearance of languages reduces our ability to understand the underlying structures of language and the range of variability they enable.

Not all global forces lead toward language homogenization. First, there is no language spoken by the majority of the world's people. Mandarin Chinese, with more than one billion speakers, is by far the most commonly spoken language, while hundreds of millions of people speak English, Spanish, Russian, French, Hindi/Urdu, Arabic, Portuguese, and several other languages. None of these languages seems likely to disappear in the foreseeable future. Second, although the number of languages spoken in the world has diminished, the diversity within each language has increased. People in New York City, Kingston, Jamaica, Glasgow in Scotland, and Mumbai, India, may all speak English, but that does not necessarily mean they can understand what each other says. Perhaps more importantly, the nature of language, the human ability to create new meanings, new words, and new grammatical structures, means that language adapts to the needs, interests, and environments of its speakers. Thus, even as globalizing forces move humans toward cultural and linguistic homogeneity, spaces are created in which linguistic and cultural diversity can flourish.

BRINGING IT BACK HOME: ENGLISH ONLY

Language has become an important political issue in America. As of 2007, 30 states have enacted legislation to make English their state's official language. Both the U.S. House of Representative and the U.S. Senate have voted to make English the national language or require the federal government to conduct all of its official business in English. Although no federal bill making English the national language has yet passed both chambers of Congress and become law, a recent survey suggests that 85 percent of Americans believe English should be the official national language (Rasmusen Reports 2006).

U.S.ENGLISH, Inc., a lobbying group that promotes English Only legislation, claims to have 1.8 million members. According to U.S.ENGLISH, Inc. (n.d.): "Official English benefits every resident of this wonderful melting pot called America. The melting pot works—because we have a common language. English is the key to opportunity in this country. It empowers immigrants and makes us truly united as a people. Common sense says that the government should teach people English rather than provide services in multiple languages. What would happen if our government had to provide services in all 322 languages spoken in the U.S.? Without a common language, how long would we remain the 'United' States?"

Many, and perhaps most, anthropologists believe the legislative program of groups such as U.S.ENGLISH, Inc., is misguided and their claims inaccurate. Graham, Jaffe, Urciuoli, and Valentine (2007) say that when people talk about language, they really are talking about race: "People in positions of social advantage feel free to say things about the language of stigmatized groups that they would never say about race or ethnicity." Furthermore, Graham et al. claim that promoters of English Only legislation assume that difficulties in communication are caused by people speaking many languages, ignoring the simple fact that sharing the same language does not create effective communication. Finally, critics of English Only legislation say that the idea of requiring official English will unify the nation and help provide answers to problems of racism gets things backwards. The underlying problem is not language, it is inequality. Official English, in the name of promoting unity and opportunity, actually disadvantages the poor and the powerless, making it harder for them to gain access to education and public services.

YOU DECIDE

1. Do you speak a language other than English as a first language? If so, do you want your children and grandchildren to speak that language? If English is your first language, did your parents or grandparents

speak a different first language? How do you feel about your abilities (or lack of ability) in that language?
2. In the United States, how closely is language linked both to American identity and to ethnic identity? To what degree can a person be a full citizen of America without speaking English as a primary language?
3. The United States has never had an official national language. Are there good reasons why this should change? Multiple languages are a great asset in the global economy. Instead of mandating English only, would it be better to mandate increased second language training for Americans?

CHAPTER SUMMARY

1. The use of language is basic to what it means to be a human being. Language is at the same time deeply biological and profoundly cultural. From a scientific point of view, no way of speaking is better or worse than any other.
2. Human language is different from the communication systems of other animals. It is complex and symbolic, and it is able to describe abstract times, places, and ideas in ways that animal communications are not.
3. Despite great variability, all human languages are based around similar patterns and show deep similarities. All are composed of a phonology (a system of sounds), morphology (a system for creating words from sounds), semantics (a system that relates words to meanings), and syntax (a system of rules for combining words into meaningful sentences).
4. Culture exerts a profound influence upon language. Environment, cultural ideas, values, and beliefs are encoded in the way people speak. The meaning of conversation usually is much more than simply the words that are spoken.
5. Cultural aspects of language are heavily influenced by wealth and identity. Privileged and stigmatized ways of speaking reflect the power dynamics of different groups. Individuals who move between social groups must often learn multiple forms of speech and the correct times and places to use them.
6. Speakers choose words to encourage others to think in certain ways. Early 20th-century theorists believed that the structure of language had a critical influence on culture, but this does not seem to be the case. Because language can be changed rapidly, it can neither force people to think in one way nor prevent them from thinking in others.

7. In addition to speaking, people communicate in many different ways. Some of these ways are through touch, the use of time, the use of space, and the use of body position. There is substantial variability in nonverbal aspects of communication both within and between cultures.
8. The sounds, words, and structures of language all are subject to change. Comparative linguists study the ways language changes and are able to describe the historical relationships among different languages. However, no agreed upon technique has been found to determine or describe very early human language.

KEY TERMS

Agglutinating language
Allophone
Artifacts
Bound morpheme
Call system
Chronemics
Comparative linguistics
Conventionality
Core vocabulary
Displacement
Free morphemes
Glottochronology
Great vowel shift
Haptics
Isolating language
Kinesics
Lexicon
Morpheme
Morphology
Phone
Phoneme
Phonology
Productivity
Proxemics
Sapir-Whorf hypothesis
Semantics
Sociolinguistics
Symbol
Syntax
Universal grammar

© Bryan and Cherry Alexander Photography

Polar bear crossing from one ice floe to another in summer pack ice. The warmer water due to climate change has led to the starvation of many polar bears.

CHAPTER 5

MAKING A LIVING

CHAPTER OUTLINE

Where Have All the Icebergs Gone?

Human Adaptation and the Environment

Major Types of Subsistence Strategies

- Foraging
- Pastoralism
- Horticulture
- Agriculture
- Industrialism
- The Global Marketplace

Bringing It Back Home: You Are What You Eat: Culture and Food Choices

- You Decide

WHERE HAVE ALL THE ICEBERGS GONE?

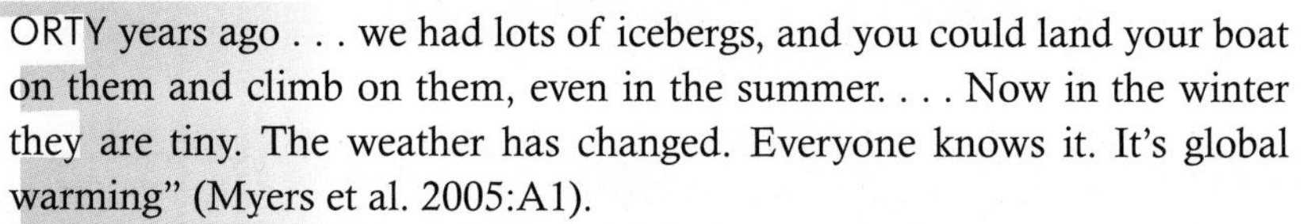

"FORTY years ago . . . we had lots of icebergs, and you could land your boat on them and climb on them, even in the summer. . . . Now in the winter they are tiny. The weather has changed. Everyone knows it. It's global warming" (Myers et al. 2005:A1).

For 6000 years, the Inuit of the Arctic hunted large land and sea animals: bowhead whales, walrus, caribou, and seal. Even in their harsh environment, Inuit knowledge and ingenious technology enabled them to be successful hunters, as they followed the seasonal availability of animals and birds. The Inuit effectively utilized the materials of their environment for survival, for example, building shelters of snow, which hold the heat and keep out the wind, and expertly fashioning layered clothing that keeps out the cold yet prevents overheating. Inuit culture and social organization are also adapted to their foraging strategy. Their cultural values emphasize cooperation and mutual aid; their religious rituals provide effective outlets for the isolation and tension of the long dark winters; and their flexible kinship organization allows local populations to expand and contract in response to the seasonal variation in resources.

The Inuit of the Arctic practice diverse foraging strategies: They hunt land animals and marine animals such as seal, walrus, and whales, which are the most important food sources. As with many other foragers, however, the 20th century and the global economy have brought significant changes in Inuit subsistence strategies (Chance 1990; Condon et al. 1996). Most Inuit now base their livelihoods on a combination of cash income from a variety of sources while maintaining their traditional subsistence foraging. By the mid-20th century, the Western demand for fox furs significantly replaced subsistence hunting with commercial trapping, providing many Inuit with guns and cash, which they then used to buy food, tobacco, tea, canvas tents, and clothing. Other nontraditional sources of Inuit income today are handicrafts, tourism, various kinds of government subsidies, and, for the Alaska Inuit, payments from the Alaska Native Claims Settlement Act.

Global warming is yet another change to which the Inuit must adapt. Essential to the Inuit traditional livelihood is the transformation of water areas into ice during the long, cold winters. Sea ice is used as a highway, formerly for dog sleds and now for snowmobiles, for building materials, and for hunting platforms. With global warming, icebergs and the permafrost are melting at an accelerating rate, making it more difficult for Inuit marine hunters to maintain their cultures and traditional ways of making a living. The shrinking ice makes it harder for polar bears to fatten up on seals, and the bears are becoming emaciated. Alaskan whale hunters in the open seas have seen walruses try to climb onto their white boats, mistaking them for ice floes. The pelts of fox, marten, and other game are thinning, and even seasoned hunters are falling into water that used to be ice.

Subsistence hunting and use of wild foods, such as moose, caribou, whales, ducks, fish, and other wildlife, continue to provide half or more of the Inuit diet. Current-day foraging techniques make significant use of modern technology, such as snowmobiles, gasoline, fishing nets, and sleeping bags. Many Inuit households enjoy modern conveniences, which requires that household members work full time or seasonally in the cash economy (Kofinas 2007).

The Inuit are well aware of the threat to their traditional subsistence activities from the potential drilling for oil in the Arctic. Some (but not all) of them have become locally active in resisting oil exploitation of the Arctic Wildlife Refuge and other Arctic areas where oil companies are now able to exploit offshore energy resources revealed by global warming (Matthiessen 2007), demanding a larger role in the management of wildlife resources. Inuit communities highly value their traditional subsistence economies beyond even the economic benefits. "The next generation . . . is not going to experience what we did," says a Canadian Inuit, "We can't pass the traditions on as our ancestors passed on to us" (Myers et al. 2005).

"Gwich'in elders long ago predicted that a day would come when the world would warm and things would not be the same with the animals. That time is now. . . ." says Matthew Gilbert of the Gwich'in, an Athabascan people of northeastern Alaska and Northwest Canada. "The lakes, the rivers, the waterfowl and, most of all, the caribou that we depend on are under threat" (Gilbert 2007).

The 8000 Gwich'in live in small villages spread across the huge subarctic tundra and forest, which contains thousands of lakes and scores of rivers. The main source of Gwich'in subsistence is the caribou herds that also occupy this area. The Gwich'in also hunt small animals for their pelts, which they sell for cash. Global warming has negatively affected the sources of Gwich'in subsistence. Immense forest fires in 2004 and 2005 laid waste to millions of acres, driving the marten (a small fur-bearing animal) north of their traditional habitat, making it harder for the Gwich'in to trap them. This has resulted in a loss of fur for clothing and a loss of cash income from the sale of marten pelts. The warmer weather also means that creeks take longer to freeze, and the ice is often too thin to take heavy loads. Thus, getting firewood in the early winter becomes difficult and dangerous. The lakes are drying out, resulting in a decline of whitefish, which feed on water plants and are an important source of nutrition for the Gwich'in in the absence of fresh produce during the long Arctic winters.

Most importantly, climate change has decreased the number of caribou, which are less healthy than they were formerly. Because of early river thaws, many caribou calves are drowned crossing the rushing river waters, the glaciers and snow pockets that provide essential resting places for mothers and their calves are disappearing, and the caribou must move further north, out of their usual territory. This makes it harder for the hunters to find them, and hunting has to begin later in the season than normal. "Because nature is the fabric of our lives, we cannot really separate 'the climate' from our human selves. . . . So when we talk about the environment and especially about the decline of caribou, we are talking about who we are and who we want to continue to be. It is a question of our very survival as a people" (Gilbert 2007).

Anthropologists seek to understand the interactions between humans and their physical environments, both the effects of the environment on culture and the effects of culture on the environment. All societies must utilize the physical environment to provide their people with the basic material requirements of life: food, clothing, and shelter. Different societies have different **subsistence strategies,** or ways of transforming the material resources of the environment into food. These subsistence strategies may be stable for hundreds, even thousands, of years, but they must change in response to new challenges in the environment.

HUMAN ADAPTATION AND THE ENVIRONMENT

Unlike most other animals, humans live in an extremely broad range of environments. Some, such as the Arctic or the Great Australian Desert, present extreme challenges to human existence and are relatively limited in the numbers of people and types of subsistence strategies they can support. The productivity of any particular environment, however, is related to the type of technology used to exploit it. For example, the Arctic can sustain only a relatively small population with the traditional Inuit technology. But with modern technology and transportation, it supports almost a million people, engaged in indigenous hunting and herding strategies as well as modern industrial pursuits.

Technology enables humans to transform a wide range of materials into sources of usable energy. As a result, humans have built many environments, such as farms and cities, and developed many different economic systems and forms of social organization. These human cultural adaptations have resulted in great increases in population, which in turn greatly intensify deleterious effects on the environment.

Until about 10,000 years ago, humans lived by **foraging**—fishing, hunting, and collecting vegetable food. As tools improved, foragers spread out into many environments and developed diverse cultures, arriving in the Americas and Australia about 25,000 years ago. About 10,000 years ago human groups in the Old World, and 4000 years later in the New World, began to domesticate plants and animals. Called the agricultural "revolution," the transition to food production was really more like a gradual evolution, although it was revolutionary in the possibilities it opened up for the development of complex social organization.

Foraging sets significant limits on population growth and density and, consequently, on the complexity of social organization. The domestication of plants and animals supported much increased populations, and **sedentary** village life became widespread. Over time, more intensive means of cultivation and animal management developed, and human labor was more closely coordinated and controlled, leading eventually to complex social forms such as the state. Within this general outline of growing control over the environment and human population increase, however, only specific environmental, cultural, and historical conditions can explain the exact sequence of events in any particular place (Diamond 1998).

Why cultivation did not arise everywhere—and why some populations, such as the aboriginal peoples of Australia or the Inuit, never made the transition from foraging to food production—has several answers. In the Arctic, climate and soil composition precluded agriculture, whereas in the fertile valleys of California, aboriginal foraging was so productive that there was little pressure to make the transition to food production. Sometimes foraging strategies actually were more dependable than cultivation or animal husbandry, which are more adversely affected by extreme drought. For example, with the introduction of the horse by the Spaniards in the 16th century, some Native-American Plains cultures, such as the Cheyenne, did so well with bison hunting that they gave up their traditional cultivation strategy. Even today, many foraging and pastoral populations resist abandoning these occupations for cultivation because they prefer the economic, social, and psychological satisfactions of a foraging or pastoral way of life. In these societies, hunting and pastoralism are highly valued occupations, intimately connected to a people's cultural identity, and in some circumstances are more productive than agriculture.

Another dramatic change in human subsistence strategies was the Industrial Revolution, which involved the replacement of human and animal energy by machines. Industrialism greatly increased human productivity: In a typical nonindustrial society, more than 80 percent of the population is directly involved in food production; in a highly industrialized society, 10 percent of the people directly produce food for the other 90 percent.

However, the price of industrialization has been high. A primary source of environmental degradation today is the consumer desires and energy needs of industrialized nations. The demands for tropical hardwoods are leading to devastating logging in tropical forests (Brosius 1999); dam building in the American Pacific Northwest impedes the ability of salmon to spawn, decreasing the food supply of Native Americans in this area (Duncan 2000); and the carbon emissions of modern transport and industrial production have already resulted in global warming affecting not just the Arctic but also areas much closer to home, such as America's shorelines and weather systems (Gore 2006).

The environmental problems resulting from industrial and postindustrial society have led to a reawakened interest and respect for the ways in which nonindustrial people have adapted. Through vast knowledge of the web of life in which they live and with ingenious, if simple, technology, many nonindustrial societies live in ways that are sustainable and create many fewer environmental problems than industrialization.

MAJOR TYPES OF SUBSISTENCE STRATEGIES

Anthropologists identify five basic types of subsistence strategies: foraging, pastoralism, horticulture, agriculture, and industrialism (Cohen 1971). Foraging depends on the use of plant and animal resources naturally available in the environment. **Pastoralism** primarily involves the care of domesticated herd animals, whose dairy and meat products are a major part of the pastoralist diet. **Horticulture** (extensive cultivation) is the production of plants using a simple, nonmechanized technology. **Agriculture** (intensive cultivation) involves the production of food using the plow, draft animals, and more complex techniques of water and soil control so that land is permanently cultivated and usually needs no fallow period. Finally, **industrialism** involves the use of machine technology and chemical processes for the production of food and other goods. Within these basic types of subsistence strategies, however, there is much diversity. Furthermore, whereas any society normally uses one dominant strategy, many societies combine strategies in order to meet their material needs. Today, no society, however seemingly remote, remains unaffected by industrialism and the global economy.

Each subsistence strategy generally supports a characteristic level of **population density** (number of people per unit of land) and has a different level of **productivity** (yield per person per unit of land) and **efficiency** (yield per person per hour of labor invested). These criteria, in turn, tend to be associated with characteristic forms of social organization and certain cultural patterns. For example, where local technology allows only limited exploitation of the environment and where safe and reliable methods of artificial contraception are unknown, cultural practices such as sexual abstinence, abortion, infanticide, late weaning, and prohibitions on sexual intercourse after the birth of a child may be used to limit population growth.

In addition to limiting population, a society can extend its resource base by exchange. Trade occurs in all types of societies and forms the basis of historical and contemporary globalization, which incorporates people all over the world as they engage in many kinds of food production, manufacturing, and financial exchanges.

Foraging

Foraging is a diverse strategy that relies on naturally available food resources. It includes the hunting of large and small game, fishing, and collecting of various plant foods. Foragers do not produce food, either directly by planting or indirectly by controlling the reproduction of animals or by keeping domestic animals for consumption of their meat or milk. Foraging strategies vary in productivity but, in general, support lower population densities than other subsistence systems. Today, only a very small proportion of the world's people live by foraging, mainly in marginal areas into which they have been pushed by expanding, militarily superior agricultural peoples and states. In the past, however, foragers occupied many diverse environments, including the Arctic tundra and the most arid deserts.

Except for societies in locations like the Arctic, foragers typically depend on vegetal food, which is usually collected by women, as well as on hunting. Foragers also engage in trade. In the Central African Ituri rain forest, Mbuti foragers have complex, hereditary exchange relationships with the Lese, their horticultural neighbors (Wilkie 1988). In exchange for meat, mushrooms, honey, building materials, medicine, and agricultural labor, the Mbuti receive manioc, plantains, peanuts, and rice, which together form more than 50 percent of their diet. The Lese also provide the Mbuti with metal for knives and arrowheads; cotton cloth, which is stronger and more colorful than traditional Mbuti bark cloth; and aluminum cooking pots, which are more durable than traditional Mbuti clay pots (Wilkie 1988:123).

While in extreme environments, such as the Great Australian desert, foragers may lead a very harsh existence. In most cases, predictable vegetal food supplemented by hunting may give foragers abundant leisure time and generally good health (Lee 1984:50–53). Some general social correlates of foraging are seasonal nomadism geared to the availability of game and wild plants, organization of the society into small camps with flexible

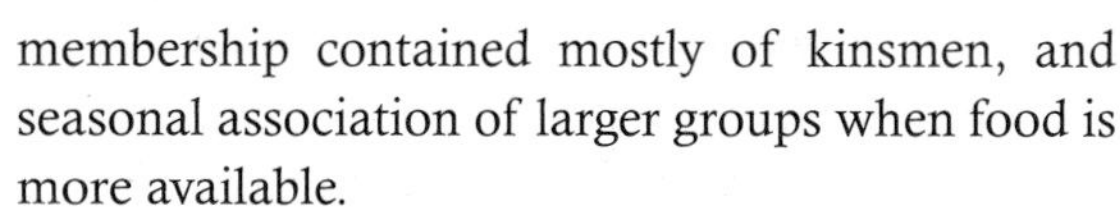
membership contained mostly of kinsmen, and seasonal association of larger groups when food is more available.

In east African cattle cultures, such as the Maasai, the blood and milk of cattle are the major dietary elements. Cattle are killed for meat only on very special ceremonial occasions.

Pastoralism

Pastoralists depend primarily on the products of domesticated herd animals. Theirs is a specialized adaptation to an environment that, because of hilly terrain, dry climate, or unsuitable soil, cannot support a large human population through agriculture but can support enough native vegetation for animals if they are allowed to range over a large area. Because human beings cannot digest grass, raising animals that can live on grasses makes pastoralism an efficient way to exploit semiarid natural grasslands that are otherwise unproductive. Unlike ranching (commercial animal husbandry), in which livestock are fed grain, which could be used to feed humans or to produce meat or milk, pastoralism does not require direct competition with humans for the same resources (Barfield 1993:13).

Pastoralists may herd cattle, sheep, goats, yaks, or camels, all of which produce both meat and milk. Because the herd animals of the New World, such as bison, could not be domesticated (except for the llama and alpaca in Peru), pastoralism did not develop as a subsistence strategy there. The major areas of pastoralism are found in East Africa (cattle), North Africa (camels), southwestern Asia (sheep and goats), central Asia (yaks), and the subarctic (caribou and reindeer).

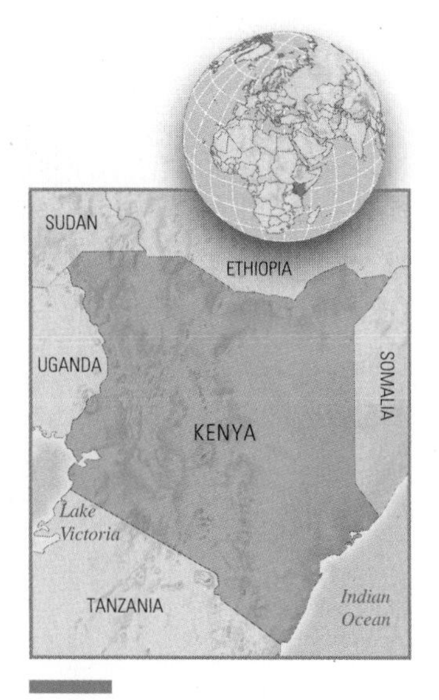

Kenya.

Pastoralism is either transhumant or nomadic. In **transhumant pastoralism,** found mostly in East Africa, men and boys move the animals regularly throughout the year to different areas as pastures become available at different altitudes or in different climatic zones, while women and children and some men remain at a permanent village site.

In **nomadic pastoralism,** the whole population—men, women, and children—moves with the herds throughout the year, and there are no permanent villages.

Pastoralism involves a complex interaction among animals, land, and people. With domestication, animals became dependent on their human keepers for pasture, water, breeding, shelter, salt, and protection from predators. Therefore, pastoralists must be highly knowledgeable about the carrying capacity of the land in proportion to the number of animals raised. They must also be able to correctly determine the number of animals needed to provide subsistence for their human populations (Barfield 1993:6).

Many pastoral nomads actually engage in mixed subsistence strategies because they cannot exist solely on the products of their herds. The survival of pastoralists depends on their relationships with their sedentary neighbors, with whom they trade meat, animals, wool, milk products, and hides for manufactured goods and for the grain that constitutes the bulk of their diet.

The key to the pastoralist economy is herd growth, which depends primarily on reproduction by female animals. The number of animals needed to support a family is a constant concern of pastoralists. Eating or selling too many animals in a single year may lead to insolvency, so pastoralists must always balance their present needs against future herd production. Pastoralism is a risky business; weather disasters such as drought or storms, disease, or theft can easily decimate a herd.

The Yarahmadzai: A Nomadic Pastoralist Society in Iran

The chief challenge for pastoralists is managing water and pasture in a sustainable way. This is illustrated by the Yarahmadzai of Baluchistan, a region in Iran (Salzman 2000). The Yarahmadzai tribal territory occupies a plateau at around 5000 feet, where the winters are cold and the summers are hot. Maximum rainfall is about 6 inches per year, most of which falls in winter; and in some years there is no rain at all. The main natural vegetation is grass, although some areas are almost completely barren.

In winter, small local groups camp together in a traditionally assigned area on the plateau. In this season there is practically no vegetation for the animals (sheep, goats, and camels) to eat, and the animals live primarily on the accumulated fat of the previous spring. The Yarahmadzai compensate for the lack of pasturage by feeding the camels with roots, the goats and sheep with grain, and the lambs and kids with dates and processed date pits. The people depend on food stores from the previous year. Because winter is the rainy season, water is normally available.

The staple Yarahmadzai food is milk, consumed in many different forms and preserved as dried milk solids and butter, which are both eaten and sold or exchanged for grain. Milk is the main source of protein, fat, calcium, and other nutrients, as the Yarahmadzai, like most other pastoral peoples, do not eat much meat. Their flocks are their capital, and the Yarahmadzai's goal is to conserve and grow their animals rather than to raise animals to eat (Salzman 2000:24).

Baluchistan, Iran.

In spring (March, April, and May), grass begins to appear and plants bud, but because of variability in the rains and water runoff, availability of pasture changes annually. When good pasture is found, the whole Yarahmadzai camp migrates. Because even good pasturage quickly gets exhausted, however, the camp migrates constantly, moving from 5 to 25 miles each time. From March to July, the animals give ample milk both for their young and for human consumption. In June and July, when pasturage begins to dry up, many Yarahmadzai migrate to areas served by government irrigation projects to harvest grain. The livestock graze on stubble and fertilize the ground with droppings. In late summer and early autumn, the Yarahmadzai migrate to the lowland desert and the groves of date palms, leaving their winter tents, goats, and sheep on the plateau in the care of young boys. During this time they live in mud huts, harvesting and eating dates and preparing date preserves for the return journey, in November, to their winter camps.

Like most contemporary pastoralists, the Yarahmadzai combine herding with other subsistence strategies in order to earn a living. During the summer and early autumn, those who farm, in addition to herding, plant grain, while the women work for cash in nearby towns.

Many pastoralists today now depend less on consuming the direct products of their herds and more on the sale of animals and of animal products for cash. Thus, they participate in a cash economy that is both local and global. Nomads in Afghanistan and Iran, for example, specialize in selling meat animals to local markets, lambskins to international buyers, and sheep intestines to meet the huge German demand for natural sausage casings (Barfield 1993:211).

Pastoralism cannot support an indefinitely increasing population, and many pastoralists have already become sedentary. But with their knowledge of their environment, their creative use of multiple resources, and the global demand for their products, pastoralism as a subsistence strategy has a strong future in exploiting the planet's large arid and semiarid zones.

Horticulture

Horticultural societies depend primarily on the production of plants using a simple, nonmechanized technology, such as hoes or digging sticks, but not draft animals, irrigation techniques, or plows. Fields are not used year after year but remain fallow for some time after being cultivated. Horticulture produces a lower yield per acre and uses less human labor than nonmechanized agriculture.

Traditionally, horticulturalists grow enough food in their fields or gardens to support the local group, but they do not produce surpluses that involve the group in a wider market system with nonagricultural populations. Population densities among horticultural peoples are generally low, usually not exceeding 150 people per square mile (Netting 1977). Despite this, horticultural villages may be quite large, ranging from 100 to 1000 people.

Horticulture may be practiced in dry lands, such as among the Hopi Indians of northeastern Arizona, who cultivate maize, beans, and squash, but is typically a tropical forest adaptation found mainly in Southeast Asia, sub-Saharan Africa, some Pacific islands, and the Amazon Basin in South America. In these environments, people practice **swidden (slash and burn) cultivation,** where a field is cleared by felling the trees and burning the brush. The burned vegetation is allowed to remain on the soil, which prevents it from drying out from the sun. The resulting bed of ash acts as a fertilizer, returning nutrients to the soil. Fields are used for a few years (1–5) and then allowed to lie fallow for a longer period (up to 20 years) so that the forest cover can be rebuilt and soil fertility restored. Swidden cultivators require five to six times as much fallow land as they are actually cultivating.

Swidden cultivation *can* have a debilitating effect on the environment if fields are cultivated before they have lain fallow long enough to recover their forest growth. Eventually, the forest will not grow back, and the tree cover will be replaced by grasslands. Because of the possibility of irreversible ecological deterioration, swidden cultivation is considered both inefficient and destructive by governments in developing nations. However, it is modern industrial strategies such as logging and giant agribusiness, not swidden cultivation, that is mainly responsible for the deterioration and disappearance of tropical forests (Sponsel 1995).

Horticulture is also a mixed subsistence strategy. Most swidden cultivators grow several crops. They may also hunt and fish or raise some domestic animals. In New Guinea, for example, domestic pigs are an important source of protein, and the horticulturalist Kofyar of Nigeria keep goats, chickens, sheep, and cows. The Yanomamo of the Amazon rain forest hunt monkeys and other forest animals.

Because of the very diverse environments of swidden cultivation, horticulturalists have diverse cultures. Most horticulturalists shift residences as they move their fields, but some occupy villages permanently or at least on a long-term basis.

The Lua': A Horticultural Society in Southeast Asia

The Lua' are a horticultural society in the mountains of northern Thailand, who depended on swidden cultivation until the 1960s. Swidden blocks around the village are cultivated in a regular rotational sequence, and each block is cultivated approximately every 10 years. Using long steel-bladed knives, the men clear their fields by felling small trees, leaving stumps about 3 feet high. Fields are cleared in January and February and allowed to dry until the end of March, the driest time of the year. On an auspicious day, decided in consultation with a Lua' ritual specialist, all the low vegetation is cleared to form a firebreak around the swidden block.

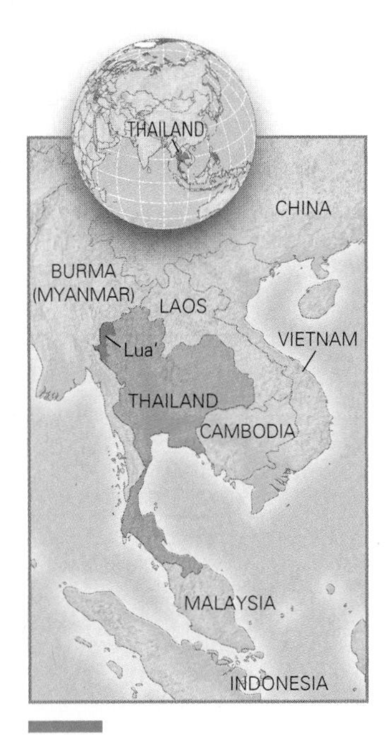

The Lua' of Northwestern Thailand.

© F. Jack Jackson/Bruce Coleman, Inc.

Swidden, or slash and burn, horticulture, as practiced traditionally in Northern Thailand, is based on a deep understanding of the forest environment. All the features of the landscape are taken into account as Lua' build their houses and plant their fields with a variety of crops used for subsistence, for cash, and for animal fodder.

First, cotton and corn are planted on the slopes of the fields, and yams are planted on the lower, wetter portions. By mid-April, upland rice, the main subsistence crop, is planted, using a 10-foot iron-tipped planting pole to loosen the soil. Different types of rice are sown in different areas of the field. Quick-ripening rice is planted near the field shelter, where it can be easily watched. Drought-resistant varieties are planted on the drier, sandier tops of the slopes, along with millet.

Mustard greens, peppers, several varieties of beans, and other vegetables are grown in gardens near the field shelters. Vine plants are grown along the creases in the hillside fields, which are more vulnerable to erosion. By May, weeding begins as mainly women and older children use a short-handled tool to scrape and hack at the weeds on the surface; weeds are not dug or pulled out by the roots. Both men and women harvest the rice, using small, handheld sickles. The rice stalks are laid out to dry for a few days before threshing, done mainly by women and young men. After winnowing, the cleaned rice is loaded into baskets for storage for future use.

Like most horticulturalists, the Lua' maintain a pattern of varied vegetation zones around the village. Mature forests are preserved, and villagers are forbidden to cut lumber or make swiddens or gardens in those areas. Uncut forest strips are maintained between swidden blocks, around the village, along stream courses and headwaters, and at the tops of ridges, all of which reduce erosion. Villagers use the plant growth of fallow fields for grazing and as traditional medicines, dyes for homespun clothing, and material for weaving baskets and building houses. The wild fruits and yams that grow on fallow land are particularly important during food shortages.

The Lua' also keep pigs, water buffalo, cattle, and chickens, which may be sold at local markets for cash. Before the 1960s, when the big fish in the streams were killed by the dumping of pesticides, fish were another important part of the Lua' diet. Hunting has also declined since World War II, although occasionally small forest animals fall into traps set in the fields meant to catch the birds and rats that could destroy the crop.

The Lua' horticultural strategy worked well until the 1960s. Since then, several factors have led to major changes. Population, formerly held in check by disease, has increased. Immigration by members of other ethnic groups (some fleeing the war in Vietnam) has resulted in greater numbers of persons in the area. In addition, the Thai government has claimed ownership of the forest and forbidden swidden agriculture. As a result, the Lua' have become intensive agriculturalists.

Now, instead of maintaining the diversity of their environment with their swidden rotation system, the Lua' are homogenizing their land use with irrigated, terraced agriculture. With the increase of cattle and human population in the area, sorghum and millet are no longer grown. Cotton planting has also declined, and today the Lua' usually buy thread for weaving and cotton clothes. Cattle grazing on the fallow land means that less grass is available for house construction, and more Lua' now roof their houses with leaves or with corrugated metal if they can afford it. The increase of cash cropping in soybeans has transformed the previously clear and free-flowing streams to muddy, polluted pools, which the Lua' now consider too dirty to wash their clothes in. Year-round irrigation has brought in year-round mosquitoes. Thus, changes in Lua' food production have brought about substantial changes in their economic, social, and ritual lifestyle.

Agriculture

Whereas horticulturalists have to increase the amount of land under cultivation in order to support a larger population, agriculture can support population increases by more intensive use of the same piece of land.

In agriculture, the same piece of land is permanently cultivated with use of the plow, draft animals, and more complex techniques of water and soil control than are used by horticulturalists. Plows are more efficient at loosening the soil than are digging sticks or hoes. The turning of the soil brings nutrients to the surface. Plowing requires a much more thorough clearing of the land, but it allows land to be used year after year.

Irrigation is also important in agriculture, which in some dry areas can be carried out only with sophisticated techniques. In hilly areas, agriculture requires some form of terracing in order to prevent crops and good soil from being washed down the hillside. Preindustrial agriculture also uses techniques of natural fertilization, selective breeding of livestock and crops, and crop rotation, all of which increase productivity.

Intensive cultivation generally supports higher population densities than horticulture. In Indonesia, for example, the island of Java, which contains only 9 percent of the Indonesian land area, is able to support more than two thirds of the Indonesian population through intensive wet rice cultivation using elaborate irrigation terraces. The Javanese population density of approximately 1250 people per square mile contrasts sharply with the maximum population density of swidden areas in Indonesia, which is about 145 persons per square mile (Geertz 1963:13).

The greater productivity of agriculture also results from more intensive use of labor. Farmers must work long and hard to make the land productive. For example, growing rice under a swidden system requires 241 worker-days per yearly crop, whereas wet rice cultivation requires 292 worker-days a year. Agriculture also requires more capital investment than horticulture. Apart from the cost of human labor, plows must be bought and draft animals raised and cared for. Although agriculturalists may have more control over food production than horticulturalists, they are more vulnerable to the environment. By depending on the intensive cultivation of one or two crops, one crop failure or a disease that strikes draft animals may become an economic disaster.

Agriculture is generally associated with sedentary villages, the rise of cities and states, occupational diversity, social stratification, and other complex forms of social organization. In contrast to horticulturalists, who grow food mainly for the subsistence of their households, farmers (agriculturalists) are enmeshed within larger complex societies. Part of their food production is used to support non–food-producing occupational specialists, such as religious or ruling elites. Rural cultivators who produce for the subsistence of their households but are also integrated into larger, complex state societies are called **peasants.**

Peasant Agriculture in Egypt

Musha, a village in Egypt, exhibits many of the characteristics typical of peasant villages (Hopkins 1987). These include the importance of the household in production, the use of a supplementary labor supply outside the household, the need of many farmers to supplement their income with nonagricultural labor, and state intervention in the production process. The multiple strategies for making a living in Musha highlight the ways in which both physical and social environments provide opportunities but also constrain and shape culture.

Musha is about 400 miles south of Cairo in the Nile Valley. In the 1980s, it had a population of about 18,000. Most village families own their houses, which they also use for storage, stabling animals, raising poultry, and some agricultural work.

In peasant villages in Egypt, a farmer makes important decisions regarding the allocation of household and extra domestic labor, purchases necessities for agriculture, schedules the use of machinery, and negotiates with the government for the sale of his crops.

Musha's farmers practice a 2-year crop rotation cycle that alternates the summer crops of cotton, maize, and sorghum with the winter crops of wheat, lentils, chickpeas, and millet. In addition, they grow fruit and vegetables for sale and for home consumption. Small farmers depend heavily on dairy production from cows, sheep, goats, and water buffalo, and they consume and sell these animals as well.

The technology of traditional agriculture in Musha relied on animal power and human effort as well as a few basic wooden tools such as the short-handled hoe for weeding and irrigation. Shallow plows and threshing sleds were pulled by cows. Donkeys carried small loads for short distances, and camels were used for larger loads and longer distances.

In the past several decades, agriculture in Musha has changed significantly. Almost all farmers now use tractors for transporting and threshing crops. They now depend on chemical fertilizers and pesticides as well as animal manure. The government has become critically involved in agriculture. In the 1960s the government constructed a network of canals to bring water from the Nile. The canal network requires the use of pumps, which are owned by groups of people who share the work of operating, maintaining, and guarding them. Farmers pay both annual fees and per-use fees for these irrigation services. One result of these changes has been an increase in the value of land leading to increased concentration of landholdings and wealth.

These changes have led to increased dependence on hired labor and equipment for landowners as well as increasing dependence on wage labor for those with little or no land. Farmers may have to hire tractors and other mechanical equipment. Wheat is often harvested by laborers who winnow, sift, measure and sack the grain, and haul it from the threshing ground back to the storeroom in the farmer's house.

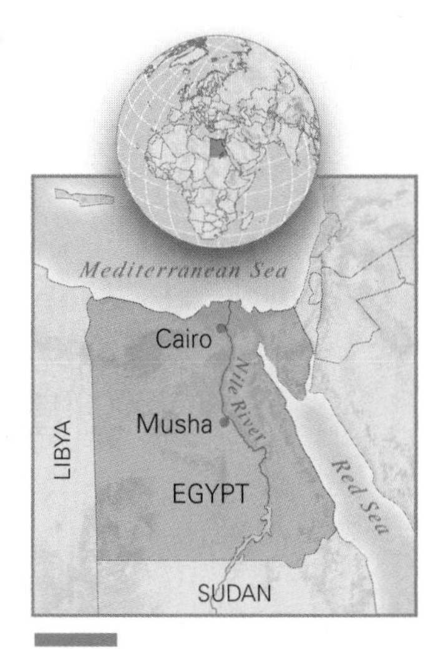

Egypt.

Wheat and cotton are the most important crops in Musha; but, because the government controls the price of wheat, growing cotton is usually more profitable. Wheat is grown for household use and for sale to merchants. Cotton is sold to the government, which subtracts the cost of services and products (such as fertilizer) that they provide from the price they pay. When prices are low, farmers pay their workers lower wages, so the poorer members of society are more affected by uncertainty than those who are wealthier.

The household is the central structure in traditional peasant agriculture. Women's primary responsibilities include housekeeping and caring for animals. Children cut clover for animals and help harvest cotton. Household heads supervise others, making agricultural purchases, hiring labor, scheduling the use of machinery, and arranging for the water flow into their fields.

In today's peasant economies, household members often work outside the agricultural sector as well. Because profits from farming are uncertain, most families have several sources of income. They sell animals as well as fruits and vegetables. However, 70 percent of village households derive their major income from activities other than farming. These include day labor, government jobs, craft trades, and specialist agricultural work as well as rents, pensions, and remittances from family members who have migrated.

Farmers today must know the traditional skills of farming as well as how to manage a wide range of other activities. They must understand local conditions and know how to respond to the complex changes and challenges taking place outside of their villages. Peasants today are part of a world economy. They are affected by global prices for the commodities they produce as well as the policies of their own national government and foreign governments. All over the world, farmers are increasingly part of a globalized, industrialized economy.

Industrialism

In industrialism, the focus of production moves away from food to the production of other goods and services. Investments in machinery and technologies of communication and information become increasingly important. In foraging, pastoralism, horticulture, and agriculture, most of the population is involved in producing food. Although the food industry is very large in industrial societies, only a very small percentage of the population is directly involved in food production. In the United States, for example, in 2005 fewer than one million people, less than one half of 1 percent of the population, had farming as their primary occupation (Census Bureau, 2008 Statistical Abstract).

Industrialism has an explosive effect on many aspects of economy, society, and culture. It has led to vastly increased population growth, expanded consumption of resources (especially energy), international expansion, occupational specialization, and a shift from subsistence strategies to wage labor. In every industrialized society, most people work for wages that they use to purchase food, goods, and services. Although cash transactions are found in other production systems, in industrial economies almost all transactions are mediated by money.

Industrial economies are based on the principles that consumption must constantly expand, and material standards of living must always rise. This contrasts with economies created by the production systems previously discussed, which put various limits on both production and consumption and thus make lighter demands on their environments. Industrialism today has vastly outgrown national boundaries. The result has been great movement of resources, capital, and population, as the whole world has gradually been drawn into the global economy, a process we call **globalization.**

Contemporary industrial and postindustrial societies are characterized by well-coordinated specialized labor forces that produce goods and services and by much smaller elite and managerial classes that oversee the day-to-day operations of the workplace and control what is produced and how it is distributed. Government bureaucracies become important economic and social strata. Increasingly, mobility, skill, and education are required for success.

Because industrialized societies generate much higher levels of inequality than societies based on foraging, pastoralism, or horticulture and because industrial systems require continued expansion, wealth and poverty become critical social issues. Unequal distributions of opportunity, economic failure, illness, and misfortune limit the life chances of vast numbers of people in industrialized societies. Conversely, economic success creates lifestyles well above poverty for large numbers and conditions of truly extraordinary wealth for a very small number. Inequalities characterize relations among as well as within nations. The creation of complex global systems of exchange between those who supply raw materials and those who use them in manufacturing as well as between manufacturers and consumers has resulted in increasing disparities of wealth around the world.

Industrialized Agriculture: The Beef Industry in the United States

Before World War II, American dinner tables were supplied with beef, pork, and chicken that came through a production chain that started with the livestock on a family farm and ended in the neighborhood retail butcher shop, where a knowledgeable homemaker (usually a woman) selected the cuts that suited her tastes and pocketbook.

Increasingly, as both parents worked outside the home, as suburban living compelled longer commutes to work, and as busy and conflicting schedules splintered family togetherness, American food culture became marked by the demand for packaged convenience meat and poultry items, which were "grazed" on at home, in drive-ins, or at fast-food restaurants or were taken on the run as mobile "fist food." Filling the ever-growing American—and global—demand for inexpensive, reliable, and widely available beef, pork, and poultry, spurred on by relentless advertising and promotion, required cost-efficient mass production methods. Such methods could most easily be used by huge transnational corporations that were able to invest huge amounts of capital in mechanization, chemical fertilizers, and assembly line processing.

Industrialized agriculture has changed America's rural culture where the factory farms and processing plants are increasingly located. The high level of capital investment required by agribusiness meant that generations-old family farms were no longer economically viable. Rural poverty increased, and young, would-be farmers saw little future for themselves. Some remained in America's rural areas and took the dangerous and poorly paid jobs offered by the corporate meat and poultry processing industry (although increasingly these jobs have gone to immigrants); others left the countryside altogether. Local chambers of commerce recruited agribusiness with free land and tax breaks, putting a greater revenue burden on farmers and small-town residents already in a downward economic spiral. Local water supplies and soil were despoiled by chemical fertilizers, and noxious fumes from the processing plants polluted the air. Thus, although some rural regions experienced short-term job increases from the meatpacking and poultry processing industries, there was a hidden cost and a long-term downside for rural communities.

Although the meat and poultry industries publicly prioritize the values of quality, safety, and productivity, they have a very long history of poor dangerous working conditions and questionable health practices. More than 100 years ago, Upton Sinclair (1906) wrote a shocking exposé of the meatpacking industry. It is alarming that many dangerous and potentially unhealthy practices remain today. Now, as then, the cost efficiency and high productivity of the industry are made possible only by cheap labor. Meatpackers need to get the maximum product out the door 24/7/365. "On the floor" this translates into a large proportion of unskilled, poorly trained, low-paid hourly workers; a speeded-up "disassembly" line; an insufficiency of lunch and bathroom breaks; and no paid "donning and doffing" time when workers can clean off the blood that bespatters them and change their clothing at the end of their shift. Management also makes significant savings by discouraging worker compensation claims or refusing to pay such claims; by "writing-up" workers as malingerers if they request absence for illness; by rigidly distinguishing job descriptions with differential pay scales down to the last penny per hour; and by intimidating workers who attempt to form or join unions (Schlosser 2005; Stull and Broadway 2004).

Work in the meat and poultry processing industries is inherently difficult and dangerous. The processing operations on the line involve thousands of panicked animals moving through a treadmill to be stun-gunned by a "knocker," axed in half by "splitters" on a moving platform, and deboned and cut up with sharp knives wielded by an assortment of specialists such as "stickers," "gutters," "tail rippers," and "head droppers," whose names suggest their roles in the process—and the possibilities for injuries. Blood, intestines, ears, hooves, and other animal by-products used for making perfumes, bonemeal, paintbrushes, and many other items that are supposed to be continually cleaned up or removed to separate locations for later use. However, they are sometimes left to decay, emitting noxious fumes. Workers report being put back on the line with flu, vomiting, or diarrhea, impacting not only their own health but the quality of the product. This was shown dramatically when, in early 2008, the Westland/Hallmark meatpacking company recalled 143 million pounds of meat, some of which was used in school lunch programs (Martin 2008). You can "have it your way," but only at a high cost!

The Global Marketplace

The contemporary world is characterized by connectedness and change of a magnitude greater than anything seen earlier. For some people, the expansion of the global economy has meant new and more satisfying means of making a living. However, these opportunities are not equally available to all peoples or to all individuals within a culture. For many people the promise of prosperity offered by the global economy has yet to be fulfilled.

Anthropology is particularly sensitive to the complex linkages among local, regional, national, and global contexts that structure the modern world. Anthropologists today can play an important role in shaping government and global economic policies that take into account the environmental impact of different ways of making a living, the values and practices of local cultures, international plant and animal conservation efforts, and corporate- and state-driven efforts to participate in global markets. In the postindustrial globalized society, new responses are called for by individuals, governments, and business as they adapt to significant changes in the production and distribution of goods. We explore some of these changes in Chapter 6 on economics.

BRINGING IT BACK HOME: YOU ARE WHAT YOU EAT: CULTURE AND FOOD CHOICES

Eating meat has many cultural connotations. For immigrants to the United States, it was associated with upward social mobility. In India under colonial British rule, it was associated with manliness. Local eating habits have worldwide ecological consequences, and Western appetites for beef have profound effects on the global environment. The proliferation of fast-food restaurants began in the United States but has expanded across the globe. This has led to an increased demand for cheap beef. This culturally patterned taste for beef has spread throughout the industrialized nations of the world, especially in Japan. The increasing global demand for cheap beef has resulted in the destruction of enormous swaths of rain forests in Central and South America and a transformation of the culture and economy of the American Midwest. From an investor's point of view, clearing tropical forests for pasturage is the best way to acquire the huge amount of land needed to raise cattle. But ecologically, cattle production is one of the worst land uses for tropical forests (Brookfield 1988). The production of enough ground beef for one hamburger requires the destruction of 200 pounds of living matter, including more than 20 plant species, 100 insect species, and dozens of bird, mammal, and reptile species. Cattle raising is also the most costly kind of food production. Producing 1 pound of beef takes 2500 gallons of water, compared with 119 gallons for corn, and 9 pounds of feed, compared with 2 pounds of feed for chicken. In the global economy, dining at your neighborhood fast-food restaurant translates into environmental consequences thousands of miles away.

In addition to its negative impact on the environment, beef consumption increases the chances of obesity and heart disease. Still, it remains an important part of the American diet: "Steak and potatoes" are still considered the iconic American meal.

In recent years, however, important food alternatives that once were out on the margins are becoming more mainstream: vegetarianism, the slow food movement, community-supported and local agriculture, and organic foods. All of these alternatives are both healthier for individuals and leave a smaller footprint on the environment (Wilk 2006). But they may cost more and may involve the difficult task of changing culturally ingrained food habits as well as buying habits. Working people may find it too difficult to fit frequent, even daily, shopping into their schedule compared to one-stop shopping at the supermarket.

YOU DECIDE

1. Discuss some of the cultural values and patterns that you think underlie America's food choices. How do these values and cultural patterns affect your own food choices? (Consider prestige, taste, nutrition, cost, availability, global and local environmental impact, religious beliefs, workers' wages and humane working conditions, and cruelty to animals that might be involved, among other factors.)
2. What cultural, social, personal, and other obstacles do you see as standing in the way of, or opening possibilities for, changes in America's food habits?
3. What are some of the interconnected changes in American culture and society that might come about as a result of substantial changes in America's food practices?

CHAPTER SUMMARY

1. All societies must adapt to their physical environments, which present different problems, opportunities, and limitations to human populations. The subsistence (food-getting) pattern of a society develops in response to seasonal variations in the environment and environmental variations over the long run, such as drought, flood, animal diseases, climate, and the presence of other groups.
2. The five major patterns of using the environment to support human populations are foraging (fishing, hunting, and gathering), pastoralism, horticulture, agriculture, and industrialism. As a whole, humankind has moved in the direction of using more complex technology, increasing its numbers, and developing more complex sociocultural systems.
3. Foraging, which relies on food naturally available in the environment, was the major food-getting pattern for 99 percent of the time humans have been on earth. Although this way of life is rapidly disappearing, foraging is still a useful adjunct to other subsistence strategies for many societies. The Inuit are a foraging culture.
4. Pastoralism involves the care of domesticated herd animals, which alone cannot provide the necessary ingredients for an adequate human diet. Because supplementary food grains are required, pastoralism either is found along with cultivation or involves trading relations with food cultivators. The Yarahmadzai are an example of a nomadic mixed pastoralist economy.

5. Horticulture typically is a tropical forest adaptation that requires the cutting and burning of jungle to clear fields for cultivation and a simple, nonmechanized technology. Fields are not used permanently but are allowed to lie fallow after several years of productivity. The Lua' are swidden cultivators in Thailand.
6. Agriculture, or intensive cultivation, involves a complex technology that includes plows, irrigation, or mechanization. Agriculture generally supports high population densities and is associated with sedentary village life and the rise of the state. Musha, an Egyptian village, is an example of peasant agriculture.
7. In industrialism, machines and chemical processes are used for the production of goods. Industrial societies require a large, mobile labor force. These societies are characterized by complex systems of exchange among all elements of the economy, by bureaucracies, and by social stratification, including a management class. The American beef industry is an example of industrialism.

KEY TERMS

Agriculture
Efficiency
Foraging (hunting and gathering)
Globalization
Horticulture
Industrialism
Nomadic pastoralism
Pastoralism
Peasants
Population density
Productivity
Sedentary
Subsistence strategies
Swidden (slash and burn) cultivation
Transhumant pastoralism

© Joan Gregg

Specialization and the creation of markets are critical aspects of the development of large-scale economies. In earlier times, cheeses were made and consumed locally. Now they enter a network of international trade. The Amsterdam Cheese Market, pictured here, is an important node in that network.

CHAPTER 6

ECONOMICS

CHAPTER OUTLINE

Ultimate Dictator

Economic Behavior

Allocating Resources

Organizing Labor

- Specialization in Complex Societies

Distribution: Systems of Exchange and Consumption

- Reciprocity
- Redistribution
- Market Exchange
- Capitalism
- Resistance to Capitalism

Bringing It Back Home: Product Anthropology

- You Decide

ULTIMATE DICTATOR

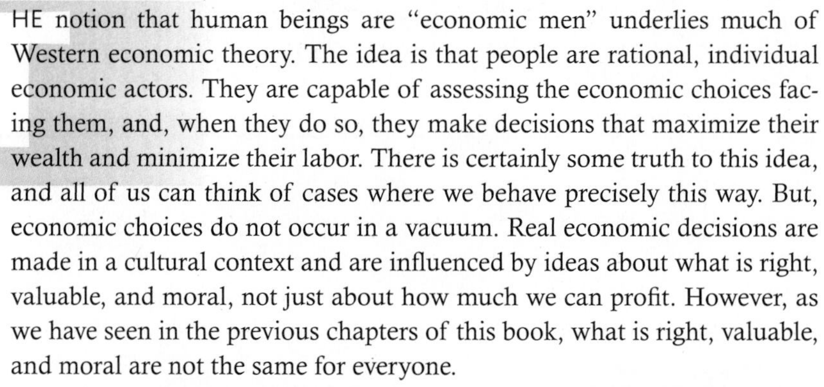

THE notion that human beings are "economic men" underlies much of Western economic theory. The idea is that people are rational, individual economic actors. They are capable of assessing the economic choices facing them, and, when they do so, they make decisions that maximize their wealth and minimize their labor. There is certainly some truth to this idea, and all of us can think of cases where we behave precisely this way. But, economic choices do not occur in a vacuum. Real economic decisions are made in a cultural context and are influenced by ideas about what is right, valuable, and moral, not just about how much we can profit. However, as we have seen in the previous chapters of this book, what is right, valuable, and moral are not the same for everyone.

Economists and anthropologists have developed interesting tools to test the degree to which people in different cultures actually behave like the "economic men" of the theory. Two examples are the dictator game and the ultimatum game.

In the dictator game, there are two individuals: a "proposer" and a "responder." The proposer is given a sum of money, say the equivalent of 1 day of wages, and is told to split it with the responder. The proposer and the responder are unknown to each other and they play the game only once, so there is no chance that generosity will be reciprocated. If people behave like "economic men" and try to maximize their wealth and minimize their work, we would expect that the proposer would keep the entire sum, offering nothing to the responder. But, in fact, that doesn't always happen. In the United States and other wealthy nations, about 30 to 40 percent of the players take the whole pot. However, most proposers leave between 20 and 30 percent for the responders. Jean Ensminger (2002) found that among the Orma, a group of cattle pastoralists living in Kenya, only 9 percent took the whole pot; the others gave an average of 31 percent to the responders.

The ultimatum game is also played with a proposer and a responder. However, in this case, the proposer offers to split a sum of money, and the responder may either accept or reject the split. If the responder accepts the split, the money is divided and the game is over. If the responder rejects the split, neither player receives any money and the game ends. As in the dictator game, players are anonymous and play only once, so generosity cannot be returned. In the ultimatum game, a respondent who behaved like "economic man" would always accept the proposer's offer since accepting the offer involves no financial cost and even a very low offer is greater than nothing. But, real people do not play like "economic men."

In the past 15 years, anthropologists and economists have played the ultimatum game with members of many different cultures. Results from 15 cultures have been reported (Henrich et al. 2004). They showed large amounts of variation between cultures and showed no culture that played the game as the "economic man" model would predict. For example, among the Machiguenga of the Peruvian Amazon, proposers rarely offered more than 15 percent, and offers were almost never rejected (Henrich 2004). American college students, on the other hand, offered 42 to 48 percent of the pot to their responders, and responders tended to reject offers of less than 30 percent.

Some of the results may seem counterintuitive. For example, in foraging groups there is a high degree of equality, but foragers were not generous game players. The Hadza, foragers who live in Tanzania, made some of the lowest proposals of any groups tested. On the other hand, industrialized economies are highly stratified and unequal, but their members are likely to offer almost half the pot to responders. In fact, the results show an interesting trend. The greater the degree to which a group is involved in a market economy, the more likely proposers were to give a larger share of the money to responders. Later in this chapter, we will explore some of the reasons why this is the case.

The results of the dictator and ultimatum games demonstrate the social and cultural dimensions of economic decision making. The fact that cross-culturally a strong majority of proposers give responders something may show that all people have a bias toward at least a little generosity. However, the systematic differences among cultures demonstrate that decisions are set in cultural contexts that determine moral and appropriate behavior and that these are different in different economic systems.

Economics is the study of the ways in which the choices people make as individuals and as members of societies combine to determine how their society uses its scarce resources to produce and distribute goods and services. But, as our example shows, this process is always set within a cultural context. How we make these decisions depends on the values we give to both goods and ideas. And that depends upon culture.

Every society must have an **economic system** in the sense that each group of people must produce, distribute, and consume. However, cultural context determines what is produced and how it is produced. Cultures establish the ways in which goods and services are distributed. And cultural values are critical in determining the meanings of consumption.

ECONOMIC BEHAVIOR

Economists assume that because human wants are unlimited and the means for achieving them are not, organizations and individuals must make decisions about the best way to apply their limited means to meet their unlimited desires. As we saw in the opening story, one way of understanding economic decisions is to assume that decision makers will always maximize their financial benefit and minimize their work (Dalton 1961). Will a business firm cut down or expand its production? Will it purchase a new machine or hire more laborers? Such decisions are assumed to be motivated by the desire to maximize profit.

However, the opening story also shows us that this understanding misses critical factors. All people live with limited means to meet their desires. As human beings, we only have so much time and so much energy to expend in meeting our desires. But, we do not always allocate our time and effort to maximize our financial wealth. Consider a choice you may make this evening. After you finish reading this chapter, you might confront a series of decisions: Should you reread it for better comprehension? Should you study for another course? Call and get a pizza delivered? Play with your kids? Socialize with your friends? You will make your choice based on some calculation of benefit. However, that benefit probably cannot be reduced to financial profit. You may believe that you will make more money if you study and get higher grades. However, your choice is set in a context in which money is unlikely to be the most important element of value; we value our friends, our children, our leisure time, and many other things as well. If you choose to socialize instead of hitting the books, your choice is not irrational, but it does not necessarily lead to greater profit. We cannot assume that you will always act to increase your material well-being. Rather, we need to find out what motivates you.

Just as you might value an evening spent with friends over an "A" in this class, members of other cultures might value family connections, cultural tradition, social prestige, leisure time, or other things over monetary profit. For example, the Hadza, mentioned earlier, live in an area of Tanzania with an abundance of animal and vegetable food. They have considerable leisure time but make no attempt to use it to increase their wealth. Although they know how to farm, they don't do it because it would require too much work (Woodburn 1968).

Leisure time is only one of the ends toward which people expend effort. They may also direct their energies toward increasing social status or respect. In Western society, **prestige** is primarily tied to increased consumption and display of goods and services, but this is not universal. In many societies, prestige is associated with giving goods away. Conspicuous consumers and stingy people become objects of scorn and may be shunned or accused of witchcraft (see Danfulani 1999; Offiong 1983 for examples). The notion that prestige can be gained through giving is well established in our own society. Universities have buildings bearing the names of their most generous donors, and Bill Gates not only is the CEO of Microsoft, he is also the head of the world's largest charitable foundation.

To understand the economies of various cultures, anthropologists face two related problems. First, they must analyze the broad institutional and social contexts within which people make decisions, and second, they must determine and evaluate the factors that motivate individual decision making.

One way we can think about any given economic system is to consider a series of fundamental issues that all societies must face. Because all societies must acquire the food and other materials necessary to their lives, all must engage in production. To do so, all societies must acquire resources, such as land and water, and all must have some system through which the rights to use such resources are allocated.

However, resources in and of themselves do nothing. Rather, people must be organized in specific ways to use resources in the production of goods and services. Thus, each society has some system of organizing their members to use the resources available to them. For example, foragers rely on the plants and animals in their environment. But, foragers never simply gather and eat the plants and animals randomly. In each group, specific groups of people do specific tasks. Most often, men hunt and women gather. Thus, they are organized to produce. Additionally, people in all societies exchange and consume the products of production. Thus, each society has a system of distribution, and in each there are distinct styles and patterns of consumption. In the remainder of this chapter we will explore how different societies tackle the problems of allocating resources, organizing labor, and distributing and consuming the results of production.

ALLOCATING RESOURCES

Productive resources are the things that members of a society need to participate in the economy, and access to them is basic to every culture. The most obvious productive resources are land, water, labor, and tools. However, knowledge is also an important productive resource. We can see the effects of access to knowledge in current-day society by looking at the relationship between university degrees and income. According to the U.S. Census Bureau (2003), the median income for high school graduates in 2003 was about $26,000. The median income for those with a college degree was almost $42,000. The median for those with masters and doctoral degrees was substantially higher. Of course, the university is not the only source of knowledge in our society. But still. . . .

An important point of contrast between economic systems is the extent to which the members of a society have access to productive resources. In general, differential access to resources develops as population and social complexity increase. Small-scale economies have a limited number of productive resources, for example, and most everyone has access to them. Large-scale societies have a great many more resources, but access to them is limited. Again, considering differential access to knowledge in the United States, we see that only 3 percent of the students at America's most selective universities come from households in the lowest 25 percent of the income scale, and only 10 percent come from the bottom 50 percent (Lexington 2005). Thus, family wealth plays a critical role in accessing knowledge and is a powerful predictor of future wealth and social position.

Access to the knowledge that allows one to make and use tools plays an important role in all societies. There may be additional important forms of knowledge that can be controlled as well, such as the knowledge of healing or of religious rituals. In preindustrial societies, however, the most basic resources are land and sometimes water. Examining the ways in which people access these particular resources can give us insight into the social organization and other aspects of a culture.

The requirements of a foraging lifestyle generally mean that a group of people must spread out over a large area. Boundaries are generally flexible so that they can be adjusted as the availability of resources change. Abundance and scarcity shape people's relationship to land. Where resources are scarce and large areas are needed to support the population, boundaries usually are not defended. Where resources are more abundant and people move less, groups may be more inclined to defend their territory (Cashdan 1989:42).

Among pastoralists, the most critical resources are livestock and land. Livestock are owned and managed by individual heads of households. Animals, in turn, produce goods that are directly consumed, such as milk. They are also kept as a form of wealth, to produce other animals and to exchange goods and services. Land and water are generally not owned. In many cases, during the summer or the rainy season, cattle graze in deserts and highland areas unsuitable for farming. In the winter or dry season, they move to areas that are occupied by settled farmers. There, agreements with landowners and village leaders allow animals to graze on crop waste and the stubble from harvested fields. Most such agreements specify rights, payments, and schedules for all parties.

In most societies characterized by horticulture (extensive cultivation), land is communally owned by an extended kin group. Designated elders or officials of the group allocate the rights to use land to individuals or heads of households. But such land may not be sold. Since almost everyone belongs to some land controlling kin group, few people are deprived of access to this basic resource. Thus, control over land is not a means by which one group can exploit or exert permanent control over another.

Extensive cultivation often involves investing a great deal of labor in clearing, cultivating, and maintaining land. Generally, the rights to cleared land and its products are vested in those who work it. Since such individuals may die while the land is still productive, some system of inheritance of use rights is usually provided. Among the Lacandon Maya, for example, individuals can farm any unused piece of land. However, clearing virgin land is difficult, so people retain rights to land they have cleared even if it is not currently in production. Maya who migrate may lose their land rights, but their families retain ownership of any fruit trees that they have planted. Should a man die after investing time and labor in clearing and planting land, his wife and children retain rights to use the land (McGee 1990).

In more politically and technologically complex societies, agriculture (intensive cultivation) dominates production. Enormous amounts of labor are invested in the land and very large quantities of food produced. When this happens, control of the land becomes an important source of wealth and power. Land ownership moves from the kin group to the individual or

In complex societies, enormous amounts of labor often are invested in land. This results in high levels of production, and land ownership becomes an important source of wealth and power. This picture shows rice paddies in Yunnan, China.

family. Within the limits of law or custom, the owner has the right to keep others off the land and to dispose of it as he or she wishes.

In societies with intensive cultivation, land and other productive resources are likely to be owned by an elite group. Landowners usually do not work their fields themselves. Most fieldwork is done by laborers who often are referred to as *peasants.* Today, peasants typically pay cash rent to their landlords, but in the past they also provided goods and services, including a portion of their agricultural production, labor, finished craft goods such as cloth, and raw material such as lumber. As a result, landowners enjoy relatively high standards of living but peasants do not.

Most current-day societies rely on intensive land cultivation, but, as we saw in Chapter 5, only a miniscule percentage of the population is involved in agriculture. Therefore, access to productive land is not important for most people. In wealthy nations, most people earn their livelihood by working for wages for businesses and other organizations that provide goods and services. These usually are organized as capitalist enterprises. We will discuss capitalism at some length later in this chapter.

ORGANIZING LABOR

In small-scale preindustrial and peasant economies, the household or some extended kin group is the basic unit of production and of consumption (White 1980). The **household** is an economic unit—a group of people united by kinship or other links who share a residence and organize production, consumption, and distribution of goods among themselves. A household is different than a family because it may include lodgers, servants, and others. Household members use most of the goods they produce themselves.

Households and kin groups do seek financial gain, but this is not their primary purpose. Their goals are often social or religious rather than monetary. Labor is not a commodity bought and sold in the market; rather, it is an important aspect of membership in a social group. The labor that people both perform and receive situates them with respect to others in their family and gives them both a sense of identity and a sense of meaning.

The gendered division of labor is a good example of the relationship between work and identity. In all human societies, some tasks are considered appropriate for women and others appropriate for men. At some level, the sexual division of labor is biological since only women can bear and nurse children. Thus, caring for infants almost always is primarily a female role and usually central to female identity (Nielsen 1990:147–168). Beyond this, few jobs are always done by men or always done by women in all societies. However, within a society, doing certain kinds of work still may be fundamental to identity. For example, in Aztec Mexico, weaving was basic to female identity. Newborn girls were presented with tools for weaving, and weaving equipment was placed with women when they died (Brumfiel 1991, 2006:866). On the other hand, in most West African societies, weaving is considered a male task.

In Western society, work also has very important social implications. Of course people work to put food on their table and a roof over their head. But, as anthropologist Pamela Crespin notes, in our society an individual's self-image and social status is bound up with work. Joblessness or the inability to earn a living wage diminishes an adult's identity and status (Crespin 2005:20). This is a particularly important issue in a nation such as the United States, where in 2003, 4.2 million families were classified as "working poor" (BLS 2005).

In economies where households are the units of production, there can be little economic growth. Households cannot easily expand or contract as the economy fluctuates. They cannot easily fire their members or acquire new ones. Thus, large-scale production and distribution systems tend not to develop under such conditions. However, as we will see in the ethnography of Turkey later in this chapter, household social relations can play an important role in an industrialized economy.

Specialization in Complex Societies

The division of labor in society becomes more specialized and complex as the population increases and agricultural production intensifies. This is particularly the case where a society is dependent on grain agriculture. Grains are hard, durable, and storable. Those who are able to control them have access to wealth and power in new and important ways. Landowners and rulers are able to support many people. Occupational specialization spreads through society as individuals are able to exchange their services or the products they produce for food and wealth. Specialists are likely to include soldiers, government officials, and members of the priesthood as well as artisans, craftsmen, and merchants.

Traditional areas of contemporary India provide an excellent example of occupational specialization. There, only people belonging to particular hereditary kinship groups can perform certain services or produce certain kinds of goods. Literally thousands of specialized activities—washing clothes, drumming at festivals, presiding over religious ceremonies, making pots, painting pictures—are traditionally performed by specific named hereditary groups.

Much of the world's population today lives in industrial or postindustrial societies, and almost everyone is a specialist of one kind or another. A quick glance at the yellow pages of the phone book of a major

American city gives a good indication of the degree of specialization in American society. Each entry represents at least one specialty.

Although specialization undoubtedly has advantages in terms of efficiency and the ability to produce large quantities of goods, it can take a large physical and emotional toll on members of a society. Since the beginnings of the industrial age, many factory jobs involved repetitious and mind-numbing labor often performed under hazardous conditions. In the American automobile plants of the early 20th century, for example, almost all skilled tasks were mechanized. Workers simply inserted pieces into machines, turned a switch and waited until the machine completed its task, removed the finished pieces, and passed them on to the next worker. The machinery determined the pace of work and the tasks performed. In the 1920s, one worker said simply, "The machine is my boss" (Meyer 2004).

Factory labor often led to new notions of identity. For example, in the 19th century, many American workers associated masculinity with skilled labor, independence, and decision-making power at work. On the assembly lines in early 20th-century America, labor was boring and monotonous, and workers had little decision-making ability. Companies such as Ford Motors, through public speeches, company policies, and employment practices, sought to redefine masculinity, associating it with "working hard in the company of other men, on a useful product, and being paid well for it" (Lewchuk 1993:852) rather than with skill and independence.

In the past 200 years, jobs have become increasingly specialized. Repetitive, monotonous factory labor, such as the work in this sneaker factory in Mexico, altered people's lives and led to new understandings of identity.

DISTRIBUTION: SYSTEMS OF EXCHANGE AND CONSUMPTION

In all societies, goods and services are exchanged. In fact, some anthropologists have long theorized that the exchange of goods is one of the fundamental bases of culture. The great French anthropologist Marcel Mauss (1924/1990) theorized that societies were held together by patterns of giving and receiving. He pointed out that because gifts invariably must be repaid, we are obligated to each other through exchange. And in many situations it is better to give than to receive.

The three main patterns of exchange are reciprocity, redistribution, and the market. Although more than one kind of exchange system exists in most societies, each system is predominantly associated with a certain kind of political and social organization (Polyani 1944). Let us look first at reciprocity.

Reciprocity

Reciprocity is the mutual give-and-take among people of similar status. Three types of reciprocity can be distinguished from one another by the degree of social distance between the exchanging partners (Sahlins 1972).

Generalized reciprocity usually is carried out among close kin and carries a high moral obligation. It involves a distribution of goods in which no overt account is kept of what is given, and no immediate or specific return is expected. In our culture, the relationship between mother and child is usually a good example. Ideally, such transactions are without any thought of self-interest.

Generalized reciprocity involving food is an important social mechanism among foraging peoples. In these societies, hunters distribute meat among members of the kin group or camp. Each person or family gets an equal share or a share dependent on its kinship relationship to the hunter. We might wonder what the hunter gets out of this arrangement. Aren't some people always in the position of providing and others always receiving? Part of the answer is that hunters gain satisfaction from accomplishing a highly skilled and difficult task (Woodburn 1998) and that this is accompanied by a degree of prestige. Additionally, because all people in the society are bound by the same rules, the system provides everyone with the opportunity to give and receive, although this does not necessarily mean that people do so equally.

Balanced reciprocity involves greater social distance than generalized reciprocity and entails a clear obligation to return, within a reasonable time limit, goods of nearly equal value to those given. In the United States, we participate in balanced reciprocity when we give gifts at weddings or birth-

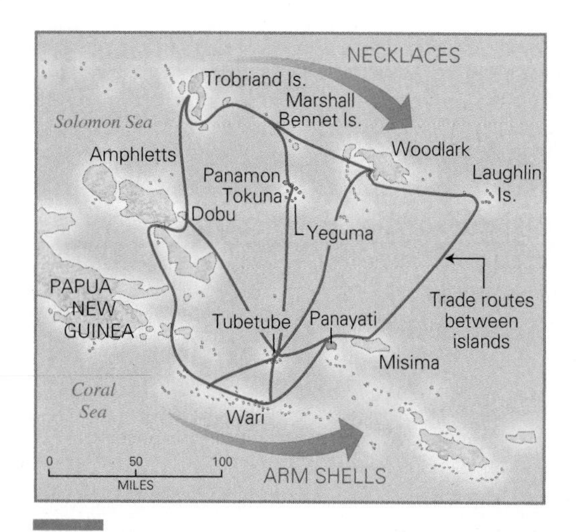

The kula trade binds people in the South Pacific in a network of reciprocal trading relationships.

days, exchange invitations, or buy a round of drinks for friends. The economic aspect of these exchanges is repressed; we say it is spirit of the gift that is important. However, we also know that accepting a gift involves the obligation to return a gift of approximately the same value. If we fail to do so, our relationship with the gift giver is unlikely to last very long.

Balanced reciprocity is often characteristic of trading relations among nonindustrialized peoples without market economies. Such trade is frequently carried out over long distances and between different tribes or villages. It is often in the hands of trading partners, men or women who have a long-standing and personalized relationship with each other.

Bronislaw Malinowski's (1922/1984) analysis of the **kula ring,** an extensive system of intertribal trade among the inhabitants of a ring of islands off New Guinea, is one of the most famous anthropological studies of reciprocal trading. The kula trade moves two types of prestige goods from island to island around the kula circle. Soulava, long necklaces of red shell, always move in a clockwise direction. Mwali, bracelets of white shell, move counterclockwise. Participants receive the necklaces or bracelets from their trading partners. Although kula items can be permanently owned and can be taken out of circulation (Weiner 1976), people generally hold them for a while and then pass them on. Kula trading partnerships are lifelong affairs, and their details are fixed by tradition.

The kula, however, is not the simple exchange of mwali for soulava. In fact, one is never traded directly for another. Instead, to receive these kula goods, traders bring gifts that may include canoes, axe blades, pottery, and pigs as well as other items. To show appreciation for these gifts, their trading partners might bestow mwali or soulava on them. To make their trading partners more likely to give them good kula items, traders are particularly likely to bring goods not found on the island where the trading is taking place. Kula trading thus increases the islanders' consumption of a wide range of goods, particularly those they do not produce. It also binds trading partners together, creating alliances that are critical in settling disputes and maintaining peace. This is particularly important because there is no formal government incorporating the different groups that take active roles in the kula.

Negative reciprocity is the unsociable extreme in exchange. It happens when trade is conducted for the purpose of material advantage and is based on the desire to get the better of a bargain. Negative reciprocity is characteristic of both impersonal and unfriendly transactions. Tribal and peasant societies often distinguish between the insider, whom it is morally wrong to cheat, and the outsider, from whom every advantage may be gained. Anthropologist Clyde Kluckhohn did important studies of the Navajo in the 1940s and 1950s. He reported that among the Navajo, the rules for interaction vary with the situation; to deceive when trading with outsiders is a morally accepted practice. Even witchcraft techniques are considered permissible in trading with members of foreign tribes (Kluckhohn 1959).

Negative reciprocity helps explain some of the findings from the ultimatum game described in the opening of this chapter. Recall that in ultimatum, one person splits a quantity of money offering a portion to another. If the second person accepts the split, they divide the money. If the second person rejects the offer, neither gets any money. Researchers found that the results of the game vary from society to society. In many kin-based societies the first person was likely to offer only a small percentage of the money and the second person usually accepted it, whereas in market-based societies the first person offered much larger percentages and the second was likely to reject small offers (Chibnik 2005; Henrich et al. 2004).

A key aspect of the ultimatum game is that the players are anonymous. The results are explained because, in kin-based societies, negative reciprocity often characterizes anonymous transactions. For players from such societies, offering little or nothing to an anonymous partner is both expected and proper. Since the second player does not expect to receive much from an anonymous person, the second player is likely to accept very small offers.

Redistribution

In **redistribution**, goods are collected from or contributed by members of a group and then given out to the group in a new pattern. Thus, redistribution involves a social center to which goods are brought and from which they are distributed. Redistribution occurs in many different contexts. In household food sharing, pooled resources are reallocated among family members. In state societies, redistribution is achieved through taxation.

Redistribution can be especially important in horticultural societies where political organization includes bigmen, self-made leaders who gain power and authority through personal achievement. Such individuals collect goods and food from their supporters. Often these items are redistributed back in communal feasts, which the bigman sponsors to sustain his political power and raise his prestige. Redistribution also occurred in some chiefdoms. In these cases, however, a distinct hierarchy was involved. Chiefs collected goods and staple foods from many communities to support their households and attendants as well as to finance large public feasts that helped solidify their power (Earle 1987).

Alaska State Library Elbridge W. Merrill Photograph Collection

Potlatches are competitive feasts held among Native Americans of the Northwest Pacific Coast. Here Tlingit chief at a potlatch pose for a photo in 1904 in Sitka, Alaska.

Potlatch feasting among Native-American groups of the Pacific Northwest, including the Kwakiutl and Tlingit, is a good example of redistribution. In these groups, potlatches were held to honor and to validate the rank of chiefs and other notables, usually in connection with births, deaths, and marriages (Rosman and Rubel 1971). A leader holding a potlatch called on his followers to supply food and other goods to be consumed and distributed during a feast to which he invited group members and rivals. The number of guests present and the amount of goods given away or destroyed revealed the wealth and prestige of the host chief. At a potlatch, the host publicly traced his line of descent and claimed the right to certain titles and privileges. Each of these claims was accompanied by the giving away, and sometimes the destruction, of large quantities of food and goods, such as blankets and carved wooden boxes. As these goods were given or destroyed, the individual and his supporters boasted of their wealth and power. In the early 20th century, Franz Boas collected speeches given at potlatches, such as:

> I am Yaqatlentlis. . . . I am Great Inviter. . . . Therefore I feel like laughing at what the lower chiefs say, for they try in vain to down me by talking against my name. Who approaches what was done by my ancestors, the chiefs? Therefore I am known by all the tribes over all the world. Only the chief my ancestor gave away property in a great feast, and all the rest can only try to imitate me. . . . (in Benedict 1961:191).

The feasting and gifts given at a potlatch demonstrated the host's right to the titles and rights he claimed and created prestige for him and his followers. Guests either acknowledged the host's claims or refuted them by staging an even larger potlatch. Thus, potlatching involved friendship but also competition and rivalry.

From an economic perspective, the drive for prestige encouraged people to produce much more than they would otherwise. This increased the amount of work they did but also the amount of food and goods they produced and consumed. Since this wealth was given to people who traveled substantial distances to come to a potlatch, it was distributed to a fairly large population and ecological area.

In the late 19th century and early 20th century, Canadian government authorities saw the potlatch as a symbol of native irrationality. They believed that investment was the key to economic success and to them, the potlatch focus on consumption and destruction of goods was both disturbing and wasteful. The result was that potlatching was outlawed between 1884 and 1951 (Bracken 1997). Since then, the potlatch has been revived but primarily as a symbol of tribal identity rather than a major element in tribal economy. Simeone (1995) and Stearns (1975), for example, report that the Tanacross and Haida people consider the potlatch a central symbol of cooperation and respect that separates native from non-native peoples.

The Pacific Northwest.

Although the term *potlatch* refers specifically to the feasting of Northwest Coast people, Rosman and Rubel (1971:xii) report that rivalrous, competitive feasting is found among many peoples. It is common, for example, throughout the Pacific Islands. We may even see some elements of it in our own society. There may be competition within families or within communities to throw the largest and most elaborate holiday parties, weddings, or coming of age celebrations (such as confirmation, bar or bat mitzvah, quinceanera). In all of these cases, the prestige that accrues to the people who give the party is a critical factor. This reminds us that there is much more to giving a gift than simply trying to determine what another person desires.

Redistribution may either increase or decrease inequality within a society. **Leveling mechanisms** are forms of redistribution that tend to decrease social inequality. They force accumulated resources or capital to be used in ways that ensure social goals are considered along with economic ones. Leveling mechanisms take many different forms. For example, if generosity rather than the accumulation of wealth is the basis for prestige, those who desire power and prestige will distribute much of their wealth. Sometimes, as with the potlatch, this is accomplished through feasting. However, there are numerous other possibilities.

Manning Nash (1961) and June Nash (1970) described a number of leveling mechanisms that operate in the village of Amatenango, in the Chiapas district of Mexico. One is the organization of production by households. As mentioned earlier, economic expansion and accumulation of wealth are limited where households, rather than business firms, are the productive units. A second is inheritance. Because all children share equally in the estate of a parent, large estates rarely persist over generations. Accusations of witchcraft are a third mechanism. People who accumulate more wealth than their neighbors or have wealth but are not generous may face such accusations, and those believed guilty of witchcraft may be killed.

Finally, in Amatenango, prosperous community members must hold religious and secular offices, called "cargos." Cargos are held for a year at a time and require their holders to perform civic duties and to pay for feasts and celebrations. Cargos are ranked, and those held by older, wealthier community members are more prestigious and more expensive. Such customs are common in southern Mexico and Central America and are referred to as **cargo systems.**

Anthropologists have shown that community obligations such as cargos help to limit the economic gap between the relatively rich and the poor, but they do not eliminate it. In fact, they may help to preserve social hierarchies (Chance and Taylor 1985). Wealthy individuals take expensive cargos that increase their prestige but do not severely impact their total wealth. They remain rich throughout their lives. The poor are generally unable to take cargos and remain poor throughout their lives. Thus, although some wealth is redistributed, economic differences are reinforced rather than equalized (Cancian 1989:147).

Market Exchange

Market exchange is the principal distribution mechanism in most of the world's societies today. Goods and services are bought and sold at a money price determined, at least in theory, by impersonal market forces.

The market involves cultural and moral assumptions that are well illustrated by the results of the ultimatum game. As we noted earlier, ultimatum players from market economies tended to offer relatively large shares of their money to their partners, and these partners tended to reject low offers, even though this penalized both players. They played this way because they shared a culturally based understanding of the market. For an impersonal market to run smoothly, most participants must believe that they will usually be treated fairly by people they do not know. People who take advantage of anonymity to enrich themselves at others' expense spoil the market and must be punished. Thus, ultimatum players from market economies are often willing to reject low offers, taking a loss to show the other player that anonymous partners must bargain and exchange fairly.

Of course, the ideal of fair and impersonal exchange is just that, an ideal. Real markets are full of conflicts, inequities, and outright cheats. In our own society there are clearly areas of commerce where people anticipate a certain amount of deceit. For example, merchants of used goods, particularly cars and machinery, often have reputations for shady practice. The continued importance of social connections among market participants is well illustrated by electronic marketplaces such as eBay, where buyers and sellers come close to true anonymity. In these cases, a sophisticated system of ratings simulates social connections and knowledge. This gives trading partners a degree of certainty that the terms of trade will be fair. But, eBay participants know that the fewer and worse the ratings of their trading partners, the greater the risk of a hostile exchange. The phrase *caveat emptor* (let the buyer beware) neatly captures the notion that the rules of even trade are not always in force.

In principle, the primary factors that set prices and wages in a market are related to supply and demand. In principle, individuals participate freely in a market, choosing what they buy and sell. However, there are many cases where these principles do not pertain. In some cases, wealthy and powerful individuals, organizations, and industries fix prices or wages, forcing people into wage labor or the market at disadvantageous terms. In other cases, cultural ideas about the proper or "just" price of a good or service are more important than supply and demand. Sometimes, governments control or influence the prices of commodities such as grain, setting them either high (to encourage farmers) or low (to feed often rebellious city dwellers cheaply).

Traders bid at the New York Stock Exchange. In a market, ideally prices are set by impersonal market forces including supply and demand.

Although markets are present in most societies, the goods and services traded in them vary greatly. As we have seen, in many societies people gain access to land, labor, and some goods through ties of kinship or obligations of reciprocity and redistribution. In such places, markets, if they exist at all, are limited to a small number of goods. In theory, in a society dominated by the market everything may be bought and sold. In practice, however, all societies limit what can be purchased legally. We live in a market-dominated society, but for moral, social, and political reasons, governments limit trade in certain goods. For example, there are restrictions on the sale of drugs, guns, children, and college degrees.

Capitalism

In the past 300 years, capitalism has become the world's predominant economic system. Capitalism expanded from northern Europe, North America, and Japan and has transformed economies worldwide, connecting them in a complex integrated international economy (Wallerstein 1995). We describe this historic process in Chapter 13, and we examine and analyze the problems and promises of the global economy in Chapter 14. Here we focus on describing capitalism and pointing out some of its most salient features.

In noncapitalist societies, most people produce goods to consume them, to trade them for other goods, or to pay rents and taxes. In capitalist societies, **firms** produce goods as a means to create wealth. For example, General Motors is not really in business to make cars. General Motors is in business to increase the wealth of its shareholders. Manufacturing automobiles is one (but only one) of the ways it achieves that end. GM is also heavily involved in banking and was historically involved in aviation, military contracting, and the production of consumer products such as refrigerators.

Productive resources become **capital** when they are used with the primary goal of increasing their owner's financial wealth. In capitalism, this becomes the most common (but not the only) use of such resources. **Capitalism** is further characterized by three fundamental attributes. First, most productive resources are owned by a small portion of the population. Banks, corporations, and wealthy individuals own the vast majority of farms, factories, and business of all kinds. Although many Americans invest in business through ownership of stocks, mutual funds, and retirement plans, ownership of substantial wealth is highly concentrated. For example, in the United States, in 2002 almost half of all households owned some stocks or mutual funds (and thus owned some share of a business). However, the median value of these investments was $65,000. Fewer than 4 percent of American households had stocks and mutual funds valued at more than half a million dollars (Investment Company Institute 2005). Thus, although a great many people held some ownership of business, the vast majority was held by a comparatively few.

The second attribute of capitalism is that most individuals' primary resource is their labor. In order to survive, people sell their labor for a salary or an hourly wage.

The third attribute is that the value of workers' contribution to production is always intended to be greater than the wages they receive. The difference between these two is the profit that accrues to those who own the productive resources, generally the shareholders of a corporation (Plattner 1989:382–384). The extremely high wages of some professional athletes and entertainers provide a good illustration of this principle. For example, Miami Heat basketball player Shaquille O'Neal earned more than $27 million in the 2004–2005 season. For the team owners, his high salary was easily justified. They believed that his presence would enable them to earn substantially more than they paid him. This proved a good guess. Mickey Arison bought The Heat for $65 million in 1995. In January 2007, the team's value was estimated at $409 million (Forbes 2007). Since a good deal of this appreciation was due to O'Neal's skill and popularity, the value of his labor was substantially greater than the wages he received.

In general, workers wish to receive as close to the full value of their labor as possible, whereas owners wish to pay as small a portion of labor's value as possible. This frequently results in conflict between the two groups.

Modern capitalist economies are dominated by market exchange, but this does not mean that people always experience their economy in terms of buying and selling at whatever price the market will bear. Capitalism always occurs within the context of other social relationships, and sometimes these provide a mask behind which it can hide. In other words, capitalist relationships are sometimes camouflaged by family ties or social obligations. When this happens, entrepreneurs may be able to extract extra profits. The production of knitted sweaters in Turkey is a good example of this.

Turkey produces many goods and services used in wealthy capitalist nations. Most of the inhabitants of Istanbul, its largest city, are part of a capitalist economy selling their labor in enterprises aimed at generating a profit. However, as Jenny B. White (1994) reports, many of them, particularly women, understand their work in terms of reciprocity and kin obligations rather than capitalism and the marketplace.

Turkey is a patrilineal and patriarchal society. Turkish women live in complex social networks characterized by social obligations and relations of reciprocity. To a great degree, they measure their worth by the work they do for family members, including parents, in-laws, husbands, and children. Being a good woman means laboring for relatives.

Married women live with their husband's family and are expected to manage the household and to keep their hands busy with knitting and other skilled tasks. Such tasks are not considered work (in the sense of work outside of the home) but are rather understood as necessary obligations of married life.

Business in Turkey is often patterned on social life, and this can be seen clearly in women's piecework. Women produce garments that are sold in the United States and other Western nations. The materials they use are generally supplied to them by an organizer, who also finds a buyer for the finished product. The organizers often are relatives, neighbors, and friends of the women who do the work.

In the neighborhood White (1994:13) investigated, almost everyone believed that women should not work for money, yet about two thirds of women are involved in piecework. How is this contradiction explained? The women who do it see piecework as a way for them to keep their hands busy and thus part of their duty as wives rather than a form of paid labor. Their work forms part of their obligation to their husband's family and to organizers with whom they have social connections, and they consider it a

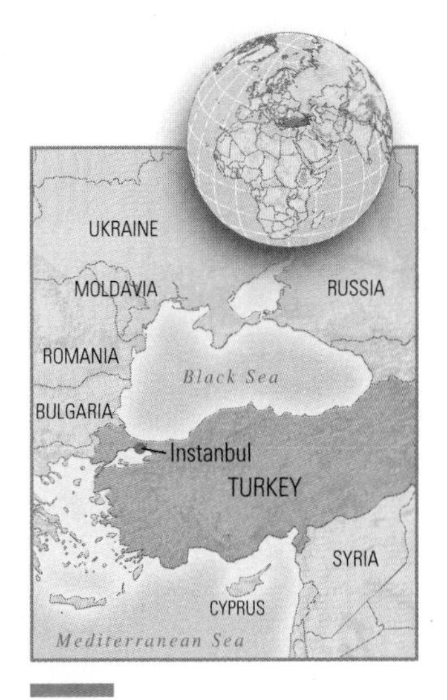

Turkey.

gift of labor. They understand the payments they receive as gifts from someone with whom they have an established social relationship.

Because the women's work is set within a context of global capitalism, work organizers may be friends and neighbors, but they are also capitalist entrepreneurs hoping to make money. In the end, women produce goods for the capitalist marketplace, and their wages ultimately derive from that market. However, these capitalist relationships are masked by social relations of balanced or generalized reciprocity with the labor organizer. Because they understand their work in terms of a social obligation, they rarely think about how much they are earning per hour or how they might use their time and talents to make more money. Thus, they are willing to accept far lower wages than might otherwise be the case.

In some ways, the system serves the women well. They are able to fill their roles as wives and in-laws, and their social connections with labor organizers may give them some degree of security from the ravages of the marketplace. This is important in a country such as Turkey, where most people are poor and social services are few. However, it is clear that the greatest beneficiaries of this system are firms and consumers in wealthy nations. The fact that reciprocity masks capitalism for poor women in Turkey allows rich consumers in Europe and America to buy hand-knitted sweaters at very low prices and the firms based in these nations to make windfall profits.

It would be difficult to find any people in the world today not affected by capitalist markets. For the most part, members of traditional societies enter the market as low-wage laborers. The wealth they produce accrues to elites within poor nations as well as to owners and consumers in wealthy nations (Wolf 1982). The case of the Turkish women illustrates some of the ways in which this process takes place. Not all societies are able to make such accommodations, however, and the expansion of capitalism and political power has been accompanied by the wide-scale destruction of traditional societies. Chapter 13 examines this process in some detail.

Resistance to Capitalism

Capitalism is a powerful economic system. It undoubtedly provides a greater number of goods and services to larger populations than do other ways of organizing an economy, but at a cost. When some individuals or groups own or control basic resources, others must inevitably be denied access to them. This results in permanently differentiated economic and social classes. Capitalism dictates that there will always be rich and poor. Often, part of the population lives in extreme poverty, without access to basic resources. In American society, this includes the homeless, the landless rural poor, and the permanently unemployed.

© Catherine Li, 2008

Garage sales, gardening, raising livestock, and doing odd jobs help many Americans avoid full participation in the capitalist economy.

Although there are probably some individuals who act as capitalists in most monetized economies, societies organized primarily by capitalism are a late development in the history of humankind. Such societies were not a natural and inevitable outcome of economic evolution. Rather, they owe their origin to the specific conditions of the Industrial Revolution in Europe in the 18th and 19th centuries and have become increasingly prevalent in the world in the past 150 years.

Although the capitalist economy has expanded in every part of the world, there probably are no countries where all of the population is directly involved in it. Noncapitalist groups remain in many areas, although they are often pushed to geographically marginal areas, such as the border between Pakistan and Afghanistan or the jungles of Brazil. In other places, issues of race, gender, and ethnicity prevent people from fully participating in the capitalist economy. However, even in these locations mass-produced goods, media, and fashions from capitalist societies are easily found.

Most Americans probably think of themselves as being in favor of capitalism, but many do not wish to actively engage in it. Individuals join the capitalist economy by selling their labor for wages. Alternatively, they might own productive resources and operate them with hired labor, reinvesting any profits to increase the value and size of their operation. However, many individuals and families in the United States resist these options.

Consider the inhabitants of Putnam County, New York (Hansen 1995). Located about 50 miles north of New York City, Putnam County has been poor since the time of the American Revolution. Even in the preindustrial era, its farms were unable to compete successfully with surrounding areas. Today, its people follow two fundamentally different strategies for survival and belong to two different but related economic systems.

Many of Putnam County's inhabitants are new residents who commute to jobs in New York City. They work for union-scale wages as police officers, firefighters, and schoolteachers, using their wages to buy houses, food, and so on. They are deeply in debt to mortgage and credit card companies but believe that higher future earnings will permit them to accommodate this financial burden. They are committed to economic and social advancement, and many hope eventually to move to more prosperous suburbs closer to the city. Members of this group are deeply committed to capitalism. They own few productive resources, sell their labor for wages, and conduct the economic aspect of their lives almost entirely through the capitalist market.

Putnam County's other residents have lived there for generations. Members of this group very rarely have full-time wage employment. They almost never visit New York City, which to them has become "a metaphor for all the world's evils" (Hansen 1995:146). Instead they follow what Halperin (1990) called a *multiple-livelihood strategy.* They acquire their land through inheritance and generally own it outright. Their lands include both forest and gardens that provide almost all of the vegetables they consume. While women work in the gardens, men hunt year-round, taking deer, rabbits, guinea fowl, and pheasants. They fish in ponds and streams and chop wood for fuel. In addition to these subsistence activities, members of this group do carpentry, electrical repair, masonry, plumbing, and other jobs. They barter these skills among themselves and sell them for cash to the commuters. They may work temporarily for wages at construction jobs. Although Putnam County's traditional residents do depend on markets for goods they cannot produce themselves or get through barter, only a small part of their total subsistence comes from the market.

Through such strategies, these residents avoid participation in the capitalist economy. Their financial goals are not to make money or to move to a higher level of consumption. They are concerned with stability rather than mobility, and they wish to live as independently as possible. Although they own productive resources such as land and equipment, these do not become capital because they are used to increase the security of their self-sufficiency rather than to accumulate wealth.

The self-sufficient residents of Putnam County remind us that culture counts. For most of us, capitalism seems both natural and inevitable, the way that society must be organized to make sense. However, the ways in which we organize our economy are the result of history, politics, economics, and individual choices—a creation of culture, not natural law.

BRINGING IT BACK HOME: PRODUCT ANTHROPOLOGY

In their book, *Creating Breakthrough Products,* Jonathan Cagan and Craig M. Vogel (2002) write that the most promising area of research is "new product ethnography." Writing in the jargon of business consulting, they say that new product ethnography uses the techniques of applied anthropology to "turn a descriptive process into a predictive field that helps to determine Value Opportunities." Product ethnographers deliver "actionable insights" into behavior and lifestyle activities and preferences that lead to product attributes (2002:107–108). In plainer English, Cagan and Vogel believe that anthropologists can offer vital services to business. New product ethnography is a way of turning the techniques and theoretical perspectives of anthropology into a resource for the corporate world. Those who promote it argue that anthropologists can and should provide vital information that helps corporations design and market products in ways that maximize their profits.

In many ways, product anthropology and other uses of anthropology in business and government are promising breakthroughs. Since the founding days of the discipline, anthropologists have wanted their voices heard by people outside the university. Now they are increasingly employed in different capacities in consumer research, product design, and marketing. On the one hand, this results in a better fit between products and consumers as well as higher profits for corporations. From the PT Cruiser (partially designed by French anthropologist G. Clotaire Rapaille) to computer software, tooth brushes, cookware, and ethnobanking (developing banking services for ethnic target groups), anthropologists have made products more friendly and business more money. As companies design products for markets around the globe, anthropologists have valuable contributions to make to design, production, and marketing. On the other hand, the involvement of anthropologists in these fields raises difficult ethical problems. For example, anthropologists mine information from their informants. If corporations then profit from this information, is payment owed to the informants? Historically, the introduction of massed produced products has destabilized craft production and destabilized local economies. Should anthropologists sell their services to corporations to promote this process? Should anthropology be a way to help corporations make more money?

YOU DECIDE

1. Historically the introduction of cheap, mass-produced manufactured goods has undercut existing economies and drawn people into the capitalist economy, generally as consumers of low-quality merchandise and low-paid wage earners. Given this, should anthropologists be involved in the design and marketing of products to groups about which they have expertise?
2. The advance of capitalism into all areas of the world has been relentless. With the aid of anthropologists, corporations can produce products that meet local needs and are marketed in culturally appropriate ways. The alternative often is inappropriate, poorly designed and poorly marketed products. Given this, can anthropologists justifiably refuse to work with corporations?
3. Perhaps the previous two questions present a false dichotomy. What are some positions that anthropologists might take between these two? Are they practicable in the real world without the security of a university appointment?

CHAPTER SUMMARY

1. Experiments in which the ultimatum and dictator games have been played in many cultures show that people's economic behavior differs from culture to culture. Some of this variation is systematic. People from market-oriented societies tend to play differently than those from societies with other forms of economic organization.
2. Economics is the study of the ways in which the choices people make combine to determine how their societies use their scarce resources to produce and distribute goods and services. People, and hence societies, make such choices differently because they value and are motivated by different goods and different principles.
3. In every society, certain goods are productive resources. Such resources generally include land, labor, and knowledge. Societies have systems by which such resources are allocated to their members. As social complexity increases, access to productive resources becomes increasingly more restricted.
4. Labor must be organized in specific ways to produce goods. In most preindustrial and peasant economies, labor is organized by the household or kin group. Work that people both perform and receive locates them with respect in their social network and often is integral to their identity.

5. As societies become more populous, the number of specialized jobs found in them increases. Current-day wealthy societies have extremely high degrees of specialization. This creates great efficiency but involves changing notions of identity and often has heavy human costs.
6. In all societies there are systems for distributing and consuming goods and services. Every society uses some combination of reciprocity, redistribution, and the market to redistribute goods and services and to provide patterns and standards for their consumption.
7. Exchange among people of similar status is characterized by reciprocity. As social distance among individuals increases, the characteristic form of reciprocity tends to change from generalized, to balanced, and, sometimes, to negative. The kula trade in the South Pacific provides an example of balanced reciprocity.
8. Redistribution is characteristic of exchange in chiefdoms as well as parts of state-level economy. Goods are collected by a central individual or office and then distributed. Potlatch among Pacific Northwest coastal Native Americans provides an example of redistribution.
9. In market exchange, goods and services are bought and sold at a money price determined, at least in theory, by the impersonal forces of supply and demand.
10. In capitalism, the owners of productive resources use them to increase their financial wealth. In capitalist societies, productive resources are held primarily by a small percentage of the population, most people sell their labor for wages, and the value of people's labor is always more than the wages they receive. Capitalism can be masked by other relationships such as reciprocity.
11. Although capitalism is ubiquitous around the world, many people resist it, avoiding wage labor and, to some degree, participation in the market. Some residents of Putnam County, New York, provide an example.

KEY TERMS

Balanced reciprocity
Capital
Capitalism
Cargo system
Economic system
Economics
Firm
Generalized reciprocity
Household

Kula ring
Leveling mechanism
Market exchange
Negative reciprocity
Potlatch
Prestige
Productive resources
Reciprocity
Redistribution

In almost all societies, marriage is a central structure in the formation of families and the linkages between wider relations. This photo of India shows a marriage ritual that contains many symbolic elements, such as the color red, which symbolizes fertility.

CHAPTER 7

MARRIAGE, FAMILY, AND KINSHIP

CHAPTER OUTLINE

A Society without Marriage: The Na of China

Forms and Functions of Marriage

Marriage Rules

- Incest Taboos
- Exogamy
- Endogamy
- Preferential Marriages
- Number of Spouses
- Choosing a Mate

The Exchange of Goods and Rights in Marriage

- Bride Service and Bridewealth
- Dowry

Family Structures, Households, and Rules of Residence

- Nuclear Families
- Composite Families
- Extended Families

Kinship Systems: Relationships through Blood and Marriage

- Rules of Descent and the Formation of Descent Groups
- Types of Unilineal Descent Groups
- Bilateral Kinship Systems

The Classification of Kin

- Principles for the Classification of Kin

Bringing It Back Home: Polygamy in the United States

- You Decide

A SOCIETY WITHOUT MARRIAGE: THE NA OF CHINA

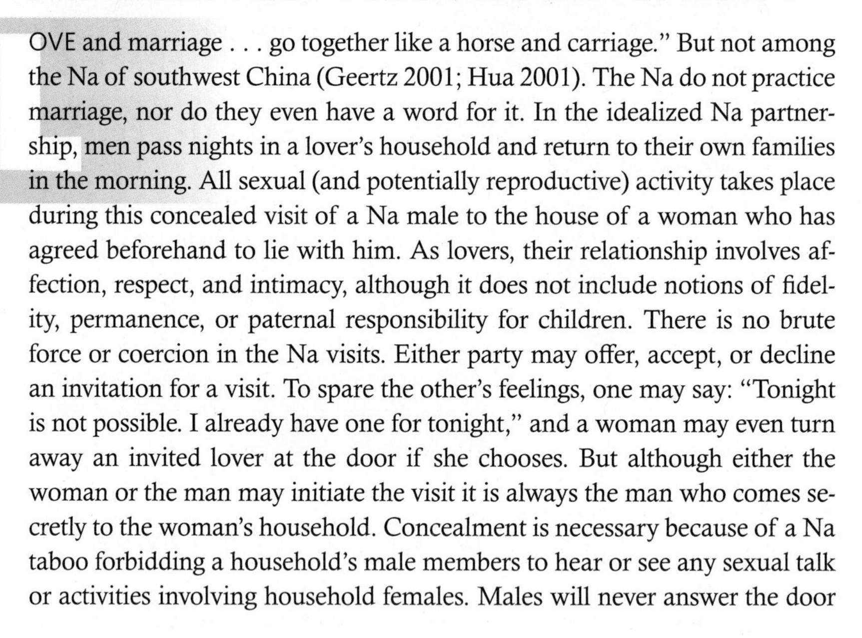

"LOVE and marriage . . . go together like a horse and carriage." But not among the Na of southwest China (Geertz 2001; Hua 2001). The Na do not practice marriage, nor do they even have a word for it. In the idealized Na partnership, men pass nights in a lover's household and return to their own families in the morning. All sexual (and potentially reproductive) activity takes place during this concealed visit of a Na male to the house of a woman who has agreed beforehand to lie with him. As lovers, their relationship involves affection, respect, and intimacy, although it does not include notions of fidelity, permanence, or paternal responsibility for children. There is no brute force or coercion in the Na visits. Either party may offer, accept, or decline an invitation for a visit. To spare the other's feelings, one may say: "Tonight is not possible. I already have one for tonight," and a woman may even turn away an invited lover at the door if she chooses. But although either the woman or the man may initiate the visit it is always the man who comes secretly to the woman's household. Concealment is necessary because of a Na taboo forbidding a household's male members to hear or see any sexual talk or activities involving household females. Males will never answer the door

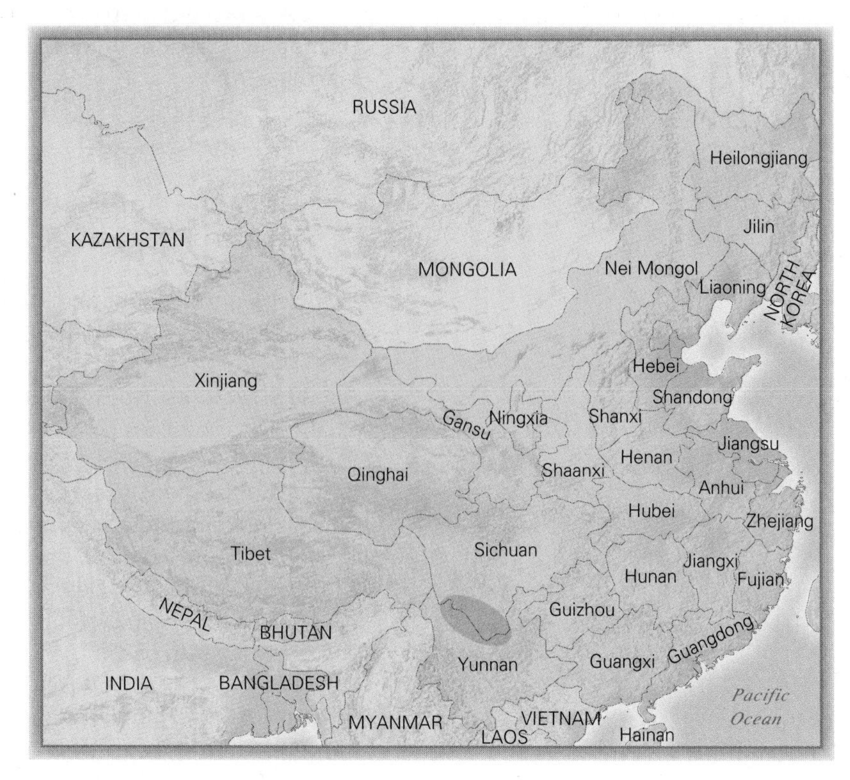

Location of the Na of China.

after dark lest they encounter a woman's lover, and the lover himself makes every effort to avoid detection, often bringing food to prevent the guard dog's barking, speaking only in whispers during intercourse, and leaving quietly before daybreak. Both women and men have multiple partners, serially or simultaneously, no records are kept of visits to ascertain paternity of children, and the Na have no word for incest, illegitimate child, infidelity, or promiscuity. Children, by a variety of fathers, stay with the mother's household for their entire lives. When a generation lacks females, a household may adopt a relative's child or encourage a son to bring his lover into the household. The only males in a Na household are relatives of different generations, who are brothers, uncles, and granduncles. There are no husbands or fathers. Where males are in short supply in a family, a woman may bring her lover home. The Na visit, which has been part of Na culture for more than a thousand years, is treated as a mutually enjoyable but singular occurrence that entails no future conditions. The Chinese state has periodically tried to change what they call this "barbarous practice," but so far without success. But as the Na adapt to the new conditions of the nation-state and the globalizing economy, they are increasingly subjected to state-sponsored public school education and media, which reflect mainstream Han mores and lifestyles and stigmatize Na practices. This, as well as their inability to name a father on official documents, may spell the end of Na visits, eliminating yet one more example of the rich diversity of human adaptive strategies.

All human societies face certain problems for which marriage, the creation of families, and kinship systems offer solutions. Every society must regulate sexual access between males and females, find satisfactory ways to organize labor, assign responsibility for child care, provide a clear framework for organizing an individual's rights and responsibilities, and provide for the transfer of property and social position between generations. The many human solutions to these challenges are guided by cultural rules, accounting for a wide variety of kinship and family systems. These systems are also guided by realities: When reality no longer meshes with the culturally defined rules, the rules themselves change.

FORMS AND FUNCTIONS OF MARRIAGE

The need to regulate sexual access stems from the potentially continuous receptivity of human males and females to sexual activity. If sexual competition was not regulated and channeled into stable relationships that were given social approval, it could cause societal conflict. These relationships need not be permanent (and in many cultures are not), and theoretically some system other than marriage could have developed. But in the absence of safe and dependable contraception throughout most of human history and with the near certainty that children would be born, a relatively stable union between a male and female that involves responsibility for children as well as economic exchange became the basis for most, but, as the Na illustrate, by no means all, human adaptations.

Marriage is the way most societies arrange both for the care of children and for the exchange of the products and services of men and women. An ongoing relationship between an adult male and an adult female provides a structure (a family) in which men provide protection and women nurse children. Men and women share the jobs of providing food and nurturing children. This creates a far more stable structure for raising children than would otherwise be the case.

In addition to forming bonds between a couple, marriage extends social alliances by linking together different families and kin groups, leading to cooperation among groups of people larger than the married couple. This expansion of the social group within which people can work together and share resources is of great advantage for the survival of the species.

Marriage refers to the customs, rules, and obligations that establish a socially endorsed relationship between adults and children and between the kin groups of the married partners. Although in most societies marriage and the subsequent formation of families rest on the biological complementarity of male and female in reproduction, both marriage and family are cultural patterns. Thus they differ in form and function both among and within human societies and change over time with changing political and economic circumstances and the life stages of individuals.

The heterosexual, monogamous marriage dominant in the United States is only one of a vast array of marriage types. Marriages built around plural spouses or same-sex relationships also fulfill the functions of marriage in satisfactory ways. The variations in forms make it difficult to find any *one* definition of marriage that will fit all cultural situations.

The Nuer and some other African societies are among the exceptions to the generalization that marriage is a bond between a man and a woman. These societies recognize an alternative form of woman–woman marriage that allows a barren woman to divorce her husband, take another woman as her wife, and arrange for a surrogate to impregnate this woman. Children born from this arrangement, which does not involve sexual relations between the wives, become members of the barren woman's natal lineage and refer to her as their father (Kilbride 2004:17). Same-sex marriage in the United States, with couples adopting children or using surrogate fertilization, is another exception to the general rule of heterosexual marriage.

In addition to marriage, the concept of the family also varies among cultures. In many societies the most important family bond is between lineal blood relations (father and children or mother and children) or between brothers and sisters rather than between husband and wife. In these societies the lineage or the clan rather than the immediate family confers legitimacy on children. Even in the United States, the definition of the family as a unit ideally defined by marriage is changing to accommodate new realities, such as the high divorce rate, same-sex commitments and domestic partnerships, the increasing number of working mothers and single-parent households, the growing number of unmarried couples living together in long-term relationships, surrogate reproduction, the growing number of childless couples, the greater number of people who never marry, and the increasing number of people who remarry after divorce or widowhood.

MARRIAGE RULES

Every society has culturally defined rules concerning sexual relations and marriage. Such rules may limit marriage to certain groups, dictate how many people an individual may marry at one time, allow for dissolving marriages, determine rules for remarriage, dictate the kinds of exchanges and rituals that legitimate marriage, and determine what rights and obligations are established by marriage. Among the most universal of these rules is the incest taboo.

Incest Taboos

An **incest taboo** categorically prohibits certain individuals from having sex with each other. The most widespread taboo is on mating between mother and son, father and daughter, and sister and brother (historical exceptions to this were the brother–sister marriages encouraged among the royalty in ancient Egypt, Peru, and Hawai'i, aimed at limiting rivalries for the throne). The taboos on mating between kin (or people classified as kin) always extend beyond the immediate family, however. Because sexual access is a basic right conferred by marriage, incest taboos effectively prohibit marriage among certain kin; again, this varies among cultures.

Anthropologists continue to debate the universality and persistence of the incest taboo, particularly as it applies to primary (or nuclear) family relationships. The origins of the taboo, its functions in contemporary societies, and the motives of individuals in respecting or violating the taboo may all have different explanations.

One popular theory is that incest taboos arose because mating between close kin is genetically harmful to the species. Population genetics has shown that inbreeding among close relatives is harmful to human populations. However, the rates of infant mortality in preindustrial and early industrial societies are very high. Therefore, accurate record keeping and sophisticated statistical techniques are necessary to detect and measure the influence of inbreeding. Since these techniques were unavailable in most places, it is unlikely that traditional peoples could have discovered and understood the connection between close inbreeding and biological disadvantage.

Preventing Family Disruption

Bronislaw Malinowski and Sigmund Freud held that the desire for sexual relations within the family is very strong. For them, the most important function of the incest taboo is preventing disruption within the nuclear family by directing sexual desires outside it. Malinowski argued that as children grow into adolescence, their natural attempts to satisfy their developing sexual urges within their families would increase the potential for family conflict and the disruption of role relationships, as fathers and sons, and mothers and daughters, competed for sexual partners.

Whereas unregulated sexual competition within the family undoubtedly would be disruptive, regulation of sexual competition among family members could be an alternative to the incest taboo. Furthermore, whereas Malinowski's theory suggests why the incest taboo exists between parents and children, it does not explain the prohibition of sexual relations between brothers and sisters.

Forming Wider Alliances

The alliance theory of the incest taboo (Lévi-Strauss 1969/1949) stresses the adaptive value of cooperation among groups larger than the nuclear family. The incest taboo on sex within the intimate family forces people to marry outside the family. This leads to joining families together into a larger social community. Since such alliances are clearly adaptive, the alliance theory can also account for the extension of the incest taboo to groups other than the nuclear family.

Exogamy

Exogamy and endogamy are marriage rules that define the acceptable range of marriage partners. **Exogamy** specifies that a person must marry outside particular groups. The incest taboo is a rule of exogamy regarding the nuclear family, but rules of exogamy also extend to wider kinship groups.

Exogamy has functions similar to the incest taboo. It reduces conflicts over sex within the cooperating group and forges useful alliances between groups larger than the primary family. These rights and obligations between groups linked by marriage are fundamental in most societies. Such ties are adaptive in extending networks of social cooperation and maintaining peaceful relationships.

The Arapesh, a horticultural society in New Guinea, clearly express the importance of exchanging women among different groups. For them, not exchanging women between families would be as unthinkable as not sharing food. When anthropologist Margaret Mead (1963:92/1935) asked an Arapesh man about marrying his own sister, he responded, "What, you would like to marry your sister? What is the matter with you? Don't you want a brother-in-law? Don't you realize that if you marry another man's sister and another man marries your sister, you will have at least two brothers-in-law, while if you marry your own sister you will have none? With whom will you hunt, with whom will you garden, with whom will you visit?"

Endogamy

Rules of **endogamy** require people to marry within certain groups. In some societies, cousins are encouraged or required to marry each other, whereas in India, castes and subcastes are endogamous groups. In the United States, although there are no named endogamous groups, so-called racial groups and social classes tend to be endogamous, based on opportunities to meet, cultural norms, and similarities in lifestyle. Endogamy is also an important rule for some religious groups in the United States, such as the Amish.

Preferential Marriages

In some societies, marriage rules involve preferences for cousin marriage. In cross-cousin marriage the preferred partners are the children of one's parents' siblings of the opposite sex—mother's brother or father's sister. Preferred cross-cousin marriage reinforces ties between kin groups established in the preceding generation, preserving the relationship between two intermarrying kin groups across generations. Parallel-cousin marriage involves children of the parents' same-sex siblings—mother's sister or father's brother—and is found in some Arab and North African Muslim societies, where the preferred marriage partner is the son *or* daughter of the father's brother. Since in Muslim Arab societies descent and inheritance are in the male line, parallel-cousin marriage helps prevent the fragmentation of family property and keeps economic resources within the family. Parallel-cousin marriage also reinforces the solidarity of brothers, but by socially isolating groups of brothers from each other, it adds to factional disputes and disunity within the larger social system (see Figure 7.1).

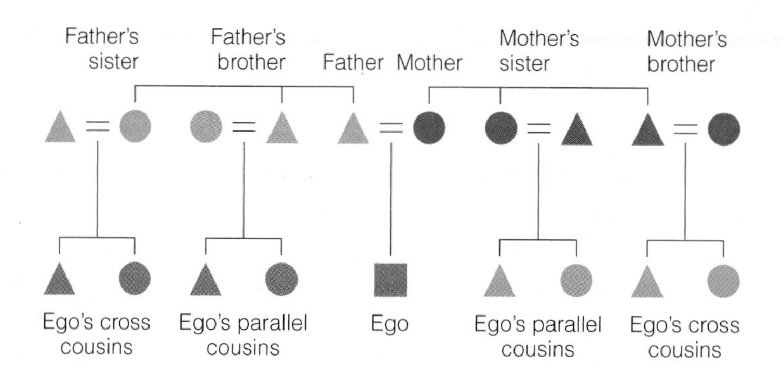

Figure 7.1

This diagram indicates the relationships of cross cousins and parallel cousins. In many cultures, these relationships determine rules of exogamy and endogamy and preferences for marriage partners.

Because cross-cousin and parallel-cousin marriage distinguish between kin who are equally biologically close, preferred cousin marriage rules demonstrate the important point that kinship rules are rooted in biological relationships but are based on culture. Each system of marriage and family formation has elements that contribute to solidarity and stability at one level of society but may be socially disruptive at another level.

Two other preferential marriage rules are the **levirate** and the **sororate.** These forms of marriage demonstrate the importance of marriage as an alliance between two groups rather than between individuals. It allows a marriage to survive the death of one of the partners with the continuance of group alliances and fulfillment of the marriage contract.

Under the levirate, a man marries the widow of his dead brother, and in some cases the children born to this union are considered children of the deceased man. Thus, the levirate enables the children to remain within the dead husband's descent group and it keeps them from being separated from their mother. In the sororate, when a woman dies her kin group supplies a sister as a wife for the widower. The sororate also means that the husband of a barren woman can marry her sister, and at least some of these children of this marriage are considered those of the first wife. If no qualifying relative is available to fulfill the levirate or the sororate, other appropriately classified kin may be substituted, or the levirate or sororate may not take place.

Number of Spouses

All societies have rules about how many spouses a person may have at one time. **Monogamy,** which permits only one man to be married to one woman at any given time, is the rule in Europe and North America, but not in most of the world's cultures. **Polygamy,** or plural marriage, includes **polygyny,** the marriage of one man to several women, and **polyandry,** the marriage of one woman to several men. About 75 percent of the world's cultures permit (and prefer) plural marriage (Murdock 1949:28). However, even in cultures in which polygyny is preferred, the male/female ratio inhibits plural wives, and where men must exchange wealth for wives, many men cannot afford more than one.

Polygyny

Polygyny has important economic and political functions in some societies. Where women are economically important, polygyny increases a man's wealth and therefore his social position. Because marriage links groups together, having several wives from different groups within a society extends a man's alliances. Thus, chiefs, headmen, and state leaders may take wives from many different groups or villages in order to increase their political power.

Polygyny is found primarily in societies where plural wives—and their children—increase both a family's labor supply and its productivity. For example, among the Tiwi of Australia, a foraging group, women's food collecting makes a very important contribution to the food supply. Thus, the more wives a man has, the better his family's standard of living (Goodale 1971).

Although Western cultural stereotypes criticize polygyny as oppressing women, the status of females in polygynous societies is not uniformly low and may even, as among the Tiwi, be relatively high and accord women a high degree of sexual and economic freedom (Goodale 1971). Where women's work is hard and monotonous, as it often is, women may welcome the addition of a co-wife because it eases their own workload and provides daily companionship. Conflict among co-wives does occur in polygynous societies and sometimes is mitigated by a preference for a man to marry sisters. In many polygynous societies, co-wives live in separate dwellings. Cultural norms requiring a man to distribute his economic resources and sexual attentions evenly among his wives as well as to separate dwellings for each wife also mitigate family conflict. Like all other cultural patterns, polygyny changes with changing economic and social circumstances. In spite of the favorable view of polygyny in many African societies, changing economic conditions, such as declining amount of available agricultural land, increasing expenses in educating children, and the social pressures of Western and Christian condemnation of polygyny, have to some extent changed its frequency or driven it underground (Kilbride 2006).

Polyandry

Polyandry is relatively rare, found mainly in Tibet, Nepal, and some indigenous groups in India. Most polyandry is fraternal: Brothers marry a single wife. In Tibet, as in other polyandrous societies, polyandry is related to a shortage of land. If brothers marry a single wife, their father's land can be kept intact within the family rather than fragmented over the generations. Polyandry may be an adaptation to a shortage of females, created by female infanticide. It is functional in societies where men are away from home for long periods of time, in that a woman has more than one husband to provide for her.

A classic example of fraternal polyandry is found among the Toda of South India. A Toda woman marries several brothers, and brothers born after the original marriage share in the marital rights. Sexual access to the wife rotates equally, with little friction or jealousy. When all the brothers and their wife share one hut, the brother who is with the wife places his cloak and staff outside as a warning to others. Determining the biological father of a child *(genitor)* is not important to the Toda. Instead, the child's legal or social father *(pater)* is determined by a ceremony called "giving the bow" held in the seventh month of pregnancy. The eldest brother usually performs this ceremony and is the pater of a woman's first three or four children. Another brother will give the bow for subsequent children. When, as occasionally happens, a woman marries several men who are not biological brothers, the wife lives with each husband for a month and the men arrange among themselves who will give the bow when she becomes pregnant. Toda polyandry may have been related to a shortage of women caused by female infanticide. As female infanticide has declined and the Toda male/female ratio has evened out, the Toda today have become largely monogamous (Rivers 1906; Walker 1986).

Choosing a Mate

In most societies, kin group interests, rather than individual desires, are the basis of mate selection. Thus, the families of the bride and groom take an important, even determinative, role in selecting their children's spouses. This practice of **arranged marriage** strongly contrasts with marriage in the United States, where individuals ideally select their own mates on the basis of sexual compatibility, emotional needs, physical attractiveness, and personality, a cluster of patterns called "romantic love."

In most societies, the economic potential of the groom is of great importance; for brides, reproductive potential, health, and looks are important criteria. In addition, each culture has its own special qualities that it emphasizes in a bride or groom. In India, where a woman is expected to live with her husband's joint family, she must be—or at least act—submissive and modest, and her domestic abilities, especially cooking, are important. In middle-class Indian families, education—but not "too much" education, as it makes women too independent—is also important, as are an ability to sing, dance, or play a musical instrument in the traditional Indian style. The qualities of the bride's family are also important: A family with a reputation for being quarrelsome or gossipy may be rejected even if the girl herself is approved (Nanda 2000a).

© Judith Pearson

Among the Wodaabe of Niger, marriages are both arranged and based on romantic attachment. At the annual Gerewol celebration, young men apply makeup, dance, and make facial expressions that best display their charms in order to capture the hearts of young women.

The "Matrimonial" section of any Indian newspaper in America today indicates that globalization and westernization have expanded the criteria for a "good match." Although a man's profession still is most important, his status as a green card holder or as a U.S. citizen is now also significant. Increasingly a woman's profession may merit inclusion as a criterion for a suitable marriage, as well as "fair skin" and a "slim" figure. Communal and caste affiliation are still important, but increasingly "caste is no bar" is included, indicating that a spouse from any caste (but in fact implying a closely related caste) is acceptable.

THE EXCHANGE OF GOODS AND RIGHTS IN MARRIAGE

The interest of the wider community in marriage is demonstrated by the ritual and ceremony surrounding it in almost every society. The presence of guests at these ceremonies bears witness to the lawfulness of the transaction, and it is these publicly witnessed and acknowledged ceremonies that distinguish marriage from other kinds of unions that resemble it. Marriage involves the transfer of certain rights and obligations, primarily involving sexual access of the partners to each other, rights over any children born to the marriage, obligations by one or both parents to care for children born to the union, and rights of the marriage partners to the economic services of the other.

In almost all societies, marriage gives the families or kin groups of the bride and groom certain rights to goods or services from each other. These may be voluntary "gifts," given perhaps as a way of winning the goodwill of those with the power to transfer marital rights. But the exchange of goods and services is often an essential and required part of the transfer of marital rights (even when called "gifts"), and if the exchanges are not completed, the rights in marriage can be forfeited.

Bride Service and Bridewealth

Three kinds of exchanges made in connection with marriage are bride service, bridewealth, and dowry. In **bride service,** most commonly found in foraging societies (Marlowe 2004) where few material goods are accumulated, the husband must work for a specified number of years for his wife's family in exchange for his marital rights. Among the Ju/'hoansi of the Kalahari Desert in Africa, this may be as long as 15 years or until the birth of the third child.

The most common form of marriage exchange is **bridewealth,** where cash or goods are given by the groom's kin to the bride's kin to seal a marriage. Bridewealth previously was called *bride price,* but this falsely conveys the idea that the marriage is merely an economic exchange (Ogbu 1978) and that women's status in such societies is devalued. In fact, in these societies daughters are valuable to their families because their bridewealth finances males' marriages.

In societies with customary bridewealth a person can claim compensation for a violation of conjugal rights only if the bridewealth has been paid. Furthermore, bridewealth paid at marriage is returned (subject to specified conditions) if a marriage is terminated.

Many studies of bridewealth emphasize its role in entitling the husband to domestic, economic, sexual, and reproductive rights, but bridewealth also confers rights on the wife. By publicly validating a marriage, bridewealth allows wives to hold their husbands accountable for violations of conjugal rights. In sanctioning these mutual rights and obligations, bridewealth stabilizes marriage by giving both families a vested interest in keeping the couple together. Nevertheless, divorce does occur in societies with bridewealth.

Although globally widespread, bridewealth transactions are particularly characteristic of Africa. Among the Kipsigis, a pastoralist/horticultural society of east Africa, the traditional bridewealth payment was livestock, but it now includes cash. First marriages are paid for by the groom's father and subsequent marriages by the groom himself, although grooms working for wages may help with the first payment (Borgerhoff Mulder 1995:576). Formerly, when agricultural land was available and crop prices were high, bridewealth was high because of the importance of women's labor in culti-

Jean Zorn

Bridewealth is the most common form of gift exchange at marriage. Among the Medlpa of New Guinea, the family of the groom gives gifts to the family of the bride to formalize a marriage. The bigman of the groom's family (left) praises the gifts while the bigman of the bride's family denigrates them. Cash and pig grease have replaced pigs and shells as the most important marriage gifts.

vation. However, bridewealth payments have declined recently because now land is scarce, crop prices are low, and women's agricultural labor has lost value. On the other hand, Kipsigis parents of girls educated beyond elementary school often demand high bridewealth, both as compensation for the high school fees they have spent on their daughters and because their increased earning potential will benefit their marital home.

Dowry

Dowry, which are goods given by the bride's family to the groom's family, is associated with private ownership of property. Among the European peasantry the dowry accompanied the bride and belonged to the newly married couple, often constituting the basic household items for their new home. This contrasts with bridewealth, which does not belong to the married couple but rather is distributed through a wider kin network.

Fewer societies give dowry compared to bridewealth. Although it is constitutionally outlawed, dowry is especially important in India, both historically and today. One interpretation of Indian dowry is that it is a voluntary gift, symbolizing affection for a beloved daughter leaving home and compensating her for the fact that traditionally she could not inherit land or property. Dowry also has been interpreted as a source of security for a woman because the jewelry given as part of her dowry is theoretically hers to keep (in practice, her husband's family usually keeps control of it). Another theory holds that dowry is a compensatory payment given by the bride's family to the groom's family as acknowledgement of their taking on an economic burden, since ideally women in India do not work outside the home. In contemporary India, with its new emphasis on consumerism and social class mobility, dowry has increasingly become a payment to the husband and his family that improves their financial and social standing. As such, insufficient dowry can be the basis of emotional blackmail of a woman's family and has been linked to wife abuse and even murder (Stone and James 2005).

FAMILY STRUCTURES, HOUSEHOLDS, AND RULES OF RESIDENCE

Two basic types of families are the elementary, or nuclear, family and the extended family. **Nuclear families** are organized around the **conjugal tie,** that is, the relationship between husband and wife. The **extended family** is based on **consanguineal,** or blood, relations extending over three or more generations.

A household, or domestic group, is not the same as a family. Although most households contain people related by blood or marriage, non-kin may be included; conversely, members of a family may be spread out over several households. Household composition is affected by the cultural rules about residence after marriage. Under **neolocal residence** rules, married couples create their own households. Under **patrilocal residence** rules (now sometimes referred to as *virilocality*), the newly married couple lives with the husband's family, whereas under **matrilocal residence** rules (now also referred to as *uxorilocal residence*), the couple lives with the wife's family. Two other rules are **avunculocal residence,** in which the couple lives with the wife's uncle's family (usually the husband's mother's brother), and **bilocal residence,** in which a couple can choose between living with the wife's family or the husband's family. Each of these residence rules is associated with different types of kinship systems. For example, avunculocal residence permits the geographical concentration of male lineage mates and the preservation of male-controlled lineage wealth in a matrilineal system.

Nuclear Families

A nuclear family, consisting of a married couple and their children, is most often associated with **neolocal residence.** Only 5 percent of the world's societies (including the United States) are traditionally neolocal. The nuclear family is adapted to making a living in a capitalist society where jobs do not generally depend on family connections and where employment and promotion often require geographical mobility. Independence and flexibility are also requirements of foraging lifestyles, and more than three quarters of all foraging groups live in nuclear families.

The Changing American Family

The nuclear family in the United States is more isolated than families in most societies. Americans tend to think of the ideal family as a neolocal unit consisting of a husband, a wife, and their children, with a high degree of domestic independence. This family form is consistent with the capitalist economy and with American cultural values of emotional bonds between husband and wife; privacy; and individualism. From the late 19th century through the 1950s, American family ideology stressed public, money-earning roles for men and domestic, child-caring roles for women. However, except for wealthy families, the reality often was different: Many American families included multiple generations, working women, and extended kin.

Beginning in the 1960s, declining salaries for men, changing cultural standards, and rising divorce rates deeply affected the American family. More women worked outside the home, and although men increasingly became involved with housework and child care, women continued to bear the greater burden of responsibility for these functions (Lamphere 1997; Pear 2006).

The American ideal of the independent nuclear family is significantly modified by the 50 percent divorce rate, although this rate is not especially high from a cross-cultural perspective. As divorce became more common, so did single-parent households. Single-mother households now account for 22 percent of all families with children, whereas single-father households account for 6 percent (Luker 1996; Simmons and O'Neill 2001).

This statistic confirms women's disproportionate share of child care. Of children living with only one parent, one in six averages a weekly visit with a divorced father, and only one in four sees the father once a month. Almost half of the children of divorced parents have not seen their biological fathers for over a year, and 10 years after a divorce more than two thirds of children have lost contact with their fathers (Hacker 2002a:22).

A significant change in the American family over the past 50 years is the increasing number of women who work outside the home. In most families, however, women still are responsible for child care and managing the home.

Divorce frequently is followed by remarriage, creating what one anthropologist has called *serial monogamy* (Tiger 1978). Divorce and remarriage enmesh nuclear families in ever larger and more complicated kinship networks, sometimes called *blended families,* which may include previously divorced spouses and their new marriage partners, children from previous marriages, and multiple sets of grandparents and other kin. In fact, marriage has declined for decades in the United States, and married couples today are in the minority of American households (Roberts 2006).

Composite Families

Composite (compound) families are aggregates of nuclear families linked by a common spouse, most often the husband. The typical composite family is a polygynist household, consisting of one man with several wives and their respective children, with each wife and her children normally occupying a separate residence. In composite families the tie between a mother and her children is particularly strong. The dynamics of the composite family typically involves the interaction of the husband with several wives, interaction between co-wives, and competition among the children of different wives over inheritance and succession.

Extended Families

The extended (consanguineal) family consists of two or more generations of male or female kin and their spouses and offspring, occupying a single household under the authority of a household head. An extended family is not just a collection of nuclear families. In the extended family system, lineal ties—the blood ties between generations (such as father and son)—are more important than the ties of marriage.

Extended families are particularly adaptive among cultivators. They are able to provide more workers than can nuclear families, which is useful both in food production and in production and marketing of handicrafts. In peasant agricultural societies where land ownership is important for both prestige and power, the extended family helps keep land intact over generations rather than parceling it out into ever smaller and more unproductive pieces among male descendants. This benefits the whole family. Although the extended family is the ideal in more than half of the world's societies, it is found most often among the landlord and prosperous merchant classes.

A patrilineal extended family is organized around the male line: a man, his sons, and the sons' wives and children. Societies with patrilineal extended families also tend to have patrilocal residence rules. A matrilineal family is organized around the female line: a woman, her daughters, and the daughters' husbands and children. Matrilineal families may have matrilocal residence rules or avunculocal residence rules.

Rules of residence as well as family type are economically adaptive. Thus, patrilocality is functional in hunting and agricultural societies where men must work cooperatively. It also may be adaptive in societies where males cooperate in warfare (Ember and Ember 1971). Where fighting between different groups or villages within a society is common, it is useful for men who will fight together to live together. Otherwise, they might wind up having to choose between defending their wife's local group, the one with whom they live, against the families into which they were born.

KINSHIP SYSTEMS: RELATIONSHIPS THROUGH BLOOD AND MARRIAGE

Kinship includes relationships established through blood, described through the idiom of blood, and relationships through marriage. Kinship determines the formation of social groups (like families), is the basis for classification of people in relation to each other, structures individual rights and obligations, and regulates behavior. Because all of these elements of social life are entwined, anthropologists refer to kinship as a system. Although a **kinship system** always rests on some kind of biological relationship, kinship systems are cultural phenomena, as indicated by the differential classification of parallel and cross cousins or the Toda concept of social fatherhood. As we will see later, kinship classifications may or may not reflect a scientifically accurate assessment of biological ties.

In small-scale, nonindustrial societies, kinship is the most important social bond. It is the basis of group formation. Kinship norms govern the most important relationships, rights, and responsibilities between individuals and groups. The extension of kinship ties is the main way of linking groups to one another and of incorporating strangers into a group. Even in modern industrialized societies, where citizenship is an important basis of rights and obligations, kinship has many important functions. It is the major context within which wealth is inherited. Kinship is important on many ritual occasions, and there is a strong sentiment that "blood is thicker than water."

Kinship systems have several functions necessary to the continuation of a society. Kinship provides continuity between generations, as kinship units care for and educate children. Kinship rules provide for the orderly transmission of property **(inheritance)** and social position **(succession)** between generations. Kinship systems define a universe of others on whom a person can depend for aid. The adaptiveness of social groups larger than the nuclear family accounts for the fact that expanded kin groups are found in so many human societies.

Kinship systems grow out of a group's history as well as its relationship to the environment and its subsistence strategies. Once in place, however, kinship systems take on a life of their own, although as economic and historical circumstances change, kinship ideologies may be manipulated and negotiated to fit the new realities.

Rules of Descent and the Formation of Descent Groups

In anthropological terminology, **descent** is a culturally established affiliation with one or both parents. Descent is an important basis of social group formation in many societies. A **descent group** is a group of consanguineal kin who are lineal descendants of a common ancestor extending beyond two generations. In nonindustrial societies, descent groups organize domestic life, enculturate children, determine the use and transfer of property and political and ritual offices, carry out religious ritual, settle disputes, engage in warfare, and structure the use of political power.

Unilineal Descent

Descent rules (sometimes called a *kinship ideology*) are either unilineal or bilateral. Under **unilineal descent,** descent group membership is based on links through *either* the paternal line or the maternal line, but not both.

Unilineal descent rules thus are either **patrilineal** or **matrilineal.** In patrilineal societies, a person belongs to the descent group of the father. In matrilineal societies, a person belongs to the descent group of the mother.

One important adaptive advantage of unilineal descent systems is that kin groups do not overlap, thus binding their members more tightly to each other. Also, unilineal descent rules provide a clearly defined group membership for everyone in the society. This allows people to more easily understand their rights of ownership, social duties, and social roles and allows them to relate to a large number of known and unknown people in the society.

Unilineal descent groups can perpetuate themselves over time even though their membership changes. Like modern corporations, **corporate descent groups** are permanent units that have an existence beyond the individuals who are members at any given time. Old members die and new ones are admitted through birth, but the integrity of the corporate group persists. Such groups can own property and manage resources, also like modern corporations.

Types Of Unilineal Descent Groups

A **lineage** is a kin group whose members trace descent from a common ancestor and who can demonstrate those genealogical links among themselves. **Patrilineages** are lineages formed by descent through the male line; **matrilineages** are formed by descent through the female line. Lineages may vary in size, from three generations upward. Related lineages may form **clans.** The common clan ancestor may be a mythological figure; sometimes, no specific ancestor is known or named.

Clans and lineages have different functions in different societies. The lineage often is a local residential or domestic group whose members cooperate on a daily basis. Clans are generally not residential units but tend to spread out over many villages. Therefore, clans often have political and religious functions rather than primarily domestic and economic ones. Clans are important in regulating marriage. In most societies, clans are exogamous, which strengthens its unilineal character. If a person married within the clan, his or her children would find it difficult to make sharp distinctions between maternal and paternal relatives. This person would not know how to act toward others, and others would not know how to act toward him or her. Clan exogamy also extends the network of peaceful social relations within a society as different clans are allied through marriage.

Patrilineal Descent Groups

In societies with patrilineal descent groups, both males and females belong to the descent group of the father, the father's father, and so on (see Figure 7.2). Thus, a man, his sisters and brothers, his own children, his brother's children (but not his sister's children), and his son's children (but not his daughter's children) all belong to the same descent group. Inheritance and succession to office move from father to son.

Whereas the status of women varies in patrilineal systems, in general, the husband is guaranteed rights and control over his wife (or wives) and children because the continuity of the descent group depends on this. Patrilineal systems most often have patrilocal rules of residence, so a wife may find herself living among strangers, which tends to undermine female solidarity and support.

The Nuer, an east African pastoral people, are a patrilineal society. All rights, privileges, obligations, and interpersonal relationships are regulated by kinship. A man, his father, his brothers, and their children are considered the closest kin. Patrilineal membership confers rights to land, requires participation in certain religious ceremonies, and determines political and judicial obligations, such as making alliances in feuds and warfare.

Lineage membership may spread over several villages, thus helping to create alliances between members of

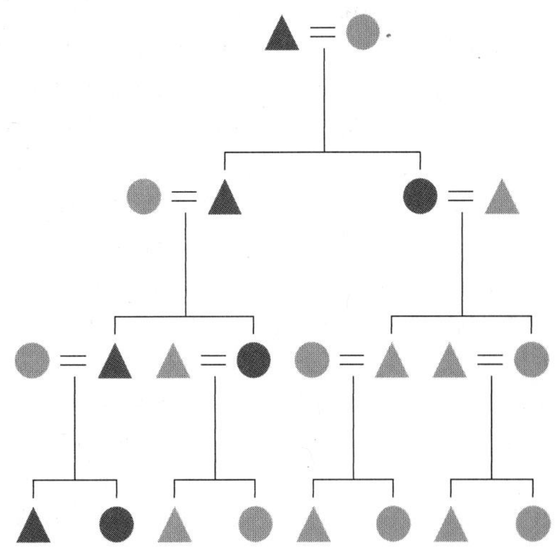

Figure 7.2

Membership in a patrilineal descent group is based on links through the father only. Sons and daughters belong to their father's descent group (shown in dark green), as do the children of sons but not of daughters.

otherwise independent villages that contain members of several different lineages. Each Nuer clan, which is viewed as composed of related lineages, not individuals, is also spread over several villages. Because a person cannot marry someone from within his or her own lineage or clan, or from the lineage of the mother, kinship relations extend widely throughout the tribe. In the absence of a centralized system of political control, these kinship-based alliances are an important mechanism of governance. Since the Nuer believe that close kin should not fight with one another, disputes within the lineage or clan tend to be kept small and settled rapidly (Evans-Pritchard 1968/1940). Because those who are not kin are perceived as potential enemies, an attack by outsiders on one lineage segment may cause all members of a clan to coalesce against a common enemy and their clan brothers (Sahlins 1961). Thus, the coalescence of the whole clan results from closer kin joining together against more distant kin.

Matrilineal Descent Groups

In matrilineal societies, the most important ties are between a woman, her mother, and her siblings. Children belong to the mother's descent group, not the father's. Thus, the membership of a matrilineal descent group (see Figure 7.3) consists of a woman, her brothers and sisters, her sisters' (but not her brothers') children, her own children, and the children of her daughters (but not of her sons).

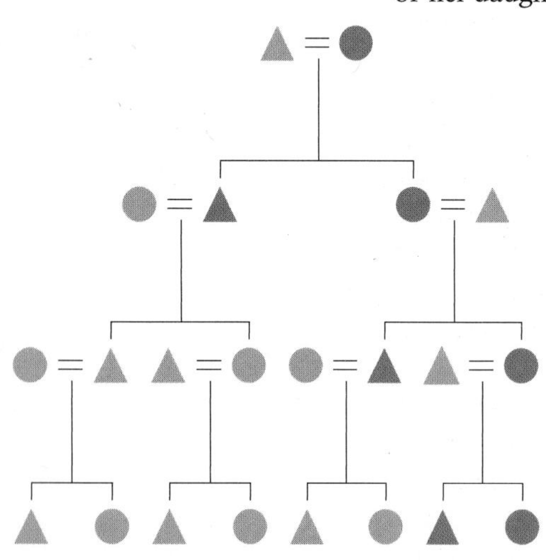

Figure 7.3

Membership in a matrilineal descent group is defined by links through the mother. Sons and daughters are members of their mother's descent group (shown in dark green), as are the children of daughters but not of sons.

In matrilineal societies, the rights and responsibilities of the father in a patrilineal society fall to a woman's brother rather than her husband. A man gains sexual and economic rights over a woman when he marries her, but he does not gain rights over her children. After marriage, a man usually goes to live with or near his wife's kin, which means that he is an outsider in the household, whereas his wife is surrounded by her kin. Because a husband's role in a matrilineal society is less important than in a patrilineal one, marriages in matrilineal societies tend to be less stable. Nevertheless, a man's position in a matrilineal society is less vulnerable than that of a woman in a patrilineal society.

In a matrilineal society, a father's relationship with his son is free of the problems of authority and control that exist between fathers and sons in a patrilineal society, as rights and responsibilities vested in male elders fall to a woman's brother rather than her husband. Although this may lessen conflict between fathers and sons, it also means that a man is committed to pass on his knowledge, property, and offices to the sons of his sister, not his own sons.

This may engender conflicts between a man and his nephews, who are subject to his control. Thus, in a matrilineal system, a man's loyalties are split between his own sons and the sons of his sister. In a patrilineal system, this tension does not occur as part of the kinship structure.

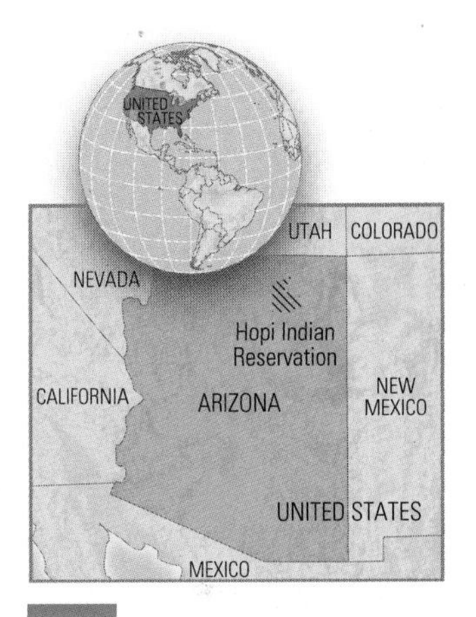

Location of the Hopi.

The Hopi, a Puebloan group in the American Southwest, are matrilineal. Hopi matrilineages are contained within matrilineal clans. The Hopi household revolves around a central and continuing core of women. The mother–daughter relationship is exceedingly close, based on blood ties, common activities, and lifelong residence together. A mother is responsible for the economic and ritual training of her daughters. Daughters offer respect, obedience, and affection to their mothers and normally live with their mother and their mother's sisters after marriage. The strongest, most permanent tie in Hopi society is between sisters, whose relationship to each other and to their mother is the foundation of the household group. The children of sisters are raised together; if one sister dies, another looks after her children. Sisters cooperate in all domestic tasks, and the few quarrels that may occur are settled by the mother's brother or by their own brothers.

Although Hopi men move into their wife's household after marriage, they are peripheral in these households and consider their mother's place as home, to which they return for many ritual and ceremonial occasions and upon separation or divorce. A son belongs to his mother's lineage and keeps much of his personal and ritual property in her home, shows respect for his mother as head of the household, and consults her on all important decisions.

As in all matrilineal societies, a Hopi man's relationship to his sister's sons is one of authority and control. He is the chief disciplinarian and has the primary responsibility for transmitting the ritual heritage of the lineage and clan. He is consulted in arranging marriages, instructs his nephews in the proper behavior toward his new relatives, and formally welcomes his niece's husband into the household. A man usually selects his most capable nephew as his successor and trains him in the duties of whatever ceremonial position he may hold.

Whereas a boy's relationship with his maternal uncle is characterized by reserve, respect, and even fear, his relationship with his father is more affectionate and involves little discipline. His obligations to his father's family involve some ritual and economic obligations, but little direct cooperation or authority. A Hopi man will prepare his sons to make a living by teaching them farming and sheep herding. He will often make gifts to his sons at the time of their marriage. In return, sons support their father in his old age. A man's relationship with his daughter also is generally affectionate but is not close, and he has few specific duties in regard to her upbringing.

Hopi matrilineal clans extend over many different villages. A Hopi man cannot marry within his own clan or within his father or his mother's father's clan. Through marriage a Hopi man acquires a wide range of relatives in addition to those resulting from his membership in his mother's clan. Kinship terms are extended to all these people, which relates a Hopi in some way to almost everyone in his village and in other villages and even to people in other Pueblo groups who have similar clans. Men play important political and religious roles in the clans, in contrast to their marginal position in domestic life (Eggan 1950).

About 5 percent of the world's cultures practice **double descent.** In this system, a person belongs both to the patrilineal group of the father and to the matrilineal group of the mother. However, these descent groups operate in different areas of life. Among the Yako of Nigeria, for example, rights to farmland, forest products, as well as some religious offices derive from membership in a patrilineal group, whereas the transfer of accumulated wealth, such as currency, livestock, tools, weapons, and household goods, is governed by matrilineal relations.

Bilateral Kinship Systems

About 40 percent of the world's societies are **non-unilineal (cognatic).** Most non-unilineal systems are bilateral; the rest are ambilineal (discussed next). Under rules of **bilateral descent,** both maternal and paternal lines are used equally as the basis for reckoning descent and for establishing the rights and obligations of kinship. Bilateral systems do not have clear-cut descent groups. Rather, they have networks of kin, called **kindreds,** that are defined only in their relation to a particular individual. Except for brothers and sisters, every individual's kindred is unique. Kindreds actually are overlapping categories of kin, rather than social groups, and thus are more difficult to organize as cooperative, kin-based collectivities. For example, because a kindred is an ego-centered network, not a social group, it cannot own land or have continuity over time.

Bilateral kinship systems seem particularly adaptive in societies where mobility and independence are important. They are basic to Western culture, including the United States, and predominate among foraging societies as well, such as the Inupiat speakers of Alaska. The flexibility of bilateral kinship systems is expressed in their **kinship terminology,** the words they use to identify different categories of kin. We're speaking here of a particular series of cultures, not culture universal.

The second type of cognatic system, found mainly in Pacific Island societies, is *ambilineal.* In these societies, individuals may choose to affiliate with either their mother's or with their father's descent group, but not simultaneously with both. Upon marriage the new couple can live with either spouse's descent group, a decision most often based on access to land, although friendship and politics also play a role.

THE CLASSIFICATION OF KIN

In all societies, kin are referred to by special terms. The total system of kinship terms and the rules for using these terms make up a *kinship classification system.* Every kinship classification system classes some relatives together (referred to by the same kinship term) and differentiates them from other relatives (called by different terms). Some kinship systems have only a small number of kinship terms, whereas others have a different term for almost every relative.

The classification of kin is related to the roles they play in society. In a kinship diagram, **ego** is the person from whose perspective the chart is drawn and viewed. If, for example, ego refers to his father and his father's brothers by the same term, his relationship with them tends to be similar. By the same token, if ego's father and father's brothers are referred to by different terms, it is expected that ego will act differently toward each of them and that they will act differently toward him. These ideals, of course, are modified (within limits) by the relationships and personalities of particular individuals.

Kinship classification is one of the most important regulators of behavior in most societies. It denotes each person's rights and obligations—how he or she must act toward others and how they must act toward him or her. Kinship classification systems are related to other aspects of culture, such as the types of social groups that are formed and the systems of marriage and inheritance.

Understanding the variety of kinship systems makes a crucial anthropological point: Although people in every society consider their own kinship classification system natural and normal, the logic underlying all kinship systems is cultural, not biological. For example, in the United States, the brothers and sisters of one's parents and their spouses are called "aunt" and "uncle," and the children of these relatives are called "cousin." Have you ever asked yourself why the same term is used for mother's sister, a relative by blood, and mother's brother's wife, a relative by marriage? Or why there are no separate terms for male and female cousins, but gender does differentiate nieces from nephews?

Principles for the Classification of Kin

Societies use a combination of some, but not all, of seven important principles of kinship classification in their kinship terminology. (1) *Generation,* which distinguishes ascending and descending generations from ego. (2) *Relative age,* where seniority counts, for example, in distinguishing older and younger brother. (3) *Lineality* versus *collaterality,* where lineal kin are related in a single line, such as grandfather–father–son, whereas **collateral kin** are descended from a common ancestor with ego but are not ego's direct ascendants or descendants, for example, siblings or cousins. (4) *Gender* differentiates relatives according to whether they are male or female; in English, for example, gender distinguishes between aunt and uncle, but not cousins. The principle of (5) *consanguineal* versus ***affinal*** kin differentiates relatives by blood in contrast to relatives by marriage, whereas the principle of the (6) *sex of linking relative* operates, for example, in differentiating between cross cousins and parallel cousins (see p. 148). Yet another principle, which distinguishes relatives from the mother's side of the family from those from the father's side, is called (7) **bifurcation,** for example, as used by societies that distinguish the mother's brother from the father's brother. These seven principles combine in different ways to form different types of kinship systems.

In making sense out of kinship systems, anthropologists attempt to understand the relationship of terminologies, rules of descent, and kinship groups to the ecological, economic, and political conditions under which different kinship systems emerge.

BRINGING IT BACK HOME: POLYGAMY IN THE UNITED STATES

In 1984, a woman and her 15-month-old baby were murdered in American Fork, Utah. Two Mormon fundamentalists and avowed polygamists, Ronald and Daniel Lafferty, admitted to the killing, justifying it as a revelation they had received from God (Krakauer 2003:171). Dan Lafferty was sentenced to life without parole. His brother Ronald was convicted and sentenced to die by a firing squad, although various appeals have kept him alive until today. More recently, Warren Jeffs, the leader of the Fundamentalist Church of Jesus Christ of Latter Day Saints (FLDS Church), was convicted as an accomplice to the rape of a 14-year-old church member by orchestrating her marriage, under duress, to her first cousin. Jeffs received a sentence of 10 years.

Although the estimated 10,000–50,000 fundamentalist Mormons are only a very small proportion of the members of the Latter Day Saints movement, these sensational cases put the Mormons once again on the national radar. In the 19th century, the Mormons had a long history of conflict with the United States. Opposition from non-Mormons and local governments forced them to move from New York to Ohio, Missouri, Illinois, and finally Utah. Following the revelations of Latter Day Saints founder Joseph Smith, Mormons permitted the practice of plural marriage from the late 1830s until they disavowed the practice in 1890. In that year, in a U.S. Supreme Court case, the court held that Mormon polygamy is "a crime against the laws, and abhorrent to the sentiments and feelings of the civilized world" (Norgren and Nanda 2006:94).

However, since that time and up until today, in defiance of federal courts, state statutes, mainstream cultural values, and excommunication by The Church of Jesus Christ of Latter Day Saints, the organization that represents the vast majority of Mormons, polygamy continues among the Mormon sect that calls itself Fundamentalist Latter Day Saints. FLDS Church members consider polygamy the sacred marriage pattern of the biblical prophets and hold that its restoration is critical to the entrance of the faithful into the celestial kingdom of God.

In the face of the sensationalist cases attributed to Mormon fundamentalism, which reinforce the already negative opinion most Americans have of polygamy, fundamentalist Mormons have campaigned to win public acceptance of their religion-based marriage practice. Those tolerant of polygamy point to the many variations in marriage and the family now existing in America as a reason to look the other way. The appearance in 2006 of a national television program called "Big Love," about a polygamous family, might indicate increasing tolerance. In his provocative book, *Plural Marriage for Our Times,* anthropologist Philip Kilbride (1994) proposes that polygamy could be a solution to some of the problems of American society. For example, he argues that infidelity in marriage often leads to divorce and that polygamy might be a better alternative because of the very damaging effects of divorce on children. He also suggests that elderly women might benefit from polygamy because of the chronic shortage of men in the oldest age categories.

Opponents of polygamy cite evidence of incest, child abuse, violence against women, rape, and the coerced marriage and sexual relations between teenage girls and much older men as reasons to continue to hold polygamy illegal. In addition to these cases, they cite the hundreds of teenaged boys who have been expelled or felt forced to leave fundamentalist Mormon polygamous families, supposedly for disobedience to religious precepts. Some former sect members and state officials argue that, in fact, such boys are forced out of the community to make more young girls available to marry older men (Eckholm 2007). With the increasing conflict in the United States over the purposes and meanings of marriage, polygamy has once again moved front and center as a subject for debate.

YOU DECIDE

1. Consider the possible advantages and disadvantages of polygamy as a form of marriage in the contemporary United States. In what ways might it be adaptive? Maladaptive?

2. Consider the historical outlawing of polygamy in the United States, in spite of the freedom of religious practice guaranteed by the U.S. Constitution. How would you build a case either for or against the continued criminalization of this religion-based form of marriage?
3. Many of the attacks on Mormon polygamy stress its oppression of women. Consider the different possible perceptions of polygamy in the United States today from a male and from a female point of view.

CHAPTER SUMMARY

1. Three major functions of marriage and the family are regulating sexual access between males and females, arranging for the exchange of services between males and females, and assigning responsibility for child care.
2. Incest taboos are prohibitions on mating between people classified as relatives. Various theories of the adaptiveness of the incest taboo are that it prevents disruption based on sexual competition within the family and that it forces people to marry out of their immediate families, extending their alliances to a larger social community.
3. All societies have marriage rules: which groups a person may marry within (endogamy); which groups they must marry outside of (exogamy); whether cousins are permitted, preferred or prohibited from marrying; the number of spouses; the exchanges of goods and services validating a marriage; and the degree of control a family or kin group has over a child's choice of spouse.
4. Two basic family types are the nuclear family, found mainly in contemporary industrial and foraging societies, and the extended family, found predominantly among cultivators.
5. A household (domestic group) usually contains members of a family. Household composition is shaped by a society's postmarital residence rules. The most common such rule is patrilocality, which requires a wife to live with her husband's family. Matrilocality, which requires a husband to live with his wife's family, is found primarily in horticultural societies. Neolocality, in which the married couple lives independently, is found in a small number of societies, including the United States.
6. Kinship systems are cultural creations that define and organize relatives by blood and marriage. A kinship system includes the kinds of groups based on kinship and the system of terms used to classify different kin. Kinship systems provide continuity between generations and define a group of people who can depend on one another for mutual aid. In traditional societies, kinship is the most important basis of social organization.

7. In many societies, descent is the basis of the formation of corporate social groups. In societies with a unilineal rule of descent, descent group membership is based on either the male or the female line. Unilineal systems are found among pastoral and cultivating societies.
8. A lineage is a group of kin whose members can trace their descent from a common ancestor. A clan is a group whose members believe they have a common ancestor but cannot trace the relationship genealogically. Lineages tend to have domestic functions; clans tend to have political and religious functions. Both lineages and clans are important in regulating marriage.
9. In patrilineal systems, a man's children and his sons' children, but not his daughters' children, belong to his lineage. In matrilineal systems, as exist, for example, among the Hopi, a woman's children belong to her lineage, not that of their father. The mother's brother has authority over his sisters' children, and relations between husband and wife are more fragile than in patrilineal societies.
10. In systems of double descent, the individual belongs to both the patrilineage of the father and the matrilineage of the mother. Each group functions in different social contexts, as described for the Yako of Nigeria.
11. In bilateral systems, the individual is equally related to mother's kin and father's kin. Bilateral systems result in the formation of kindreds, which are overlapping kinship networks, rather than a permanent group of kin. Bilateral kinship is found predominantly among foragers and in modern industrialized states.
12. Kinship terminology groups together or distinguishes relatives according to various principles, such as generation, relative age, lineality or collaterality, gender, consanguinity or affinity, bifurcation, and sex of the linking relative. Different societies may use all or some of these principles in classifying kin. Each type of kinship classification system reflects the particular kinship group that is most important in the society.

KEY TERMS

Affinal
Arranged marriage
Avunculocal residence
Bifurcation
Bilateral descent
Bilocal residence
Bride service

Bridewealth
Clan
Collateral kin
Composite (compound) family
Conjugal tie
Consanguineal
Corporate descent group
Descent
Descent group
Double descent
Dowry
Ego
Endogamy
Exogamy
Extended family
Incest taboos
Inheritance
Kindred
Kinship
Kinship system
Kinship terminology
Levirate
Lineage
Marriage
Matrilineage
Matrilineal descent
Matrilocal residence
Monogamy
Neolocal residence
Non-unilineal (cognatic) descent
Nuclear family
Patrilineage
Patrilineal descent
Patrilocal residence
Polyandry
Polygamy
Polygyny
Sororate
Succession
Unilineal descent

© Serena Nanda

The hijras of India are one of many examples of sex/gender alternatives that transcend the dichotomy of male and female, man and woman.

CHAPTER 8

SEX AND GENDER

CHAPTER OUTLINE

Neither Man nor Woman: The Hijras of India

Sex and Gender as Cultural Constructions

Cultural Variation in Sexual Behavior

Male and Female Rites of Passage
- Male Rites of Passage
- Female Rites of Passage

Power and Prestige: Gender Stratification

Gender Relations: Complex and Variable
- Gender Relations in Foraging Societies
- Gender Relations in Horticultural Societies
- Gender Relations in Pastoral and Agricultural Societies
- Gender Relations in the Global Economy

Bringing It Back Home: Female Genital Operations and International Human Rights
- You Decide

NEITHER MAN NOR WOMAN: THE HIJRAS OF INDIA

SALIMA, born intersexed, is a real hijra. Accepting that Salima was "neither one thing nor the other," Salima's mother sent her to join the hijras when Salima was about 12 years old. In her early teens, Salima, along with a group of her "sister" hijras, began to beg and perform the traditional hijra *badhai.* They would seek out families where a wedding was taking place or where a child had been born. Salima played the *dholak,* the two-sided drum that accompanies every hijra performance. Salima told me she doesn't remember much about her childhood, but she does know that her mother was very sad about her birth, that she was born "neither here nor there." "But from my childhood, I am like this," Salima said. "From my birth my [male sex] organ was very small. My mother took me to doctors but they told her it was no good, your child is not a man and not a woman. This is God's gift. So when I came to the age of knowing, they gave me to the hijras. And I have been living with them ever since, as you see me now."

The **hijras** are an ambiguous gender role in India. Although born male, they are considered neither man nor woman. Hijras undergo an operation in which their genitals are surgically removed. This "operation" accounts for the popular designation of hijras as eunuchs. Hijras consider this operation a rebirth, and it is carried out as an act of devotion to the Hindu Mother Goddess. After the operation, hijras are believed to incorporate the goddess' powers of procreation. Thus, their presence is required at weddings and at the birth of a child.

Hijra performances involve clapping, drumming, and the tinkle of ankle bells, which announce their arrival. Tossing their spangled scarves, flashing their heavy jewelry, and beating their drums, the hijras sing and dance, making comic, ribald gestures and striking sexually suggestive feminine poses, causing laughter by the men and more discreet embarrassed giggling behind their hands by the women. In celebrating childbirth, the dancers take the infant from his mother's arms and bless him with wishes for prosperity and virility, meanwhile examining his genitals to confirm that he is a fully formed male infant. At the end of their performance the hijras are given their traditional payment of money, cloth, and sweets, satisfied with having once again confirmed their importance in Indian society.

Because they are born male, hijras are mainly perceived as "not man," but they are also thought of as "man plus woman." They adopt women's clothing, gestures, and behaviors. They must wear their hair long, like women, and they have a special language that includes feminine expressions, intonations, and female kinship terms. But hijras are also "not woman" mainly because they cannot bear children.

As neither man nor woman, hijras identify with the many ambiguous **gender roles** and figures in Hindu mythology and Indian culture: male deities who change into or disguise themselves as females temporarily, deities who have both male and female characteristics, male religious devotees who dress and act as women in religious ceremonies, eunuchs who served in the Muslim courts, and the ascetics, or holy men of India, whose renunciation of all sexuality paradoxically becomes the source of their power to bless others with fertility. Indian culture thus not only accommodates such androgynous figures as the hijras but views them as meaningful, sacred, and even powerful (Nanda 1999).

India is only one of the many societies throughout the world where cultural support is given to individuals who transcend or bridge the differences between male and female (Herdt 1996; Nanda 2000b). Among these are the *mahu* of Polynesia (Besnier 1996; Matzner 2001), the *xanith* of Oman on the Saudi Arabian peninsula (Wikan 1977), the *two-spirit* found in many Native-American tribes (Roscoe 1995/1991; Whitehead 1981; Williams 1986), the *travesti* of Brazil (Kulick 1998), the *kathoey* of Thailand (Costa and Matzner 2007), and the *waria* of Indonesia (Boellstorff 2004; Graham 2006), just to name a few. Most of these roles involve males who adopt women's work, dress, and behavior, but there are female alternative gender roles as well (Blackwood 1998).

Among some subarctic groups, for example, people depended on sons to feed the family through big game hunting. A family that had daughters and no sons would select a daughter to "be like a man." When the youngest daughter was about 5 years old, the parents performed a transformation ceremony in which they tied the dried ovaries of a bear to a belt the child always wore. This was believed to prevent menstruation, protect her from pregnancy, and give her luck on the hunt. From then on, she dressed like a male, trained like a male, and often developed great strength and became an outstanding hunter (Williams 1996:202). For these native peoples, being male or female included both biological elements, such as menstruation and the ability to become pregnant, and cultural features, such as the ability to hunt.

You might wonder why anthropologists study such esoteric topics as alternative genders and what we can learn from them. After all, the division of humans into two opposite sexes—male and female—appears to be a basic characteristic of human biology, a natural and inevitable aspect of human life. Sex assignment, which takes place at birth, is assumed to be permanent over a person's lifetime. Most of us take for granted that sex is the same as gender and that people come in two opposing and unchangeable categories. But, although it is true that every culture acknowledges the biological differences between male and female, there is great cultural variety in both the number of sexes and genders a society constructs and the ways in which sex and gender are defined.

SEX AND GENDER AS CULTURAL CONSTRUCTIONS

A basic anthropological concept is the distinction between the biological and cultural aspects of being male or female. **Sex** refers to the biological differences between male and female, particularly the visible differences in external genitalia and the related difference in the role each sex plays in the reproductive process. **Gender** is the cultural and social classification of masculine and feminine. In other words, gender is the social, cultural, and psychological constructs that different societies superimpose on the biological differences of sex (Worthman 1995:598). Every culture recognizes distinctions between male and female, but cultures differ in the meanings attached to these categories, the supposed sources of the differences between them, and the relationship of these categories to other cultural and social facts. And, as we saw in the opening of this chapter, in many cultures, genders are not limited to masculine and feminine.

Gender and gender relations are among the basic building blocks of culture and society, central to social relations of power, individual and group identities, formation of kinship and other groups, and attribution of meaning and value. This makes gender a central interest of contemporary anthropology. Understanding that gender roles are not biologically determined but rather are culturally constructed raises new questions about the culturally patterned nature of women's and men's lives in all cultures, including our own.

Cross-cultural ethnography demonstrates that not only do different cultures incorporate different genders beyond those of man and woman, but that concepts of masculine and feminine also vary among cultures. Thus, in order to grasp the potential and the limits of diversity in human life, we must look at the full range of human societies—particularly those outside Western historical, cultural, and economic traditions. When we broaden our perspective on sex and gender beyond our own society, we see that culture counts. Gender is culturally constructed and extraordinarily diverse, as are the relationships between sex and gender.

The work of anthropologist Margaret Mead was essential in developing the now central anthropological principle that gender is a cultural construction. In the 1930s, Mead (1935/1963) began to question the biologically determined nature of gender. She organized her ethnographic research around the question of whether the characteristics defined as masculine and feminine in Western culture, specifically the United States, were universal. In her studies of three groups in New Guinea—the Arapesh, the Mundugamor, and the Tchambuli—Mead found that the whole repertoire of behaviors, emotions, and roles that go into being masculine and feminine is patterned by culture. Among the Arapesh, men and women both were expected to act in ways that Americans considered "naturally" feminine. Both sexes were concerned with taking care of children and nurturing. Neither sex was expected to be aggressive. In Mundugamor society, both sexes were what American culture would call "masculine": aggressive, violent, and with little interest in children. Among the Tchambuli, the personalities of men and women were different from each other but opposite to American conceptions of masculine and feminine. Women had the major economic role and showed common sense and business shrewdness. Men were more interested in esthetics. They spent much time decorating themselves and gossiping. Their feelings were easily hurt, and they sulked a lot.

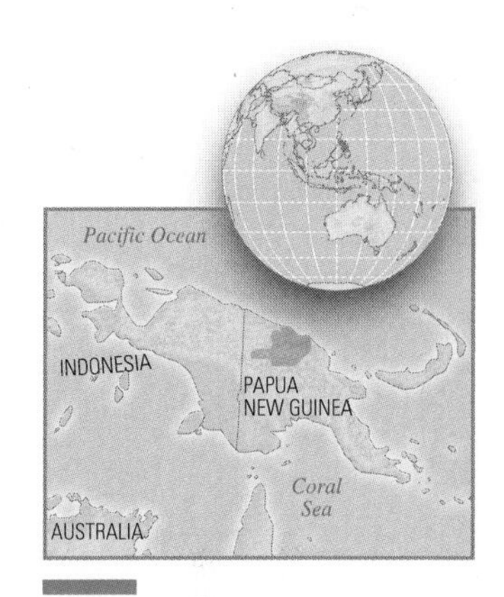

Location of the Arapesh, the Mundugamor, and the Tchambuli.

Although Mead's ethnographic descriptions of these societies were later criticized and superseded (di Leonardo 1998:213–215, 2003; Roscoe 2003), her work made a lasting contribution by raising the issue of the great diversity in cultural definitions of masculine and feminine and by calling attention to the ways in which gender and gender relations are **cultural constructions.** A society's **gender ideology,** that is, its totality of ideas about sex, gender, the natures of men and women, including their sexuality, and the relations between the genders, is significant not only in its own right but because it is a core element in a society's gender stratification system, a subject discussed later in this chapter.

CULTURAL VARIATION IN SEXUAL BEHAVIOR

Understanding gender systems as culturally constructed also helps explain the cultural variations in definitions of appropriate sexual behavior. Although sexual activity is most often viewed as "doing what comes naturally," a cross-cultural perspective demonstrates that human sexual activity is patterned by a culture's gender ideology and influenced by learning.

Culture patterns the habitual responses of different peoples to different parts of the body. What is erotic in some cultures is considered disgusting in others. Kissing, for example, is not universal. The Tahitians learned to kiss from the Europeans; before this cultural contact, Tahitians began sexual intimacy by sniffing. Among the Alaskan Inuit, sniffing the hollow in another's cheek can be both a pattern of sexual as well as nonsexual behavior. When an adult asks a child to do this, it is affectionate and innocent, whereas among adults it is considered quite erotic. Like a kiss in our own culture, it is the social construction of behavior that counts.

Sexual foreplay is also culturally diverse. In the Trobriand Islands, a couple expresses affection by inspecting each other's hair for lice, a practice Westerners may find disgusting. But to the Trobrianders, the European habit of a couple going on a picnic with a knapsack of prepared food is equally disgusting, although it is perfectly acceptable for a Trobriand boy and girl to gather wild foods together as a prelude to sexual activity (Malinowski 1929b:327, 335).

Who is considered an appropriate sexual partner also differs among cultures. In some societies, like the United States, homosexual activity is generally considered shameful or abnormal, but elsewhere it is a matter of indifference or approval.

Among the Sambia of New Guinea, what Americans call homosexual practice is culturally central in the sex/gender system, not as an aspect of sexual orientation but as a core ritual in male initiation considered essential for the development of adult masculinity. In Sambian culture, women are viewed as dangerous creatures that pollute men, deplete them of their masculinity substance, and are inferior in every way except for reproduction capabilities. The Sambia believe that women are naturally fertile and mature naturally without external aid, whereas males do not naturally mature as fast or as competently as females. The Sambia believe that males cannot attain puberty or become "strong men" without semen. They further believe that male bodies do not naturally produce semen, so it must be externally and artificially introduced into the body. This they do by magical ritual treatments, which include homosexual fellatio during the boys' initiations, as a way of the boys consuming semen from adult men. Only repeated inseminations of this kind are considered capable of conferring on young boys the reproductive competence that results in manliness, necessary to become a vigorous warrior and a father. As adults, these men are expected to make heterosexual marriages (Herdt 1981, 1996:431–436). Among ancient Greeks, homosexual relationships were considered to be superior to those between men and women, whereas in many cultures, the male who takes the dominant role in same-sex relationships is not considered homosexual. The many cultures in which same-sex relationships are viewed as normal variants of human sexuality strongly contrast with the varied and constantly changing ways that homosexuality has been seen in modern Europe and with the dominant cultural ideology in the United States, where consistent heterosexuality is considered essential to masculine identity.

The ages at which sexual response is believed to begin and end, the ways in which people make themselves attractive, the importance of sexual activity in human life, and its variation according to gender—all these are patterned and regulated by culture and affect sexual response and behavior. A comparison of the cultures of the Irish of Inis Beag and the Polynesians of Mangaia makes clear the role of culture in sexuality.

Anthropologist John Messenger (1971:15) describes Inis Beag as "one of the most sexually naive of the world's societies." Sex is never discussed at home when children are near, and parents provide practically no sexual instruction to children. Adults believe that "after marriage nature takes its course." (As we shall see, "nature" takes a very different course in Inis Beag than it does in Polynesia!) Women are expected to endure but not enjoy sexual relations; to refuse to have intercourse is considered a mortal sin among this Roman Catholic people. There appears to be widespread ignorance in Inis Beag of the female capacity for orgasm, which in any case is considered deviant behavior. Nudity is abhorred, and there is no tradition of "dirty jokes." The main style of dancing allows little bodily contact among the participants; even so, some girls refuse to dance because it means touching a boy. The separation of the sexes begins very early in Inis Beag and lasts into adulthood. Other cultural patterns related to sexual repression here are the virtual absence of sexual foreplay, the belief that sexual activity weakens a man, the absence of premarital sex, the high percentage of celibate males, and the extraordinarily late age of marriage. According to a female informant, "Men can wait a long time before wanting 'it' but we [women] can wait a lot longer" (Messenger 1971:16).

Although the idea of total sexual freedom in the South Sea Islands is a Western myth, Mangaia, as described by Donald Marshall (1971), presents a strong contrast to Inis Beag. In this Polynesian culture, sexual intercourse is one of the major interests of life. Although sex is not discussed at home, sexual information is taught to boys and girls at puberty by the elders of the group. For adolescent boys, a 2-week period of formal instruction about the techniques of intercourse is followed by a culturally approved experience with a mature woman in the village. After this, the boy is considered a man. This contrasts with Inis Beag, where a man is considered a "lad" until he is about 40. In Mangaia there is continual public reference to sexual activity; sexual jokes, expressions, and references are expected as part of the preliminaries to public meetings. And yet, in public, sex segregation is the norm. Boys and girls should not be seen together in public, but practically every girl and boy has had intercourse before marriage. The act of sexual intercourse itself is the focus of sexual activity. What Westerners call sexual foreplay generally follows intercourse in Mangaia. Both men and women are expected to take pleasure in the sexual act and to have an orgasm. Female frigidity and male celibacy are practically unknown. The contrast between Inis Beag and Mangaia indicates clearly that societies' different attitudes pattern the sexual responsiveness of males and females in each society.

A culture's gender ideology always includes ideas about sexuality, and most societies view males and females as different in this respect. These differences are often used to justify men's control over women's sexuality, and they become a basis for gender stratification, constraints on women's lives, and discrimination against women. This control may take forms such as seclusion of women (Hale 1989), cultural emphasis on honor and shame as related to female sexuality (Brandes 1981), and male control institutionalized in law and organized religion, over marriage, divorce, adultery, concepts and treatment of rape (Sanday 1992), and abortion. Society's control of female sexuality is often inscribed on female bodies, as in female circumcision in some African societies (Barnes-Dean 1989), Chinese foot binding (Anagnost 1989), and *sati* (now outlawed in India), the traditional Hindu practice of a woman burning herself on her husband's funeral pyre (Narasimhan 1990).

In many cultures, control of female sexuality is central to the cultural understanding of masculinity (Gilmore 1996). This pattern may have its roots in religious beliefs. It is central in Islam and in many circum-Mediterranean cultures. Anthropologist Stanley Brandes (1981) links this pattern in southern Spain to early and medieval Christianity. "Women are the Devil," a butcher in San Blas, Andalusia, tells him, "because when Eve

The hijab, or headscarf, worn by these Malaysian girls is one means by which some Muslims accommodate the Islamic requirement for women to dress modestly. Wearing the headscarf has become a political issue in Turkey and in many European countries, which have large numbers of Muslim immigrants.

fell to the temptation of the serpent in the Garden of Eden, she then went on to tempt Adam to eat the apple of the tree of knowledge. . . . [Woman] was that way from the beginning, and she has been trying to tempt and dominate man ever since."

For San Blas men, this biblical story justifies the view that men are more virtuous than women, are more pure (because man sinned only after he was tempted by woman), and are closer to God. Consistent with this view, men in San Blas view women as "seductresses and whores," possessed of insatiable, lustful appetites, who can break down a man's control over his passions and lead him into temptation. Women possess goodness only in their role as mothers, an idealized, pure version of womanhood. Otherwise they are devils who threaten family unity and honor. The ability of women to undermine the reputation of their family and kin group through lustful sexuality underlies the male ambivalence toward women that permeates San Blas social life. This attitude extends to widows, who are seen as having driven their husbands to premature deaths by sapping their strength through demands for frequent sexual activity and heavy physical labor (Brandes 1981:225).

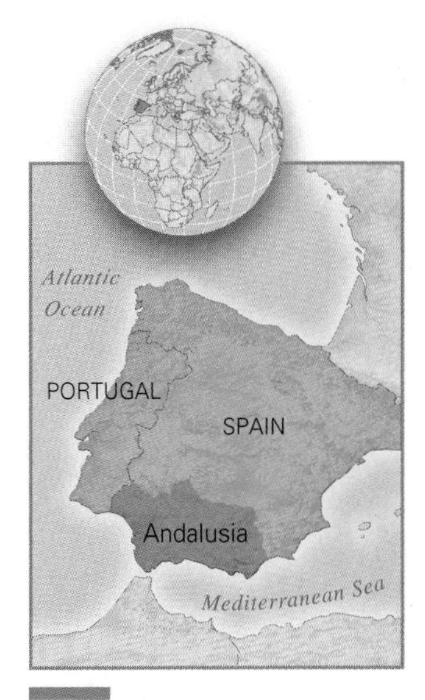

Andalusia.

The cultural construction of manhood in San Blas explicitly opposes the cultural construction of women. Men most fear that their wives, driven by insatiable sexuality, will be unfaithful, will emasculate them, and will ruin the honor of their families. They counter this fear by adhering to an image of manliness that centers on aggressive sexuality, a willingness to confront and compete with other men in public, and the demonstrated drive and ability to be successful in their marital and economic lives.

Where this culturally constructed contrast between men and women is part of a gender ideology, it is expressed in many cultural patterns, for example, the use of space, which is constructed in gender terms: Women belong to the home, and men to the streets, bars, and other public spaces (Gilmore 1996).

MALE AND FEMALE RITES OF PASSAGE

In all cultures the role expectations of individuals change at different points in life, as new capacities unfold or old ones diminish. At each of these points, individuals must learn what is necessary for these new roles. In many societies, the transition from one social status to another is formalized by special **rites of passage,** which move individuals publicly and ceremonially from one stage of life to the next (see Chapter 12, p. 271). One of the most widespread rites of passage signals the transition from childhood to adult gender roles (van Gennep 1960).

Male Rites of Passage

Male rites of passage, which are very widespread, have important psychological and sociological functions. They reinforce the social order by dramatizing cultural values in a public context; they express and affirm male relationships, male solidarity, and, sometimes, male dominance; they publicly validate a change of status from child to adult; and they transmit the cultural knowledge necessary to being a responsible adult male in the society.

Male rites of passage often involve an extended period during which boys are separated from the larger society. This separation emphasizes the importance of an individual's responsibility to his kinship group as well as the larger community (Hart 1967). These rites often include painful practices such as scarification or circumcision that symbolize the formal transition from child to adult. Such rites may also include difficult and dangerous tasks, such as killing a large animal, which test a boy's preparation for the obligations of male adulthood.

Male rites of passage have been interpreted as a means of psychologically separating boys from identification with their mothers, particularly in societies where such identifications are intense and accompanied by hostility toward their fathers (Whiting, Kluckhohn, and Anthony 1967). These rites have also been interpreted as a symbolic appropriation of female reproductive capacities, as among the Sambia of New Guinea, for example, where male initiation into adulthood is explicitly described as a rebirth which "makes boys into men" (Herdt 1981). In New Guinea, fertility is frequently a male as well as a female principle, and male rites of passage may be viewed as a fertility cult in which men celebrate and ritually reproduce their control over the fertility of crops, animals, and humans.

The widespread (but not universal) cultural pattern in which men must *prove* themselves to be virile, successful in competition with other men, daring, heroic, and aggressive (whether on the streets, in bars, or in warfare) means that male rites of passage often involve "proving manhood" (Gilmore 1990). Where formal rites are absent, proving manhood may occur in informal but nevertheless culturally patterned ways. In Chuuk, Micronesia (formerly the U.S. territory of Truk), for example, male adolescents engage in excessive drinking and violent brawling as an expression of a cultural concept of masculinity that is defined by competitiveness, assertiveness, risk-taking in the face of danger, physical strength, and physical violence (Marshall 1979).

Anthropologist David Gilmore calls the widespread male need to publicly test and prove one's manhood, the **manhood puzzle.** Why, he asks, is the state of manhood regarded as so uncertain or precarious that the transformation of a male into a "real man" requires trials of skill or endurance, or special rituals? As part of the answer, Gilmore suggests that cultural patterns of "proving manhood" help ensure that men will fulfill their roles as procreators, providers, and protectors of their families. This essential contribution to society, he argues, is at the heart of the *"macho"* masculine role and accounts for its intensity, near universality, and persistence.

These questions about possible universals in the construction of masculinity (and femininity) are interesting and important, but we need to remember that one problem with a universalist view of masculinity is that it does not recognize the plurality of masculinities within a culture or the differences among cultures (Conway-Long 1994; Gutmann 1996).

Female Rites of Passage

Female rites of passage, until recently somewhat neglected in the anthropological literature, actually occur in more societies than do male rites, although they are generally less spectacular and intense. Female initiation into adulthood often is performed at *menarche* (first menstruation), but there is much cross-cultural variability (Lutkehaus and Roscoe 1995). Sometimes the initiate is isolated from society; sometimes she is the center of attention. Some rituals are elaborate and take years to perform; others are performed with little ceremony.

As with boys' rites, there are multiple interpretations for girls' initiation rites. Since these rites occur more frequently in matrilocal societies where the young girl continues her childhood tasks in her mother's home, one of their important functions is to publicly announce a girl's status change, as she will now carry out these tasks as a responsible adult. The rites demonstrate a girl's public acceptance of her new legal role (Brown 1965). The rites may also teach girls what they need to know to function as effective adults. Among the Bemba of Africa, women explain the elaborate girls' rite of passage, Chisungu, as a way to make the girls "clever," a word that translates as intelligent and socially competent (Richards 1956:125).

In addition to transmitting cultural skills and traditions and publicly moving girls from one social status to another, female rites of passage serve to channel sexuality into adult reproduction. In some New Guinea societies, painful scarification culturally calls attention to the connections among beauty, sexuality, and power and is explained as motivating girls to bear and rear children, strengthening their fortitude, and providing them with the capacity for the hard work necessary to assist their husbands in gathering wealth. Although many New Guinea female rites of passage highlight the differences between males and females, they also may convey the message that the sexes are complementary and dependent on each other in making their contribution, as a father or a mother, to reproducing society as a whole.

POWER AND PRESTIGE: GENDER STRATIFICATION

A central concern of the anthropology of gender is the nature of **gender stratification.** Although anthropologists have long debated whether male dominance is universal and, if so, why, contemporary examinations of gender stratification focus on the intersection of many aspects of women's status to explain the great variety of gender stratification systems in the world's cultures. These interacting dimensions include the social and cultural significance of women's roles as mothers, sisters, wives, and daughters; women's economic contributions in different types of societies; informal as well as formal sources of women's power and influence; development of women's identities; and changes in all these dimensions as a result of historical factors, particularly colonialism, technological and economic change, and globalization.

One early anthropological theory that addresses the widespread, perhaps even universal, subordination of women to men is called the **private/public dichotomy.** This theory holds that female subordination is based on women's universal role as mothers and homemakers. In this view, all societies are divided into a less prestigious domestic (private) world, inhabited by women, and a more prestigious public world, dominated by men (Rosaldo and Lamphere 1974). However, subsequent research revealed that the private/public dichotomy is not universal but rather is most characteristic of the highly gender stratified 19th-century capitalist societies, such as those of Victorian Europe and the United States, where productive relationships moved out of the household and middle-class women (but not working-class women) retreated into the home, where they were supposed to concern themselves solely with domestic affairs, repress their sexuality, bear children, and accept a subordinate and dependent role (Martin 1987; see also Lamphere 2005 for a reevaluation of this theory). The private/public dichotomy also seemed less applicable to smaller-scale, non-Western societies where home and family and economics and politics were not so easily separated. The public/domestic opposition tended to be intensified by the impact of capitalism, Christianity, and colonialism—either directly, as European administrators recognized only male political leaders, or indirectly with the devaluing of women's economic contributions, as well as reflecting the dominant Christian view of the ideal family as nuclear and patriarchal (Lockwood 2005:504).

Ernestine Friedl (1975), in an influential reexamination of the private/public dichotomy, put emphasis on other factors, particularly economic ones, such as the degree to which women control the distribution and exchange of goods and services outside the domestic unit. She pointed out that in foraging societies, male control over the distribution of meat within the larger community is a source of their greater power, whereas in horticultural societies, men clear the forest for new gardens; thus, they exercise control over the allocation of land, and this increases their power relative to women. Friedl further noted that since small children can also be cared for by older children, neighbors, relatives, and others, women's low status could not be explained by their obligations for child rearing. Rather, she held, cultural norms regarding family size and systems of child care are adapted to women's productive roles in society rather than their workloads being an adaptation to pregnancy and child care. For example, between 1960 and 2006, the average number of children under 18 present in American households with children dropped from 2.19 to 1.82 (U.S. Census Bureau 2006). We might ask, for example, if this is related to the fact that most American wives now feel they need to work outside the home.

In theorizing about widespread male dominance, anthropologists have also used controlled cross-cultural comparison. Peggy Sanday (1981), for example, concluded that male dominance was *not* universal but occurred in connection with ecological stress and warfare. She showed that where the survival of the group rests more on male actions, such as warfare, women accept male dominance for the sake of social and cultural survival. Still other anthropologists emphasize the cultural and historical variation in women's status, particularly the effects of capitalism and European colonialism on many non-Western societies, which appeared to be more gender equalitarian before European contact (Leacock 1981).

GENDER RELATIONS: COMPLEX AND VARIABLE

In earlier gender studies, there was intense debate over which gender dominated a society. Male dominance, called **patriarchy,** was considered universal, or almost universal. **Matriarchy,** or female dominance in a society, was held by some anthropologists to exist in some societies. Although female power, as we see next, does find a place in many societies, sometimes in official, explicit ways and other times in more implicit, subtle ways, it is generally agreed that in no society does matriarchy hold sway in the extreme versions characteristic of patriarchy. Today, with greater understanding of the complexity and variability in gender stratification systems, anthropologists have moved from the question of whether male dominance is universal to explanations of gender stratification in particular societies. This has led to a closer examination of the sexual division of labor in different types of societies and an examination of the informal as well as formal bases of female power.

Gender Relations in Foraging Societies

Earlier anthropological descriptions of foraging societies viewed male hunting as the major source of the food supply, providing the basis of male dominance in these societies. Contemporary ethnographic studies have modified this view. In many foraging societies, such as the Tiwi of Australia and the Ju'/hoansi of the Kalahari Desert in Namibia (Africa), women make very significant contributions to the food supply by gathering vegetable foods (Hart and Pilling 1960; Lee 2003). In other societies, like the Agta of the Philippines, women also substantially contributed to the food supply by hunting (Estioko-Griffin 1986), although in different ways and for different kinds of animals than hunted by the men. These contributions by women to the society's food supply were an important source of female power.

The Tlingit of the Northwest Coast of North America is a foraging society in which women traditionally had equal power and prestige with men. Important Tlingit social roles are based on individual ability, training,

Among the foraging Agta of the Philippines, men frequently hunt large animals alone. But Agta women also hunt. The women hunt in groups and often are more successful than men in bringing home game.

and personality rather than on gender (Klein 1995). Both Tlingit women and men achieve prestige through their own efforts and their own kin relationships. Women may be heads of clans or tribes, and Tlingit aristocrats are both male and female. Titles of high rank are used for both men and women, and the ideal marriage is between a man and woman of equal rank. The prestige the Tlingit achieved through extensive trade with other coastal societies is open to both men and women. Although in the past long-distance trade centered on men, women often accompanied the men, acting as negotiators and handling the money, and both girls and boys were—and are today—expected to "work, save, get wealth and goods" (Klein 1995:35).

Gender egalitarianism continues to be a core Tlingit cultural value. Today, women occupy the highest offices of the native corporations administering Tlingit land and are employed in government, social action groups, business and cultural organizations, and voluntary associations (Klein 1976). Tlingit women take advantage of educational opportunities and easily enter modern professions. Unlike many non-Western societies where European contact diminished women's economic roles and influence (see the Nukumanu, later), modernization has expanded Tlingit women's roles, and modern gender egalitarianism is not experienced as diminishing men, who encourage their wives and daughters to go into public life.

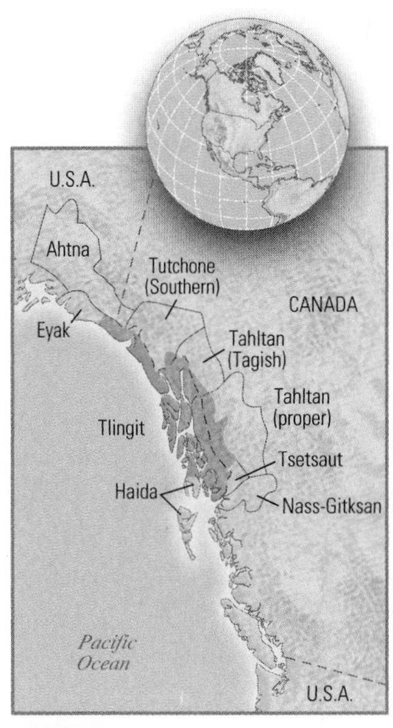

The Tlingit, on the Northwest Coast of North America.

Gender Relations in Horticultural Societies

Generally speaking, women have more autonomy and power in egalitarian foraging societies, such as those in native North America (Klein and Ackerman 1995), some tribal populations in southeast Asia (Ong 1989), and some hunters and gatherers in Africa (Shostak 1983), than in horticultural, pastoral, or agricultural societies, but again, there is great cross-cultural variation. For example, the Iroquois of the eastern United States are highly egalitarian (Brown 1975), whereas the Yanomamo of Venezuela and Brazil are highly sex segregated and male dominated (Chagnon 1997), as are most societies in highland New Guinea (Strathern 1995, but see Lepowsky 1993).

A high degree of sex segregation, paralleled by the importance of males in ritual, is associated with male dominance in some horticultural societies. Among the Mundurucu of South America, for example, adolescent boys are initiated into the men's cult and thereafter spend most of their lives in the men's house, only visiting their wives, who live with the children in their own huts in the village. The men's cults exclude women and are surrounded by great secrecy. The men's house itself usually is the most imposing structure in the village and houses the cult paraphernalia and sacred musical instruments. These instruments, which often are flutelike (shaped like the male genitals), are the symbolic expressions of male dominance and solidarity (Murphy and Murphy 1974). Among the indigenous peoples of Australia, similar cults are associated with circumcision rites for newly initiated boys. Sometimes the myths that explain the cult's origin include an explanation of why women are excluded from them, why women are considered socially inferior to men, and why men and women have different roles in these societies.

The solidarity of women in horticultural societies usually is not formalized in cults or associations but is based on the cooperation of domestic life and strong interpersonal bonds among female kin. In sub-Saharan Africa, for example, the most important economic and emotional ties for both men and women are more likely to be between generations (consanguineal ties) than between spouses (conjugal ties). Women's most important ties are with their children, particularly their sons, on whom women depend for emotional support and security in old age (Potash 1989:199). Women, like men, also use kinship ties with their natal groups to gain access to land, gain support in marital disputes, and participate in ritual activities (Sacks 1982). In many parts of West Africa, however, women's power is expressed through political office (Kaplan 1997) and also formally organized secret societies, such as the Sande society of Sierra Leone (MacCormack 1974). Contemporary ethnography demonstrates that women's power and influence sometimes go beyond their economic contributions, their significant roles within households and families, and even beyond formal political offices sometimes occupied by women. An important dimension of female power may rest on female alliances and participation in networks and groups outside the household. These collectivities provide arenas for entertainment, prestige, influence, and self-esteem. Anthropologist Annette Weiner (1976), for example, demonstrated the important exchanges among women in the Trobriand Islands, where the emphasis on male kula exchanges had excluded any anthropological attention to women's participation in exchange networks.

The impact of European expansion on women in horticultural societies varied. Generally, women's role declined as indigenous economies shifted from subsistence horticulture to cash crops sold in the world market, as illustrated in Nukumanu, a Polynesian atoll. Before European contact, Nukumanu subsistence depended on the abundant marine life and a few indigenous plants, such as coconut, pandanus, and taro (a starchy root). Women's primary responsibilities were domestic, whereas men contributed food acquired at longer distances from the home through fishing, collecting shellfish, and collecting and husking coconuts. Men also made canoes and constructed new buildings, whereas women cooked food and collected and prepared leaves for thatch. Both women's and men's roles were highly valued in traditional Nukumanu society. Women exclusively controlled and cultivated swamp taro lands, which were inherited matrilineally. Matrilocality added to women's status, whereas men's power came from their economic contribution and their exclusive occupation of formal positions of power in the chiefly hierarchy.

With the advent of German colonial occupation in the 1880s, most of Nukumanu was turned over to the production of copra (dried coconut meat). Wage laborers were brought in from nearby islands, commercially marketed foods such as wheat flour and rice supplanted taro, and men's wages were needed to buy coffee, tea, and sugar (once luxury items). As a result, women's traditional sphere of influence and their status declined, while men's spheres of power expanded (Feinberg 1986). The traditional segregation of men's and women's activities also intensified. Kareve (a potent alcoholic beverage made from fermented coconut sap) was introduced in the 1950s, and men's economic activities, such as canoe building, took on a social aspect involving drinking. Because kareve production and consumption takes up much of men's leisure time and excludes women, sexual segregation increased.

As taro declined in importance, women's collective activities became more individualized, leaving them more isolated and dependent on their husbands and brothers than previously. Male–female tensions also increase partly as a result of kareve drinking, which many women vehemently oppose. The traditional tendency for men to travel off the island more than women also lowered women's status, and even today it is primarily men who go overseas for wage labor and higher education. More recently, however, more women are leaving the island to take advantage of opening educational and career opportunities, and the prestige, money, and social influence of such women may move Nukumanu back toward its tradition of sexual egalitarianism.

Gender Relations in Pastoral and Agricultural Societies

Pastoral and agricultural societies tend to be male dominated, although there is some variation. In pastoral societies, women's status depends on the degree to which the society combines herding with cultivation, its specific historical situation, and the diffusion of cultural ideas, such as Islam. Generally speaking, women's contribution to the food supply in pastoral societies is small (Martin and Voorhies 1975). Men do almost all the herding and most of the dairy work as well. Male dominance in pastoral society is partly based on the required strength to handle large animals, but females sometimes do handle smaller animals, engage in dairy work, carry water, and process animal by-products such as milk, wool, and hides (O'Kelly and Carney 1986). Pastoral societies generally do not have the rigid distinction between public and domestic roles of agricultural societies. Herder's camps typically are divided into male and female spaces, but both men and women work in public, somewhat blurring the private/public dichotomy.

In pastoral societies, men predominantly own and have control over the disposition of livestock, which is an important source of power and prestige. However, the disposition of herds is always subject to kinship rules and responsibilities, and animals may be jointly held by men and by women. Still, the male economic dominance in pastoral societies seems to give rise to general social and cultural male dominance, reinforced by patricentric kinship systems and the need for defense through warfare (Sanday 1981).

Again, this generalization is subject to variation. Among the Tuareg of the Central Sahara, for example, women generally have high prestige and substantial influence (Rasmussen 2005). The Tuareg, who are Muslims of Berber origin, herd camels, sheep, goats, and donkeys. As a matrilineal society, Tuareg women enjoy considerable rights and privileges. They do not veil their faces, they have social and economic independence and can own property, and they have freedom of movement. There is only minimal separation of women from men. Women are singers and musicians and organize many social events. They traditionally have enjoyed freedom of choice in sexual involvements, although this has been somewhat modified among those Tuareg who are more devout Muslims. The traditionally high status of Tuareg women, and matrilineality itself, is also undermined today by the migration of men to cities, where they work for wages, and the incorporation of the Tuareg into larger nation-states, with their patrilineal cultures. Cities, however, may also provide increasing opportunities and freedom for Tuareg women. Although the Tuareg appear to be an unusual exception to the generally patriarchal nature of pastoral—and Muslim—societies, they are an essential reminder that gender roles vary greatly, even within similar economic types of societies and within religious traditions.

With the transition to agriculture, the direct female contribution in food production generally drops drastically, though this varies. Agricultural work by women declines with the introduction of plow agriculture, but women have an important productive contribution in wet rice agriculture. Generally, agricultural societies are a good example of the principle that women lose status in society as the importance of their economic contribution declines. The decline of women's participation in agriculture is also generally accompanied by their increasing isolation in domestic work in the home and increasing numbers of children (Ember 1983). The transformation of agricultural production through machine technology reduces the overall labor force, and since most machinery is operated by men, this particularly affects women, who are disproportionately excluded from the productive process. The inequality between the sexes is also apparent in the lower wages paid to women as agricultural laborers and in the concentration of women in the labor-intensive aspects of agriculture such as weeding, transplanting, and harvesting. This situation is exacerbated as societies increasingly rely on cash economies and the marketplace. It is relatively easy for men to enter the cash economy, selling their crops or animals to buy goods and services. It is far more difficult for women, who thus become more dependent on men. For example, in Zinacantan, Mexico, men control cash crops and participate in the market. As a result, they now are able to purchase many of the goods and services that women used to contribute to the household. Zinacantec women are increasingly dependent on men, but men are less and less dependent on women (Flood 1994).

The lower status for women is often exacerbated by foreign aid and development programs that, while increasing production in the man's sphere of work, tend to be more restrictive on women. Economic development is intended to improve people's lives, but such projects often fail to take women's economic contributions into account. Frequently they increase gender inequality, worsening women's position in their societies (Moser 1993; Warren and Borque 1989). Some development projects have resulted in more prestige, income, and autonomy for women. These include projects promoting the global marketing of women's textiles and pottery in Mexico and Guatemala. However, in some cases this has led to greater tension and even violence between men and women (Nash 1993, 1994:15). As anthropologists increasingly point out, the impact of development projects on women is a result of the interplay of specific material and cultural conditions in a particular society (Lockwood 2005).

Gender Relations in the Global Economy

Women's status in modern, stratified societies varies greatly and is affected in various ways by economic development, political ideology, and globalization. Women have been highly involved in the global economy, primarily through the expansion of industrial production by multinational corporations in Latin America, Asia, and Africa. As rural lifestyles and agriculture are replaced by urban lifestyles and industrial production, women may benefit relative to men. For example, in Mata Chico, Peru, in the 1930s, access to land was critical, and the only way for women to get land was to marry. By the 1980s, Peru was increasingly urbanized, and many occupations were available to both men and women. Since women could support themselves and their children through employment in urban areas, they began to remain single longer and in some cases chose to not marry at all (Vincent 1998).

Although they may benefit financially from factory labor, these benefits often come at a high price. Women are exploited as cheap labor and work under sweatshop conditions in factories producing for the global market in Asia, on the U.S./Mexican border, and in many other places, as illustrated by anthropologist Pun Ngai's (2005) study of a microchip factory in China.

The young women workers Ngai studied are called *dagongmei.* They spend 15 hours per day on the job, resulting not only in boredom but also physical ailments, such as menstrual pain and anemia. Those who weld microchips suffer eyesight problems, whereas those who wash plates with acids are constantly at risk for chemical poisoning. The dagongmei sleep in dormitory-type accommodations, called *cagehouses,* which, along with other expenses such as overpriced consumer goods and medical care, are deducted from their already low wages.

Dagongmei work and live under very strict rules. They must wait their turn to go to the restroom, they are thoroughly searched before they can leave the factory premises, and security guards wielding electric batons guard their locked quarters at night. In China a residence permit is required to live in a particular city, but dagongmei are denied residential rights even if they have worked in the same city for more than 10 years. When unemployment hits, the dagongmei are targeted to be sent back to their rural villages. After years of urban living and participation in a consumer-oriented global lifestyle, dagongmei find it difficult to readapt to village life. Dagongmei receive little sympathy in China, especially from men who say they are taking away their jobs. And times are getting harder economically for dagongmei as well. China's increasing participation in the global economy has led to increasing urban migration, while at the same time privatization of factories has led to significant downsizing of the workforce.

Still, dagongmei see advantages in their work. It gives them a wider view of the world and permits some escape from the rigid patriarchal structure of the village. Some dagongmei, by pooling their earnings, have managed to open small factories themselves. Others have ambitions for a business career or for improving their education. Few of them succeed, but globalization has opened new doors for these new women workers, although its effect on gender equality is most often uncertain.

Even in societies in Europe, Japan, and the United States, nations that are much further along on the path of economic development, the status of women is by no means equal to that of men.

In the United States, for example, the view that women should be excluded from all but domestic and child-rearing roles has historically been culturally dominant and remains so among many Americans today (Norgren and Nanda 2006). Although it is true that women have made great strides in professions such as law, medicine, and academe, there is still much stereotyping and discrimination. More women than men may go to medical school, but they tend to take on less prestigious medical specializations after graduation. Even in academic anthropology, where women like Margaret Mead and Ruth Benedict are among our most influential and celebrated elders, women's rates of promotion to full professor lag behind the rates of men. The constraints on women's roles in civic participation, such as serving on jury duty and in public office, have been legally overthrown to a large extent, yet the numbers of women in Congress is decidedly small, and, as of this writing, there has yet to be a female president or vice president. Domestic violence and sexual harassment of women are other significant problems, again based on an American cultural pattern that values masculine aggression and control over women. But it is perhaps in the struggle for reproductive autonomy, in the right to choose whether or not to end a pregnancy, that cultural patterns defining women's roles as domestic and reproductive emerge most strongly. The American debate over abortion is really a cultural debate about the meaning of life, the nature of women, and the limits of gender equality (Ginsburg 1989). In the United States, as in all societies, gender stratification is a complex issue. It consists of social, economic, and political dimensions, it is embedded in culture, and it affects both men and women and the relationships between them.

BRINGING IT BACK HOME: FEMALE GENITAL OPERATIONS AND INTERNATIONAL HUMAN RIGHTS

Approximately 100 million females in the world today, mainly in Africa and the Middle East, undergo some form of female genital operations, the ritual cutting of a girl's genitals. These practices vary in intensity from a ritualized drawing of blood to infibulation, the removal of almost all of the genitals, stitching together of the wound, and leaving only a small opening for passing urine and menstrual flow. Where practiced, female genital operations are viewed as essential gender rites. They are intended to preserve a girl's virginity before marriage, to symbolize her role as a marriageable member of society, and to emphasize her moral and economic value to her patrilineage (Barnes and Boddy 1995; Walley 1997).

Scientific evidence demonstrates that female genital cutting substantially raises the likelihood of a woman's death in childbirth. The name of

© Welsh/Getty Images

During female initiation, elders impart important information to girls that allows them to participate as responsible adults in their society. Where female initiation involves circumcision, as among the Kikuyu of Kenya, elder women give girls the necessary emotional support to help them get through this very painful ritual.

the rites themselves is a subject of debate. Many anthropologists, feminists, and international health and children's organizations condemn the more extreme forms of female genital operations, which they call *genital mutilation,* as a violation of the human rights of women and children (Seddon 1993). Sometimes the rite is called *female circumcision,* a label that seems to make it parallel to male circumcision, when in fact female genital cutting is much more invasive and painful and has more frequent debilitating effects on health than does cutting the male foreskin.

Another point of view, held by both some anthropologists and some members of cultures that practice this ritual, urge that the practice not be condemned outright but rather examined carefully in its cultural context, both for greater understanding of its variety as well as the positive values it has in connection with marriage within particular societies (Gruenbaum 2001). Indeed, from the perspective of some women in some African societies, female genital cutting is an affirmation of the value of women in traditional society (Walley 1997). Today, many women from societies where female genital rituals are practiced are migrating to Europe and the United States, giving this once local cultural pattern a global dimension. Although some women have fled their countries for fear of being forced to undergo some form of genital cutting, others wish to preserve this practice in their new countries. As a result of the diffusion of female genital cutting, these practices now are outlawed by several European countries and by the United States.

Female genital operations reveal the difficulty of steering a just course between the demands of multiculturalism and cultural relativity, which emphasize respect or at least understanding of local cultural patterns in their cultural context, and the concept of universal rights, incorporated into the United National Universal Declaration of Human Rights, which specifically includes the protection of women against gender-specific violence.

Although some women from societies that practice female genital operations defend them as affirming a woman's value and enhancing traditional cultural cohesion, others from those cultures speak out against it (El Saadawi 1980). But even for many African women who oppose female circumcision, denunciation of the practice by outsiders is resented as yet another Eurocentric assault on African cultural integrity by former colonial powers. Some anthropologists also decry this as a form of cultural imperialism and, more importantly, as an obstacle to reforming the practice or finding more effective ways to eliminate it (Gruenbaum 2001).

YOU DECIDE

1. Should female circumcision be outlawed globally as a violation of women's and children's rights, even if it is a valued cultural tradition in many societies?
2. Because female circumcision is most often associated with religious belief, does outlawing the practice in the United States impermissibly violate our Constitution's freedom of religion clause?
3. What can anthropologists contribute to the debate over female genital operations and other debates that pit universal human rights, especially regarding women, against local cultural patterns? What does the example of female genital operations suggest about the possible limits of the anthropological principle of cultural relativism?

CHAPTER SUMMARY

1. An important anthropological principle is that gender is not biologically determined but is culturally constructed. This is demonstrated by the presence of alternative genders in different societies and by the culturally variable definitions of femininity and masculinity in different cultures.
2. *Sex* refers to biological differences between male and female; *gender* refers to the social classification of masculine and feminine and the roles that people assume.
3. Views about the nature of male and female sexuality are part of gender ideologies. Many cultures perceive women as sexually voracious, and attempts to control female sexuality are embedded in gender hierarchies. Sexuality, however, although rooted in biology, is patterned by culture.
4. Many societies have rites of passage for males and females, in which boys and girls are transformed into adult men and women. These rites have many social and psychological functions, such as the transmission of cultural knowledge, the public acceptance of the obligations of adulthood, and the reaffirmation of cultural values, including gender hierarchies.

5. A male-dominated gender stratification system is one in which men are dominant, reap most of the social and material rewards of society, and control the autonomy of women. Gender stratification systems differ in foraging, horticultural, agricultural, and industrial societies. These have changed through the impact of European colonialism on non-European societies and as a result of contemporary globalization.

KEY TERMS

Cultural construction of gender
Gender
Gender ideology
Gender role
Gender stratification
Hijra
Manhood puzzle
Matriarchy
Patriarchy
Private/public dichotomy
Rite of passage
Sex

In Ghana, the Asante kingdom persisted through the period of British colonialism and continues today. Here, the paramount chiefs surround the sixth Ashanti king (Asantehene) of his dynasty, Osei Tutu II, for his enthronement ceremonies in Kumasi.

CHAPTER 9

POLITICAL ORGANIZATION

CHAPTER OUTLINE

Wealth and Power in the Asante State

Political Organization

- Power and Authority
- The Political Process
- Political Organization and Social Complexity

Social Control and Conflict Management

Types of Political Organization

- Band Societies
- Tribal Societies
- Chiefdoms
- State Societies

Bringing It Back Home: Do Good Fences Make Good Neighbors?

- You Decide

WEALTH AND POWER IN THE ASANTE STATE

POLITICAL organization in all societies is buttressed by a set of cultural values that give meaning to the distribution of power. In complex state societies, this cultural justification often has to do with sustaining the position of wealthy elites. When Charles Wilson, head of General Motors in 1955, told a U.S. Senate Committee investigating corporate profits that "What's good for the country is good for General Motors and vice versa," he was invoking an American cultural value that the nation and corporations mutually benefit through the accumulation of wealth in the hands of a business elite.

This cultural value is also central in the West African state of Asante, where political power was closely linked to the individual accumulation of wealth. The Asante state, which emerged out of the military conquest of surrounding tribes in 1701, rested on a highly productive economy of intensive cultivation, accessible deposits of gold, and the slave trade with Europe.

Asante social stratification consisted of slaves, peasants, urban specialists, government officials, and, at the top, with the ultimate power, the Asantehene and his royal family. Social stratification was based on individual competition, achievement, and the accumulation of wealth, all of which were directly or indirectly controlled by the king. The state appointed office holders and military leaders and loaned them money, thus putting them in debt to the king. If they invested well and became wealthy they were publicly acknowledged as contributors to the glory of the state, through their participation in public rituals, their right to use certain official titles, or their right to display certain ritual insignia. Access to all of these symbolic expressions of power and wealth was controlled by the king. Wealthy people, who went bankrupt, on the other hand, were held responsible for undermining the public good and were denied these symbols of power.

In the Asante state, free and slave agricultural labor was organized and managed by the state in order to support the urban elites and the government bureaucrats. These in turn supported the king, who was the source of their wealth. The state justified its control over the redistribution of wealth, especially gold, by actively promoting the cultural value that the wealthy deserved to hold power and that this benefited the whole society.

The state enhanced its own wealth through its discretionary use of both law and custom. First, it accepted only gold for payment of fines and taxes. Those who couldn't pay had to give land and laborers to the state. Fines and taxes were then used to give financial rewards to powerful political officeholders. The state also enriched itself by permitting an individual

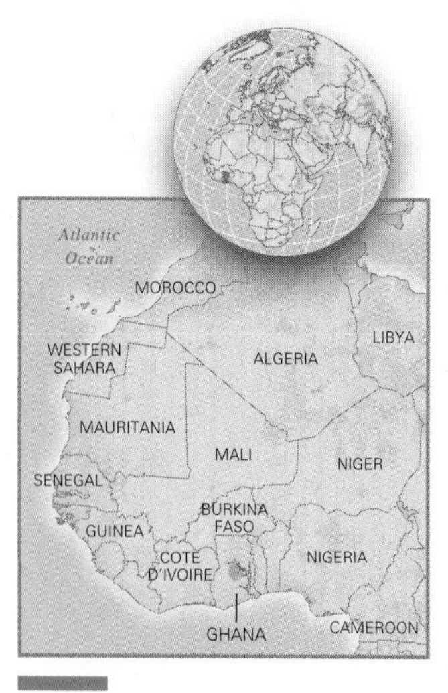

The Ashanti of Ghana.

to buy himself out of a death sentence with a payment of gold to the state. The Asante also had an "estate tax" through which the state took part of an individual's land upon his death. This not only enriched the wealth of the state but also prevented an hereditary nobility from emerging as a threat to the king's power. Thus did the Asante state create and use power to maintain its political authority and its concentration of wealth, demonstrating that the accumulation of wealth and political authority rightfully went hand in hand.

This description of the Asante state illuminates the concept of political organization. It demonstrates how the distribution and use of power interacts with other aspects of society and the role of culture in maintaining and contesting the political status quo.

POLITICAL ORGANIZATION

Political organization is about power. The Asante state is just one example of how power is used in one society to address a universal problem of human societies: how to maintain themselves over time with a minimum of social disorder and social discontent. This means that every society must make and implement decisions affecting the whole society; provide a means of managing conflicts, dissent, and deviance; and generally regulate behavior so that it is consistent with social order. **Political organization** refers to the ways in which power is used in all societies so that they can maintain themselves collectively over time. Like other responses to universal human problems, societies do this in many different ways, and this diversity is a primary interest of anthropology.

Power and Authority

Any discussion of political organization must focus on power: what it is, who has it, how it is used, and how it is related to other cultural patterns and social institutions in a society. **Power** is the ability to exercise one's will over others, that is, to cause individuals or groups to take actions that, of their own accord, they might otherwise not take. The source of power is ultimately based on the control of resources that people need or desire.

Power is not the same as authority. **Authority** can be defined as the socially approved use of power. It is based on personal characteristics such as honor, status, knowledge, ability, respect, and/or the holding of formal public office. For example, political leaders may have authority based on their occupation of public office, but they may also wield power through their control of resources and/or control over the use of force or knowledge. Power can exist without authority: An armed robber certainly has power but is denied authority.

The shared values and beliefs that legitimize the distribution and uses of power and authority in a particular society are called its **political ideology.** A political ideology may be widely shared throughout a society, although it may not be held by everyone. The sources of power may be coercive (based on force or the threat of force), consensual, or, more likely, both. One difference among types of political organization is the degree to which they rely on coercion or consensus to achieve social order.

The Political Process

Political process refers to how groups and individuals use power and authority to achieve various public goals. Public goals, such as exploiting particular water sources for cattle, building a road, or increasing a society's goods through trade, may benefit the larger society, or they may benefit only smaller groups or a small number of individuals. Decisions and activities by groups and individuals may be motivated by material profit, prestige, altruism, survival, or any combination of motives, usually justified, however, by reference to the public good. This is illustrated in the description of Asante society and also in the comments of Charles Wilson, former head of General Motors.

Formal political institutions and informal systems of alliance are both sources of power and authority. Among the Hopi, for example, as in other matrilineal societies (p. 161), women's power is interwoven with their formal roles in the kinship, ceremonial, and economic systems. In many West African societies, women as well as men exercised power through their membership in formal associations. Among the Yoruba of Nigeria, certain offices were reserved to represent women's interests (Matory 1994), whereas among the Mende of Sierra Leone, women could be paramount chiefs. Like men, women belonged to secret societies called Sande, which wielded a great deal of power (Hoffer 1974).

The study of political process emphasizes how power changes hands and how new kinds of political organization and ideologies develop. Different kinds of power and authority can be used to stabilize a social order, avoid or resolve conflicts, and promote the general welfare, but they can also contest prevailing political ideologies and change or even destroy existing political systems. Groups, or **factions,** informal alliances within a group or society, as well as governments use diverse means to gain their ends. These may include violence and terror as well as behind-the-scenes manipulation, peaceful protest, the ballot box, and political lobbying.

Political processes are the ways in which different, often conflicting groups in society mobilize to achieve their goals. This peaceful protest is directed against the American invasion of Iraq.

Two important political processes involving conflict are **rebellion,** which is the attempt of one group to reallocate power and resources within an existing political structure, and **revolution,** which is an attempt to overthrow the existing political structure and put another type of political structure in its place. The 2005 riots of African and Arabs in France are referred to as a rebellion; their participants were not seeking to overthrow the French society but to gain a larger presence in it. Rebellion and revolution are sometimes related. The American Revolution, for example, started out as a rebellion but became a revolution.

Political Organization and Social Complexity

Societies vary in their systems of political organization. One useful way to look at this diversity is to examine a society's **social complexity.** Social complexity refers to the degree to which political roles, institutions, and processes are centralized and differentiated from or embedded within other social institutions. In smaller-scale nonindustrial societies typically studied by anthropologists (bands, tribes, and chiefdoms), the uses of power and authority, the decision making, and the coordination and regulation of human behavior are more highly integrated than in contemporary societies. In these societies, power and authority do not operate independently but are embedded in other social institutions such as kinship, economics, and religion. In many of these societies, for example, **leadership,** the ability to direct an enterprise, may be a function of political office (authority), but it may also be based on an individual's position as the head of a family, lineage, or clan; on supernatural connections and interventions; or on economic roles in the distribution of goods.

In the mid-20th century, anthropologist Elman Service (1962) developed a typology of social complexity that identified four main types of societies: bands, tribes, chiefdoms, and states. Each of these was associated with a characteristic way in which people make a living, a dominant principle of economic exchange (see Chapter 6), characteristic forms of leadership and social control, and different systems of social differentiation. **Social differentiation** refers to the relative access individuals and groups have to basic material resources, wealth, power, and prestige. Anthropologists have defined three ideal types of social differentiation: egalitarian societies, rank societies, and stratified societies. Although individuals in every society are not equally talented, attractive, or skilled, some societies do not formally recognize these inequalities, and these distinctions do not affect access to important resources.

In **egalitarian societies,** individual (as well as age and gender distinctions) are recognized, but no individual or group is barred from access to material resources or has power over others. There are no rules of inheritance by which some individuals accumulate material goods or prestige passed down over generations. Unlike egalitarian societies, **rank societies** recognize formal differences among individuals and groups in prestige and symbolic resources, and these may be passed on through inheritance. However, there are no important restrictions on access to basic resources, and all individuals can obtain the material necessities for survival through their membership in kinship groups.

In **stratified societies** there are formal and permanent social and economic inequalities. Wealth, prestige, and office frequently are passed down over generations, establishing relatively permanent elites. **Elites** are those who have differential access to all culturally valued resources, whether power, wealth, or prestige, and they possessively protect their control over these resources. In stratified societies, some individuals and groups are also systemically denied access to the basic material resources needed to survive. Thus, stratified societies are characterized by permanent and wide differences among groups and individuals in their standard of living, security, prestige, political power, and opportunity to fulfill one's potential. The Asante state is an example of a stratified society.

In reference to the previous typology, generally speaking **bands** are foragers, usually egalitarian, who exchange goods through generalized reciprocity. There is little social differentiation, and their political institutions are embedded in other aspects of society, such as kinship and religion. **Tribes** are horticulturalists or herders, generally egalitarian, who have balanced reciprocity as their major means of exchange. The political organization of tribes is closely intertwined with other social institutions. Thus, power and authority are mainly rooted in religious or kinship roles, but there are also some social roles that are specifically political.

Chiefdoms are rank societies characterized by the political office of the chief. Redistribution, mainly through the chief, is the central mechanism of exchange, and there are important differences in wealth and status among society's members. Chiefdoms are generally found among productive horticulturalists and herders.

State societies usually are based on agriculture, industry, or, in the contemporary world, a postindustrial service economy. States are dominated by market exchange and have a high degree of social stratification. In state societies, many institutions have strictly political functions, which are differentiated from other aspects of society. Among them are government agencies, courts, and political parties.

Although political organization, social differentiation, and social complexity can be analyzed separately, in reality they intersect with each other in significant ways. In addition, history, geography, and culture must also be taken into account. For example, the Asante state shares similarities with other state societies but also exhibits its own particular cultural and social features (discussed later).

Although many critics reject the evolutionary implications of this typology (the idea that societies develop from simpler bands to more complex states), we present it here as a preliminary way of grasping some of the many details of the varieties of political organization.

SOCIAL CONTROL AND CONFLICT MANAGEMENT

Conflict is present in all societies and all must have ways of managing it and persuading individuals to conform to (at least most of) society's norms. A major basis for conformity in most societies, particularly those organized through kinship and face-to-face social relations, is the internalization of norms and values. This process begins in childhood, but it is lifelong. In complex, socially stratified state societies, behavior is also regulated by the internalization of norms, but added to this is the control of the state over many social institutions and regulatory processes, particularly including the mobilization of force. **Deviants,** or those who transgress society's rules, are handled differently in different types of societies.

Informal mechanisms of social control, such as gossip, ridicule, and avoidance, are effective because most people value the esteem of (at least some) others. These informal mechanisms work mainly in face-to-face or small societies or communities, but they also effectively operate in informal groups within complex societies such as housing developments, the workplace, or local voluntary associations (Merry 1981). Fear of witchcraft accusations or other supernatural interventions are other effective social control mechanisms (Evans-Pritchard 1958; Lemert 1997; Seitlyn 1993) that often are directed at people who stand above the group, are malicious, have a nasty temper, or refuse to share according to group norms. Avoidance is another informal way of dealing with social deviants. In small-scale societies, where most activities are cooperative, a person shunned by others is at a great disadvantage, both psychologically and economically. In complex societies, avoidance is effective in smaller groups within larger institutions, such as the workplace in an industrial society, or in certain small subcultures, such as the Amish in the United States.

When social control is implemented through the systematic application of force by a constituted authority in society, we use the term **law** (Moore 1978:220). Sometimes law enters the picture when a social norm is so important that its violation authorizes the community, or some part of it, to punish an offender, resolve a conflict, or redress a wrong. In other cases, laws are the result of both individual and collective interest as well as political maneuvering. In every society, some offenses are considered so disruptive that force or the threat of force is applied. In this sense, law is universal, although in small-scale societies it is most often embedded in other social institutions, such as the kinship system, and most often directed at maintaining existing social relationships. In more complex societies, law's functions belong to separate legal institutions, such as a constituted police force, courts, and prisons, and may be more adversarial, resulting in "winners and losers" rather than repairing damaged social relationships.

TYPES OF POLITICAL ORGANIZATION

Band Societies

A band is a small group of people (usually 20–50) belonging to extended families who live together and are loosely associated with the territory in which they make a living. Foragers are primarily organized into bands and mainly use generalized or balanced reciprocity as mechanisms of exchange (Chapter 6). Band societies have minimal role specialization and few differences of wealth, prestige, or power. Bands are fairly independent of one another, with few higher levels of social integration or centralized mechanisms of leadership. Bands tend to be exogamous, with ties between them established mainly by marriage. Bilateral kinship systems link individuals to many different bands through ties of blood and marriage. Trading relations also link individuals to other band members. Membership in bands is flexible, and people may change their residence from one band to another fairly easily. The flexibility of band organization is particularly adaptive for a foraging way of life and low population density.

Band societies have no formal leadership; decision making is by consensus. Leaders in foraging bands usually are older men and women whose experience, knowledge of group traditions, special skills or success in foraging, and generosity are a source of prestige. Leaders cannot enforce their decisions; they can only persuade. They attract others to their leadership on the basis of past performance. Thus, among some Inuit, the local leader is called "The One to Whom All Listen," "He Who Thinks," or "He Who Knows Everything Best."

Social order in band societies is primarily maintained informally through gossip, ridicule, avoidance, or, in some cases, as among the Inuit, supernatural interventions and sanctions, such as public confession directed by a shaman (Balikci 1970). This practice leads to an interesting example of culture clash. When Inuit people go before American courts, they may behave according to Inuit social norms, freely admitting their guilt. But this is contrary to what is required (and what lawyers advise their clients) in the adversarial legal system of the United States. In Inuit bands, disputes are sometimes resolved through public contests that involve physical action, such as head butting or boxing, or verbal contests, such as song duels, where the weapons are words—"little, sharp words like the wooden splinters which I hack off with my ax" (Hoebel 1974:93).

Band societies *do* contain individual violence, such as the frequent fights over women among the Ju'hoansi hunters of the Kalahari Desert in Africa, but because of the low level of technology, lack of formal leadership, and other ecological factors, warfare is largely absent in band societies. Bands have no formal organization for **war,** no position of warrior, little or no production for war, and no cultural or social support for sustained armed conflict (Lee 2003). When conflict gets too disruptive, bands may break up into smaller units as a way of separating people in extended conflict with one another, thus preventing prolonged hostilities (Turnbull 1968).

Tribal Societies

A tribe is a culturally distinct population whose members think of themselves as descended from the same ancestor or as part of the same "people." Tribes are found primarily among pastoralists and horticulturalists. Their characteristic economic institutions are reciprocity and redistribution, although, as part of larger states, they may participate in market systems as well. Like bands, tribes are basically egalitarian, with no important differences among members in wealth, status, and power. Also like bands, most tribes do not have distinct or centralized political institutions or roles. Power and social control are embedded in other institutions, such as kinship or religion.

Tribes usually are organized into unilineal kin groups (see p. 158), which are the "owners" of basic economic resources and the units of political activity. The emergence of local kin groups larger than the nuclear family is consistent with the larger populations of horticultural and pastoral societies compared to foraging band societies.

The effective political unit in tribal societies is a shifting one. Most of the time, the local units of a tribe operate independently. In some societies, the local units may be in a state of ongoing violent conflict among themselves. A higher-level unity among tribal segments most often occurs in response to the threat of attack from another society or the opportunity to attack another society.

Among the Nuer of East Africa, lineages at different levels (from minimal to maximal) will join each other to attack a common enemy (see p. 159; Evans-Pritchard 1940/1968). This coalescing of lineages directs the energies of the society upward, away from competition between close kin, to an outside enemy. Lineage segments on the borders of other tribes know that if they attack an enemy, they will be helped by other lineages related to them at these higher levels of organization. This kind of tribal integration works particularly well when stronger tribes want to expand into nearby territories held by weaker tribes (see Figure 9.1).

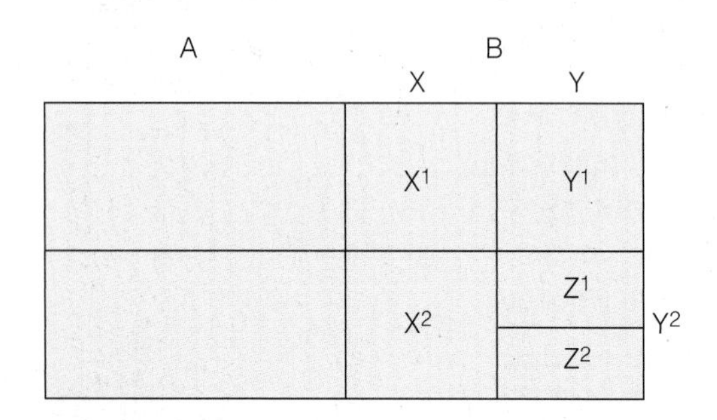

Figure 9.1

The organization of the Nuer and other tribes with segmentary lineage systems. The tribe is divided into two groups, A and B. These are further divided into subgroups. Here, Z^1 and Z^2 are subgroups of Y^2. Groups Y^1 and Y^2 are subgroups of Y, and Y is a subgroup of B. This organization helps both to contain and to expand conflict. A conflict between individuals that belong to the same larger group, Z^1 and Z^2 for example, is contained within that larger group, Y^2. A conflict between individuals or families that are members of different larger groups quickly expands to include all members of those groups. For example, should a member of Y^2 quarrel with a member of X^2, all members of Y and X will be involved (Evans-Pritchard 1940/1968).

Other types of groups help integrate tribal societies beyond simple kinship affiliation. Two of these are age sets and age grades. An **age set** is a named group of people of similar age and sex who move through some or all of life's stages together. Age sets are mainly male and have political and military functions. Because their members come from different kinship groups, they are an important basis for wider social integration throughout the society. In a society with **age grades,** individuals, again, usually males, follow a well-ordered progression through a series of statuses, such as childhood, warrior, adult, and seniors. Among the Maasai of Kenya and Tanzania, age grades are an important integrating mechanism. After childhood, boys are initiated into the warrior stage, which lasts about 15 years. It is a time of training in social, political, and military skills, traditionally geared toward warfare and cattle raiding. The warriors then ceremonially graduate to a less active status, during which they can marry and ultimately retire into the age grade of elderhood. The solidarity, shared identity, sense of unity, and cooperation of Maasai age grades, reinforced by periodic gatherings and great ceremonies, lend political coherence to a people who live dispersed from one another and have no centralized government (Galaty 1986). This central cultural feature in Maasai society may be in decline, however, as young men now seem to prefer going to school over becoming warriors.

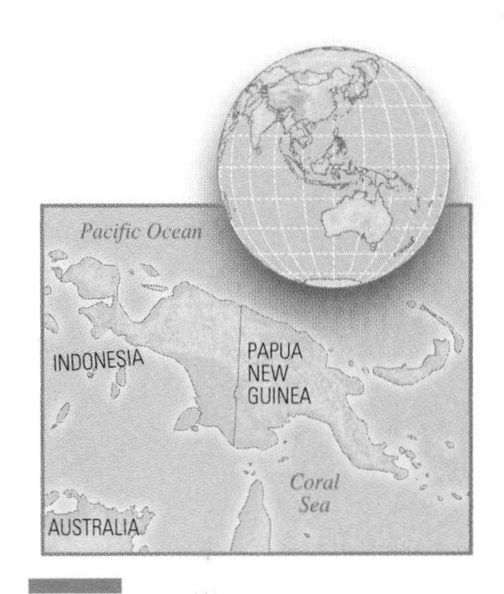

New Guinea

Other kinds of associations, such as military societies among some Plains Indian tribes in North America and **secret societies,** such as the Poro society for males and the Sande society for females, found in West Africa, also help integrate tribal societies (Sahlins 1961).

Tribal societies have leaders but no centralized government and few positions of authority. In Melanesia and New Guinea, a characteristic form of leadership is the **bigman**—a self-made leader who gains power and authority through personal achievements rather than through holding office. A bigman starts out as the leader of a small, localized kin group. He builds up his capital, mainly in the form of pigs, and attracts followers through generous loans, sponsoring feasts, purchasing high ranks in secret societies, helping his military allies, paying bridewealth for young men seeking wives, and other initiatives. These actions increase his reputation and put other people under obligation to him, thus further extending his alliances and influence.

The bigman is an informal leader in many Melanesian cultures. Much of his influence is based on his ability to distribute resources, of which pigs are the most important.

Although the bigman is a form of tribal leadership above the local level, it is a fragile mechanism of tribal integration. It does not involve the creation of a permanent office but rather depends on the personality and constant striving of an individual (somewhat like the most popular boy or girl in an American high school). Bigmen rise and fall; with their deaths, their support disperses. One of the reasons why bigmen are vulnerable is that they must spur their local group on to ever greater production if they are to hold their own against other bigmen in the tribe. To maintain prestige, a bigman must give his competitors more than they can give him. Excessive giving to competitors means the bigman must begin to withhold gifts to his followers. The resulting discontent may lead to defection among his followers or even murder of the bigman. Being a bigman is not like holding political office: The status cannot be inherited. Each individual who aspires to be a bigman must begin anew to amass the wealth and forge the internal and external social relationships on which bigman status depends (Sahlins 1971).

Tribes have a variety of (mainly) informal and some formal mechanisms for controlling deviant behavior and settling conflicts. **Compensation**—a payment demanded by an aggrieved party to compensate for damage—is found in New Guinea, among other places. Compensation is based on the severity of the act that precipitated the dispute, and the individual's kin group shares in the payment. Payment of compensation generally implies acceptance of responsibility by the donors and willingness to terminate the dispute by the recipients (Scaglion 1981). When payments become too inflated, however, rather than resolving conflicts, they become the basis for further disputes (Ottley and Zorn 1983).

Mediation, a common form of tribal conflict management, is particularly effective between parties with ongoing social relationships. Mediation aims to resolve disputes so that the prior social relationship between the disputants is maintained and harmony is restored to the social order. Mediation involves a third party, either a go-between or even the whole community, in resolving conflict between the disputants.

Through the work of anthropologist James Gibbs, the moot courts of the Kpelle of West Africa are widely known. In these courts, the whole community participates in the dispute process, asking questions of the disputants and witnesses. A specially appointed mediator controls the proceedings and, after everyone has been heard, proposes a solution to the conflict that expresses the consensus of the disputing parties and the audience. The party at fault apologizes to the other party, and a ritual distribution of food and drink unites the group, as the mediator stresses the importance of the restoration of community harmony (Gibbs 1988).

Anthropological studies of mediation and other alternative forms of conflict resolution have become widely known in the United States today. Because these methods of addressing conflict are less costly, are less time consuming, and result in better postconflict relationships than American adversarial court procedures, they have been applied to a wide range of disputes where disputants are in long-term relationships, such as between neighbors, between work mates, and within families (Fry and Bjorkqvist 1997).

Warfare in Tribal Societies

Despite the wide variety of nonviolent methods of conflict resolution, tribal societies seem prone to a high degree of warfare, a fact for which anthropologists have suggested various explanations. In the absence of strong mechanisms for tribal integration through peaceful means and the absence of strong motivations to produce food beyond immediate needs, warfare may regulate the balance between population and resources in tribal societies. With slash and burn horticulture, for example, it is much harder to clear forest for cultivation than to work land that has already been used. Thus, a local group may prefer to take land from other groups, by force if necessary, rather than expand into virgin forest.

Warfare is also a way for societies to expand when they are experiencing a population increase or have reached the limits of expansion into unoccupied land (Vayda 1976). Tribal warfare can also be linked to social structure. Patrilineality and patrilocality promote male solidarity, which enables the use of force in resolving local conflicts. In contrast, matrilineal, matrilocal societies emphasize the solidarity of women, who remain in the village of their birth. This solidarity enables men to engage in warfare carried out over long distances, as occurred among the Iroquois (Ember and Ember 1971). Although anthropologists may not agree about the specific causes of warfare, there is a general consensus that warfare is grounded in historical, material, cultural, social, and ecological conditions and not in any biologically based human instinct for aggression.

One tribal society that experiences both warfare and a high level of personal violence is the Yanomamo of the Amazon areas of Venezuela and Brazil. Anthropologist Napoleon Chagnon (1997) argues that violence by men against women, violence among men in the same village, and warfare between villages are central to Yanomamo culture. Chagnon explains ongoing Yanomamo warfare and their military ideology as a way of preserving village autonomy. The high degree of violent conflict between men within villages leads to the division of villages into hostile camps. In order to survive as an independent unit in an environment of constant warfare, a village adopts a hostile and aggressive stance toward other villages, perpetuating intervillage warfare in an endless cycle.

However, the explanation for the high degree of Yanomamo violence described by Chagnon has been challenged by other anthropologists. William Divale and Marvin Harris (1976) argue that tribal warfare in horticultural societies like the Yanomamo regulates population—not by causing deaths in battles but indirectly through female infanticide. In societies with constant warfare, there is a cultural preference for fierce and aggressive males who can become warriors. Because male children are preferred over females, female infants are often killed. The shortage of women that results from female infanticide among the Yanomamo provides a strong conscious motivation for warfare—when asked, the Yanomamo say they fight for women, not for land—and a continuing "reason" to keep fighting among themselves. In a Yanomamo raid on another village, as many women as possible are captured.

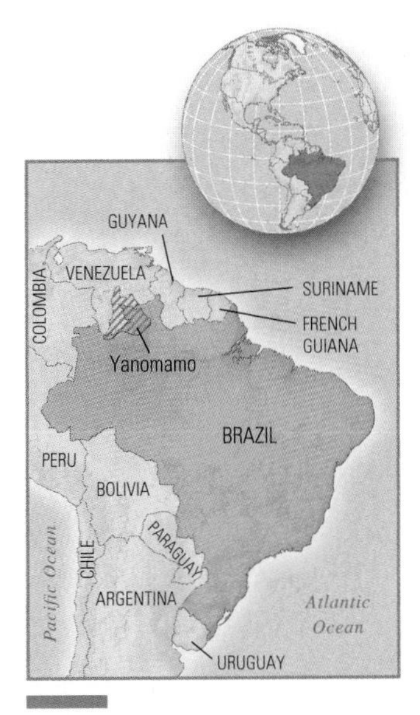

The Yanomamo.

Yanomamo warfare may also be the result of European contact. According to Brian Ferguson (1992), the buildup of the extreme Yanomamo violence documented by Napoleon Chagnon in the 1960s was precipitated in the 1940s as a result of severe depopulation due to European disease epidemics, fatal malnutrition, and intensified competition over European goods. The high death rate led to disruption of Yanomamo family life, and negotiating marriages became particularly difficult due to the deaths of adult males. In addition, the Yanomamo desire for European manufactured goods—particularly metal machetes, axes, and knives, which are very useful for horticulturalists—increased competition among Yanomamo males, and the introduction of firearms substantially increased the number of fatalities in warfare. Whereas previously such goods were traded into even remote Yanomamo villages, by the 1960s the desire to acquire these goods led to the increasing settlement of Yanomamo around European outposts such as missionary stations. This led to the depletion of game, a highly desired food for Yanomamo cultivators who were also hunters. With the depletion of game, cultural norms of reciprocity broke down, meat was less likely to be shared, and conflict within villages increased. This, in turn, led to enmity between villages. The increasing intervillage warfare reinforced the low status of Yanomamo women and helped further male violence against them, perpetuating the cycle of female infanticide, shortage of women, and raids for women, described by Divale and Harris and by Chagnon. Thus, historical factors complement other explanations of Yanomamo "fierceness" and raise the question about how fierce the Yanomamo actually are.

Chiefdoms

Although there is a great diversity among chiefdoms (Earle 1987), a chiefdom can be defined as "an autonomous political unit comprising a number of villages or communities under the permanent control of a paramount chief" (Carneiro 1981:45). Two main characteristics distinguish chiefdoms from tribes. First, unlike a tribe, in which all social segments are structurally and functionally similar, chiefdoms are made up of social parts that are structurally and functionally different from one another. Chiefdoms have been called the first step in integrating villages as units within a multicommunity political organization (Carneiro 1981).

The second distinguishing characteristic of chiefdoms is centralized leadership. Chiefdoms vary greatly in their social complexity (Peoples 1990). Some have monumental architecture, distinct ceremonial centers, elaborate systems of social stratification, and large settlements that functioned as administrative centers, surrounded by smaller villages. Each geographical unit within a chiefdom may have its own chief or council.

Chiefdoms, like tribes, are organized through kinship ties. However, whereas tribes tend to be **acephalous,** that is, they do not have a centralized government, chiefdoms, in contrast, have centralized leadership vested in the political office of the chief. Chiefs are born to that office and often are sustained in it by religious authority. Chiefdoms keep lengthy genealogical records of the names and acts of specific chiefs, which are used to verify claims to rank and chiefly title.

Rank societies normally are based on highly productive horticulture or pastoralism (or occasionally, as among the Kwakiutl and other foraging groups on the Northwest Coast of North America, on an abundance of wild food, such as salmon), which permits sufficient accumulation of food so that a surplus can be appropriated by chiefs and redistributed throughout the society. Redistribution is the characteristic mode of exchange in rank societies, although balanced reciprocity is also important.

Anthropologists generally argue that the rise of a centralized governing center (that is, a chief with political authority) is related to redistributive exchange. In redistribution, goods move into the center (the chief) and are redistributed in feasts and rituals. Ideally, the economic surplus appropriated by a chief is dispersed throughout the whole society and is a primary support of the chief's power and prestige, although chiefs may also control their communities by coercion or despotism (Earle 1987). In addition to redistributing food, the chief also deploys labor, making for a higher level of economic productivity. Internal violence within chiefdoms is lower than in tribes because the chief has authority to make judgments, punish deviant individuals, and resolve disputes.

Some of the most complex chiefdoms were found in Polynesia. In Tahiti, society was divided into the Ariki, who were the immediate families of the chiefs of the most important lineages in the larger districts; the Raatira, who were the heads of less important lineages and their families; and the Manahune, which included the remainder of the population. Social rank in Tahiti had economic, political, and religious aspects. Mana, a spiritual power, was possessed by all people, but in different degrees depending on rank (see Chapter 12, p. 270). The Ariki had the most mana because they were closest to the ancestral gods from which mana comes. An elaborate body of taboos separated those with more mana from those with less and also regulated social relations among the three ranks. Higher-ranked people could not eat with those of lower rank. Men had a higher rank than women and children and could not eat with them. The highest-ranking Ariki was so sacred that anything he touched became poison for those below him. In some Polynesian islands, the highest chief was kept completely away from other people and even used a special vocabulary that no one else was allowed to use.

In the Trobriand Islands the power of a chief to punish people is achieved partly by hiring sorcerers to kill the offender by magic. Trobriand subsistence depends on the success of gardening, and the principal power of the Trobriand chief lies in his control of garden magic. As garden magician, he not only organizes the efforts of the villagers under his control but also performs the rituals considered necessary for success at every step in the gardening process: preparing the fields, planting, and harvesting. The ultimate power of the Trobriand chief is his magical control of rain. It is believed that he can produce a prolonged drought, which will cause many people to starve. This power is used when the chief is angry as a means of collective punishment and enforcement of his will (Malinowski 1935).

Although a chief's authority is backed by his control of symbolic, supernatural, administrative, economic, and military power, violent competition for the office of chief sometimes occurs. Chiefdoms may be rendered unstable if the burdens the chief imposes on the people greatly exceed the services they receive from him. Chiefs generally suppress any attempt at rebellion or threats from competitors and deal harshly with those who try to take their power. To emphasize the importance of this office for the society, offenses against a chief are often punished by death.

State Societies

A **state** is a hierarchical (socially stratified), centralized form of political organization in which a central government has a legal monopoly over the use of force. Generally speaking, state societies are based on agriculture and industrialism, but there is also much diversity. The Asante state, you recall, was based on income from gold mining and the slave trade as well as cultivation.

Unlike chiefdoms, where ranking is based on kinship, in state societies **citizenship** rather than kinship regulates social relations between the different social strata and defines a person's rights and duties. Groups based on territory become central, and individuals belong to states by virtue of being born in a specific locale (or of parents from that locale). Because of this, the state has an ability to expand without splitting, by incorporating a variety of political units, classes, and ethnic groups. Thus, states can become much more populous, heterogeneous, and powerful than any other kind of political organization.

States are characterized by **government:** an interrelated set of status roles that become separate from other aspects of social organization, such as kinship. Central to the functioning of governments is a **bureaucracy,** an administrative hierarchy characterized by specialization of function and fixed rules. We've all run into those! And although most of us complain mightily about them when our car is towed or at income tax time, bureaucracy is the backbone of government in state societies.

The administrative divisions of a state are territorial units, cities, districts, and so on. Each unit has its own government specifically concerned with making and enforcing public policy, although these governments are not independent of the central government.

States engage in many functions that keep societies going. For example, the state intervenes in many aspects of the economic process. Through taxation, it redistributes wealth and can stimulate or discourage various sorts of production. It can order people to work on roads and buildings and to serve in armies, thus affecting the workforce available for other occupations. The state also intervenes in the exchange and distribution of goods and services. It protects the distribution of goods by making travel safe for traders as they move from one place to another and by keeping peace in the marketplace. The many economic, coordinating, and controlling functions of states, in peace and war, require extensive record keeping, giving rise to writing and systems of weights and measures. In some states, cities arose as administrative, religious, and economic centers. These centers then stimulated important cultural achievements in science, art, architecture, and philosophy.

Nation-states intensify national identities by presenting history in emotionally intense ways, such as this sculpture of United States Marines raising the flag at the Battle of Iwo Jima in World War II.

A key characteristic of state societies is the government's monopoly over the use of force. Most modern states use a code of law to make clear how and when force will be used and to forbid individuals or groups to use force except under its authorization. Laws (usually written) are passed by authorized legislative bodies and enforced by formal and specialized institutions. Courts and police forces, for example, have the authority to impose all kinds of punishments on deviants: fines, confiscation of property, imprisonment, and even death. In practice, in authoritarian states, the ruler may "become the law," implementing and enforcing those laws that suit his or her own purposes. States frequently are involved in warfare, and this can increase both their power and the degree to which they are centralized. During war, states may attempt to regulate daily life and internal conflict. They may take control over information and channels of communication. This strengthens not only the war effort but also the power of the state.

The origin of the state, one of humankind's most significant cultural achievements, cannot be explained

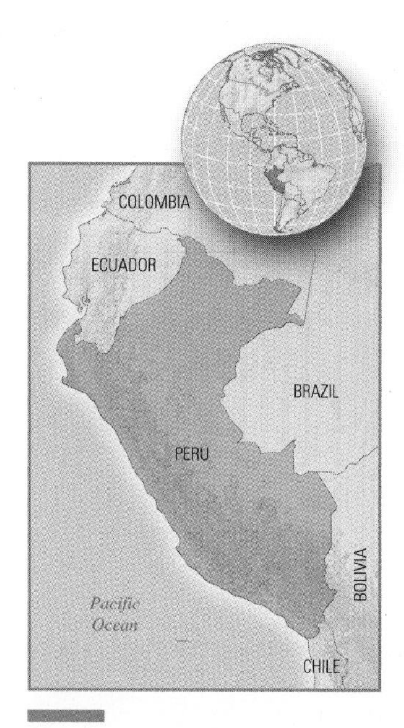

Peru.

by any one theory of cause and effect. States have evolved in different ways in different historical and ecological circumstances. Pre-state societies in various situations respond to selective pressures by changing some of their internal structures, by subduing a competing group, or by establishing themselves as dominant in a region. This initial shift sets off a chain reaction that may lead to state formation.

In pre-Columbian Peru, for example, anthropologist Robert Carneiro (1970) emphasizes the importance of ecological factors in the emergence of the Inca Empire. In this area, independent, dispersed farming villages were confined to narrow valleys bounded by the sea, the desert, or the mountains. As the population grew, villages split and populations dispersed until all the available land was used up. At this point, more intensive methods of agriculture were applied to land already being farmed, and previously unusable land was brought under cultivation by terracing and irrigation. As the population continued to increase, pressure for land intensified, resulting in war. Because of the constraints of the environment, villages that lost wars had nowhere to go. In order to remain on their land, they had to accept a politically subordinate role. As more villages were defeated, the political organization of the area became more complex and chiefdoms developed. The warring units were now larger, and as conquest of larger areas continued, centralization of authority increased. Finally, the entire area was brought under the control of one chief. The next step was the conquest of weaker valley chiefdoms by stronger ones until powerful empires emerged, most notably that of the Inca.

The State and Social Stratification

The productivity of intensive cultivation enables a state's government to appropriate an economic surplus through taxation. The spending of this surplus encourages the development of cities, economic and occupational specialization, and extensive trade.

With the emergence of specialized, non–food-producing elites, social stratification becomes a key fact of social life, and economic and social inequalities are built into the system. In state societies, unlike in chiefdoms, only a part of the surplus goes back to the people directly. The rest, as we saw among the Asante, is used to support the activities of the state itself, such as maintaining administrative bureaucracies, standing armies, artists, craft workers, and a priesthood as well as supporting the ruling class in a luxurious lifestyle that differs substantially from that of ordinary people.

In state societies, elites almost always are a numerical minority, so the question arises: How do they manage to dominate? One of the ways elites try to ensure their continued dominance is through hegemony (Gramsci 1971). **Hegemony** refers to the dominance the state achieves through the internalization of elite values by those in the larger society. Hegemonic cultural ideologies explain the existing social order as being in the interest of the larger society, a process we see among the Asante and expressed by Charles Wilson as well. For example, the American cultural ideology of the individual as responsible for his or her own economic failure or success and the mystification of the ways in which the American economic and political system contributes to, or even creates, poverty are examples of how hegemony contributes to the status quo of nation-states and the continued dominance of elites.

Hegemony, however, must be constantly reinforced, and the state cannot count on permanent stability. Social stratification creates powerful elites as well as less powerful and oppressed peoples. Thus, states always face the risk that these latter will rebel against the social order. For this reason, political and cultural ideas that support elite practices are also reinforced by the threat of coercion (Nagengast 1994:116). For example, in the spring of 2008, as food and commodity prices rose around the world, the poor rioted in nations including Indonesia, Guinea, Haiti, Morocco, and many others. In each case, the government used armed troops and policemen to quell the rioting (Bradsher 2008).

Anthropological theories tend to emphasize either conflict (Fried 1967) or integration (Service 1971) as the dominant factor in the emergence of the state. Integration theories emphasize the benefits of the state to its members: its ability to provide the stability needed for growth and technological development, protection of the rights of its citizens, effective mechanisms for peaceful settlement of disputes, protection of trade and financial arrangements, defense against external enemies, and ability to expand. Conflict theories tend to emphasize the emergence of the state as directly connected with protecting the power and privileges of an elite class through coercive power and management of political ideology. We need look no further than the newspaper headlines or the TV news to see the political processes involved in the emergence of states, the failures of states, and perhaps also the transcendence of states in our increasingly politically and economically globalized world.

As we see in this chapter, political organization is intimately tied up with access to and distribution of resources. In Chapters 10 and 11 we explore further the connections between power and social stratification in complex societies, first in relation to class and caste and second in relation to race and ethnicity.

BRINGING IT BACK HOME: DO GOOD FENCES MAKE GOOD NEIGHBORS?

Contemporary states view a fixed and secure border as essential to sovereignty and national security. They accept the notion that states have a right and responsibility to restrict and control immigration. In many states today, including the United States, immigration has become a hotly debated issue regarding both economics and national security.

In the United States, most of the passionate talk about immigration concerns the border with Mexico, which has become increasingly militarized in an effort to keep out undocumented workers. The border has become a place of political theater, an arena in which the American debate over immigration is dramatically played out (Chavez 1998).

Politicians often justify the militarization of borders through the rhetoric of protecting domestic labor markets and, in the United States since 9/11, protecting the nation from terrorism. In spite of fencing, lighting, use of infrared scopes, underground sensors, increased law enforcement, and vigilante groups, hundreds of thousands of undocumented Mexicans continue to cross the border in search of work. They are encouraged by employers who use them as a source of cheap labor. Although there are supposedly penalties for employers who exploit undocumented workers in this way, in fact there are far too few law enforcement officers to make such penalties meaningful. Thus, while the debate over undocumented immigration generates much heat, most of it is aimed at the undocumented immigrants themselves rather than the employers of such workers who are subject to much less vigilance.

The latest proposal to control undocumented migration is the erection of a double-layered 700-mile-long border fence. Thus far, measures such as the fence have only succeeded in directing immigration to more difficult and dangerous terrain, making the immigrants even more vulnerable to exploitation (Chavez 1998:196; Holthouse 2005).

The border fence is a controversial project that highlights the clash of interests and cultures in the American Southwest. Seventy five miles of the border, at one of its most vulnerable points, is located on the Tohono O'odham Reservation, not far from Tucson, Arizona. The Tohono O'odham oppose the wall, saying they need to freely cross the border to visit friends and relatives in Mexico, take their children to school, gather traditional foods, and visit religious sites to perform rituals, all of which they have been doing for years. Their cultural concerns also focus on the wall's restricting the free range of deer, wild horses, coyotes, jackrabbits, and other animals they revere and regard as kin. "In our tradition we are taught to be concerned about every living thing as if they were people. We don't want that wall," said one tribal council member.

The Tohono O'odham cooperate extensively with the U.S. border patrol and the Department of Homeland Security in patrolling the border. The federal government is the trustee of all Indian lands, so it could build the fence through the reservation without tribal permission, but that would jeopardize the valuable help the Tohono O'odham now gives the government (Archibold 2006).

YOU DECIDE

1. Do you think human movement between states should be free and unrestricted? Why or why not? If you believe that there should be restriction of immigration, how would you determine an appropriate immigration policy for the United States (see Chapter 11, p. 257).
2. To what extent, if any, do you believe that the rhetoric against undocumented immigrants from Mexico is a disguised form of anti-Latino racism? What, in your view, is the real core of the perspective that immigration across the U.S. border with Mexico is a problem? What kinds of solutions would you suggest to the problem of undocumented immigration? Do you think, for example, that the construction of the border fence will make a substantial contribution in addressing this problem? Why or why not?
3. Decisions made by states often pit groups in society against each other. In this case, do you think the need to prevent undocumented immigrants and the threats of terrorists crossing the border justifies overriding the cultural values of the Tohono O'odham? How would you mediate the conflict between the U.S. government and the Tohono O'odham over the building of a wall on their reservation?

CHAPTER SUMMARY

1. A key focus in anthropological understanding of political organization is power: who has it, what its sources are, how it is related to other aspects of culture, especially political ideology, and how it is used to achieve public goals.
2. Social control in all societies is affected through formal sanctions such as exile and death. In state-level societies, punishments often are meted out by courts, judges, police, and other institutionalized forms of regulation. Conformity is also achieved through informal means such as gossip, ridicule, and ostracism.

3. Political organization is closely related to social differentiation, which in turn is related to the dominant pattern of making a living and exchanging goods and services. Band societies, which are characteristic of foragers, are egalitarian and dominated by generalized reciprocity.
4. Tribal societies, found among pastoralists and horticulturalists, also tend to be egalitarian and operate through generalized reciprocity as well as balanced reciprocity. Although tribal societies have many different nonviolent means of resolving conflicts within the society, they also have a high degree of warfare.
5. Chiefdoms, which are found in highly productive horticultural societies and among pastoralists, are called *rank societies.* Although kinship integrates the society, social units are socially ranked, and social position may be inherited. The chief is a central office, supported by his position as one who redistributes goods within the society.
6. The most complex form of political organization is the state, found mainly in agricultural and industrial societies and associated with social stratification. Social, political, and economic inequality are institutionalized and maintained through a combination of internalized controls (hegemony) and force. Kinship ties between the upper and lower classes no longer serve to integrate the society, and there is a wide gap in standards of living.

KEY TERMS

Acephalous
Age grades
Age set
Authority
Band
Bigman
Bureaucracy
Chiefdom
Citizenship
Compensation
Deviants
Egalitarian society
Elites
Factions
Government
Hegemony
Law

Leadership
Mediation
Political ideology
Political organization
Political process
Power
Rank society
Rebellion
Revolution
Secret societies
Social complexity
Social differentiation
State
Stratified society
Tribe
War

© Joan Gregg

Americans protest increasing inequality. In the United States, job loss and declining income have most affected the working and middle classes.

CHAPTER 10

INEQUALITIES: CLASS AND CASTE

CHAPTER OUTLINE

The American Dream

Explaining Social Stratification

Criteria of Stratification: Power, Wealth, and Prestige

Ascription and Achievement

Class Systems

- The American Class System
- Class Stratification in China

Caste

- The Caste System in India

Bringing It Back Home: Government Responsibility versus the Gospel of Wealth

- You Decide

THE AMERICAN DREAM

GLORIA Castillo, 22, a child of undocumented immigrants, is married, with two children, from a tough neighborhood in Dallas, Texas. She works the night shift at the Drive-Through window at a highway Burger King, from 10:30 PM to 6:30 AM, for $252 a week before taxes, and receives no health care benefits. To help make ends meet, she has a second job, earning $150 a night for the $1\frac{1}{2}$ hours it takes her to clean three bathrooms in a local bar. Her husband works at an auto parts place during the day, so Gloria takes the children, age 7 and 8, for a fast-food breakfast before dropping them at school, returns home, sleeps till 2, picks up the kids, prepares their frozen-food dinners, puts them to bed at 7, spends a few hours with her husband, and leaves for work. On Saturdays she attends a community college, working toward a degree as a paralegal. "I got dreams," she says (LeDuff 2006b).

Adam, son of a welfare mother, dropped out of school after the 10th grade and was turned down for a job at a fast-food restaurant in his inner-city neighborhood. Now he is earning $70,000 a year with full benefits as a union driver for an express delivery firm. Ebony, a young woman lucky enough to land a job at the same fast-food chain, is now a receptionist for a fancy law firm, studying at night for her BA in political science.

Jamilla, an unmarried mother who quit her fast-food kitchen job to go on welfare completed her GED, worked her way through culinary school, and now holds a well-paying job in a fancy restaurant in an upscale Fifth Avenue department store (Newman 2006).

After 10 years of conducting cancer research, Robert Glassman, a physician, was earning about $190,000 annually. But at age 45, he decided he wasn't making enough money, so he joined a Wall Street business firm hiring doctors as consultants. Today, in his current position as an adviser on medical investments, he's worth over $20 million. John Moon, whose parents were immigrants from South Korea, has a PhD in Economics from Harvard. He set out to be a professor of finance and landed a job with an elite New England college, earning a salary in the low six figures. But that salary was no match for the Wall Street offers that came his way, and he decided to trade in academia for work at a private equity firm. Moon is now among the very rich. Although he lives relatively unostentatiously, he and his wife, who left her job as a lawyer to stay at home to care for their two children, are renovating a newly bought co-op apartment on Park Avenue in Manhattan (Uchitelle 2006).

Meanwhile, as U.S. factories close, thousands of workers lose their jobs. Aaron Kemp, who worked for 8 years at the Maytag factory in Galesburg, Illinois, before it closed, says, "I wanted to work at a decent job and earn a decent wage, with decent benefits, so I can raise my kids, give them a decent education and maybe take them out to Pizza Hut on a Friday night. I don't need a Mercedes, just a ho-hum existence, and now," he says, "it seems hard to even do that" (Moberg 2006). Some of the Maytag jobs moved to Mexico and some to a Maytag factory in Newton, Iowa. In October 2007, the Iowa factory closed, putting several thousand people out of work (Uchitelle 2007). One of these people was Steve Schober, an industrial designer who had worked at Maytag for 25 years. Now, at age 52, with 6 months' severance pay as a cushion, he started his own design firm, working from his home. As a freelancer, his annual income plunged from the low six figures he earned at Maytag to $25,000. Half his current income goes to pay for health insurance for himself and his children, and $1000 a month pays for their home mortgage. Even with his wife earning $30,000 as a schoolteacher who receives her own medical benefits, the Schobers now have to cut into their savings, which they had been planning to use for their children's college tuition. They shop more cautiously and recently had a garage sale for stuff they previously would have given away. Both Mr. Schober and his wife have taken part-time jobs "to help the cash flow," says Mrs. Schober.

These stories put an individual face on social stratification in the United States. We earlier looked at gender as a dimension of social inequality. In this chapter and the next, we look at other dimensions of social stratification—class, caste, race and ethnicity—as these intersect in our own and other complex societies. **Social stratification** refers to a relatively permanent unequal distribution of goods and services in a society. The ways in which this distribution takes place depends on the organization of production, cultural values, and the access that different individuals and groups have to the means for achieving social goals in society. Two types of social stratification systems are *class systems* and *caste systems.*

A **class** is a category of persons who all have about the same opportunity to obtain economic resources, power, and prestige and who are ranked high and low in relation to each other. In a **class system** there are possibilities for movement between the classes or social strata, called **social mobility.** Sometimes class systems are called *open systems,* although even in the most open systems there are always constraints, however subtle, on movement from one class to another. A closed stratification system is one in which there is little or no possibility of social mobility or movement between strata. These are called caste systems and are discussed later.

EXPLAINING SOCIAL STRATIFICATION

Social stratification is related to social complexity. As we saw in Chapter 9, social stratification is one of the criteria by which states, the most socially complex types of societies, are defined. No society has ever devised a successful means of organizing a large population without stratification and inequality.

There are two basic perspectives on social stratification. One theory, called **functionalism** holds that, at least in societies with some mobility between social classes, social stratification may have some social functions. In this functionalist perspective, the promise of economic and social rewards for effort, although resulting in inequalities, motivates people to increase their efforts and to engage in difficult, risky jobs as well as jobs requiring long and arduous training. This benefits the whole society. For example, society as a whole benefits from motivating some people to become medical doctors, a career that is very highly paid but requires 11 or more years of education and training. The prestige and wealth that accrue to doctors are critical motivators impelling individuals to enter this profession.

But social stratification and inequality do not always serve the general good. Not all of society's most difficult jobs are well rewarded. In the United States, for example, schoolteachers, nurses, and many other professionals do difficult jobs that require substantial training, yet they are not well compensated financially. Nor are many of the low-prestige "dirty jobs" that are nevertheless basic to the functioning of society well paid. Nor does social stratification necessarily result in recruiting the most able people to the most demanding positions, as those of us who have ever had an incompetent boss can attest!

From a functionalist perspective, in order for society to enjoy the full benefits of inequality, all of a society's members must have the same economic and social opportunities. But a level playing field does not exist in any complex society: Family background and connections, gender, ethnicity, race, accumulated wealth, and other factors play important roles in determining the sorts of opportunities available to individuals in all stratified societies.

Furthermore, although it is obvious that in societies such as the United States financial wealth is a powerful motivating force, money's ability to motivate may have limits. A person making $25,000 a year probably would agree to work harder or undertake more training for a salary of $50,000 a year, but would a person making $400,000 a year take on additional work and training for $450,000 a year? Yet $50,000 is still a great deal of money.

Beyond all these considerations is an issue of the human spirit. Although inequality seems inevitable in large-scale social systems, resentment, however repressed, always seems to accompany substantial inequalities (Scott 1992), especially when the inequalities are based on ascribed factors such as race, gender, caste, or other attributes an individual is born with and cannot change (Berreman 1988). But even in a stratified system where change in one's status is theoretically possible, resentment between people of different levels of wealth and power is likely, especially if the inequalities become large. Anthropologist Gerald Berreman (1981:4–5) calls unfair systems of social stratification "painful, damaging, and unjust" and attributes much of the conflict in modern societies—crime, terrorism, ethnic conflict, civil war, and international war—to organized and systemic inequality.

The idea that social stratification causes conflict and instability, known as **conflict theory,** is central to the work of Karl Marx. In conflict theory, social stratification results from the constant struggle for scarce goods and services in complex societies. Inequalities exist because those individuals and groups who have acquired power, wealth, and prestige use their assets and their power to maintain control over the apparatus of the state, particularly its institutions of coercion and ideology. When these attempts to establish dominance falter or are challenged, elites may fall back on the threat of force or its actual use to maintain the status quo. This emphasis on conflict and change provides an essential dimension in the understanding of social stratification.

Conflict theory also enables us to understand some of the hidden motivations of social actors and to assess institutions by what they actually do as well as by what they say their intentions are. However, just as the functional view of inequality may lead theorists to ignore the possibility of structural conflict, conflict theorists may sometimes ignore the mechanisms that promote solidarity across caste, ethnic, and class lines.

CRITERIA OF STRATIFICATION: POWER, WEALTH, AND PRESTIGE

The social stratification system of any society depends on the complex interaction of the three main dimensions of stratification: power, wealth, and prestige. Anthropologists analyze **power** (the ability to control resources in one's own interest) by examining its sources, the channels through which it is exercised, and the goals it is deployed to achieve (see Chapter 9). For example, in the United States, we might discuss the different sources, uses, and goals of power among corporate presidents, elected public officials, entertainment celebrities, and heads of organized crime families. From a cross-cultural perspective, we might compare the sources and uses of power of an American president, the Prime Minister of France, and the chairman of the Communist party in the People's Republic of China.

Wealth is the accumulation of material resources or access to the means of producing these resources. For Karl Marx and those who follow his thinking, understanding how wealth is produced, distributed, and accumulated is the critical factor in explaining social stratification. Marx differentiated two main social classes in capitalist society on the basis of wealth: the *capitalists,* who own the means of production, and the *workers,* who must sell their labor in order to survive. According to Marx, the relationship of individuals to the means of production is critical in determining how much power and prestige they have.

Although wealth is not the sole criterion of social status even in capitalist societies, it can eventually translate into high social position and power. Wealth enables people to send their children to the most prestigious schools, buy homes in the best neighborhoods, and join the right social clubs. It enables people to gain access to important politicians by giving large campaign contributions. It may also allow them to run for political office themselves.

Prestige, or social honor, is the third dimension of social stratification. Prestige is related to income; accumulated wealth; power; personal characteristics, such as integrity; family history; and the display of material goods. Not all wealth, in and of itself, is a source of prestige. For example, people who earn their incomes illegally have less prestige than do those whose incomes are legally earned. The head of an illegal gambling syndicate or drug distribution network may make hundreds of millions of dollars but has little prestige. On the other hand, few winners of the Nobel Peace Prize made much money but they surely have great prestige. And committing oneself to poverty, as India's great leader, Mahatma Gandhi, did, may paradoxically be a source of great prestige.

One of the most important sources of prestige is occupation, both for its relation to income and the cultural values attached to it. In complex societies, occupations are ranked, and different societies rank occupations differently. In the Hindu caste system, for example, occupations are ranked according to their level of spiritual purity or pollution, a concept formally absent from occupational rankings in the United States. Americans do, however, make some connections between prestige and the "dirt" involved in various occupations; this connection is the subject of "Dirty Jobs," a popular television program.

As socioeconomic conditions change, the value system that supports a particular system of occupational prestige also may change. In 18th-century Europe, surgery was performed by barbers and was a lower-class occupation. In contemporary North America, surgeons rank very high in prestige, both because they make a great deal of money and because the occupation requires great skill and training. In the People's Republic of China (discussed next), the prestige and power associated with different occupations has almost completely reversed itself from traditional Chinese society. Before the Communist Revolution, China followed a Confucian value system, in which scholars had the highest honor. After the revolution, workers were honored, and scholars often were explicitly ridiculed and despised. Today, with China's growing free-market practices and increasing economic role in globalization, businesspeople, previously a target of socialist contempt, are highly regarded.

Social scientists have long debated whether prestige or class is more important in explaining the behavior of people in complex, stratified societies. Karl Marx argued for the primacy of economic or class interests, whereas Max Weber, a German sociologist of the late 19th century, argued for the importance of other social group memberships, such as the family. Whereas Marx thought that people were (or should be) most conscious of their class membership (their economic status), Weber believed that people may value prestige and the symbolic aspects of status even more than their economic position. Weber further argued that political action can be motivated by a group's desire to defend its social position as well as, or even in opposition to, its economic self-interest. For example, poor whites in the American South did not join poor blacks in working for improvement of their common economic position because they were more committed to maintaining status differences based on color. More recently, it has been suggested that many working-class people in the United States, who would have benefited from some of the policies of a Democratic president, nevertheless voted for a Republican based on what are called "social issues," such as gay marriage and a woman's right to choose (Frank 2004).

ASCRIPTION AND ACHIEVEMENT

In comparing stratification systems in different cultures or over time, anthropologists differentiate between systems of **ascribed status,** based on birth, and systems of **achieved status,** (ideally) based on a person's own efforts to achieve social position. Race and sex are ascribed statuses; wife, college professor, criminal, and artist are achieved statuses. Although societies may be primarily based on achievement **(open systems)** or ascription **(closed systems),** most societies contain both. In less socially complex societies, most important statuses, such as kinship, may be ascribed, but prestige may also be based on individual achievement.

CLASS SYSTEMS

In open social systems, or class systems, the different strata (classes) are not sharply separated from one another but form a continuum. Social status is dependent on both achievement and ascription. Ideally, in a social class system, social mobility—the (upward) movement from one class to another through various means such as education, marriage, good luck, hard work, or taking risks—is possible for all of society's members.

In reality, however, in most societies including the United States, social mobility is limited for most people, and class status tends to be largely ascribed rather than achieved. You might ask, for example, what are the constraints on Gloria Castillo's family that affect the probability that it will move up in the American class system in spite of her obvious hard work and determination?

The American Class System

A core American cultural value is the "American Dream," the idea that self-sufficiency and social success, perhaps even great wealth and power, is possible for all. The cultural premise underlying the American Dream is that if one works hard, there are endless opportunities, open to all, to improve one's social position and material standard of living and to improve those of one's children. American culture is so wedded to the possibilities for upward social mobility that many Americans, including many social scientists, deny that a class system even exists (Durrenberger 2001:4, 2006).

The American Dream is closely tied to other core American values, such as individualism, meritocracy, the work ethic, optimism, pragmatism, a national faith in progress and achievement, and a belief in the ability of individuals to control the circumstances of their lives. One corollary of the American Dream is that low-class status is mainly viewed as a weakness in the individual rather than as an aspect of social structure or cultural opportunities and restraints.

Although belief in the American Dream and an open society is strong among all the diverse racial and ethnic groups in the United States (*New York Times* 2005), social science evidence demonstrates that educational achievement, levels of indebtedness, income, and wealth accumulation are significantly linked, not just to an individual's class status but also to his or her race, ethnicity, and gender.

Furthermore, the American emphasis on upward social mobility implies that downward mobility is rare or absent. In fact, as described in our chapter opening description of Maytag workers, downward social mobility does occur and is becoming more widespread, as productive jobs leave the country and health care costs squeeze working- and middle-class families. It is important to see, although it is very often ignored in the popular culture, that contrary to the idea that those who experience downward socioeconomic mobility "have only themselves to blame," systemic factors such as downsizing, job outsourcing, and the increasing costs of a college education and health care outweigh individual factors in explaining inequality.

For example, homelessness is significantly related to the lack of affordable housing and to the wage-depressing competition for low-skill jobs in many urban areas (Lyon-Callo 2004) (see Chapter 1, "You Decide").

Cultural patterns are tenacious, though. In spite of the fact that there is far less upward social mobility in the United States than there used to be, belief in the American Dream remains strong, reinforced by the celebrity of self-made billionaires, the stories of upward mobility presented in the media, and the lives of people, some of you reading this chapter, who are experiencing upward mobility yourselves.

The Material Basis of Class in the United States

Class matters! And, as most Americans agree, income is the most important determinant of social class. Income is the gateway to a middle-class lifestyle and serves as the basis for family economic security. Over the long term, sufficient and steady income is essential toward saving and accumulating assets.

From 1979 to 2001, there was an extraordinary jump in income inequality in the United States. During that period, the after-tax income of the top 1 percent of American households jumped 139 percent to more than $700,000, the income of the middle fifth of households rose only 17 percent to $43,700, and the income of the poorest fifth rose only 9 percent. In 2004, the chief executives at the 100 largest companies in California took home a collective $1.1 billion, an increase of nearly 20 percent. For most workers, only during the speculative bubble of the 1990s did income rise above inflation. Reductions in pensions have also increased the prospect of financial insecurity in retirement. Tax cuts under President George W. Bush have exacerbated this inequality: the 400 taxpayers with the highest incomes—over $87 million a year each—now pay income tax and Medicare and Social Security taxes amounting to the same percentage of their incomes as people making $50,000 to $75,000 a year.

Income and accumulated wealth have a tremendous impact on people's lives. Good health, quality health care in illness, and the life span itself are affected by social class (Scott 2005). The high and rising costs of pharmaceuticals and medical care are merely one aspect of the different life chances available to the poor, the middle class, and the wealthy. People with higher education and income are less likely to have and to die of heart disease, strokes, diabetes, and many types of cancer (Scott 2005). They are more likely to benefit from advances in medicine, to have more useful information about medicine, and to be covered by health insurance. In addition, they are less likely to smoke and are more likely to be less overweight, to exercise more, and to eat healthier food than do people in the lower classes.

Life chances are the opportunities that people have to fulfill their potential in society. Sufficient and steady family income is the essential gateway to increasing life chances. It is the basis of a decent standard of living, including access to food, clothing, shelter, health care, a quality education, and the accumulation of some resources or equity as a safety net for emergencies. In our society these things make social advancement possible. Conversely, insufficient and irregular income negatively affects not only one's own life chances but also those of one's children.

Social mobility itself is a life chance that depends on where one already is in the class system. People born into positions of wealth, high status, and power strive to maintain those positions and often have the means to keep others from achieving upward mobility. Rich and powerful people have a better chance of maintaining their position over generations than people born into the middle class have of reaching these positions, and middle-class people have a better chance of improving their own and their children's life chances than do people in the working or poorer classes (Bowles et al. 2005; Corak 2004; Frank and Cook 1996; Lareau 2003; Neckerman 2004).

In *Falling from Grace: Downward Mobility in the Age of Affluence,* anthropologist Katherine Newman (1999) defines the downwardly mobile middle class as people who had secure jobs, comfortable homes, and reason to believe that the future would be one of continued prosperity for themselves and their children. Through job loss, they experienced not only economic decline but also a decline in prestige. They lost their place in society and, with it, their sense of honor and self-esteem. Downward mobility is almost institutionally invisible. The media most often focus on the lives of the rich and famous and those in the business world who make fantastic salaries. American culture provides many rituals and symbols of upward mobility and success in the form of displays of wealth and status, but there are no such occasions to mark status deterioration. As Newman observes, "Downward mobility is a hidden dimension of our society's experience because it . . . does not fit into our cultural universe."

The experience of environmental disasters and pollution is also affected by social class. This was tragically demonstrated by Hurricane Katrina. In New Orleans, death came most often for the poor: those who had no private transportation, no credit cards, no wealthy relatives to rely on, no home insurance, and no resources to evacuate the young and the aged. As anthropologist Neil Smith notes, not just the effect of the hurricane but the government's response to it deepened the social grooves already built into New Orleans society (Paredes 2006; Smith 2005:9).

A similar story is told by anthropologist Melissa Checker (2005), who documents the environmental pollution in a poor African-American community on the outskirts of Augusta, Georgia. Surrounded by nine polluting industries, community residents began to notice that local people were getting sick and dying at an alarming rate. The information about the poisoned land made their property impossible to sell, so the inhabitants were caught in a deadly bind: too poor to move and often too poor for health care. Checker perceptively notes that the environmental movement itself is impacted by class: The white middle class focuses on landscape preservation, while poorer communities, like that in Augusta, organize against toxic waste dumping, which more directly affects them.

© Nubar Alexanian/Stock, Boston, LLC

In the United States today, among members of the middle class, personal and class identity are closely tied to an abundance of material goods. However, members of the middle class vary substantially in both salaries and accumulation of wealth.

Social Classes as Subcultures

Social class has a cultural as well as a material dimension. It is characterized by differences in attitudes, behavior, consumption patterns, lifestyle, and values. The members of a social class tend to share similar life experiences, occupational roles, values, educational backgrounds, affiliations, leisure activities, buying habits, religious affiliation, and political views.

On the surface, the cultural aspects of social class seem to be blurring because of some interesting contradictions. On the one hand, while income and wealth inequalities are rising, class-related lifestyles, expressed in consumer purchasing is, in many dimensions, growing more similar. This is partly because cheaper consumer goods are more easily available, thanks to globalization; because of easy credit (which, as the recent increase in home foreclosures indicate, turned out to have a high price); and because more people within a household are working, contributing to slightly increasing median household incomes (*New York Times* 2005:135). For example, a middle-class family may own a flat-screen TV, drive a BMW, buy expensive chocolates, take a Caribbean cruise, and will almost certainly have a cell phone. Meanwhile, the wealthy may buy wine at Costco and adopt a more casual dress style of jeans and a sweatshirt.

But these surface lifestyle similarities blurring class lines is only a small part of the story. Money does make a lifestyle. As luxury has gone down market, the market produces ever more expensive luxury goods that are affordable only for those with great incomes and wealth: $4000 handbags, $130,000 Hummer automobiles, and $12,000 mother/baby diamond bracelet sets. Even more than material goods, class differences are expressed in personal services and exclusive experiences: personal chefs and personal trainers, face lifts and other cosmetic surgery, $400 per hour tutors for the children, who in any case will be attending private schools, and the most expensive homes, often in gated communities. And while the middle class may be taking group tours to Europe or Caribbean cruises, the rich are shelling out $50,000 for a 10-day, private jet tour of the seven most wonderful sights in the world sponsored by National Geographic (Newman and Chen 2007).

Although American class differences are now less reliable in predicting political choice or religious affiliation, they are still very significant in such things as family structure and educational achievement. The upper classes are more likely to be married before they have children, they have fewer children, and they have them later in life. All these factors impinge on the possibilities of upward social mobility (*New York Times* 2005:125). As Katherine Newman notes, family circumstances is one of the most important factors determining whether those in the category she calls the "near poor," who have household incomes between $20,000 and $40,000 a year for a family of four, can make it into the middle class (Newman and Chen 2007). "Women with children and no one to help them with those kids [are] much more likely to get trapped—they [can't] get more education which limit[s] their job options [and] their contact with the labor market [is] more fragile and episodic" (Press 2007:23).

One of the factors clouding the importance of class in America is that, compared to the rest of the world, a high standard of material comfort is widely spread throughout the classes, even if much of it is based on growing debt obligations. As one social scientist explained it: "Being born in the elite in the U.S. gives you . . . privileges that very few people in the world have . . . , but being born poor in the U.S. gives you disadvantages unlike anything in Western Europe, Japan, and Canada" (Scott and Leonhardt 2005).

Beyond participating in shared cultural patterns, members of a social class also tend to associate more with one another than with people in other classes. Thus, the lifestyle and interactional dimensions of social class reinforce one another. Through interaction based on common residence and schooling, religious participation, voluntary associations, and other social institutions, people learn the lifestyle of their social class. Because lifestyle is an important part of sociability, informal and intimate social relationships, such as friendship and marriage, also tend to bring together people from the same social class. This partly explains why classes are endogamous.

Class Stratification in China

China.

Like the United States, the People's Republic of China is ideologically committed to a society in which opportunity and wealth are widespread. However, China has followed a very different path than the United States. China was an empire with rigidly defined social classes: peasants, a small trading and artisan class, a legal and governing bureaucracy appointed through rigorous written examinations, and an emperor, his court, and his relatives. Intellectuals and administrators were highly regarded, merchants and soldiers were disrespected, and peasants had no status beyond the produce they contributed to the state. In the mid-20th century, following a protracted war, Mao Zedong's Chinese Communist Party came to power, declaring a new state, the People's Republic of China (PRC). Between 1950 and the mid-1970s, the PRC attempted to maintain its power and create a "classless" Marxist society. This process probably cost between 20 and 40 million lives but did eliminate much economic stratification. After Mao's death in 1976, the PRC adopted a program of rapid liberalization and since that time has moved steadily toward capitalist relations of production.

However, the price of economic liberalization has been increasing inequality and social differentiation. This is particularly the case for the rural poor, few of whom have the skills to meet the demands of urban living. As a result, they are cut off from the privileges of urban life, such as universal education, high-quality health care, and individual family housing. Villagers who do come to the city face a variety of obstacles. They often do not know how to negotiate for proper wages or how to redress grievances when they are cheated.

Those peasants who remained in the countryside after liberalization lost access to free housing, health care, farm machinery, and other necessary services. Although some government loans were provided, they were not as substantial as the benefits given to city dwellers. Some farmers have been able to produce goods for sale at the new free-market prices, and some villages were able to form farming cooperatives that were more economically viable than individual farming. Although China's gross domestic product grew by over 9 percent in the 1990s and other economic indicators showed that both urban and rural Chinese had significantly increased their standard of living, the gap between rural and urban incomes remained larger than international standards and is growing wider.

Income inequalities in the PRC are also increased by the decentralization of authority that permits local provincial and district offices substantial autonomy in economic affairs. Certain towns and cities with a head start in industry did well. One town became the sock supplier to two thirds of the world (you are probably wearing one of those pair of socks as you read this), but decentralization also increased opportunities for corruption since government officials, subject to less scrutiny from the capital, used the opportunity to enrich themselves at the expense of others.

An especially serious aspect of rural poverty is the enormous emigration of rural villagers to urban areas in order to find wage-earning jobs that will help them support their families in the countryside. Since peasants must now pay for schooling, health care, and other basic services, agriculture alone frequently provides inadequate income. Typically, the father and sometimes both parents must migrate to an urban area for factory work and send money back home for their household, which typically consists of their child and the grandparents. Rural families are split up for years at a time. "We have more freedom now than we did when we had a communal life," says one villager," but where rich city people call their one child 'little sun,' we call ours 'left behind, growing up without their parents'" (Yardley 2004).

In just one generation, these changes, mediated through China's exploding participation in the global economy, produced a rising inequality of social classes. As capitalism moves forward, those who have made it in the new society live side by side with the have-nots. Some foreign and Chinese economists argue that it is normal and even beneficial in the transition period to a modern economy that "a few get rich quickly" as an incentive to others, but this view is not yet embedded into Chinese culture. Rather, the Chinese government boasts of its efforts to bring the poorest of China's rural regions a share of the wealth so blatantly enjoyed by a small percentage. Yet surveys of government officials show that the widening income gap has potential for stirring unrest and is an area of great concern. It is clear that the Chinese motto for the new economy, "to get rich is glorious," has not fulfilled its promise equally to all sectors of society.

CASTE

In contrast to class systems, which are largely, or at least theoretically, based on achieved statuses, a **caste system** is based on birth, or ascribed status. A person belongs to the caste of his or her parents and cannot move from one caste to another. In a class system, people from different classes may marry. In fact, marriage may be one route to upward social mobility. In a caste system, a person can marry only within his or her caste. In other words, caste is hereditary, and castes are endogamous. This is why caste systems are called *closed stratification systems.*

Castes are ranked in relation to one another and are usually associated, although more in the past than today, with a traditional occupation. A caste system, then, consists of ranked, culturally distinct, interdependent, endogamous groups. Unlike class systems, in which no clear boundaries exist between the different classes, a caste system has definite boundaries between castes.

The caste system of India is perhaps the best known and is the model upon which the characteristics of a caste system are based. However, caste systems do exist in other cultures. In many West African societies, blacksmiths, praise singers, and leather workers function as endogamous castes. In traditional European society, peasants and nobility were endogamous castes. In Japan, the Burakumin people represent a separate caste (see p. 243). Indeed, before the 1950's era of civil rights, black/white relations in the American South contained many elements of a caste system. The ascribed status of race prohibited people from intermarrying, eating together, and interacting with each other in ways very similar to that of the Indian caste system (Dollard 1937).

The Caste System in India

The unique elements of the Indian caste system are its complexity, its relation to Hindu religious beliefs and rituals, and the degree to which the castes (or, more properly, the subcastes) are cohesive and self-regulating groups. Hinduism refers to four caste categories, called *varna,* ranked according to their ritual purity, which is based on their traditional occupations. The highest ranked varna, the Brahmins, are priests and scholars; next highest is the Kshatriyas, the ruling and warrior caste; third ranked are the Vaisyas, or merchants; and fourth are the Shudras, or menial workers and artisans. Below these four varnas is a fifth group, previously called untouchables, who perform spiritually polluting work such as cleaning latrines or tanning leather and are considered so ritually impure that their mere touch, or even shadow, contaminates the purity of the higher castes. A person's birth into any one of these caste categories is believed to be a reward or punishment for the quality of his or her actions in a previous life. The term "untouchability" is now officially rejected in India, and the previously named untouchables are now called *harijans,* or children of God, and officially are called *dalits.*

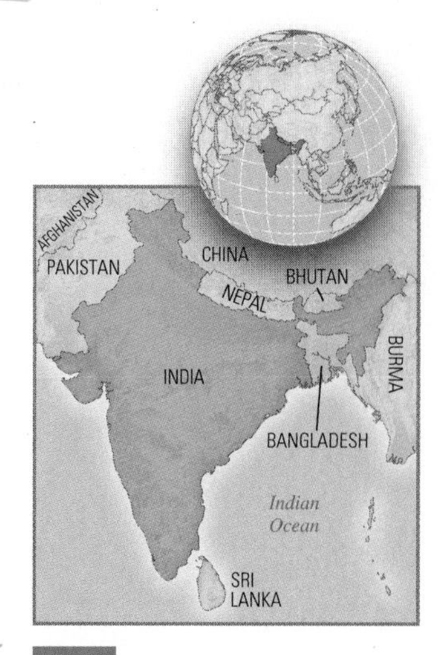

India.

The social interactions between castes is governed by strict rules of behavior that help maintain caste boundaries. Under these rules, members of different castes do not eat with one another, and a higher-caste person will not accept most kinds of food or drink from a lower-caste person. In Indian villages, dalits are spatially and socially segregated, are prohibited from drawing water from the same wells that are used by higher castes, and cannot enter high-caste temples.

In its rural setting, the Indian caste system has an important economic dimension, involving traditional exchanges of goods and services

In India, the upper-caste view that the lowest castes are content in their socioeconomic position is contradicted by the many protests of dalits against the unfairness of the caste system.

between higher and lower castes. Families of various artisan and serving castes, such as carpenters, potters, blacksmiths, water carriers, and leather workers, perform their services for high-caste landowning families. In return they receive food, grain, clothing, fodder for animals, butter, milk, small amounts of cash, and many other things. These relationships between families may carry over for several generations. Higher castes often extol these relationships as mutually beneficial. Landowners have a steady supply of available workers while the serving castes gain a relatively reliable source of subsistence. The lower castes tend to emphasize the exploitation of the system rather than its mutual benefits.

Although Indian castes are ranked on the basis of prestige rather than wealth, the gains of high-caste position are not merely symbolic. Economic relationships are very significant in holding the caste system together. The higher castes benefit materially as well as symbolically from their higher status and are in a better position to exercise political power in their own self-interest. The lower castes appear to accept their low position without question, but their conformity largely hinges on their awareness that economic sanctions and physical force will be used against them if they try to break out of their caste position. Indeed, in both local and regional arenas, violent conflict between castes has been frequent, especially in rural India.

Two justifications for the caste system serve the upper caste interests and help maintain elite hegemony. One is the functional view of the caste system as benefiting the upper and lower castes equally. Even more important, however, is the Hindu religious belief that individuals occupy social positions based on the virtue of their actions in a previous life. Just as elite hegemony is maintained in the American class system by the widely accepted ideology among all classes that an individual achieves success by his or her own hard work, willingness to take risks, and intelligence, so in the Indian caste system the upper castes benefit from the widely shared belief in social position reflecting an individual's spiritual achievement. In both the American class system and the Indian caste system, the workings of economics and politics in furthering the interests of some strata over others are obscured.

Changes in the Caste System

Unlike a class system, social mobility and the dynamics of change in the Indian caste system rely primarily on group effort rather than individual effort. A caste that has been economically successful in some new occupation may try to raise its prestige by adopting the customs of a higher caste, claiming a new rank for itself. These new behavior patterns are formulated by caste councils, and nonconforming members will be publicly censured or even outcaste. As part of its striving for social mobility, a lower caste may invent an origin myth, claiming it originally belonged to a higher-ranked varna.

The Camars, a dalit caste of leather workers in Agra (site of the Taj Mahal), vividly illustrate social mobility in a caste system (Lynch 1969). Traditionally, Camars were shoemakers, and with an increased demand for shoes both in India and abroad, some of them became fairly wealthy. This stimulated the Camars to try to raise their caste ranking with a claim to be Kshatriyas (the warrior caste). In an effort to get this claim accepted by the higher castes, the Camars outlawed the eating of beef and buffalo among their members and adopted some high-caste rituals. But these attempts were not acknowledged by the high castes, who persisted in maintaining caste boundaries on eating, drinking, and marriage.

Subsequently, the Camars tried a different strategy: conversion to Buddhism. Instead of trying to raise their status within the Hindu caste system, they sought to improve their position by putting themselves outside the caste system altogether. At the same time, however, they wanted to retain their status as a special caste in order to be eligible for the benefits of affirmative action offered by the Indian government. Indeed, the affirmative action requirements for dalits and other lower castes is one of the important bases for maintenance of the caste system.

As partly illustrated by dalit social mobility, important changes in the caste system have occurred in India in the past 50 years (Fuller 1995). The Indian constitution of 1950 outlawed dalit status as well as the many social practices associated with untouchability. In rural as well as urban India, caste ranking appears to be less sharply defined than formerly, at least within the higher-caste categories. This is partly the result of the increasing differentiation of wealth, prestige, and power *within* each caste.

Perhaps the biggest change has occurred in the traditional connection between caste and occupations. New occupations, such as factory work, government service, information technology, and the professions, which are not caste related, have opened opportunities, especially for the middle-

and lower-level castes. At the same time, many low-caste occupations, such as potter and drummer, have declined.

At the same time that occupation and caste are becoming increasingly disconnected, the higher castes have mainly benefited by these new openings in the professions and information technology through their previous accumulation of capital, their higher education, their business and social contacts, and their ability to speak English, which has given them opportunities outsourced by American and multinational companies. Today, members of the middle-class "intelligentsia" feel almost no obligation to follow their caste's traditional occupation (Beteille 1998).

At an ideological level, there has been a significant change in the public discourse about caste (Fuller 1995). Differences in caste are now referred to in public as cultural differences rather than as a hierarchy based on spiritual purity and pollution. Corresponding to these new trends of public discourse, the more neutral terms "community" and "association" are replacing the term *jati* (which literally means *species* but refers to subcaste). At the same time, the strict maintenance of many caste boundaries—in eating and drinking in the same public places, particularly in cities—has weakened, but many caste-related boundaries remain at private gatherings.

The extent to which the new public discourse on caste reflects a real change in attitude is unclear. The urban upper classes, whose occupations make caste largely irrelevant, may dismiss notions of caste hierarchy, but for the lower castes these ideas are still very relevant. In private, people still speak of caste in a spiritual framework, and both "love matches" and arranged marriages still take place primarily within the caste or within closely aligned subcastes. This along with the affirmative action measures of the Indian government that attempt to raise the position of the lowest castes suggests that caste as a building block of Indian society will not disappear in the near future.

In the contemporary world globalization, neoliberal economic policies and the rise of multinational corporations, among others factors, have a significant impact on systems of social stratification. India is now experiencing economic growth that is greatly expanding its urban middle class (which at this point is almost equivalent to the entire population of the United States), while a free-market ideology has meant cutbacks on government-supported education and medical care, which disproportionately affect the poor. In addition, with the Indian government's hands tied by the free trade policies of international institutions such as the World Trade Organization, millions of cotton farmers are impoverished by a global system of trade in which the agricultural products of heavily subsidized farmers in the United States and Europe depress international prices. This has resulted in the suicide of thousands of cotton farmers in central India (Mishra 2006:50).

India's new economic growth has meant that class, with its expression in luxury consumerism as well as caste, now is a significant factor in the Indian system of social stratification (Luce 2007). Nevertheless, caste remains a dominant factor even when it is sometimes overcome by exceptional individuals.

The economic changes we call globalization—in India, China, the United States, and indeed most of the world—have led to increasing prosperity for some but also increasing economic inequality (Schneider 2002). Social mobility is not equally distributed throughout all social and economic classes, and stratification has become more unequal both within and between nations. In Chapter 11 we examine other aspects of social stratification, race, and ethnicity, keeping in mind that in each society the dimensions of social stratification—gender, class, race, and ethnicity—interact differently and grow out of specific cultural, economic, and historical circumstances.

BRINGING IT BACK HOME: GOVERNMENT RESPONSIBILITY VERSUS THE GOSPEL OF WEALTH

For many people, the American Dream of social mobility continues to be a core value of American culture. But statistical and ethnographic evidence shows growing income inequalities and declining opportunity for economic advancement for many Americans. Members of the lower and middle classes are increasingly leading a precipitous existence.

The expansion of the American middle class from the 1940s to the 1970s was to a large extent based on government policies and programs, including the GI Bill, Social Security, unemployment insurance, a progressive income tax, and federal mortgage assistance programs. It involved a cultural vision that held that government should attempt to improve citizens' economic security and increase their economic opportunities. Those who support this view hold that these policies put more money in the hands of consumers and that this leads to increased demand for goods, a growing economy, and a more just and equitable distribution of wealth. Furthermore, they argue that as people experience improvement in their economic life, they will become more invested in the core values of our democratic society and more willing to participate to keep these values alive.

Competing with this view is the vision sometimes called the "gospel of wealth," a phrase coined by the late 19th-century capitalist Andrew

Carnegie. Carnegie, and others like him, claimed the best government was the least government. They argued that government regulations stifle entrepreneurial initiative; that progressive taxation and policies, like a minimum wage, undermine investment in the economy by small businesses and large corporations; and that government entitlement programs, like Social Security, welfare, and health care, lead to laziness and a declining sense of individual responsibility. On the other hand, they say, policies that increase corporate profits lead to higher rates of economic growth, providing opportunities and jobs, and ultimately benefit the most people. Privatization, whether in the form of individual savings accounts, private health care, or school vouchers, is sound economic doctrine and will give people responsibility for their actions and their future. As a result, they will become more invested in the core values of our democratic society and more willing to participate to keep these values alive.

YOU DECIDE

1. What is your American Dream? Do you believe that education, hard work, and high personal character will be rewarded with a higher material standard of living for yourself and your children—or not? What evidence do you use for your view in your own life or those of other people you know?
2. What impact do you think government policies (for example, regarding child care or family leave; availability of credit; home ownership; business or college loans) have had on your own success in life or your social position in the American stratification system? Have these policies opened up or constrained the possibilities for your achieving your American Dream?
3. What kind of role, if any, do you think government policies and programs should play in shaping the social stratification system of the United States? Give reasons for your answer.

CHAPTER SUMMARY

1. A functionalist view of social stratification is that it works to the benefit of the whole society because it motivates people to undertake all the jobs necessary for the society to survive. However, social stratification also causes conflict as different social strata, with opposing interests, clash with one another over goals and resources.
2. The major dimensions of social stratification are power, wealth, and prestige, which are closely tied to occupation. The particular value system of a culture determines how these interact to determine where a person is placed in the stratification system.

3. Two major types of stratification systems are class and caste. In a class system, social position is largely achieved, although it is also partly determined by the class into which a person is born. People can move between social classes, which are ranked from most powerful to least powerful. Social classes are largely based on differences of income and wealth but also are characterized by different lifestyles and cultural differences.
4. The culture of the United States emphasizes "the American Dream," that is, the idea that a person can and should improve his or her life chances and material wealth. Although many Americans feel that class is unimportant in the United States, there are important material differences and differences in life chances in different social classes. Inequality between social classes is increasing, as is downward social mobility.
5. The People's Republic of China has moved from its ideology of a classless socialist society under Mao Zedong to one in which the pursuit of wealth is encouraged. The result has been steep and increasing inequalities. Economic disparities between men and women, between different occupational positions, and particularly between rural and urban populations have widened enormously, causing many social disruptions.
6. In a caste system, social position is largely ascribed (based on birth). Boundaries between castes are sharply defined, and marriage is within the caste. The caste system in India is based on Hindu ideas of ritual purity and pollution. The boundaries of caste in India are maintained by prohibitions on many kinds of social interactions, such as sharing food, as well as by cultural differences.
7. The positions of subcastes within the larger caste hierarchy as well as the importance of the caste system itself have changed in India with independence. The Indian constitution incorporates protection of individual rights and affirmative action for lower castes, particularly former untouchables. Other factors for change include the widening of economic and occupational opportunities, particularly in urban India.

KEY TERMS

Achieved status
Ascribed status
Caste system
Class
Class system

Closed system
Conflict theory
Functionalism
Life chances
Open system
Power
Prestige
Social mobility
Social stratification
Wealth

Cultural Survival

Cultural Survival is an organization of anthropologists that tries to help indigenous peoples adapt to the modern world.

CHAPTER 11

INEQUALITIES: RACE AND ETHNICITY

CHAPTER OUTLINE

Trouble in Paradise

The Cultural Construction of Race

Racial Stratification Systems

- Cultural Construction of Race in the United States
- Racial Classification in Brazil

Ethnicity and Ethnic Stratification

Ethnicity and the Nation State

- Ethnic Conflict
- Ethnic Stratification and Indigenous Peoples
- Ethnicity and Immigration in the United States

Bringing It Back Home: Class, Ethnicity, Race, and Educational Achievement

- You Decide

TROUBLE IN PARADISE

ON a pitch-dark Sunday morning, September 13, 1931, in Honolulu, Hawai'i, an elegantly dressed woman walking alone waved down a car. As the driver lowered his window, the woman, whose face was bruised, peered inside and asked, "Are you white people?" When the driver said yes, she said "Thank God," climbed in the car and directed them to drive her home. Within 24 hours, everyone in Honolulu heard the shocking story of a young navy officer's wife, Thalia Massie, who claimed she was gang raped by a carload of native Hawaiians (Stannard 2005:7–8). The ensuing rape trial and subsequent events, known as the Massie Case, was a national media sensation, playing on the obsessive fears in America, and particularly the South, over the assault of white womanhood by blacks and other "people of color."

As the rape investigation proceeded, five young men identified by Thalia Massie were arrested: two Native Hawaiians, two Japanese, and one Chinese. The prosecutor explicitly played on white fears regarding the vulnerability of "white womanhood" attacked by "lust-sodden beasts," as he called the defendants, urging the jury to "protect its women" and justify their manhood by voting guilty. In the face of the lies, contradictions, distortions, and suppression of evidence by the prosecution, the racially and ethnically mixed jury, after deliberating 97 hours, was deadlocked. The judge was forced to call a mistrial, allowing the defendants to go free on bail. In the storm of outrage that followed, prominent whites, including high-level Naval officers, many from the South, called the verdict the "shame of Honolulu" and claimed that Thalia Massie was another victim of Hawai'i's "half-breed natives" who had voted along racial lines. Sailors roamed Honolulu looking for trouble—and they found it. Horace Ida, one of the Japanese defendants, was abducted at gunpoint, badly beaten up, and left by the roadside, his life saved only by a passing motorist. But worse was yet to come. In early January 1932, Thalia Massie's socialite mother, Thalia's husband, and two sailors kidnapped and killed Joe Kahahawai, one of the Hawaiian defendants. On their way to dump Joe's dead body into the ocean, the four were stopped and arrested for murder by a passing policeman. The national media went wild with headlines such as "Honor Killing in Honolulu Threatens Race War," focusing on Hawai'i as an unsafe place for white women. In the South, many called for lynch law against the rape defendants (p. 274). One Navy official declared that "Hawaiians or any dark-skinned person" was deserving of the same treatment whites accorded blacks in the South (p. 394).

The four accused of the murder were defended by the famous lawyer, Clarence Darrow. In his closing argument, Darrow reminded the jury of the "unwritten law"—the widely shared American belief that a man has a right to kill another man who has assaulted his wife, especially when the rape victim was white and the rapist was not (p. 376). A compromise verdict was reached: The ethnically mixed jury found the four defendants guilty of manslaughter, and the judge sentenced them to 10 years of hard labor. Hawai'i's governor, under tremendous political pressure from the white community to pardon the defendants, commuted their sentence to 1 hour in custody. The defendants were then spirited off to a navy ship sailing to San Francisco (p. 390).

But the Massie case was not quite over. Under pressure, the governor ordered the Pinkerton Agency to investigate Thalia Massie's original rape charges. The Pinkerton report overwhelming demonstrated that the defendants were not guilty and indeed questioned whether Thalia Massie was raped at all. There was significant local pressure on the governor to retry the original rape case or to drop the charges against the defendants. With the support of John Kelley, the local prosecutor, Judge Charles Davis did just that on February 13, 1933 (Stannard 2005:398–399).

With this, the Massie case officially ended, but its impact permanently transformed the ethnic, racial, political, and class structure of Hawai'i. At the top of this structure were the minority of whites, or *haoles,* who owned most of the land and who dominated business, the media, the territorial government, and the Navy establishment at Pearl Harbor. Most of Hawai'i's population were immigrants of Portuguese, Filipino, Chinese, and Japanese descent. They occupied the lowest rungs of society as oppressed plantation workers or as urban slum dwellers. Despite their common class interests, these immigrant groups kept largely to themselves, working separately rather than joining together, even in their occasional protests against their working conditions. Whites viewed native Hawaiians somewhat more favorably than the immigrant groups, but economically they were little better off and, like the immigrants, were both derided and feared as racial "others."

In response to the Massie case and especially the killing of Joe Kahahawai, a new racial and ethnic social structure emerged. The beginnings of solidarity appeared among the various immigrant populations and the native Hawaiians, along with a new, inclusive concept of racial/ethnic identity. This social transformation was reflected in language. The term *local* had always referred to any longtime resident of the islands, with no reference to race or ethnicity. But, in the wake of the Massie trial, it took on an expanded and more potent meaning, now referring only to native Hawaiians and longtime Pacific Islander and Asian residents. Haoles, whatever their character, could never be "local."

The Massie case also changed Hawai'i's political structure. Formerly overwhelmingly Republican, prominent haoles in the legal community, the press, and the government began to speak out against the arrogance of the entrenched white oligarchy. At the same time, Hawaiian, Japanese, Chinese, Filipino, and Portuguese community leaders began finding common political ground. Along with the rest of the nation, Hawaii turned overwhelmingly Democratic in the 1932 elections, for both local and territorial offices. Native Hawaiians, who previously had supported the Republicans, partly out of a fear of political dominance by the Japanese, now also voted Democratic. The new ethnic solidarity was also reflected in the increasing success of the labor movement. Where previously ethnic separatism had undermined the success of labor protests, now strikes by combined ethnic groups of workers succeeded both on the plantations and on the docks.

The impact of the Massie case in transforming the racial, ethnic, and class configuration in Hawai'i illustrates the important role of culture and history in constructing categories of race and ethnicity. It demonstrates how these identities interact in different systems of social inequality and how they can and do change over time. We need to hold this concept of the cultural construction of race and ethnicity in mind as we examine the various issues discussed in this chapter.

THE CULTURAL CONSTRUCTION OF RACE

As noted in Chapter 1, race is a culturally constructed category, based on *perceived* physical differences, which implies hereditary differences between peoples and is used to justify social stratification. But although race is a culturally constructed category, it becomes a social fact that has enormous impact on the way people are treated and on the circumstances of their lives.

Caste, class, or ethnic differences often are conceptualized in racial terms, even when there are no objective physical differences, such as skin color, between groups so contrasted. As recently as the 19th century, the English described the Irish as a race of utter savages, truly barbarous and brutish. According to the Victorian theologian and novelist Charles Kingsley, the Irish were "human chimpanzees." Kingsley wrote that "to see white chimpanzees is dreadful; if they were black, one would not feel it so much, but their skins, except where tanned by exposure, are as white as ours" (Curtis 1968:84). It was this idea of a "degenerate Irish race," along with class and religion, that the British used to justify their domination over Ireland. As the Irish migrated to the United States, the notion of their cultural and biological inferiority was commonly expressed in the language of race (Shanklin 1994:3–7).

In Japan, the concept of race is applied to the Burakumin, a stigmatized and oppressed group. The Japanese believe that the Burakumin are innately physically and morally distinct from other Japanese, but in fact there are no physical differences between them. Thus, the Burakumin are an "invisible race," distinguished only by differences in family name, occupation, place of residence, and lifestyle. In spite of their official emancipation in 1871, the racial stigma of the Burakumin lives on (De Vos and Wagatsuma 1966).

Many systems of inherited stratification, whether racial, ethnic, or caste based, symbolize these social distinctions in terms of biological or racial differences, which are then associated with traits of culture, character, morality, intelligence, personality, and purity that are seen as natural, inherited, and unalterable—in a word, ascribed. Although it is socially easier to distinguish a race when individuals differ in obvious physical characteristics, the Japanese–Burakumin relationship and the English perceptions of the Irish demonstrate that a lack of observable physical differences does not prohibit the invention of racial categories or the emergence of racial stratification systems.

RACIAL STRATIFICATION SYSTEMS

One way to explore the cultural nature of racial systems is to compare the understandings of race in different societies. In some systems of racial stratification race is viewed as a continuum. In Brazil there are many shades of "color," and a different name and status is accorded to each. In other systems, race is largely defined as a binary opposition between black and white, as in the United States. In yet other systems, as in South Africa under **apartheid**, multiple exclusive racial classifications—black, white, colored, and Asian—were formally recognized. Their members were segregated, treated differently in law and life, and occupied different and almost exclusive statuses within the society (Marx 1998).

The United States and Brazil are both societies where there is a close connection between racial classification and social stratification, yet both nations understand race in very different ways.

Cultural Construction of Race in the United States

In the United States race is culturally constructed largely on the basis of a few observable traits, such as skin color and hair texture and presumed ancestry. Apart from a few regional variations on race (for example, the Anglo-Hispanic distinction in the American Southwest and the complex racial/ethnic system in Hawai'i, described previously), historically the

North American system of racial stratification primarily divides people into blacks and whites. This dichotomy ignores two realities: first, skin color actually forms a continuum; and second, widespread racial mixing has occurred historically and continues in the present. Indeed, recent trends show that this cultural view of a racial dichotomy is changing. In the 2000 U.S. Census, for the first time people were permitted to self-identify as more than one race. Seven million people, almost half of whom were under 18, chose to do so (Boynton 2006).

The culturally constructed nature of the American binary of race is revealed in antebellum Southern court decisions. For the purposes of school segregation, courts held that the Chinese were white but that individuals with at least 1⁄32 "Negro blood" were black, even if their skin color was indistinguishable from whites (Dominguez 1986:3). In an ironic comment on the American racial classification system, Haitian dictator Papa Doc Duvalier once told an American reporter that 96 percent of Haitians were white. Surprised and puzzled, the reporter asked on what grounds he arrived at this percentage. Duvalier explained that Haiti used the same procedure for counting whites—a "drop" of white blood—that Americans used for counting blacks (Hirschfeld 1996).

In the United States, we think of race mainly in terms of African, Hispanic/Latino, Asian, or Native Americans—that is, minority races. But white also is a racial identity. Because white is a cultural norm in the United States, however, the privileges and advantages that go with it are largely invisible and taken for granted (Allen 1997; Frankenberg 1993; Hartigan 1997; Hill 1998).

For whites, ordinary experiences such as shopping, buying or renting a place to live, finding a hairdresser, or using a credit card do not generally involve a reflection on their racial identity. But for African Americans, Hispanic/Latino Americans, Asian Americans, and Native Americans, these everyday activities cannot be taken for granted (McIntosh 1999).

The binary form of American racial classification grew out of specific historical conditions, especially slavery and reconstruction (Foner 1988). The racial stereotypes that reinforced slavery and later segregation were also, shamefully, supported by the then emerging biological and social sciences. Many scientific statements legitimized races as hierarchically arranged natural categories, characterized by physical, cultural, and moral differences (Smedley 1998). Even today in the United States, pseudoscientific publications linking race and intelligence, such as *The Bell Curve* (Herrnstein and Murray 1994) maintain great popularity, even though little evidence supports their hypotheses and their thesis has been soundly critiqued by anthropologists (Nisbett 2007; http://www.understandingRACE.org).

Race is misguided as a scientific concept, but race as a social fact is centrally implicated in the American social stratification system. Race impacts on every aspect of life, indeed, on the very chance of life itself, as we saw earlier on the effects of Hurricane Katrina (see Chapter 10, p. 226). This is particularly demonstrated by statistics showing higher mortality rates of both infants and mothers among African Americans (Chelala 2006; Stolberg 1999). A black male baby born in the United States today will live 7 years less than a white male baby (Calman et al. 2005:8). Racial disparities with regard to access to health care and health care outcomes also are revealed. Cancer survival rates, death rates due to heart disease and human immunodeficiency virus (HIV)/acquired immunodeficiency syndrome (AIDS), and complications from diseases such as diabetes, loss of a limb, or kidney disease, all are substantially higher for African Americans than for whites. The causes of these and many other health disparities are clearly linked to unequal treatment and health care, itself linked significantly to medical insurance. In New York City, 30 percent of African Americans, Latinos, and "other" New Yorkers are uninsured compared to 17 percent of whites. People who are covered by Medicaid are treated differently by health care institutions. For example, they are more likely to be seen by rotating medical students and interns and thus less likely to receive coordinated medical care (Calman 2005:25).

Racial stratification also affects job and educational opportunities open to racial minorities; access to fair credit, salary levels, accumulation of wealth, all of which affect social mobility; home ownership, mortgage rates, and housing foreclosures; use of public spaces; levels and types of violence, and interactions with law enforcement and the criminal justice system, where black males, followed by Latino males, are much more likely to have spent time in prison (Bajaj and Nixon 2006; *Class Matters,* New York Times; Harrison 1998). These are just some of the ways in which race and class interact in the United States (Reed 2006).

Racial Classification in Brazil

Like the United States, Brazil had a plantation economy whose core was African slave labor. After 1888, when Brazil abolished slavery, the Brazilian government followed a policy of "whitening" by encouraging immigration of Europeans and teaching only Euro-Brazilian history and culture (dos Santos 2002). At the same time, Brazil did not encode racial distinctions in law, and interracial marriage and sexual relations were not illegal (Goldstein 1999; Sheriff 2001). In contrast, the United States legally barred interracial marriage until the courts struck down this law (which existed in 16 states) in 1967.

In Brazil, interracial sex and marriage were much more common than in the United States. Today, individuals of African descent account for about 45 percent of the total population of Brazil, yet only about

© Joan Gregg

In Brazil, in contrast to the United States, race is a continuum, not a dichotomy.

15 percent of these people identify themselves as *preta* (black) on the census forms. The rest self identify as *parda* (brown, of partially African ancestry). This self-identification is tied to social stratification. Brazilian understandings of race may be flexible, but the distribution of wealth and education in Brazil is profoundly unequal. Brazilian stratification is racially structured, with whites at the top, blacks at the bottom, and *parda* somewhere between the two.

Brazilian racial classification is extremely complex, particularly within the part of the population that self-identifies as African descended. For example, in a community studied by Conrad Kottak (1992:67), almost all the villagers were of slave ancestry, and most would have been considered black in the United States. But here, almost half identified themselves as mulatto, a commonly used intermediate category between black and white. Unlike in the United States, where race is determined by ancestry, in this village brothers and sisters were often classified as belonging to different races. These Brazilian villagers also used many more criteria than North Americans to assign race, including skin color, nose length and shape, eye color and shape, hair type and color, and shape of the lips. The villagers used 10 to 15 different racial terms to describe people, such as mulatto, *mulatto claro* (light mulatto), or *sarara,* meaning a person with reddish skin and light curly hair. These terms were applied inconsistently, and there was wide disagreement among the villagers in placing themselves and others in racially defined categories. Such decisions frequently were mediated by class and status.

Throughout Latin America, many nations promote their mixed ethnic heritage as a central aspect of their national identity. This is true of Brazil, where "mixed blood" has long been central to political ideology. In the 1940s, the influential Brazilian anthropologist and politician Gilberto Freyre promoted the idea that "Brazillianness" was the result of mixing between people of European, African, and indigenous ancestry (Bailey and Telles 2006; Freyre 1946). Freyre, who had been a student of Franz Boas at Columbia University, adopted many of his understandings of race and racial equality (Sánchez-Eppler 1992). Freyre's work and other trends in Brazilian society gave race mixing in Brazil a positive connotation, whereas in the United States, historically race mixing has had mainly negative connotations.

Brazilian politicians and some social scientists used Freyre's work to promote the notion that Brazil was a racial democracy. In the 1970 census, the military government declined to ask people's race, arguing that because there was no race issue in Brazil, there was no need to ask the question (Bailey and Telles 2006:77). The public denial of race in Brazil has had both positive and negative effects. On the one hand, the linkage between Brazilian identity and mixed ancestry probably has made it easier for many Brazilians to negotiate their identity. It has also led to a society where, at least in theory, opportunity is open to people of diverse physical characteristics. On the other hand, the persistent denial that race is a social issue has led to a widespread refusal to take discrimination and racial stratification seriously (Reichman 1995).

This is an important flaw in Brazilian society, as studies show that racial inequality exacts a high toll. On every measure of social and economic well-being, Brazilians who self-identify as having African ancestry are far worse off than are those who self-identify as white. Their illiteracy rates are far higher and their wages are far lower. Higher education is almost exclusively the domain of white Brazilians. In the United Nations Human Development Index (HDI) for all nations in 2000, which measures national quality of life, Brazil ranked 74th in the world. However, if the same methodology were used to rank its white and African-descended populations separately, the white population would rank 48th and the African-descended population would rank 108th (Roland 2001).

In Brazil the educational disparities between whites and nonwhites are much greater than in the United States, a difference based partly on different traditions of public education (Andrews 1992:243). In the United States, providing education is a major obligation of the state and local governments, but in Brazil, governments have assumed this responsibility only since World War II. Thus, the general level of education in Brazil for both whites and nonwhites is much lower than in the United States. Brazil has a high rate of illiteracy, and higher education is almost entirely the province of white elites (Berman, in Danaher and Shellenberger 1995:91). In contrast, most Americans, white and black, are literate, and most are high-school graduates, although educational disparities between blacks and whites continue and the percentage of the black population enrolling in college lags far behind that of whites, a trend exacerbated in states, like California, where affirmative action has been banned by voter referendums (see You Decide).

This comparison between the Brazilian and American racial stratification systems indicates that racial inequality is a serious issue in both societies in spite of their very different cultural constructions of race.

ETHNICITY AND ETHNIC STRATIFICATION

The term **ethnicity** often appears in the media as the cause of conflict and violence—between the Irish and the English in Northern Ireland, between the Hutu and the Tutsi in Central Africa, between Hindus and Muslims in India, between Tamils and Sinhalese in Sri Lanka, between French and English speakers in Canada; between Bosnians and Serbs, Croatians, and Albanians in the former nation of Yugoslavia; between Kurds, Shi'a, and Sunni Muslims in Iraq; and between the Basques and the Spanish in Spain, among many others.

Ethnicity refers to *perceived* differences, such as culture, religion, language, national origin, by which groups of people distinguish themselves and are distinguished from others in the same social environment. Unlike the concept of race, which always involves perceived *physical* differences, ethnicity refers to perceived *cultural* differences. **Ethnic identity,** which is an ethnically based sense of self, is an important identification in contemporary society, but it intersects with other sources of identity, such as age, gender, nation, race, and social class.

Ethnic groups are categories of people who view themselves as sharing an ethnic identity that differentiates them from other groups or from the larger society as a whole. **Ethnic boundaries** are the perceived cultural attributes by which ethnic groups distinguish themselves from others. The perception that a person belongs to a particular ethnic group, and the emergence of particular ethnic groups and identities, evolves from the interaction of a group with other groups and with the larger society. This interaction, although couched in symbolic cultural terms, is significantly shaped by competition and conflict over resources, hence the term *ethnic stratification.*

In popular culture, ethnicity and ethnic identity are often viewed as based on a timeless division of people that rests on a "bedrock" of cultural difference from others (Meier and Ribera 1993). Ethnicity is understood as based on "primordial" or "natural" ties that stem from "common blood, religion, language, attachment to a place, or customs" and passed down largely unchanged from generation to generation (Geertz 1973b:277).

From this perspective, called **essentialism,** ethnicity appears as an independent force that explains why people act collectively in certain ways, whether voting as a political bloc, protecting economic interests, going to war with other ethnic groups, or rebelling against national governments. In the context of group conflicts, ethnicity is viewed as "a clinging to old loyalties" and as the cause of a group's resistance to various aspects of modern life.

The anthropological view of ethnicity emphasizes its social construction: Ethnic groups and ethnic conflict are seen as socially constructed.

Ethnicity becomes more or less important and takes particular shape under specific historical, demographic, and economic conditions (De Vos and Romanucci-Ross 1995). This **social constructionist** view of ethnicity is illustrated by the changing ethnic landscape in Hawaii after the Massie case. From this perspective, ethnic group identity and ethnic boundaries are not fossilized "age-old" patterns, but they are repeatedly reinterpreted over time and intersect with changing political and economic circumstances. Social constructionists might say, then, that ethnicity rests less on a bedrock of culture than it does on the shifting sands of history and political power, specifically, social interactions with other ethnic groups (Barth 1998/1969). Although cultural differences between groups in society do exist, it is relationships between groups—which may be competitive or cooperative, may involve conflict, or may be some combination of these factors—that are the most significant components of the process of ethnic group formation and definition. With this orientation, anthropologists today ask questions about the circumstances that elicit or mobilize ethnicity as a vehicle for association, collective action, and personal identity and investigate how ethnic groups emerge, change, and disappear in response to changing conditions in the economic and social environment.

ETHNICITY AND THE NATION STATE

The most important contemporary context for the emergence, conflict, change, and disappearance of ethnic groups and ethnic identity is the **nation-state.** Nation-states are governments and territories that are identified with (relatively) culturally homogeneous populations and national histories. A nation is popularly felt by its members to be a natural entity based on bonds of common descent, language, culture, history, and territory, but in fact all modern nation-states are composed of many ethnic (and other) groups. Benedict Anderson (1991) calls nation-states "imagined communities" because an act of imagination is needed to weld the many disparate groups that actually make up the state into a coherent national community. Anthropologists are interested in the historical circumstances under which nation-states evolve, the processes by which they are constructed and maintained, and the circumstances under which they are challenged and destabilized (Stolcke 1995).

One way in which nation-states construct national identities is by drawing boundaries between spatially defined insiders and outsiders (Bornstein 2002; Handler 1988). Regardless of some cultural differences, people who live within these boundaries are viewed as having an essential natural identity, based on a common language and shared customs and culture. People outside the national boundary are viewed as essentially

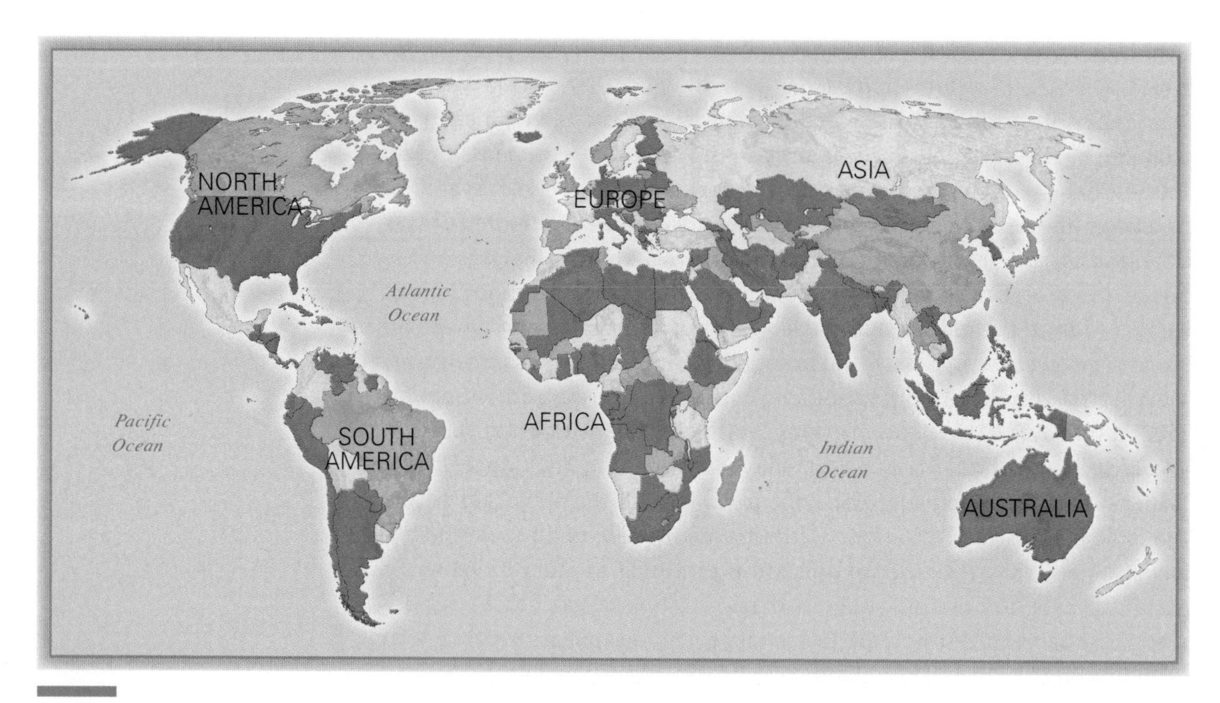

World maps reinforce the importance of the nation-state as a territorial unit.

different, having their own national identities. The importance of the spatial dimension of the nation-state is continually impressed on us by colorful world maps, which visually represent the world of nations as a discrete spatial partitioning of territory (Alonso 1994:382). Additionally, nations often erect physical boundaries to define their territory and to separate insiders from outsiders. The Great Wall of China and the Berlin Wall are two historic examples of this separation. The current controversy over the building of a fence along the border between the United States and Mexico demonstrates that this continues to be a powerful idea (see p. 212).

Nation-states are constructed by attaching people to time as well as to space. A common interpretation of the past is essential in creating national identities. This is problematic because different groups within the nation likely have different interpretations of its history. Because of this, the creation of national histories often is marked by struggles over which version of history will prevail (Friedman 1992). "Tradition," "the past," "history," and "social memory" all are actively invented and reinvented in accordance with contemporary national interests and reproduced through rituals, symbols, ceremonies, memorials, and representations in museums and other cultural institutions (Hobsbawm and Ranger 1983; Nanda 2004; White 1997). Coronations, inaugurations, daily pledging of allegiance to the flag, or singing of the national anthems—ceremonies that link the nation's dead to its living and thus the past to the present, such as Veterans

Day and Memorial Day—all are essential to maintaining the nation-state. Constructing national identities has been particularly problematic for postcolonial states, whose artificial colonial boundaries encompassed many different ethnic groups (see Chapter 13), but it also is true in older nations. After World War II, the ethnic homogeneity of many nation-states was achieved by the coerced migration of ethnic minorities (Judt 2005). In Canada, because of the dual influence of English and French culture, the search for Canadian national identity is ongoing, occasionally flaring up in demands for French-speaking Quebecois separatism (Handler 1988). In November 2006, the Canadian House of Commons overwhelmingly passed a motion declaring Quebec "a nation within Canada."

Although the nation-state always seeks to repress the invented or imagined nature of national unity (Foster 1991:238), it has many sources of power in shaping ethnicities, fostering some group identities and marginalizing or disparaging others. In their attempts to establish hegemony (see Chapter 9, "Political Organization," p. 211), the invention and implementation of a national identity, with its associated rites and symbols, are carried out by nationalist elites, intellectuals, politicians, and institutions supported by the state. For example, states use education, law, and the media to create a national culture and identity that become the only authorized representations of society.

Through law, the state can criminalize certain aspects of minority cultures. In the past the United States suppressed many Native-American rituals, such as the potlatch or the use of peyote for religious purposes, and the United States continues to suppress many contemporary aspects of Native-American culture (Bracey 2006). Marijuana use among Rastafarians continues to be criminalized, even though it is used for religious purposes, and the acceptability of polygamous families among Fundamentalist Mormons is a matter of continuing debate (Norgren and Nanda 2006). The mere use of the term cultural *mainstream* conveys a level of lesser acceptance of subcultures, even though the mainstream, like the subcultures, is a cultural artifact, and its content is constantly changing.

The state may shape ethnicity by incorporating, for its own purposes, elements of subcultures into the national culture. In many nations of Central and South America, indigenous Indian ethnicity, if not totally repressed, is defined in ways that serve state purposes. Indians may be identified with a fossilized past as a folkloric irrelevance, a tourist commodity, or a backward culture standing in the way of national development (Alonso 1994:398). Only a few nations, most recently Bolivia, with the election of Evo Morales as its president, have raised indigenous Indian ethnicity to a central place in national identity and political leadership (Guillermierpietro 2006).

Ethnic Conflict

Much ethnic conflict today is tied to the rise, maintenance, and collapse of the nation-state (Stolcke 1995). Although contemporary ethnic conflicts often are presented as natural eruptions of age-old ethnic hatreds, many such conflicts in fact are rooted not in some distant past but in relatively recent circumstances, shaped by contemporary political events and conflicts over economic resources. Ambitious politicians often promote ethnic identity, building constituencies from groups that hope to gain increased access to economic and political power. Such individuals mobilize a rhetoric of historical abuses and inequities, arousing fears of victimization among members of different groups who, in the past, lived fairly amicably together.

One example is the former Yugoslavia, a multiethnic state, which was part of the Ottoman Empire ruled by Muslim Turks until after World War II, when Yugoslavia became a nation. Conflict between the Turks and Christian Europeans was a central force generating Serb nationalism in the 19th and 20th centuries. Yugoslavia had been held together by a powerful central government frequently backed by the Soviet Union. However, after the death of Dictator Josip Tito and the collapse of the Soviet Union the nation disintegrated into ethnic violence. Throughout the 1990s bitter conflicts among different ethnic and religious groups led to deaths numbering in the hundreds of thousands. By the early 2000s, six new nations, divided largely along ethnic lines, had emerged from the former Yugoslavia. Recently, a seventh, Kosovo, has appeared. But ethnic conflict of the 1990s was not "caused" by the cultural distinctions and past conflicts among Yugoslavia's ethnic groups—Serbs, Croats, Bosnians (many of whom are Muslim), Macedonians, and Albanians. Rather, a selectively remembered past of cultural differences was mobilized in contemporary struggles over economic and political power, which began in the 1980s (Gilliland 1995; Judt 2005:665–684; Maybury-Lewis 1997; Ramet 1996).

Ethnic violence in the former Yugoslavia began as a result of the political exploitation of relatively small cultural differences between Croats and Serbs.

The emergence of Croatia is a good example of the way ethnic nationalism can become a means of expressing political and economic issues. In 1981, after the death of Yugoslav leader

Tito, the new political leadership introduced an economic austerity program in an attempt to shore up the nation's import–export imbalance. The resulting shortages of consumer goods undermined faith in the government, and people depended even more than usual on kinship and friendship networks within their ethnic groups in order to survive. Hostility was mainly directed toward the national government, which exploited long-standing cultural differences among the main ethnic groups to secure its own political power. The Croat nationalist leader Franjo Tudjman gained supporters by urging Croats to claim their national rights against Serbs, Muslims, and others, reigniting the bitter divisions between the Croats, who supported Hitler in World War II, and the resistance, which was primarily Serb. In 1990, after the breakup of the Yugoslav Communist Party, Tudjman led his own nationalist party to victory in Croatian elections and declared an independent state in Croatia, resulting in the bloody war with Serbia that ended with Croatian independence.

Within this context, old attributes of cultural similarity were transformed into markers of difference. For example, Croats and Serbs both are Christian but they belong to different sects: the Croats are Catholic and the Serbs Eastern Orthodox. They speak the same language but they use different writing systems. Croatians now call their language Croatian rather than Serbo-Croatian, as it was formerly called (Gilliland 1995:202). The actual cultural differences between Serbs and Croats, which are slight, did not cause the ethnic conflict but rather became its vehicle.

This, of course, is not the whole story of ethnic conflicts. In many cases, there are significant long-standing cultural and religious differences among groups who generally live in mutual tolerance. These differences may erupt in violence. In some cases, such differences may be exploited by politicians or nationalist groups with their own political interests in mind. The conflicts in Kashmir, a territory disputed over by Pakistan and India, is an example of this situation. In other cases, such as with many indigenous peoples (described later), ethnic conflict and ethnic violence arise from years, even centuries, of mistreatment of cultural minorities by the state or by elites.

Ethnic Stratification and Indigenous Peoples

In much of the world today, particularly in North and South America, Africa, and parts of Asia, indigenous peoples are an important part of the ethnic landscape. **Indigenous peoples** are those small-scale societies designated as bands, tribes, and chiefdoms that occupied their land prior to European contact. Generally, indigenous people are closely identified with their land, are relatively egalitarian, manage resources at the community level, and (previously) had high levels of economic self-sufficiency. They consider themselves distinct from other sectors of society now living in their territories and today function as nondominant sectors of the larger nation-states of which they are a part. Indigenous societies today are determined to preserve and transmit their lands and culture to future generations in order to continue their existence as a people, which frequently brings them into conflict with the nation-state (Lee 2000).

Indigenous peoples today are in a struggle for autonomy and survival in a world dominated by nation-states and a global capitalist economy (Bodley 1999). The assault against indigenous peoples began with European invasion and conquest in the 15th century. Many indigenous societies completely disappeared as a result of epidemics, frontier violence, and military conquest; others survived as remnants in marginal geographic areas (see Chapter 13). As late as 1800, approximately 50 percent of the world's territory and 20 percent of the global population were still controlled by indigenous societies (Bodley 2000:398). The destruction of indigenous peoples intensified rapidly by the mid-19th century as new frontiers were opened up in nations such as the United States, Australia, and Brazil. Although there was much resistance, in most places indigenous peoples were no match for the military and economic power of nation-states. After World War II, many indigenous peoples were incorporated into new postcolonial states, such as in Indonesia, Malaysia, and India, and few independent, self-sufficient indigenous societies remained (Maybury-Lewis 1997).

The incorporation of indigenous peoples into modern nation-states involved at least partial destruction of their political and economic autonomy. Because indigenous peoples must maintain control over their land base and subsistence resources in order to remain self-sufficient and politically autonomous, their political defeat was usually accompanied by their economic marginalization. Europeans appropriated their land, and, without their land base, indigenous peoples were pushed into participation in the global market economy and forced to give up their traditional livelihoods.

Participation by indigenous peoples in larger economies was—and is—furthered by the "pull" of their desire for Western goods. However, whenever indigenous people were reluctant to acquiesce to colonial agendas, including participation in capitalist consumer-oriented economies, colonialists always fell back on threatened or actual coercion through military conquest.

The colonial agenda was also imposed on indigenous peoples through Western law. European colonial powers defined acceptable behavior and enforced that behavior through the establishment of written penal codes, constitutions, and Western-style courts, with severe sanctions for nonconformity (Merry 1991, 2000). A wide array of indigenous cultural practices—

witchcraft accusations, use of peyote and marijuana in religious contexts, potlatching, drumming, dancing, warfare, collective land tenure, headhunting, slash and burn horticulture, transvestism, and many others—were outlawed in the name of social reform and the European civilizing mission (Merry 1991). Sexual practices of indigenous peoples often were criminalized as uncivilized and un-Christian (W. Roscoe 1995).

After World War II, the establishment of the United Nations provided an international framework within which the concept of human rights was steadily expanded to include indigenous peoples as cultural groups and to legitimize their struggle for self-determination. Since the United Nations policy worked within the framework of the nation-state, however, it did little to support indigenous rights in any substantial way. Some of this has changed with the passage, on September 13, 2007, of the Declaration on the Rights of Indigenous Peoples. However, in addition to the United States, Australia, Canada, and New Zealand, who did not sign the declaration, there were 11 abstentions and much controversy over some of its principles. For example, Canada fears that the commitment of the declaration to land rights for aboriginal peoples will open up new land claims. Namibia claims that the special privileges for the San people unfairly disadvantages non-San citizens and undermines the territorial integrity of Namibia.

National policies reflecting neglect or hostility toward indigenous peoples frequently were based on the expectation that indigenous peoples eventually would disappear as they were assimilated into national cultures and participated in national and global economic programs. This also was the presumption of international financial organizations, such as the World Bank and the International Monetary Fund, whose lending practices supported economic "development" programs that adversely affected the subsistence economies of indigenous peoples (Bodley 2000:378).

National policies of cultural assimilation also contributed to the losses of indigenous peoples. In the United States, assimilation was the dominant American policy toward Native Americans, although even groups, like the Cherokee, that had adopted many "American" cultural patterns were still subject to removal and appropriation of their land by whites (Norgren 1996; Wallace 1999). By the mid-19th century, when they were forced onto reservations, Native Americans became a captive audience for the teaching of American values of individualism, Christianity, privately owned agricultural production, and the English language by missionaries and Indian agents of the U.S. government. Native Americans were forced to send their children to American boarding schools, often hundreds of miles from their local communities, permanently alienating these children from their native cultures and languages. Although these policies did succeed in weakening Native-American cultures and languages and traumatizing many individual Native Americans, they did not succeed in transforming Native Americans into assimilated American yeoman farmers. Only in the 1930s, under the directorship of John Collier, an anthropologist who headed the Bureau of Indian Affairs, were government policies reversed to support the strengthening of Indian cultures and societies (Norgren and Nanda 2006). In the 1960s, with the emergence of the civil rights movement, Native Americans again mounted a struggle, still ongoing, to reclaim their cultures, with only partial success.

Many anthropologists, most notably the organization Cultural Survival, actively participate with indigenous peoples in their struggles for justice. Cultural Survival actively works to increase the ability of indigenous peoples to improve their position within multiethnic or culturally pluralist nation-states. It helps indigenous peoples retain their cultural identities while they adapt gradually to the changes accompanying national economic development (Maybury-Lewis 1993).

Ethnicity and Immigration in the United States

Although the cultural diversity of the United States is partially based on conquest (of Native Americans, Native Hawaiians, and Mexicans) and the importation of African Americans as slaves, the dominant American narrative of ethnicity is largely based on the national origins of its many groups of voluntary immigrants. Only in the mid-20th century did African Americans, Native Americans, and Latinos reassert their cultural identities as part of a civil rights movement, broadening definitions of ethnicity to reach beyond immigration.

No one criterion of ethnic identity holds for all groups in the United States. Language is an important ethnic boundary marker for some Latino/Hispanics but no longer is an important marker for many older ethnic groups of European origin. Rather, more subtle ethnic patterns, such as food preferences, verbal and nonverbal means of communication, the experience of health, illness, and pain, occupational choices, and voting patterns give substance to the many ethnic identities in the United States today (Cerroni-Long 1993; Schensul 1997).

U.S. immigration history is an essential context for understanding contemporary constructions of American ethnicity and the relations between ethnic groups (Ryan 1999). There is no single immigrant experience because different groups faced historically different circumstances (di Leonardo 1984; Lamphere 1992). Depending on historical circumstances, national origin, and the degree to which the immigrant culture was perceived as alien, immigrants have met with greater or lesser hostility from those already established here.

The continuous process of immigrant adaptation in the United States intersects with the continuous, self-conscious project of creating an American national identity—a process that started with the American Revolution (Wallace 1999). Thus, although ethnicity in the United States led to the equation of ethnicity with national origin, this concept was not equally applied to all nationalities. English national origin, for example, was not seen as ethnic but as the American norm.

Public debate on immigration has been a consistent feature of American cultural and political life, taking different forms in different historical periods. Early idealistic visions of America as a land of economic opportunity and political freedom for immigrants from Europe were actually narrowly defined to encompass mainly those from northern and western Europe. In considering questions of citizenship in the creation of the United States Constitution, the framers effectively limited it to those who were "free and white (and male)." By the 1830s, increasing immigration of Irish Catholics and Germans to the United States heightened earlier concerns that the new immigrants would undermine American republicanism, either because their previous poverty in Europe had denied them the experience of political freedom or because their authoritarian religion would make them hostile to it and draw their loyalties elsewhere (Gjerde 1998). In addition, some Americans feared that an influx of immigrants would result in lower urban wages or that immigrants would flood and then dominate the western part of the country. These concerns coalesced in strongly anti-Catholic and anti-immigrant nativist movements and today are an important source of the debate over both undocumented and legal immigration.

Between 1850 and 1910, many immigrants gravitated to cities, where they lived in ethnic (actually multiethnic)—and poor—neighborhoods, generating the fear that they would be corrupted by urban political machines. On the basis of common culture and national origin, immigrants formed social and ethnic institutions that helped them retain some of their ethnic culture and separateness from the larger society and at the same time mediated their connections with it.

The largest and most varied immigration to the United States occurred between 1880 and the 1920s. In this period the cultural discourse on immigration moved from ethnicity to race. African Americans were always viewed as a racial group, but by 1880 racial typologies became fashionable (a process in which anthropologists unfortunately played a role) and were applied to Europeans as well. Southern and eastern Europeans were racially distinguished from the Nordic races from northern and western Europe. By the 1920s, restrictive immigration laws effectively limited immigration to these "Nordic" groups.

Proponents of restrictive immigration claimed that members of different races could never become good American citizens and that the United States would "degenerate" if it incorporated them. Nations such as England, viewed as culturally and politically similar to the United States, were allowed almost unrestricted immigration, whereas nations of eastern Europe, including Greece and Poland, were allowed only minimal immigration. Immigration of Asians and persons from the Middle East were all but completely halted. The nexus between national origin and race in this period led to several Supreme Court cases in which the Court grappled with the definition of "whiteness" as immigrants from India, Lebanon, and other places appealed their denial of entry into the United States based on their "nonwhite" racial status (K. Moore 2000; Lopez 2006).

Models of Adaptation

At the turn of the 20th century, the dominant vision of responding to immigration was **assimilation**—the view that immigrants should abandon their cultural distinctiveness and become "mainstream" Americans. Urban settlement houses, public schools, and citizenship classes were designed to teach immigrants "American" ways and to motivate them to abandon the cultural patterns they brought from their homelands.

By the 1950s it was clear that although much of the cultural distinctiveness of ethnic groups in the United States had been lost in the so-called "melting pot," ethnic groups themselves persisted, now mainly as interest groups organized around political goals and mobilized for gaining access to economic resources (Glazer and Moynihan 1970). After the civil rights movement at midcentury, concepts of ethnicity and its relation to American nationhood changed again. **Multiculturalism,** which embraces cultural diversity as a positive value that added richness to the whole society, emerged to contest older, assimilationist views. A new Immigration and Nationality Act, passed in 1965 and explicitly aimed at reversing the discriminatory basis of earlier immigration laws, greatly expanded the number of people permitted to immigrate from previously discriminated against nations, abolished immigration quotas, gave high priority to the social goal of family unification, and put refugee immigration on a more structured basis (Fix and Passel 1994; Lamphere 1992:Introduction). Although the new law resulted in a historic high of immigration, the percentage of the United States population that is foreign born (about 8.5 percent) actually is about half what it was at its historic peak (Fix and Passel 1994). The major change has the increase of immigrants from the Middle East, the Indian subcontinent, China, Korea, the Caribbean, and parts of Central and South America, groups previously discriminated against.

The changed economic circumstances from the early 1900s have changed the immigrant experience and society's response to immigration. In the present era of economic contraction, with the loss of jobs resulting from globalization and corporate downsizing and the widespread exploitation of undocumented immigrants working for lower wages in many American industries, a new intense debate over immigration, particularly of undocumented immigrants, is again emerging (Benson 1999; Schlosser 2005; Stull, Broadway, and Erickson 1992), resulting in passage of state "English Only" laws and bans on providing social services to undocumented immigrants (Norgren and Nanda 2006).

At the same time, improved communications and cheaper airfares make it easier for new immigrants to retain closer social and economic ties with their families and cultures in their homelands. This pattern of transnationalism (Glick-Schiller, Basch, and Szanton-Blanc 1992) has also changed immigrant experiences.

Some of the changing dimensions of contemporary immigration are illustrated by Chinese immigrants to the United States. In 1882, the United States passed the Chinese Exclusion Act in an attempt to keep out the Chinese, who were perceived not only as racially and culturally inassimilable but also as an economic threat. Today most (but by no means all) Chinese immigrants are educated, technically skilled, urban people. Those from Taiwan or Hong Kong, motivated primarily by economic and educational opportunities, frequently arrive with access to capital, professional training, and experience or with expertise in manufacturing, finance, or engineering. Many are relatively westernized and proficient in English, a crucial factor in their successful adaptation, as is their adherence to maintaining many Chinese cultural values like family solidarity, entrepreneurship, hard work, and drive for higher education (Wong 1988). All of these factors contributed to their successful adaptation, and indeed they are now often referred to as the "model minority."

In today's increasingly globalized world, with its large migrations of populations, immigration now is also an intensely emotional issue in many European nations. For example, France experienced widespread and violent riots from the second generation of North African and African immigrants in 2005 (Ireland 2005). The rioters were mainly children of immigrants who had been recruited to France as manual laborers and factory workers to replace the declining French labor force in the expanding economy after World War II. Despite promises of the French government, these immigrants and their families were never integrated into French society. Rather, they were largely "warehoused" in high-rise, low-income ghettos at the edge of many French cities. With the subsequent decline in the French economy in the 1980s, this second generation of immigrants, who are French citizens, experience job discrimination, subsequent high unemployment, and intense alienation from French society. Because most of these immigrants are Muslim, religious and cultural differences add to the tensions in French society. As in Germany and the Netherlands, conflicts, sometimes violent, emerge over issues such as the building of mosques and the wearing of head scarves by Muslim women (Bowen 2007; Buruma 2006).

Race, religion, and ethnicity are important dimensions of individual and national identity and contemporary social stratification systems. In Chapter 12 we explore in greater depth the concept of religion and the roles religion plays in both identity formation and social structures.

BRINGING IT BACK HOME: CLASS, ETHNICITY, RACE, AND EDUCATIONAL ACHIEVEMENT

During the mid-term election campaigns of 2006, Senator John Kerry said, "You know, education, if you make the most of it . . . you can do well. If you don't, you get stuck in Iraq." The statement caused a furor but also revealed a truth about the widespread view that educational achievement is essential for success and social mobility in the United States today.

In explaining the differences in educational achievements among different American minority groups, anthropologist John Ogbu argues for the importance of culture. Ogbu differentiates between what he calls *voluntary minorities,* those who came to the United States voluntarily in order to better their lives, and *involuntary minorities,* those who were brought here as slaves or incorporated through military policies of expansion. According to Ogbu, voluntary minorities believe they will be able to improve their current position and emphasize education as an important means of getting ahead (Gibson and Ogbu 1991:211–218).

In contrast, involuntary minorities, which include African Americans and Mexican Americans, view the social hierarchy of the United States as unfair, permanent, and systematically discriminatory. They are less likely to believe that success in education will lead them to success in life. Ogbu (and others, see Patterson 2006) hold that many students from involuntary minorities cope with their subordinated social status by creating a secondary culture, in which peer group values of cool behavior are more important than academic achievement. This "oppositional culture" contributes to academic failure likely.

Other social scientists acknowledge that inner-city cultures may undermine educational achievement but emphasize that these cultural patterns have their source in the poverty of inner-city neighborhoods; discriminatory educational policies such as low expectations of minority students; overcrowded and underfunded schools; and less qualified teachers (Gibson 1997; Mateu-Gelabert and Lune 2003, 2007). Under these conditions, inner-city schools are easily permeated by the street culture of violence. Indeed, as anthropologist Philippe Bourgois, in his study of East Harlem, New York, points out, the school itself is a significant place for learning the necessary skills for surviving on the streets of inner cities: fist fighting, verbal jousting, and strategic cruelty at the expense of weaker classmates. At the same time, much social science research notes that most inner-city residents support mainstream cultural norms and behaviors, especially educational achievement (Anderson 1999; Mateu-Gelabert 2003).

Thus, where an oppositional cultural model puts the burden on inner-city students to change their culture, the model's critics emphasize that educational achievement among minorities must depend on a fairer distribution of resources, more equitable educational policies, and the transformation of schools into safer, more disciplined environments.

YOU DECIDE

1. How important do you think educational achievement is to success in later life in the United States? Do you agree with cultural model of Ogbu or that of his critics as an explanation for the differential educational achievements of various minorities in America? Explain your answers.
2. What factors, such as culture, family, community, material accumulation, or other, do you see as most important in your own educational achievement?
3. What do you think are/were the most important obstacles you experienced in your drive toward educational achievement? To what extent do you think the obstacles and advantages of a good education are affected by minority status in America? Discuss this with regard to your own experience and that of other groups.

CHAPTER SUMMARY

1. The chapter opening story of Hawai'i illustrates that racial and ethnic categories are culturally constructed, that they must be understood in specific historical circumstances, and that they change over time.
2. Race is a culturally constructed category that refers to groups of people perceived as sharing similar physical and other characteristics transmitted by heredity. Although scientifically invalid, racial categories are important in many systems of social stratification.
3. The binary system of the United States and the multiracial system of Brazil are alternative ways of constructing race, but both systems incorporate racism and racial inequalities.

4. Ethnicity involves perceived cultural distinctions between groups. The essentialist view of ethnicity emphasizes the emotional sense of collective selfhood based on shared cultural traits. The social constructionist perspective views ethnicity, ethnic groups, and ethnic boundaries as contingent and dynamic cultural constructions.
5. Through its access to greater resources, control over its population, passage of laws, control of media, and other means, states are important actors in shaping ethnicity and ethnic conflict.
6. Indigenous peoples are important ethnic groups in many contemporary nation-states, with whom they may be in conflict over land, law, and repression of their traditional cultures.
7. The cultural diversity of the United States has largely been framed in terms of ethnicity based on the national origins of immigrants. Debates over assimilation, multiculturalism, and discrimination, both in the United States as well as many European nations, are important elements of current national immigration policies.

KEY TERMS

Apartheid
Assimilation model
Essentialism
Ethnic boundaries
Ethnic groups
Ethnic identity
Ethnicity
Indigenous peoples
Multiculturalism
Nation-state
Social constructionism (of ethnicity)

Among the Mentawai of Indonesia, shamans read the entrails of chickens and pigs to diagnose and then cure illness.

CHAPTER 12

RELIGION

CHAPTER OUTLINE

Cargo Cults

Defining Religion

Some Functions of Religion

- The Search for Order and Meaning
- Reducing Anxiety and Increasing Control
- Reinforcing or Challenging the Social Order

Characteristics of Religion

- Sacred Narratives
- Symbols and Symbolism
- Supernatural Beings, Powers, States, and Qualities
- Rituals and Ways of Addressing the Supernatural
- Religious Practitioners

Religion and Change

- Varieties of Religious Prophecies: Revitalization Movements

Bringing It Back Home: Religion, Art, and Censorship

- You Decide

CARGO CULTS

IGH on a mountain top in New Guinea, a group of men are performing a ritual around the body of a small plane that crashed there years ago. Their ritual is aimed at ensuring the arrival of "cargo," their word for the trade goods of Western culture that are the focus of their desires, stimulated by the encounters with Europeans, Americans, and Japanese over the past hundred years. Outsiders frequently promised wealth, equality, and political power, but members of these groups soon realized that their words did not match reality. Not only did Melanesians fail to gain wealth and power, but, in many cases, they grew poorer and were more deeply oppressed under colonial rule.

And so, all over Melanesia, rituals were performed to gain the secret knowledge that the Melanesians knew was the source of the power and wealth of the white outsiders, just as it was in their own society. Melanesians observed that whites did not seem to work but instead made "secret signs" on scraps of paper, built strange structures, and behaved in strange ways. For example, they built airports and seaports with towers and wires, and they drilled soldiers to march in formation. When they did these things, planes and ships arrived, disgorging a seemingly endless supply of material goods. Melanesians, who did so much hard physical labor, got nothing. Plainly, the whites knew the secrets of cargo and were keeping it from the islanders. If Melanesians could learn the secret knowledge and rituals of cargo, they believed they could rid their societies of oppressive colonial governments and gain access to this immense wealth for themselves.

Cargo cults usually began with a local prophet who announced that the world was about to end in a terrible catastrophe, after which God (or the ancestors, or a local culture hero) would appear, and a paradise on earth would begin. The end of the world could be caused or hastened by the performance of ritual that copied what they had observed the whites to do. In some places the faithful sat around tables dressed in European clothes, making signs on paper. In others they drilled with wooden rifles and built wharves, storehouses, airfields, and lookout towers in the hopes that such ritual would cause planes to land or ships to dock and disgorge cargo (Lindstrom 1993).

Cargo cults are not limited to Melanesia. In the United States and Latin America, millions of followers of prosperity theology or the Word-Faith movement believe that God wants Christians to be wealthy (Van Biema and Chu 2006). Promoted by Oral Roberts and other televangelists, the movement teaches their adherents that if they give money (the more the better) to movement churches and pray with sincerity, devotion, and frequency, God will reward them with cash and other material wealth, such as cars and houses. In other words, if they perform the correct rituals, they will receive cargo. If they remain poor, it is because they failed to properly ask God for wealth.

But perhaps cargo is not merely a cult in the United States but is central to our culture. Westerners do seem obsessed with cargo: an endless desire for consumer goods and the belief that buying specific brands of cars, drinks, or clothing will make them forever young, sexy, and powerful. Some might say that this is as likely to happen as it is for cargo to descend from the skies in Melanesia.

DEFINING RELIGION

All societies have spiritual beliefs and practices that anthropologists refer to as *religion.* Yet because of the great diversity of these beliefs and practices, defining religion is surprisingly difficult. Most definitions focus on the supernatural. Because Westerners make a clear distinction between natural and supernatural, this seems logical. But some religions explicitly deny that supernatural beings exist, whereas others do not distinguish them from what Westerners call the natural.

The phenomena that anthropologists identify as religion share five common characteristics. First, religions are composed of sacred stories that members believe are important. Second, religions make extensive use of symbols and symbolism. Third, religions propose the existence of beings, powers, states, places, and qualities that cannot be measured by any agreed upon scientific means—they are nonempirical (for convenience we refer to the nonempirical as supernatural, even though, as previously noted, this term is problematic). Fourth, religions include rituals and specific means of addressing the supernatural. Fifth, all societies include individuals who are particularly expert in the practice of religion. And, religions, like all patterns of culture, are subject to change. Thus, we might define **religion** as a social institution characterized by sacred stories; symbols and symbolism; the proposed existence of supernatural beings, powers, states, places, and qualities; rituals and means of addressing the supernatural; and specific practitioners.

Early anthropologists were primarily interested in the development of religion from **animism**—the belief that all living and nonliving objects are imbued with spirit—through polytheism and finally monotheism, which they held represented the increasingly evolved levels of logic and rationality. However, this view has been discredited: No religion is more or less logical or evolved than any other. Anthropologists today are more interested in exploring religion in terms of its functions, its symbolism, and its relation to both social stability and change than its origins.

SOME FUNCTIONS OF RELIGION

Religion has many and varied functions in society. One is to provide meaning and order in people's lives; another is to reduce individual and social anxiety and to give people a feeling of control over their destinies. Religion promotes and reinforces the status quo, but it can also do the opposite. Religion sometimes makes people profoundly fearful and can be used to contest the status quo, catalyzing radical politics and sometimes even murderous violence.

The Search for Order and Meaning

A basic function of religion is to explain important aspects of the physical and social environment and to give them meaning. Thus religions provide a **cosmology** or framework for interpreting events and experiences. This may include the creation of the universe, the origin of society, the relationship of individuals and groups to one another, and the relation of humankind to nature. It certainly will include beliefs about the nature of life and death: whether we live once, as taught in the Judeo-Christian-Muslim tradition, or we have many lives, as taught in Hinduism and Buddhism. By defining the place of the individual in society and through the establishment of moral codes, religions provide people with a sense of personal identity, a sense of belonging, and a standard of behavior. When people suffer a profound personal loss or when life loses meaning because of radically changed circumstances or catastrophic events, religion can supply a new identity or new responses that become the basis for personal and cultural survival.

Reducing Anxiety and Increasing Control

Many religious practices, such as prayer, sacrifice, magic, and other rituals, aim at ensuring success in human activities by calling on the help of supernatural beings, particularly where forces impinging on individuals and groups appear unpredictable and risky. These religious practices can achieve results indirectly, for example, by altering the emotional state of those who practice them (or whom they are practiced upon) and reducing or increasing their anxiety. The practice of "magical death" in many parts of Melanesia, for example, a sorcerer ritually imitates throwing a magical stick in the direction of the intended victim with an expression of passionate hatred on his face, is very often effective because of its psychological effects. Anthropologist Walter Cannon (1942) concluded that death was usually caused by the victim's extreme terror, which led to despair, appetite loss, and vulnerability to heart attack. Biomedical evidence of the past

60 years confirms Cannon's views about the strong connection between our psychological and physiological states and details the specific biochemical pathways through which such reactions can occur (Flamm 2002; Sternberg 2002; Tessman and Tessman 2000).

Reinforcing or Challenging the Social Order

Religion, culture, and society tend to reinforce each other, and religion generally works to preserve the social order. Through religion, dominant cultural beliefs about good and evil are reinforced by supernatural means of social control. Sacred stories and rituals provide a rationale for the present social order and give social values religious authority. Religious ritual intensifies social solidarity by creating an atmosphere in which people experience their common identity in emotionally moving ways. Finally, religion is an important institution for transmitting cultural values and knowledge.

Religion can provide an escape from reality. Through religious belief in a glorious future or the coming of a savior, powerless people who live in harsh and deprived circumstances can create an illusion of power. In these circumstances, religion may provide an outlet for individual frustration, resentment, and anger, thus deflecting opposition to the state. However, religion can also focus this same frustration, resentment, and anger against political or social targets, thus catalyzing rebellion and revolution.

CHARACTERISTICS OF RELIGION

As previously noted, all religions traditions share certain similarities. They involve stories—sacred narratives and myths. They have symbols. They are characterized by nonempirical or supernatural beings and states. There are rituals, and there are practitioners who perform the rituals. We explore each of these characteristics in this section. In addition, religions change, another subject we examine in this chapter.

Sacred Narratives

Fundamental to all religions are **myths** or *sacred narratives.* Using symbolic, poetic, and sometimes esoteric language, myths describe and explain the cosmos and are powerful forms of communication. They also may have a sacred power that is evoked when they are told or performed. Myths may be stories of heroic deeds or historic events, or they may be explanations of the origins of a people, the world, or particular aspects of a culture. The term *myth* is often taken to refer to false beliefs, although this is not necessarily correct. By explaining that things came to be the way they are through the activities of sacred beings, myths legitimize beliefs, values, and customs, particularly those having to do with ethical relations and social organization. In pointing out these connections, Bronislaw Malinowski (1992:146) noted that "These stories are not merely idle tales, but a hard-worked active force; the function of myth, briefly, is to strengthen tradition and endow it with a greater value and prestige by tracing it back to a higher, better, more supernatural reality of initial events."

For example, the Hopi, an agricultural people who live in Arizona and New Mexico, subsist mainly on blue corn, a variety that is more difficult to grow than other varieties of corn but is stronger and more resistant to damage. According to Hopi belief, before their ancestors appeared on the earth's surface, they were given their choice of subsistence activities. The ancestors chose blue corn and were taught the techniques for growing it by the god Maasaw. The Hopi believe that in growing blue corn, they recreate the feelings of humility and harmony their ancestors experienced when they first chose this form of agriculture. Thus, the Hopi live their religious understanding of the world as they grow blue corn. The stories that accompany this action reinforce social traditions and enhance solidarity.

Symbols and Symbolism

Religious stories depend on symbolism, which may be expressed in words; in material objects such as masks, statues, paintings, costumes, or body decorations; by objects in the physical environment; or through performance, dance, and music. The use of symbolism is one of the strongest similarities between religion and art. Indeed, art is very often used to express religious ideas.

Some religious symbols may have supernatural power in and of themselves, such as the masks used in African ceremonies or the wafers used in Catholic communion. Part of the power of religious symbols (like art) is that they pack many different and sometimes contradictory meanings into a single word, idea, object, or performance.

The multiple meanings of religious symbols imbue them with great power, which explains why their desecration evokes such strong responses.

Symbolic representation allows people to grasp the often complex and abstract ideas of a religion without much concern or knowledge of the underlying theology. The Christian ritual of the communion service, for example, symbolizes the New Testament story of the Last Supper, which communicates the abstract idea of communion with god. In Hinduism, this idea is represented in plays, paintings, and sculptures as the love between the divine Krishna, in the form of a cowherd, and the milkmaids, particularly Radha, who are devoted to him. The dramatic reenactments and devotional singing about the love of Krishna and Radha offer paths to communion with god that ordinary people can understand and participate in.

Supernatural Beings, Powers, States, and Qualities

Although many religions do not separate the natural from the supernatural, all religions propose that there are important beings, powers, emotional states, or qualities that exist apart from human beings. Spirits are often imbued with positive or negative emotions, which affect their actions on the material world and toward human beings.

In religious ritual, humans may be transformed into supernatural beings. This masked dancer from Cote d'Ivoire is not just a person wearing a mask but a person who has become a supernatural being.

In many hunting societies, rituals are directed toward pleasing the animals that provide food so that they will allow themselves to be killed. The Netsilik Inuit believe that a neglected animal soul might become angry and refuse to be killed, resulting in hunting failures, or even become a bloodthirsty monster that terrorizes people (Balikci 1970:200–201). Among the Inupiaq speakers of Alaska, when a bowhead whale is brought to shore, its tongue is cut out and put back in the water so the whale can go back to its family and tell them what good treatment he or she had at the hands of the hunters.

The term **god (or deity)** is generally used for a named spirit believed to have created or to have control of some aspect of the world. High gods, that is, gods understood as the creator of the world and as the ultimate power in it, are present in only about half of all societies (Levinson 1996:229). In about one third of these societies, such gods are distant and withdrawn, having little interest in people. Prayer to them is unnecessary, and they can be reached only through prayer to lesser spirits, as among the Ibo of Nigeria (Uchendu 1965:94).

Polytheism refers to belief in many gods; and **monotheism** to a belief in a single god. The difference between these two may not be as great as it seems. In polytheistic religions, the many gods may really be different aspects of one god. India has millions of gods, yet Indians understand that in some way these are all aspects of one divine essence. Conversely, in monotheistic religions, the one god may have several aspects, as in the Christian belief in God the Father, God the Son, and God the Holy Spirit, which are still viewed as part of a single, unitary God.

In addition to supernatural beings, religions posit the existence of supernatural states, qualities, or powers, such as the enlightenment of Buddhist tradition, the saintliness of Catholicism, or the nirvana of the Hindus. Belief in **mana,** a powerful supernatural quality, exists throughout the Pacific. Mana may be concentrated in individuals, such as the Tahitian chief (see Chapter 9, p. 207) or in objects and places. Mana is like electricity: It is powerful, but it is dangerous if it is not approached with caution. That is why a belief in mana often is associated with an elaborate system of taboos, or prohibitions.

Rituals and Ways of Addressing the Supernatural

People enact their religion through **ritual,** a ceremonial act or a repeated stylized gesture used for specific occasions involving the use of religious symbols (Cunningham et al. 1995). Religious rituals may involve the telling or acting out of sacred stories; the use of music, dance, drugs, or pain to move worshipers to a state of trance; or the use of ritual objects to convey religious messages.

The stories, symbols, and objects of worship that make up the content of religious rituals are exceedingly diverse, yet there are commonalities. Most religious rituals involve a combination of prayer, sacrifices, and magic to contact and control supernatural spirits and powers. Despite great diversity, however, some types of rituals, such as rites of passage and rites of intensification, are extremely widespread, if not universal.

The Power of the Liminal

Liminal objects, places, people, or statuses, which fall between clear-cut categories, are often used as religious symbols. For example, hair is widely believed to contain supernatural power (as in the Hebrew Testament story of Samson and Delilah), perhaps because it is a boundary between the self and the not-self. It is both part of a person and is separable from the person. Doorways and gates, which separate the inside from the outside, are also widespread liminal symbols that often represent opposing moral categories, such as good and evil and pure and impure. Because boundaries and liminal symbols contain supernatural power, they are often used in religious ritual and are surrounded by taboos.

The importance of liminality is often central in rites of passage. **Rites of passage** are public events that mark the transition of a person from one social status to another. They include birth, puberty, marriage, and death and may include many other transitions as well (see Chapter 8, p. 177 on gender initiation rites). Rites of passage involve three phases. In **separation,** the person or group is ritually detached from a former status. In the liminal phase, the person has been detached from the old status but has not yet attached to a new one; the person is in limbo, "neither here nor there." The liminal stage mediates between separation and the third stage, **reincorporation,** in which the passage from one status to another is symbolically completed (van Gennep 1960). After reincorporation, the person takes on the rights and obligations of his or her new social status.

Liminality may also take the form of role reversals, that is, behavior that would be virtually unthinkable under normal circumstances but is required for certain rituals. Traditionally, for example, many Japanese festivals included ritual transvestism, where community members dance in the clothing of the opposite sex (Norbeck 1974:51). In the Wubwang'u ritual among the Ndembu of Zambia, men and women publicly insult each other's sexual abilities and extol their own, but no one is allowed to take offense (Turner 1969:78–79). Ritual role reversals include class as well as gender. In *Holi,* the Hindu harvest festival, members of the lower class and castes throw colored powder (and, in the old days, excrement and urine) at males of the middle and upper classes.

Anthropologist Victor Turner (1969) argues that liminal symbols and rituals involve the dissolution of many of the structured and hierarchical classifications that normally separate people in society, such as caste, class, or kinship categories. Anthropologists often refer to these rituals and symbols as **antistructure** because they put people in a temporary state of equality and oneness, which Turner called **communitas.** In communitas, the wealthy and the poor, the powerful and the powerless are, for a short time, equals. An example of communitas in the United States is the incredibly diverse crowd of over a million people who gather on New Year's Eve to watch the falling of the illuminated ball in the center of Times Square.

Although all societies must be structured to provide order and meaning, according to Turner (1969:131), antistructure—the temporary ritual dissolution of the established order—also is important, helping people to more fully realize the oneness of the self and the other.

Turner's ideas about antistructure and communitas are provocative. However, critics charge that although the rituals and symbols of antistructure seem to convey at least temporary equality, people in higher statuses experience the unity of communitas more than the powerless do. The powerless may use liminal symbols and rituals of reversal to subvert the social order (even if temporarily), expressing feelings not of oneness but of conflict with the powerful. Where liminal groups exist (whether temporarily, during rituals or religious festivals, or permanently) in association with certain occupations, they frequently have low status and an ambiguous nature. Paradoxically, this is the source of their supernatural power and their perceived subversion of the social order, as illustrated by the hijras of India (see Chapter 8, p. 170), whose sexual ambiguity contains the power both to bless and to curse.

Rites of Intensification

Rites of intensification are rituals directed toward reinforcing the values and norms of the community and strengthening group identity and well-being. Through these rituals the community maintains continuity with the past, enhances the feeling of social unity in the present, and renews the sentiments on which social cohesion depends (Elkin 1967).

A classic anthropological example of rites of intensification is the **totemism** of the Australian aborigines. A totem is an object, animal species, or feature of the natural world that is associated with a particular descent (kinship) group. In aboriginal Australia, people are grouped into lodges, each of which is linked with a totemic species in the natural environment that members of the group are generally prohibited from eating.

In their religious rituals, members of the same lodge assemble to celebrate their totem. The ceremonies explain the origin of the totem (and hence of the group) and reenact the time of the ancestors. Through singing and dancing, both performers and onlookers are transported to an ecstatic state ". . . in which a man does not recognize himself any longer . . . [and feels] himself dominated and carried away by some sort of external power. . . . [E]verything is just as though he really were transported into a special world" (Durkheim 1961/1915:247–251). Emile Durkheim, a pioneer in the anthropological study of religion, believed that totems were symbols of common social identity. When people worshiped totems, they were at the same time worshipping the moral and social order of their society. The ecstatic religious experience of their shared identity helped to bind the members of their society together.

The religious rituals of the Australian aborigines may seem exotic, but Americans participate in many similar observances, some religious but many secular, to the same effect. The rallies associated with college football games are a good example. If the game is "good" or the school has "spirit," these gatherings produce enormous excitement among their fans and transport them to "a special world," increasing collective identity and intensifying loyalty to the school (and hopefully motivating financial donations from them as alumni). Schools, like Australian descent groups, also have totems (animal mascots).

Prayer, Sacrifice, and Magic

Prayer, sacrifices, and magic are found in most religious traditions. Although theoretically differentiated by the degree of control that humans believe they exert over the spirit world, the distinctions between them are more a matter of degree than of exclusive classification.

Prayer is any conversation held with spirits and gods in which people petition, invoke, praise, give thanks, dedicate, supplicate, intercede, confess, repent, and bless (Levinson 1996). A defining feature of prayer is that people believe the results depend on the will of the spirit world rather than on actions performed by humans. When prayer involves requests, the failure of a spirit to respond to a request is understood as resulting from its disinclination rather than from improper human action. Prayer may be done without any expectation of a particular response from the beings or forces prayed to. There are many forms of prayer. In the West, prayer mainly involves words recited aloud or silently, but in Buddhist tradition people may pray by hoisting flags or spinning wheels with prayers written inside them.

Sacrifice occurs when people make offerings to gods or spirits to increase their spiritual purity or the efficacy of their prayers. People may sacrifice the first fruits of a harvest, animal lives, or, on occasion, human lives, an important ritual among the Aztec of Mexico. Changes in behavior are often offered as sacrifices, as in the Muslim practice of fasting for Ramadan or the Christian practice of giving up something for Lent, a sacrifice intended to help the worshipper identify with Jesus, show devotion, and increase purity. In many religions people make a vow to carry out a certain kind of behavior, such as going on a pilgrimage or building a place of worship, if a prayer is answered.

Among many east African cattle pastoralists, such as the Nuer or Pokot, cattle sacrifices are central to religion, and cattle are killed and eaten only in the context of religious ritual. This practice, like other religious rituals, may be adaptive in that, in the absence of refrigeration, sacrifices and feasts offer access to fresh meat, which is not otherwise eaten. Furthermore, a feast where the meat of a sacrificed animal is offered to the whole community makes the best use of the meat that one family could not eat by itself. Because the portions are distributed according to age and sex using a rigid formula, meat can be shared without quarreling over the supply (Schneider 1973). In addition, the religious taboo that a person who eats ritually slaughtered meat may not take milk on the same day results in making milk more available to those who have no meat.

With **magic,** people attempt to mechanistically control supernatural forces. When people do magic, they believe that their words and actions *compel* the spirit world to behave in certain ways. Failure of a magical request is understood to result from incorrect performance of the ritual rather than the refusal of spirits to act, as in prayer.

Imitation and contagion are two of the most common magical practices. In **imitative magic,** the procedure performed resembles the result desired. A vodou doll is a form of imitative magic based on the principle that mistreatment of a doll-like image of a person will cause injury to that person. **Contagious magic** is based on the idea that an object that has been in contact with a person retains a magical connection with that person. For example, one might attempt to increase the effectiveness of a vodou doll by attaching a piece of clothing, hair, or other object belonging to the person he or she wishes to injure. People in the United States often attribute special power and meaning to objects that have come in contact with famous or notorious people. Signed baseballs, bits of costumes worn by movie stars, and pens used to sign famous documents all become collector's items and are imbued with special power and importance.

In many cultures, magical practices accompany most human activities. Among the people of the Asaro Valley in Highland New Guinea, when a child is born, its umbilical cord is buried so that it cannot later be used by a sorcerer to cause harm. In order to prevent the infant's crying at night, a bundle of sweet-smelling grass is placed on the mother's head, and her wish for uninterrupted sleep is blown into the grass. The grass then is crushed over the head of the child who, in breathing its aroma, also breathes in the mother's command not to cry. In cultures where magic is not universally used, it may accompany the most risky activities. Professional baseball players in the United States are more likely to use magic for hitting and pitching, the least predictable aspects of the game. Few magical practices are invoked in outfielding, which has little uncertainty. For example, after each pitch one major league pitcher would reach into his back pocket to touch a crucifix and then straighten his cap. Detroit Tigers infielder Tim Maring wore the same clothes and put them on exactly in the same order each day during a batting streak. One baseball myth is that eating certain foods will give the ball "eyes," that is, the ball will seek the gaps between fielders, so eating certain foods on the day of a game is another example of baseball magic (Gmelch 2000).

Divination is a widespread ritual practice directed toward obtaining useful, hidden, or unknown information from a supernatural authority. Divination may be used to predict the future, diagnose disease, find hidden objects, or discover something about the past. In many cultures, divination is used to discover who committed a crime. Many Americans are familiar with divination techniques such as tarot cards, palmistry, flipping coins, and reading auras.

Divination makes people more confident in their choices when they do not have all the information they need or when several alternative courses of action appear equal. It may be practiced when a group must make a decision about which there is disagreement. If the choice is made by divination, no member of the group feels rejected.

Religious Practitioners

Every society includes people who are believed to have a special relationship with the religious world and who organize and lead major ritual events. Of the many kinds of religious practitioners, two main types are shamans and priests.

Shamans

Shamans are part-time practitioners who otherwise work like other members of their communities. Their shamanic activities are reserved for specific ceremonies, times of illness, or crises. Learning to be a shaman may involve arduous training, but such study is never sufficient. The distinctive characteristic of shamans is that they have direct personal experiences of the supernatural that other members of the community accept as authentic. Shamans use prayer, meditation, song, dance, pain, drugs, or any combination of techniques to achieve trance states in which they understand themselves (and are understood by their followers) as able to enter into the real world of the supernatural. They may use such contact to search for guidance for themselves or for their group, to heal the sick, or to divine the future.

Almost all societies have some shamans, but in foraging and tribal societies shamans are likely to be the only religious practitioners. In some cultures, almost every adult is expected to achieve direct contact with the supernatural. In some Native-American societies, this was achieved through a vision quest in which individuals developed a special relationship with a particular spirit from whom they received special kinds of power and knowledge and who acted as a personal protector or guardian. The vision seeker might fast, might isolate himself or herself at a lonely spot, or might use self-mutilation to intensify his or her emotional state in order to receive the vision.

Particularly before the advent of modern medicine, many societies treated illness by means that today would be considered primarily spiritual rather than medical. Illnesses were thought to be caused by broken taboos, sorcery, witchcraft, or spiritual imbalance, and shamans had an important role in curing. The shaman, usually in a trance, would travel into the supernatural world to discover the source of illness and how to cure it.

In the modern world, shamanic curing often exists alongside modern technological medicine. People go to shamans for healing when they have diseases that are not recognized by modern medicine, they lack money to pay for modern medical treatment, or they have tried such treatment and it has failed. Shamanistic curing can have important therapeutic effects. Shamans frequently treat their patients with drugs from the culture's traditional pharmacopoeia, and some (but not all) of these have been shown scientifically to be effective (Fábrega 1997:144). Shamanic curing ritual also uses symbolism and dramatic action to bring together cultural beliefs and religious practices in a way that enables patients to understand the source of their illness. Such rituals present a coherent model of sickness and health, explaining how patients got ill and how they may become well again, and these models can exert a powerful curative force (Roberts, Kewman, Mercier, and Hovell 1993).

Priests

In most state societies, religion is a formally established institution consisting of a series of ranked offices that exist independently of the people who fill them (a *bureaucracy*). Anthropologically, a **priest** is a person who is formally elected, appointed, or hired to a full-time religious office. Priests are responsible for performing certain rituals on behalf of individuals, groups, or the entire community.

Priests are most often associated with high and powerful gods. Where priests exist, there is a division between the lay and priestly roles; laypersons participate in ritual largely as passive respondents or as an audience rather than as managers or performers. Jewish rabbis, Muslim imams, Christian ministers, and Hindu *purohits* all fit the definition of priests.

People generally become priests through training and apprenticeship and are certified by their religious hierarchy. Although in mainstream religious denominations in the United States priests need not have ecstatic religious experiences, this is not universally true. Although ultimately the priest's authority derives from a priestly office, in some cultures, like the ancient Maya, priestly office may also give a person the right to seek direct ecstatic contact with gods and spirits.

The Maya of Mexico was a state society in which temples were elaborate public stages for rituals performed by priests.

Generally, state societies attempt to suppress independent shamans or to bring them under bureaucratic control, as their ability to directly contact the supernatural without certification by any institutionalized religion challenges both church and state authority.

Witches and Sorcerers

Belief in the existence of witches and sorcerers is widespread but not universal. In some societies, **witchcraft** is understood as a physical aspect of a person. People are witches because their bodies contain a magical witchcraft substance. They generally acquire this substance through inheritance. If a person's body contains the witchcraft substance, his or her malevolent thoughts will result in misfortune among those around him or her.

The Azande of East Africa, a classic example, believe that witches' bodies contain a substance called *mangu,* which allows them to cause misfortune and death to others (Evans-Pritchard 1958/1937). People who have the witchcraft substance may not be aware that they are witches and are believed to be unable to prevent themselves from causing evil. They are suspected of witchcraft when evil befalls those around them, particularly family members.

Sorcery is the conscious manipulation of words and ritual objects with the intent of magically causing either harm or good; an example is the magical death described earlier (see p. 266).

Although people do actually practice witchcraft and sorcery, their main effects on society are through witchcraft accusations. Leveling witchcraft accusations against friends and neighbors is common in many cultures and serves various purposes. The most common form of witchcraft accusation serves to stigmatize differences. People who do not fit into conventional social categories are often suspected of witchcraft, exemplified by the Western image of the witch as an evil old hag dressed in black. In traditional western European society, social norms dictated that women should have husbands and children (or alternatively become nuns). Impoverished women who remained in the community yet were unmarried or widowed without children violated this social convention and might be subject to witchcraft accusations (Brain 1989; Horsley 1979). Although witches are sometimes killed, they also are sometimes allowed to remain in a community, serving as valuable negative role models, examples of what not to be. The lesson that a young girl might derive from the witch is you should get married and have children or you might end up accused of being a witch.

Witchcraft and sorcery accusations may be used to scapegoat. In times of great social change when war, disease, calamity, or technological change undermines the social order, people's lives lose meaning. Under such circumstances, a community may turn to witchcraft accusations, blaming their misfortunes on the presence of evildoers—witches and sorcerers who must be found and destroyed in order to reassert normality.

In Europe, for example, the witch craze, which resulted in the death of thousands of men and women, occurred primarily in the 16th and 17th centuries, a time of great artistic and technological achievement but also of great social disasters (Hester 1988). Plague swept repeatedly through Europe, and the medieval social and religious order collapsed in war and chaos. Under these circumstances, people were willing to believe that witches were the cause of their misery and to pursue reprisals against people they suspected of witchcraft.

RELIGION AND CHANGE

The function of religion as a force to preserve the social order is particularly evident in socially stratified societies, where the elite may invoke religious authority to control the poor. In such situations, the priesthood and religion act not only as a means of regulating behavior, which is a function of religion in all societies, but also as a way of maintaining social, economic, and political inequalities. These religious beliefs may rationalize the lower social position of their more powerless members and emphasize an afterlife in which their suffering will be rewarded.

However, religion can also be a catalyst for social change. When a religious image of the social order fails to match the daily experience of its followers, **prophets** may emerge who create new religious ideas or call for a purification of existing practices. Sometimes prophecies encourage people to invest themselves in purely magical practices that have little real effect on the social order, such as the Melanesian cargo cult described earlier. But prophets may also urge their followers to pursue their goals through political or military means, which may result in rapid social change. The American civil rights movement and the Iranian revolution are examples of social movements in which religion played a critical role in cultural change.

Prophecy and the founding of new religions often occur among oppressed groups and among people caught in the grip of rapid social change (as a result of colonization, disease, technological change, etc.) that results in feelings of hopelessness and extreme alienation. People may come to believe that their religious practices are no longer powerful or that their religious beliefs are simply wrong. Under these conditions, prophets may emerge, and new religions may be created. Religious fervor may then be exploited, cynically or sincerely, by political or religious leaders to promote new political, economic, and/or social policies that challenge those of the mainstream.

The rise of religious fundamentalism throughout much of the world today calls attention to the potential of religion in affecting social or political change. A useful definition that captures its diversity is that **fundamentalism** is "a proclamation of reclaimed authority over a sacred tradition which is to be reinstated as an antidote for a society that has strayed from its cultural moorings" (Hadden and Shupe 1989). In spite of their diversity, there are some general similarities among religious fundamentalists. They tend to see religion as the basis for both personal and communal identity; to believe that there is a single unified truth and that they can possess and understand it; and to envision themselves as fighting in a cosmic struggle of good against evil, in which they are a persecuted minority.

The rise and contemporary expansion of religious fundamentalism throughout the world may grow out of the truly revolutionary changes over the last 50 years. One such change is the modern technology and global capitalism that now permeates all societies, bringing together people of disparate cultures in a vast global network, disrupting communities and creating new inequalities. Faced with profound change, some people look for the stability and certainty that religious fundamentalism promises.

Religious movements vary in the effectiveness with which they bring social and political change, and indeed along with the rise of religious fundamentalism there has been a growing secularism, especially in Europe but also elsewhere, as the expansion of scientific knowledge challenges religious belief and proves adaptive in many areas of life (Dawkins 2006).

Even religions that do not effect change in people's lives in the material world nonetheless may create powerful new identities among their members, even to the extent of leading to individual or mass suicide, as in Jonestown, Guyana, in 1978 (Asad 2007).

Varieties of Religious Prophecies: Revitalization Movements

Nativistic religions, one type of **revitalization movement,** are aimed at restoring a past golden age when things seem better than they are at present. Nativistic prophets claim that the present life has degenerated because people have fallen away from the ways of their ancestors and that the glorious past can be regained if certain practices are followed.

The Ghost Dance, a late 19th-century nativistic religious movement that arose among the Plains Indians of the United States, was a response to the disastrous effects of European invasion. Disease, warfare, and technological change had undermined native cultures. As a result, many prophets emerged whose visions were directly related to the effects of the expansion of Euro-American power (Wallace 1970). In 1889, the prophet Wovoka had a vision in which "he saw God, with all the people who had died long ago engaged in their old time sports and occupations, all happy and forever young" (Mooney 1973/1896:771). Wovoka taught that the arrival of paradise could be hastened by specific rituals, including dances, songs, and the wearing of specially designed "ghost shirts," which some followers believed had the power to protect them from bullets. Although Wovoka called for peace with the whites, he also taught that the whites either would be carried away by high winds or would become Indians, and he urged Indians to return to their traditional practices (Lesser 1933).

The Ghost Dance prophecy spread widely among Native Americans, especially the Sioux, for whom the conditions of conquest and reservation life were experienced as particularly oppressive. After their defeat of General Custer at the Little Bighorn in 1876, they had been restricted to agriculture on their nonproductive reservations and nearly starved to death. Thus, Wowoka's vision of the disappearance of their oppressors and the return of traditional ways was compelling. U.S. government agents became increasingly frightened that the Ghost Dance movement would lead to a Sioux war against the whites. They ordered the Sioux to stop the dance; some Sioux did, but others fled into the badlands and continued to perform the Ghost Dance and to await the cataclysm that would sweep their oppressors from the Plains. In December 1890, the Seventh Cavalry captured the last remaining band of Ghost Dancers at Wounded Knee. In the ensuing battle about 350 Sioux Ghost Dancers, including many women and children, were killed. This battle effectively ended the Ghost Dance, although it continued among small groups even up until the 1960s.

Vitalistic Prophecies

Vitalistic prophecies hold that the golden age is in the future—not the past—and that it can be achieved by following the teachings of the prophet. The Rastafarian religion, a vitalist movement originating in Jamaica in the 1930s, has gained many adherents worldwide. In the 1930s, the Jamaican peasantry was being incorporated as wage labor into the emerging capitalist economy, replacing the peasant economy that was organized around a system of localized, small-scale exchanges involving interpersonal networks of extended kin. Capitalism exacerbated both poverty and racial stratification, as whites and mulattos accumulated wealth at the expense of black peasants.

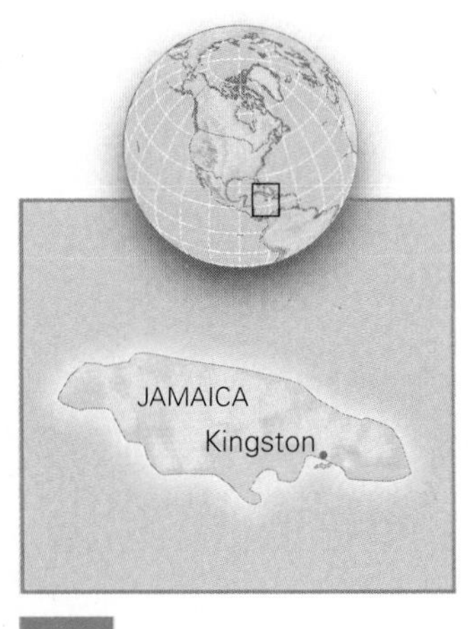

Jamaica.

In 1930, Ras (Duke) Tafari was crowned Emperor Haile Selassie I of Ethiopia and was proclaimed "King of Kings" and "Lion of Judah." The splendid coronation ceremonies at which European dignitaries paid homage to the new emperor drew enormous publicity in Jamaica. One result was a prophetic revelation by Leonard Howell, who, returning to Jamaica after serving in the United States Army, declared that the coronation of Haile Selassie fulfilled biblical prophecies. Haile Selassie was the messiah and was the hope of freedom for all black people (Lewis 1998). Howell and other Rasta leaders founded communities in Jamaica, celebrating what they understood as traditional African values such as cooperative work efforts, respect for life, and the unity of all peoples of African descent. Haile Selassie became their central symbol.

Rastafarians reject the values of capitalist society and the competitive marketplace. They emphasize the repatriation of blacks to Africa, a concept mainly understood symbolically as a call to live what Rastafarians believe are African lifestyles in whichever country they find themselves.

Two other important symbols of Rastafarian culture are a special vocabulary, which subverts language to emphasize Rasta values, and the use of marijuana as a method of religious illumination. Whereas ganja (marijuana) had been used by working-class Jamaicans as a stimulant and incentive to work (in contrast to its leisure time uses in mainstream American society), the Rastafarians reversed these meanings. Marijuana is used to stimulate discussion at "reasoning sessions," where Rastafarians interpret biblical passages and share their beliefs about freedom, slavery, colonialism, and racism. They believe ganja allows them to see through the evils of the bourgeois world, to understand the roots of their oppression, and to verify the authenticity of the Rasta lifestyle. In addition, many Rastafarians engage in the illegal sale of marijuana, using personal networks for growing it, preparing it for sale, and distributing it. This underground economy provides Rastafarians with a livelihood that allows them independence and freedom from the capitalist system, a position they value highly, although it has brought them trouble from law enforcement (Norgren and Nanda 2006).

Rastafarians are members of a religion that resists the imposition of much of the contemporary culture of capitalism.

Rastafarians reject much of the social and psychological orientation of modern society, which they call *Babylon,* referring to the captivity and enslavement of the Israelites by the Babylonians recorded in the Hebrew bible. Despite harassment by authorities, their religion and culture allow them to survive in a manner consistent with their own world view.

Messianic and Millenarian Religions

Many of the revitalization movements found among oppressed peoples are **messianic:** They focus on the coming of a special individual who will usher in a utopian world. Other religions of the oppressed are **millenarian,** envisioning a future cataclysm or disaster that will destroy the current world and establish in its wake a world characterized by their version of justice. In many messianic and millenarian religions, such as the holiness churches found among coal miners and other rural poor in Appalachia, members participate in rituals and experience states of ecstasy that give them direct access to supernatural power. Church members cite biblical passages as the basis for their practices of faith healing, glossolalia (speaking in tongues), drinking poison, and handling poisonous snakes. Holiness church congregations view these activities as demonstrations of the power of God, working through people whose beliefs allow them to become God's instruments (Burton 1993; Covington 1995).

Many of these revitalistic religions involve religious **syncretism,** in which two or more religious traditions are merged. For example, the Rastafarians use both Christian and non-Christian elements in their religious symbols and rituals. In some cases, syncretism involves practices in which the beliefs, symbols, and rituals of one religion are hidden behind similar attributes of another. A good example is Santeria, an African-based religion that originated in Cuba and now is widespread throughout Latin America and the United States among the middle and the lower classes (Murphy 1989). Santeria emerged from a slave society in which Europeans attempted to suppress African religions. The slaves resisted by combining African religion, Catholicism, and French spiritualism to create a new religion (Lefever 1996). They identified African deities, called *orichas,* with Catholic saints and used them for traditional purposes: curing, casting spells, and influencing other aspects of the worshiper's life. In this way, they could appear to their masters to be practicing Catholicism as they actually continued to practice their own religions.

Religion offers principles embedded in stories, symbols, and interpretations that become the core of culture for their many followers. Religion can support the status quo but it also is a powerful force for change. Religious beliefs and practices can have powerful political impacts, or they can function mainly as a source of personal satisfaction and deflect individuals from seeking political change. In the contemporary world, cultural anthropology makes an important contribution to our understanding of religious diversity and some of the functions it serves.

BRINGING IT BACK HOME: RELIGION, ART, AND CENSORSHIP

". . . this show is disgusting," said New York City's then (1999) Mayor Rudolph Giuliani, commenting on an art exhibit called "Sensation," at the Brooklyn Museum of Art. He was referring specifically to a painting by the African artist Chris Ofili called "The Holy Virgin Mary." The painting depicted a Black Madonna in a colorful flowing robe, dabbed with a clump of elephant dung and surrounded with images of women's buttocks and genitals clipped from pornographic magazines (Steiner 2002).

"Roman Catholic parish vows to fight [museum] committee's decision to retain controversial artwork" ran a newspaper headline in response to a computer-generated collage by artist Alma Lopez of the Virgin of Guadalupe clad in a floral garment resembling a bikini, with a bare midriff, included in the Cyber Arte exhibition at the Museum of International Folk Art, in Santa Fe (Associated Press 2003).

". . . disrespectful, in bad taste . . . provocative . . . comes close to blasphemy," said Roman Catholic leaders, supported by Jews and Muslims, regarding pop singer Madonna's decision to stage a mock crucifixion, standing on a mirrored cross wearing a crown of thorns, as part of her concert in Rome in 2000.

For many religious believers these examples of art using religious symbolism are deeply offensive. As individuals and institutions they lobby, often successfully, to have shows closed and artworks removed. NBC television declined to show pictures of Madonna mounting the cross to avoid "confrontation with religious groups."

The Bill of Rights guarantees both freedom of religious practice and freedom from the imposition of religious conformity by the government. Our constitutionally based freedom of speech also seems to guarantee that the government could not censor what some people might find offensive to their religious beliefs. In an age of growing religious fervor we can expect to see greater confrontation on issues involving religion.

YOU DECIDE

1. On what bases might you find the three examples previously described as offensive? Have you ever seen a representation of your own religion that you found offensive? What, if anything, did you do about it, and why? If you were the mayor of New York City, the CEO of NBC, or a member of the Board of the Santa Fe Museum, how would you have responded to the artistic representations of religion previously described? On what principles or cultural values would you base your actions?
2. Who should decide if the public representation of a religion is offensive? If a majority in a community finds a religious representation offensive, should it be censored? Why or why not? What differences and/or similarities do you see between government censorship of an offensive religious representation and that of a corporation such as NBC?
3. Is it relevant that the representations previously described are claimed as artistic by their creators? Is it relevant that all the artists are Catholic? Why or why not? What do you think might be the intent of the artists in their various representations of their religion?

CHAPTER SUMMARY

1. Although the great diversity in beliefs and practices worldwide makes religion difficult to define, all religions include sacred stories, include supernatural beings, powers, and states, enact rituals, and include specialized practitioners. Religious ideas are expressed symbolically so that abstract ideas can be more easily understood by most people.
2. Religion has many functions. Through religion, societies create meaning and order in the world, explain aspects of the physical and social environment, reduce anxiety in risky situations, increase social solidarity, transmit cultural traditions, ensure conformity, maintain social inequalities, and regulate the relationship of a group of people to their natural environment.
3. Most religions assume the world to be populated with gods and spirits who have life, personality, and power. People, objects, or places may be imbued with spiritual power, called *mana*. Religious rituals, which include prayer, sacrifice, and magic, are enacted to communicate with, manipulate, and influence religious powers. Two common types of religious ritual are rites of passage and rites of intensification.
4. Shamans and priests are two major types of religions practitioners who are charged with taking leading roles in performing religious ritual for other members of their society. Witches and sorcerers are those in a society who use their powers to harm people through magical means.
5. Religion is often used to resist cultural domination. In situations where people experience extreme oppression and the loss of cultural and personal identity, religious revitalization movements, such as Melanesian Cargo Cults, the Native-American Ghost Dance, and the Rastafarian religion, may emerge to construct new cultural and personal identities, although they may or may not substantially affect economic and political structures.

KEY TERMS

Animism
Antistructure
Communitas
Contagious magic
Cosmology

Divination
Fundamentalism
God (deity)
Imitative magic
Liminal
Magic
Mana
Messianic
Millenarian
Monotheism
Myths (sacred narratives)
Polytheism
Prayer
Priest
Prophet
Reincorporation
Religion
Revitalization movement
Rite of intensification
Rite of passage
Ritual
Sacrifice
Separation
Shaman
Sorcery
Syncretism
Totemism
Witchcraft

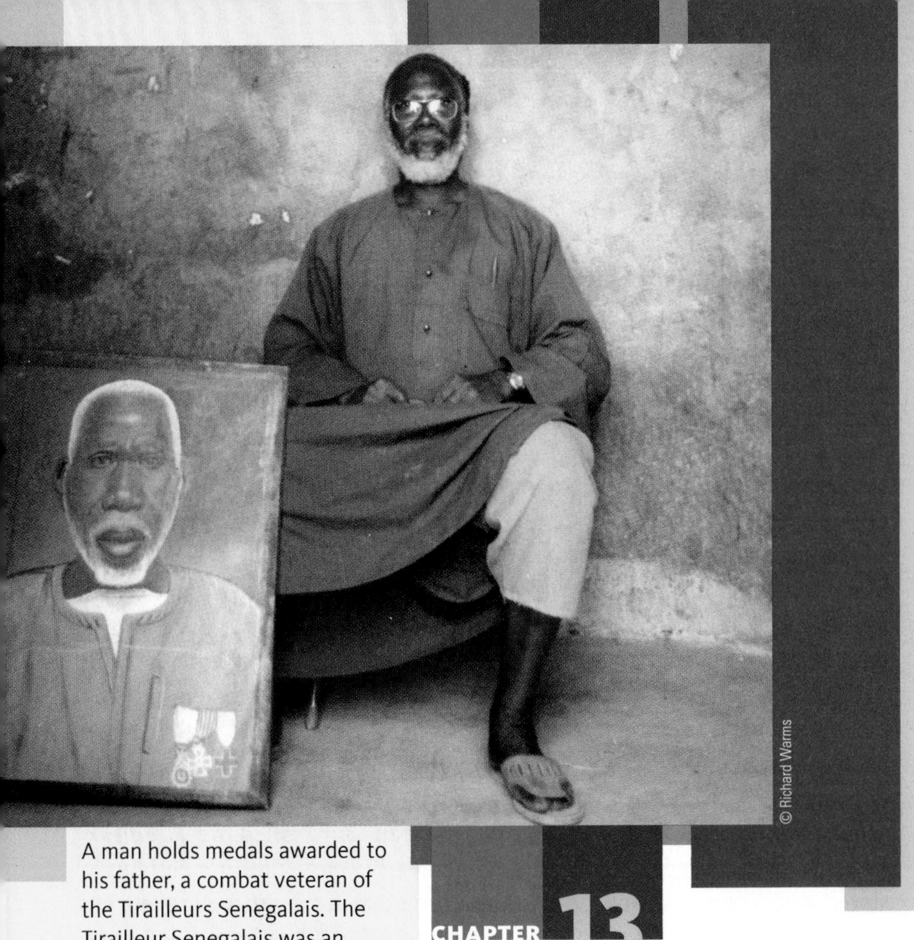

A man holds medals awarded to his father, a combat veteran of the Tirailleurs Senegalais. The Tirailleur Senegalais was an army the French drafted and recruited from their colonial possessions in West Africa between the 1850s and 1960.

CHAPTER 13

POWER, CONQUEST, AND A WORLD SYSTEM

CHAPTER OUTLINE

Veterans of Colonial Armies

Making the Modern World

European Expansion: Motives and Methods

- Pillage
- Forced Labor
- Joint Stock Companies

The Era of Colonialism

- Colonization 1500 to 1800
- Colonizing in the 19th Century
- Colonialism and Anthropology

Decolonization

Bringing It Back Home: Celebrating Ghana's 50th Anniversary

- You Decide

VETERANS OF COLONIAL ARMIES

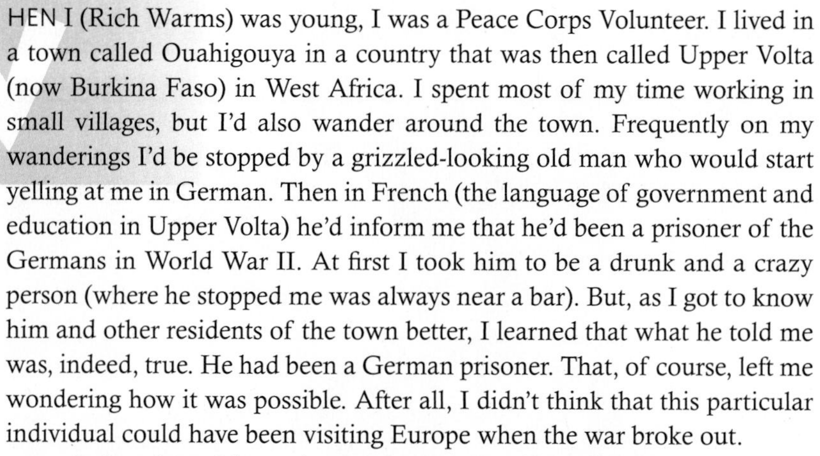

WHEN I (Rich Warms) was young, I was a Peace Corps Volunteer. I lived in a town called Ouahigouya in a country that was then called Upper Volta (now Burkina Faso) in West Africa. I spent most of my time working in small villages, but I'd also wander around the town. Frequently on my wanderings I'd be stopped by a grizzled-looking old man who would start yelling at me in German. Then in French (the language of government and education in Upper Volta) he'd inform me that he'd been a prisoner of the Germans in World War II. At first I took him to be a drunk and a crazy person (where he stopped me was always near a bar). But, as I got to know him and other residents of the town better, I learned that what he told me was, indeed, true. He had been a German prisoner. That, of course, left me wondering how it was possible. After all, I didn't think that this particular individual could have been visiting Europe when the war broke out.

As I spoke to him and, over the 15 years that followed, to many others like him, I learned a story that had been left out of my high school and college history lessons. I learned that starting in the second half of the 19th century, France began to create a black African army called the ***Tirailleurs Senegalais*** or Senegalese Riflemen. In the early years, the French bought slaves to fill the army ranks. But as time progressed, they turned to levying a draft on their colonies and then, finally, after World War II, to a volunteer force. First they used this army to conquer the areas that became French colonies in Africa. Later, they used these troops to fight in the trenches in World War I and to suppress rebellion in various colonial possessions. In World War II, African troops were essential to the conquest of North Africa and Italy and to taking back France itself. When people think of Charles DeGaulle's Free French forces of that war, they generally summon up a Hollywood image of a white guy in a beret. In fact, before the last phase of the liberation of France in 1944, most Free French forces were black Africans and more likely to be called Mahamadou than Pierre. In the late years of French colonialism, it was African troops, among others, who fought at the battle of Dien Bien Phu that in 1954 ended the French colonial venture in Vietnam.

In the 1990s, I interviewed more than 50 surviving members of the Tirailleurs Senegalais. The stories they told were fantastic, even unbelievable. Dragged out of small African villages and sent to fight in Europe and elsewhere around the globe, they faced horrors and cultural shock that nothing could have prepared them for. Some cracked under the strain, responding with violent outbursts and, when they made it home, with drunkenness and insanity. However, most learned to adapt. When they got home they sometimes put their language skills, organizational skills, and bravery to new uses, playing important roles in their communities. But many are also deeply aggrieved. They feel neglected by history and, in particular, by France. In 1991, Mory Samake, a veteran of World War II, told me:

> Look, when you work for someone, he's got to recognize your efforts. They treat us like their dogs. They are white, we are black but we are all equal. If someone cuts my hand and someone cuts one of their hands, the blood is just the same. When we were there fighting the war, no one said "this one is white, this one is black". We didn't go to fight with ill will. We gave our blood and our bodies so that France could be liberated. But now, since they have their freedom, they have thrown us away, forgotten us. If you eat the meat, you throw away the bone. France has done just that to us.

The story of the Tirailleurs Senegalais and Mory Samake's anger with the French remind us of several extremely important points. A cliché has it that history is written by the winners. It might be more accurate to say that history is written by the powerful and often presented as a narrative of their inevitable triumph. But such a history ignores inconvenient truths or relegates them to footnotes and appendices. The relation between wealth and poverty and between the powerful and the powerless, or, in this case, between the colonized and the colonizer, are among the most important of these.

Even though we are all aware that things change, most of the time, most people tend to treat the world as static. We assume that the social arrangements we see today, the distribution of wealth and poverty, of power and powerlessness, are of great historical depth. When we think of history at all, we tend to think of the histories of individual nations. But thinking about the world this way fails to account for change and limits our understanding. Our world is the current result of large-scale historic processes that involved the ebb and flow of wealth and power, not only among nations but among different areas of the world. These processes have had a particularly important impact on the kinds of small-scale, seemingly isolated societies that anthropologists often study.

We all know that the pace of change has been extremely rapid in the past several centuries. We know less about the patterns of change and their effects on cultures around the world. The story of these patterns is complex and diverse; it is a story of contact between cultures. A significant part of the story concerns the expansion of the affluence and power of places that are now wealthy, principally the nations of northern Europe and the colonies settled by their English-speaking (and sometimes French-speaking) subjects and citizens.

The expansion of European power occurred in thousands of locations and had many different effects. Sometimes cultural contact was accidentally genocidal, sometimes intentionally so. Many traditional cultures have been destroyed, but others have prospered, although in altered forms. Members of different cultures often confronted each other through a veil of ignorance, suspicion, and accusations of savagery. But sometimes common interests, common enemies, mutual curiosity, and occasionally friendship among people overrode their differences.

In this chapter, we describe the overall pattern of change during the past several hundred years. In the broadest sense, this involved the incorporation of relatively separate cultures and economies into a vast, chaotic, yet integrated world economic system. The formation of this system resulted in enormous inequality both within and among nations as wealth and labor flowed from one area of the world to another. It created the financial accumulation necessary for the industrial revolution and the development of capitalism. In this era, empires rose and fell as powers competed for dominance within their own borders and with each other. The Ottoman Empire as well as the growth of Russia and of Japan played critical roles in the story. However, it was the expanding influence and power of western European states that probably had the greatest impact worldwide. For that reason, we begin with a bird's-eye view of Europe and the rest of the world as it might have appeared in 1400.

MAKING THE MODERN WORLD

As surprising as it may seem now, a visitor touring the world on the eve of European expansion in 1400 might well have been amused by the notion that European societies would soon become enormously wealthy and powerful. Other areas of the globe would have seemed much more likely prospects for power. Europeans had devised oceangoing vessels, but Arab and Chinese ships regularly made much longer voyages. The cities of India and China made those of Europe look like mere villages. Almost no European states could effectively administer more than a few hundred square kilometers. Certainly there was nothing that could compare to China's vast wealth and centralized bureaucracy. Europeans were masters of cathedral and castle construction, but other than that, their technology was backward. War, plague, and economic depression were the order of the day (Scammell 1989). Moreover, other areas of the world seemed to be growing in wealth and power. Despite occasional setbacks, the Islamic powers had expanded steadily in the five centuries leading up to 1400, and Muslim societies stretched from Spain to Indonesia. Not only had these empires preserved the scholarship of India and the ancient Mediterranean civilizations, but they had greatly increased knowledge in astronomy, mathematics, medicine, chemistry, zoology, mineralogy, and meteorology (Lapidus 1988:96, 241–252).

China also had an extraordinarily ancient and powerful civilization. As late as 1793, Emperor Ch'ien Lung, believing China to be the most powerful state in the world (or perhaps showing bravado in the face of foreign traders), responded to a British delegation's attempt to open trade by writing to King George II: "Our dynasty's majestic virtue has penetrated into every country under heaven and kings of all nations have offered their costly tribute by land and sea. As your Ambassador can see for himself, we possess all things . . . we have never valued ingenious articles, nor do we have the slightest need of your country's manufacturers" (Peyrefitte 1992:288–292). Unfortunately for the Chinese, by the time the emperor wrote this letter, it was no longer accurate. Within a half century, at the end of the First Opium War, Britain virtually controlled China.

EUROPEAN EXPANSION: MOTIVES AND METHODS

From slow beginnings in the 15th century, European power grew rapidly from the 16th to the 10th centuries. Many theories have been suggested to account for the causes and motives of European expansion. Although it was often a cover for more worldly aims, the desire of the pious to Christianize the world was certainly a motivating factor. The archives of the Jesuit order include more than 15,000 letters, written between 1550 and 1771, from people who wanted to be missionaries (Scammell 1989:60). The desire to find a wide variety of wonders, both real and imagined, was also important. The Portuguese looked for routes to the very real wealth of Eastern empires, such as China, but also for the mythical kingdom of Prester John, a powerful but hidden Christian monarch, the fountain of youth, and the seven cities of Cibola.

Beyond this, there was always the desire for wealth. Nations and nobles quickly lost their aversion to exploration as gold and diamonds were discovered. The poor and oppressed of Europe saw opportunities for wealth and respect in the colonies. There, they sometimes fulfilled their dreams of wealth by re-creating the very social order they had fled.

Europeans were aided in their pursuit of expansion by various social and technological developments. These included the rise of a banking and merchant class, a growing population, and the development of the caravel, a new ship that was better at sailing into the wind. Two other developments, the **monoculture plantation** and the **joint stock company,** were to have critical impacts on the world's people.

In many cases, however, the key advantage Europeans had over other people was the diseases they carried. Almost every time Europeans met others who had been isolated from the European, African, and Asian land masses, they brought death and cultural destruction in the form of microbes. In many instances, virtually the entire native population perished of imported diseases within 20 years. Although Europeans too died of diseases, they did so in far smaller numbers (Karlen 1995; Newson 1999; Palkovich 1994; Wolf 1982).

The European search for wealth depended on tactics that, in their basic form, were ancient. Two of the quickest ways to accumulate wealth are to steal it from others and to get other people to work for you for free. State societies have always practiced these methods. War, slavery, exploitation, and inequality were present in most of the world before European contact, so there was nothing fundamentally new about their use by Europeans. However, no earlier empire had been able to practice these tactics on the scale of the European nations. All previous empires, however large, were regional affairs. European expansion, for the first time in history, linked the entire world into an economic system. This system created much of the wealth of Europe and ultimately that of many of today's industrialized nations. At the same time, it systematically impoverished much of the world.

Pillage

One of the most important means of wealth transfer was **pillage.** In the early years of expansion, Europeans were driven by the search for precious metals, particularly gold and silver. When they found such valuables, they moved quickly to seize them. Metals belonging to indigenous peoples were soon dispatched back to Europe, and mines were placed under European control. The profits of these enterprises were enormous. For example, in 1531, Pizarro captured the Inca emperor Atahuallpa and received $88.5 million in gold and $2.5 million in silver (current value) as his ransom. A gang of Indian smiths worked nine forges day and night to melt down this treasure, which was then shipped back to Spain (Duncan 1995:158). In the early 17th century, 58,000 Indian workers were forced into silver mining in the town of Potosi in the Peruvian Andes (Wolf 1982:136). Between 1500 and 1660, Spanish colonies in the Americas exported 300 tons of gold and 25,000 tons of silver (Scammell 1989:133). At current prices, this would be worth about $23.5 billion.

Such looting was not limited to the New World. After the British East India Company came to power in India, it plundered the treasury of Bengal, sending wealth back to investors in England (Wolf 1982:244). In addition, art, artifacts, curiosities, and occasionally human bodies were stolen around the world and sent to museums and private collections in Europe.

Forced Labor

Forced labor was another key element of European expansion. The most notorious example was African slavery, but impressing local inhabitants for labor, debt servitude, and other forms of peonage was common. Europeans forced both the peoples whose lands they conquered and their own lower classes into vassalage. Europeans did not invent slavery in general or African slavery in particular. For example, non-Europeans probably exported more than seven million African slaves to the Islamic world between 650 and 1600 (Lovejoy 1983). However, Europeans did practice African slavery on a larger scale than any people before them. Between the end of the 15th century and the end of the 19th century, approximately 11.7 million slaves were exported from Africa to the Americas. More than six million left Africa in the 19th century alone (Coquery-Vidrovitch 1988). No one really knows how many died in the process of capturing and transferring slaves within Africa. Estimates vary from one to five individuals died for every slave successfully landed in the Americas.

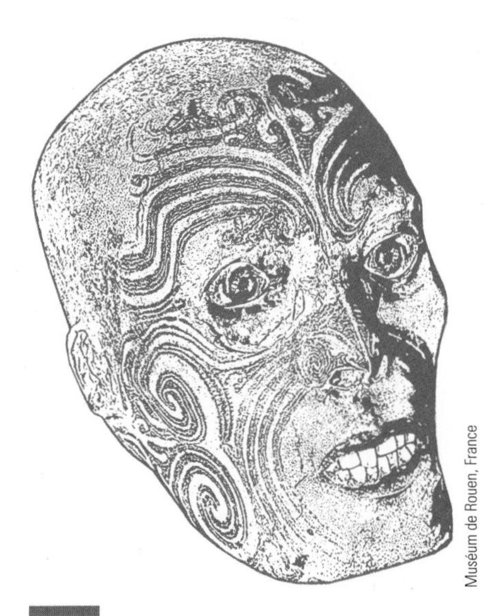
Muséum de Rouen, France

Drawing of a mummified Maori head. This head has been in the collection of the Museum of Natural History at Rouen, France. In 2007, the mayor of Rouen offered to return the head to New Zealand in "atonement" for the trafficking of human remains that occurred in the colonial era. However, the French government prevented the return of the head.

The massive transport of people had two important economic effects. First, the use of slave labor was extremely profitable for both slave shippers and plantation owners. Second, slave labor created continuous warfare and impoverishment in the areas from which slaves were drawn. Although some undoubtedly grew rich on the profits of slavery, the loss of so many people and the violence and political instability resulting from the capture and transport of slaves radically altered African societies (Coquery-Vidrovitch 1988).

The demand for slaves was created by monoculture plantations—farms devoted to the production of a single crop for sale to distant consumers. Sugar and cotton produced in the Americas and spices produced in Asia were sold to consumers located primarily in Europe. Through the 19th century, sugar was the most important monoculture crop. British consumption of sugar increased some 2500 percent between 1650 and 1800. Between 1800 and 1890, sugar production grew another 2500 percent, from 245,000 tons to more than six million tons per year (Mintz 1985:73). The massive amount of labor required for the growing and processing of sugar was largely provided by slaves. Between 1701 and 1810, for example, Barbados, a small island given over almost entirely to sugar production, imported 252,500 slaves, almost all of whom were involved in growing and processing sugar (Mintz 1985:53).

Joint Stock Companies

The joint stock company was another innovation that allowed extremely rapid European expansion and led to enormous abuses of power. Most early European exploration was financed and supported by aristocratic governments or small private firms. By the turn of the 17th century, however, the British and Dutch had established joint stock companies. The French, Swedes, Danes, Germans, and Portuguese followed by midcentury. The best known of these companies include the Dutch East India Company (founded 1629), the British East India Company (founded 1600), the Massachusetts Bay Company (founded 1629), and the Hudson's Bay Company (founded in 1670).

Joint stock companies were the predecessors of today's publicly held corporations. The idea was simple. In order to raise the capital necessary for large-scale ventures, companies would sell shares. Each share entitled its purchaser to a portion of the profits (or losses) from the company's business. Exploration and trade by joint stock companies had critical advantages over earlier forms. First, a great deal of capital could be raised rapidly, so business ventures could be much larger than previously possible. Second, although the motives of aristocratic government often included the search for prestige and missionary zeal, joint stock companies existed to provide profits to their shareholders and were relatively single minded in pursuit of that goal. Since they frequently were empowered to raise armies and conduct wars, they could have devastating effects on the societies they penetrated.

The **Dutch East India Company (VOC,** after its initials in Dutch) is a model example of a joint stock company. Based on money raised from the sale of shares, the VOC was chartered by the Dutch government to hold the monopoly on all Dutch trade with the societies of the Indian and Pacific Oceans. Shares in the VOC were available on reasonable terms and were held by a wide cross-section of Dutch society (Scammell 1989:101). In many ways, the company functioned as a government. Led by a board of directors called the **Heeren XVII** (the Lords Seventeen), it was empowered to make treaties with local rulers in the name of the Dutch Republic, occupy lands, levy taxes, raise armies, and declare war. The fundamental difference was that governments were to some degree beholden to those they governed, whereas the VOC was interested solely in returning dividends to its shareholders. Through the 17th and early 18th centuries, the VOC distributed annual dividends of 15.5 to 50 percent. It returned dividends of 40 percent per year for six consecutive years from 1715 to 1720

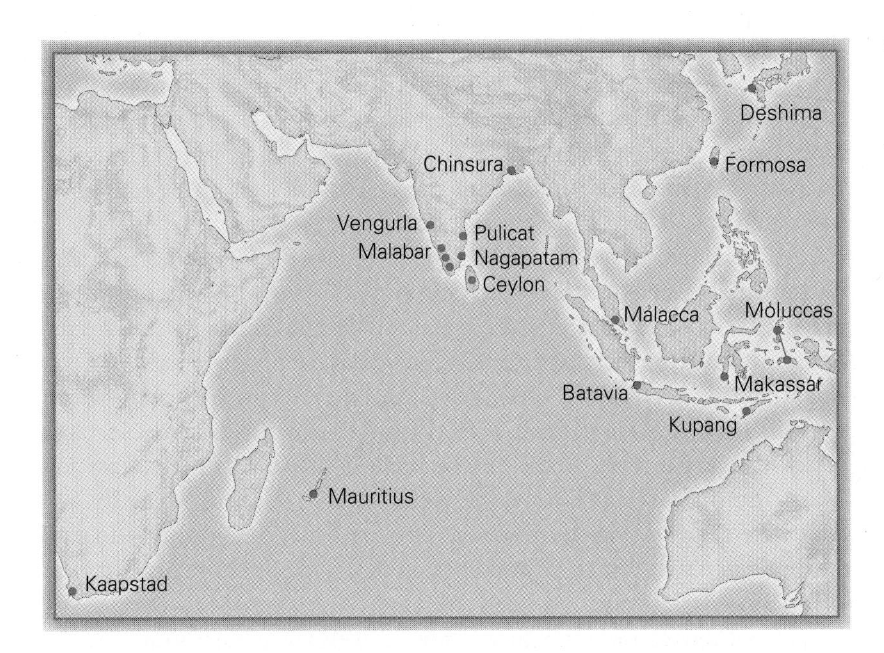

Principal holdings of the Dutch East India Company in the Pacific in the 1660s.

(Boxer 1965:46). By comparison, the average annual dividend paid by a Standard and Poor's 500 stock index between 1960 and 2007 was between 2 and 5 percent.

Through the 17th century, the VOC used its powers to seize control of many of the Indian Ocean islands. Among these were Java, including the port of Jakarta (which became their headquarters, renamed Batavia), Sri Lanka (Ceylon), and Malacca. In addition, the VOC acquired the right to control the production and trade of the most valuable spices of the area (cloves, nutmeg, and mace) and took brutal steps to maintain this monopoly. For example, during the 1620s, virtually the entire population of the nutmeg-producing island of Banda was deported, driven away, starved to death, or massacred. They were replaced with Dutch colonists using slave labor (Ricklefs 1993:30). By the 1670s, the Dutch had gained complete control of all spice production in what is now Indonesia (Wolf 1982).

Natives of this region did not submit passively to VOC control, and the company did not have a clear-cut military advantage. Instead, the VOC rapidly (and ultimately disastrously) became embroiled in the area's wars. For example, in the 17th century, the Maratram Dynasty controlled most of central Java. In 1677, when the dynasty faced rebellion, the VOC intervened on its behalf in hopes of cash payments and trade concessions. In a bloody campaign, the combined VOC and dynasty forces crushed the rebellion and established Emperor Amangkurat II on the throne. Trouble ensued when the VOC received neither payments nor concessions. An armed force that it sent in 1686 to make its demands was defeated by

Amangkurat II. The company was unable to recoup its losses or to claim its trading privileges (Ricklefs 1990). This was just the beginning of a series of extremely brutal wars pitting different factions of Javanese kingdoms against each other and against the VOC. Kingdoms alternately allied with and fought against the VOC as their interests dictated. These conflicts lasted until 1757.

The company often acted with extraordinary brutality. The treatment of the Chinese in Batavia is a good example. The Chinese had come to Batavia as traders, skilled artisans, sugar millers, and shopkeepers. Despite harsh measures against them, by 1740 roughly 15,000 lived there. VOC officials believed they were plotting rebellion, and after an incident in which several Europeans were killed, VOC governor general Adriaan Valckenier hinted that a massacre would not be unwelcome. In the melee that followed, Europeans and their slaves killed 10,000 Chinese. The Chinese quarter of the city burned for several days, and the VOC was able to stop the looting only by paying its soldiers a premium to return to duty (Ricklefs 1993:90).

The burden of continual warfare, as well as corruption and inefficiency, forced the VOC into serious financial difficulties. By the last quarter of the 18th century, large areas of coastal Java had been depopulated by years of warfare, but the VOC had not succeeded in controlling the principal kingdoms of the island. The Heeren XVII were dismissed by the Netherlands government in 1796 after an investigation revealed corruption and mismanagement in all quarters. On December 31, 1799, the VOC was formally dissolved, and its possessions were turned over to the Batavian Republic, a Dutch client state of France.

The story of the VOC was, in large measure, repeated by other mercantilist trading firms organized by the British, French, Germans, Portuguese, Danes, and Swedes. In each case, companies generated enormous profits but eventually fell into disarray and either were dissolved or were taken over by their national governments. Despite their eventual failure, the trading companies placed fantastic riches in the hands of European elites. Europeans invested this wealth in many different ways: in the arts, in luxury goods, in architecture, but also in science and industry. This supply of wealth became one of the sources for the Industrial Revolution and the rise of capitalism itself.

The effects were far less pleasant for the regions in which the trading companies operated. The VOC and other trading companies left poverty and chaos in their wakes. In every case, Europeans fundamentally altered the communities with which they came into contact. Frequently, brutal policies and disease destroyed entire cultures. However, in most cases, societies were not simply overrun. Before the 19th century, Europeans did not have a truly decisive technological advantage over others. Instead,

Europeans collaborated with local elites, which often were able to use their contact with the foreigners to increase their own wealth and power. However, as a whole, their societies suffered.

THE ERA OF COLONIALISM

Colonialism differs in important ways from the earlier expansion of European power. Whereas much of the initial phase of European expansion was carried out by private companies and often took the form of raid and pillage, colonialism involved the active possession of foreign territory by European governments. **Colonies** were created when nations established and maintained political domination over geographically separate areas and political units (Kohn 1958).

There were several different types of European colonies. Some, as in Africa, existed primarily to exploit native people and resources. In other areas, such as North America and Australia, the key goal was the settlement of surplus European population. Still other locales, such as Yemen, which borders on the Red Sea and thus controlled shipping through the Suez Canal, were seized because they occupied key strategic locations.

At one time or another, much of the world came under direct European colonization, but the timing of colonialism varied from place to place. The Americas were colonized in the 1500s and 1600s, but most other areas of the world did not come under colonial control until the 19th century. As long as Europeans confronted others with broadly similar weaponry and military tactics, the result was indecisive, and local governments were able to retain autonomy and power. By the 19th century, however, the Industrial Revolution gave Europeans (and their North American descendants) decisive advantage in both technological sophistication and quantity of arms. Although European colonizers faced frequent rebellions and proved unable to entirely subdue guerrilla activity in all places, no other government or army could offer effective resistance to them.

Colonization 1500 to 1800

As we have seen, before the 1800s, very little of Africa or Asia was colonized. In these places, Europeans were able to establish small coastal settlements, but these existed largely because they were profitable for both Europeans and at least some local elites. In most cases, local powers had the ability to expel Europeans or to strictly limit their activities. Relatively few Europeans settled permanently in such colonies.

In the Americas, the situation was radically different. There, Europeans quickly established colonies and immigrated in large numbers. For example, between 1492 and 1600, more than 55,000 Spaniards immigrated to the New World. In the 50 years that followed, another quarter million joined them (Boyd-Bowman 1975). By comparison, in the first half of the 19th century, the total Dutch population of Indonesia, Holland's most important colonial possession, was about 2100 (Zeegers et al. 2004).

Although there was stiff resistance to European expansion in the Americas and Indian wars continued until the late 19th century, Europeans were quickly victorious almost everywhere they wanted to expand. The main reason for rapid European success was disease. Europeans, Africans, and Asians shared similar diseases and immunities. New World natives did not. In the wake of contact, up to 95 percent of the total population of the New World died (Karlen 1995; Palkovich 1994; Wolf 1982).

Although occasionally epidemics may have been caused intentionally, neither Europeans nor natives had any knowledge of contagion or germs. The vast majority of deaths were not premeditated. However, Europeans came to see the handiwork of God in the disappearance of native populations. God clearly intended them to populate the Americas and was removing the native population to make that possible.

New World natives lacked immunity to European diseases for two principal reasons. First, the key diseases that killed indigenous populations, such as smallpox, influenza, and tuberculosis, require large reservoirs of population, in some cases up to a half million individuals (Diamond 1992). Many North American groups were too small to sustain such crowd diseases and therefore lacked immunity to them. Second, although some Central and South American groups did have large populations, most crowd diseases originate in domesticated animals, which were largely absent from the Americas.

Cortés's conquest of Mexico is a good example of the effects of disease. When Cortés first appeared in 1519, the Aztec leader Montezuma, following his tradition, gave Cortés gifts and opened the city of Tenochtitlán to the Spanish. When it became clear that the Spanish were their enemies, the Aztecs expelled them from the city in a fierce battle that cost the Spanish and their allies perhaps two thirds of their total army. By the time Cortés returned in 1521, a smallpox epidemic had killed up to half the Aztecs. Even after such crushing losses to disease, the Spanish conquest of Tenochtitlán took more than 4 months to accomplish (Berdan 1982; Clendinnen 1991; Karlen 1995). Had the Aztecs not been devastated by disease, they might have again defeated Cortés.

The die-off of Native Americans had dire effects throughout the Americas. The increasing population of Europeans and the diminishing population of natives assured that resistance could not be very effective. When Winthrop, the first governor of Massachusetts, declared that the settlers had fair title to the land because it was *vacuum domicilium* (empty land), he was creating a legal fiction (he was well aware of the natives and their need for agricultural and hunting land), but he also knew that the native population was declining sharply.

If not for disease, the European experience in the Americas probably would have been very similar to its experience in Asia and Africa. Rather than establishing control over vast amounts of territory, Europeans probably would have been confined to small coastal settlements and would have been involved in protracted battles with powerful local kingdoms.

Colonizing in the 19th Century

By the beginning of the 19th century, industrialization was underway in Europe and North America. This had two immediate consequences. First, it enabled Europeans and Americans to produce weapons in greater quantity and quality than any other people. Second, it created an enormous demand for raw materials that could not be satisfied in Europe. In addition, discoveries in medicine, particularly vaccines and antimalarial drugs, improved the odds of survival for Europeans in places previously considered pestilential. Thus, Europeans had both motives and means to colonize.

By 1900, most nations in the Americas had achieved independence. However, much of the rest of the world was under colonial rule. Many areas not formally colonized, such as China, were dominated by European powers.

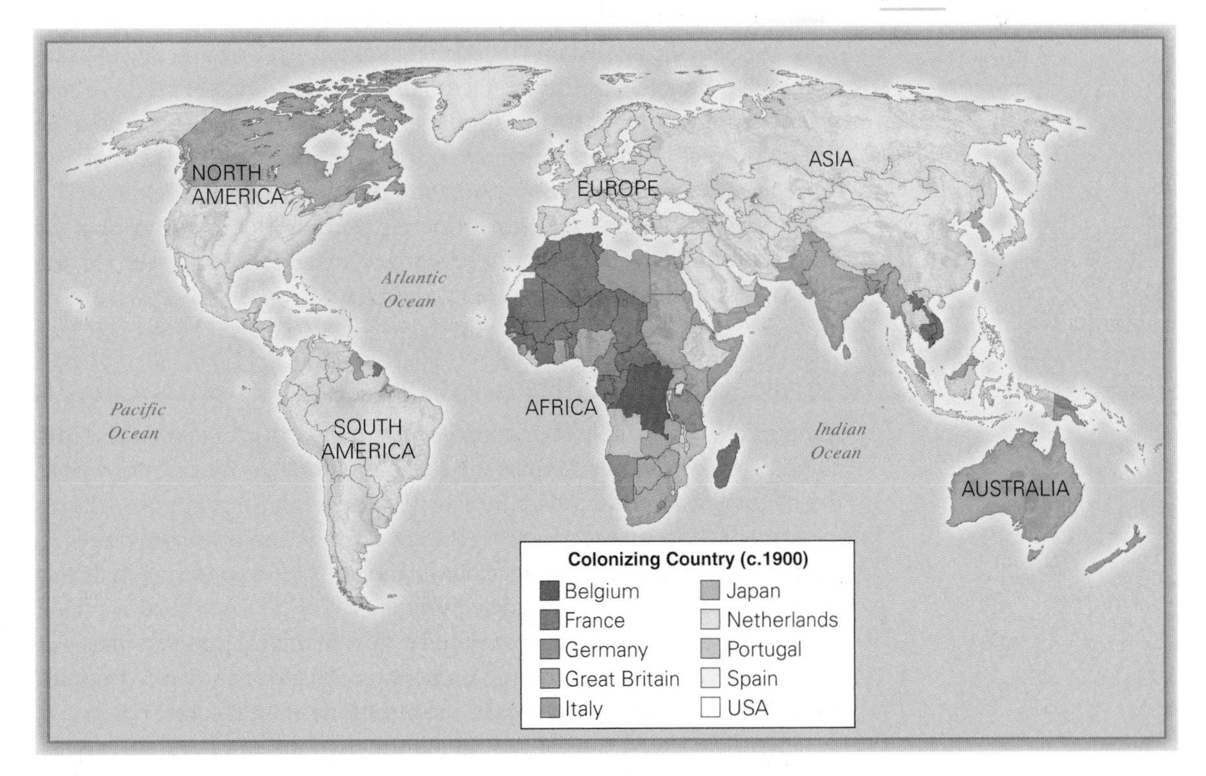

Acting in their own self-interest, Europeans and Americans generally did not move rapidly to place other areas under their colonial control. The primary goal of European expansion was the pursuit of wealth and plunder. Mercantilist firms were rapid cost-effective ways to get them. The financial burden of establishing companies such as the VOC was borne by their shareholders. However, colonizing an area required some level of government expenditure. At the very least this included government officials and the troops to back them, all of whom had to be equipped and paid out of government funds. In most cases, infrastructure such as roads, bridges, and railways had to be built. These were expensive undertakings, and European taxpayers and governments were generally not enthusiastic about funding them.

Most often, European governments felt forced to assume colonial control either because of the scandals surrounding the collapse of mercantile companies or out of fear that their national commercial interests were threatened, generally by other European nations. It was this fear that led to the Berlin conference partitioning Africa among European powers in the late 19th century.

After European governments had established colonies, they had to sell this fact both to their own populations and to those they colonized. They defended their actions by cloaking them in the ideology of social betterment. In Britain, citizens were encouraged, in the words of the poet Rudyard Kipling, to take up "the white man's burden" of bringing civilization to the "savage." In France, the population was told that it had a "*mission civilisatrice,*" a civilizing mission that would both help the "savages" in the colonized areas and increase French political and cultural power throughout the world. The government portrayed its colonial practices as "*rayonnement,*" lighting the way for others. In the colonies, as we will see next, subjects were taught that they were colonized for their own good and that their societies would advance as a result.

Making Colonialism Pay

Once colonies were seized, they had to be administered and they had to be made profitable. Colonizing powers hoped that tax revenues from colonial subjects would support the cost of colonial government as well as the construction of various public works. However, in many cases taxes were insufficient, and taxpayers in the colonizing country were required to make up the difference between colonial income and expenses. Despite this situation, colonies were extremely profitable.

Colonies gave businesses based in the colonizing country places in which they could operate free of competition. This was particularly important for Britain and France, two of the most important colonial powers. In the late 1700s, the Industrial Revolution began in Britain, but by the end of the 19th century, its factories were aging. New, more efficient industrial processes developed in the United States and Germany enabled these countries to produce cheaper manufactured goods (Allitt 2002). France came to industrialization relatively late and had a relatively weak road and rail network. As a result, France too had difficulty competing with the United States, Germany, and Britain. Colonies created a zone of protection for older British industry and newer French manufacturers, thus enabling high profits for firms in these nations.

The costs of the colonies were born (unequally) by subject colonial populations and by colonizing country taxpayers. The windfall profits from colonialism went to shareholders of companies operating in the colonies.

Finding ways to extract taxes and create the conditions in which corporations could make money often meant the systematic undermining of indigenous ways of life. Although the newly colonized communities had traded with other communities and frequently with Europeans for centuries, trading generally accounted for only a small percentage of their economy. For the most part, their economic relations were drawn along kinship lines, and most of their production was for their own consumption. For colonialism to be profitable, these patterns had to change. Colonial subjects had to be made to produce the goods that colonizing societies wanted and to labor in ways that would be profitable to the colonizers. From the colonizers' perspective, the key problem was finding ways to cause these changes. Some of the methods they used were control of local leaders, forced labor, forced production of particular commodities, taxation, and direct propaganda through education.

Sometimes colonial powers seized direct control of the political leadership, but this was expensive, and foreign colonial leaders often lacked sufficient knowledge of local language and culture. More often colonialists ruled indirectly through native leaders. Promises of power and wealth as well as the realization that colonial governments held the reins of power and were unlikely to lose them any time soon drew colonial subjects to support them. In some cases, colonial powers offered education, employment, and improved status to people who were oppressed or outcast in precolonial society; and these individuals were particularly drawn to support the colonizers.

A well-organized chain of command was needed for colonial powers to rule effectively. In hierarchical societies where kings or chiefs already existed, this did not pose a difficult problem. Most often, local elites sympathetic to the colonizers were able to retain a degree of power, although they became answerable to the colonial authorities. Those unsympathetic to colonial rule were rapidly replaced. Regions where precolonial relationships were largely egalitarian posed a more difficult problem. If there was no chief or there were many coreigning chiefs, establishing colonial authority was far more difficult. Colonizers tried to solve this problem by creating new chiefly offices. Sometimes colonialists and missionaries forged entire new ethnic groups, lumping together people with different traditions and even different languages (Harries 1987). For example, the Bété, an ethnic group of the central Ivory Coast in Africa, did not exist before the era of colonialism but was created by the actions of colonial and postcolonial governments (Dozon 1985). In the long run, these policies of indirect rule created the preconditions for instability and violence. Political leaders were compromised by their close connections with colonial authorities, losing the confidence and respect of those they purported to lead. Ethnic groups created for the purposes of colonial rule tended to fragment when that rule diminished.

One of the most direct ways that European governments tried to make their colonies profitable was by requiring ***corvée* labor**—unpaid work demanded of native populations. Until World War II, most colonial governments insisted on substantial labor from their subjects. The British often compelled subjects to work for up to 1 month per year, the Dutch 2 months. In 1926, the French enacted a law that permitted an annual draft of labor for their West African colonies. Conscripts were compelled to work for 3 years on bridge and road building, irrigation projects, and other public works. Mortality rates during the 3 years of forced labor often were very high, making forced labor one of the most hated institutions of colonialism. Natives resisted colonial demands by concealing workers or by fleeing from authorities when such work was demanded (Evans 2000; Ishemo 1995).

Even when subject populations were not forced into labor gangs, economic and social policies of colonial regimes required them to radically alter their cultures. For example, Portuguese colonial policy in Mozambique forced almost one million peasants to grow cotton. The colonial government controlled what these growers produced, where they lived, with whom they traded, and how they organized their labor. Although a few growers prospered, the great majority became impoverished and struggled to survive against famine and hardship (Isaacman 1996). By the 1960s, the brutality and terror used by the colonial regime resulted in a civil war that continued into the 1990s.

At the turn of the century, conditions were perhaps worst in the Congo, ruled between 1885 and 1908 as the personal property of King Leopold of Belgium. There, each native owed the government 40 hours of labor per month in exchange for a token wage (Bodley 1999:116). Failure to work sufficiently or to produce the proper quantities of goods (particularly rubber) were met with extreme measures. Leopold's subjects were held hostage, were beaten or whipped, had their hands cut off, and, in many cases, were killed outright. By the time the Belgian government stripped Leopold of his control of Congo, between four and eight million Congolese had been killed or had starved to death (Hochschild 1998).

In addition to forced labor and forced production, the British and French both drafted natives into their armed forces. They used these armies to capture and control their colonies, fight colonial wars, and augment their regular armies wherever needed. The *Tirailleurs Senegalais* were described at the opening of this chapter. Additional *Tirailleurs* units included groups from Algeria, Morocco, Madagascar, Vietnam, Cambodia, and other French colonial possessions. In East Africa, the British drafted and recruited the King's African Rifles. In India, the British created an entire army led by British officers but consisting almost entirely of colonial subjects drawn primarily from ethnic groups the British considered particularly warlike. About 1.3 million members of the Indian Army served in World War I, primarily on the Western Front but also in the Middle East (UK National Archives).

Anti-Slavery International Reg Charity 1039160

From 1885 to 1908, Congo was the property of King Leopold II of Belgium. Atrocities committed during that era cost the lives of four to eight million Congolese. Punishments for disobedience or failure to meet payment quotas included chopping off children's hands.

Although particular projects might use forced labor, to make a colony truly profitable, colonial masters also used other methods to encourage the population to work for them voluntarily or to produce the goods they desired. Taxation was a key mechanism for accomplishing this goal. Taxation was needed to support the colonial government, but since colonizers knew that colonial economies were small and their tax receipts low, they rarely expected taxes to provide the full cost of governing. However, taxing colonial subjects had another purpose: to force them into the market system. Taxes generally had to be paid in colonial money, which native subjects could obtain only by working for a colonist or by producing something that the colonists wanted to buy. This participation in the market and wage labor was viewed as the essential precondition for "civilizing" the natives.

Taxation often forced colonial subjects into a vicious cycle of dependency on the market system. To raise money for taxes, subjects had to work directly for the colonizers or produce things that colonizers desired. But spending time on these tasks meant that less time could be spent making goods or raising crops for one's own consumption. This in turn meant that increasingly food and goods had to be purchased from the market, which was dominated by companies owned by colonialists.

In addition to policies aimed at forcing subjects to take part in an economy centered in the industrial world, colonial governments took more direct aim at cultures through educational policies. Colonial education was often designed to convince subjects that they were the cultural, moral, and intellectual inferiors of those who ruled them. For example, education in 19th-century India encouraged children to aspire to be like the ideal Englishman (Viswanathan 1988). In France's African colonies, children were directly taught to obey their colonial masters, as illustrated in this passage from a turn-of-the-century reader designed to teach French to schoolchildren and used in the colonies:

> It is . . . an advantage for a native to work for a white man, because the Whites are better educated, more advanced in civilization than the natives, and because, thanks to them, the natives will make more rapid progress. . . and become one day really useful men. . . . You who are intelligent and industrious, my children, always help the Whites in their task (cited in Bodley 1999:104).

Education was often aimed at the children of elites. These children were taught that, although they might never reach the level of the colonists, they were considerably more advanced than their uneducated countrymen. In France's African colonies, individuals who were educated and assimilated to French culture were known both by the French and by themselves as *evolues,* or evolved people. This increased the perception of the uneducated and unassimilated as being backward and primitive. Thus, schooling both reinforced the colonizers' position and created a subservient educated class convinced of its superiority (Kelly 1986).

Colonialism and Anthropology

The origins and practice of modern anthropology are bound up with the colonial era. Both anthropology and 19th-century colonialism are products of the 18th-century age of European enlightenment, the romantic retrenchment of the 19th century, the Industrial Revolution, the birth of modern science, and other historical and philosophical forces. For example, the evolutionary theories of 19th-century anthropologists described a world in which all societies were evolving toward perfection. This idea shows elements of enlightenment rationality (they were systematizing knowledge and trying to discover laws of social development) and 19th-century romanticism (nations were moving toward perfection) and was very clearly influenced by the scientific theories of Charles Darwin and the social theories of Herbert Spencer. It was also a convenient philosophy that could be pressed into service as a rationale for colonization (Ghosh 1991; Godelier 1993).

One of the most important impacts colonialism had on anthropology was in determining the locations of fieldwork. British Commonwealth anthropologists tended to work in British colonies, French anthropologists in their colonies, and Americans within U.S. borders, in areas "protected" by the Monroe Doctrine or in areas of American influence and control in the Pacific. In some cases, colonialism may have played a role in determining the topics of anthropological research. Studies of indigenous political systems or law were of particular interest to colonial governments. Colonialism and, more importantly, the discourse of rationalism and science also tended to promote a kind of anthropology where the anthropologist speaks as an active authority claiming to objectively describe essentially passive subjects.

In the first half of the 20th century, colonial governments faced with the practical problems of governing their possessions sometimes relied on information provided by anthropologists. Anthropologists, anxious to find funding for their research, argued that their studies had practical value to colonial administrators (Malinowski 1929a, for example). However, anthropology did not come into being to promote or enable colonialism, which would have gone on with or without it (Burton 1992).

Anthropologists did not generally question the political reality of colonialism, but they often self-consciously tried to advance the interests of the people they studied. Most anthropological research was financed by private charitable organizations with reformist agendas and not by governments (Goody 1995). The result was that colonial officials generally mistrusted anthropologists, believing they were much too sympathetic to colonial subjects (Prah 1990).

DECOLONIZATION

The eras of Western expansion and colonization radically and permanently changed the world. By the time of World War II, all peoples had been affected by Western expansion and their cultures altered by this experience. Some, attempting to resist foreign influences and protect their ways of life, had moved as far away from outsiders as possible (for example, see Breusers 1999). However, most people lived in societies where the presence and influence of outsiders, their demands for goods and labor, and their attempts to change culture were fundamental facts of life.

Most of the nations of the Americas had gained their independence in the 18th and 19th centuries. In Africa and Asia, independence from European colonialism was not achieved until after World War II. Many nations that were part of the Soviet Union only received their independence in the late 1980s and early 1990s. Some colonies persist today, although usually with the consent of the majority of their residents. For example, Britain has some 14 "overseas territories," including Bermuda, Gibraltar, and the Pitcairn Islands. French "overseas departments" include Martinique and French Guiana. U.S. "organized unincorporated territo-

National Archives Photo No. 306-RNT-57-18116

Kwame Nkrumah, Ghana's first president, proclaims independence on March 6, 1957.

ries" include American Samoa and Guam. Many consider the U.S. relationship with Puerto Rico colonial as well (Grosfoguel 2003; Melendez 1993).

There were as many reasons for the granting of independence as there were for exploration and colonialism, but three are of particular importance: civil disobedience, changing political structures, and changing economic structures.

Governing colonies was never a simple affair, and from the beginning there was rebellion against colonial rule. Strikes, acts of terrorism, and in some places guerrilla warfare were common throughout the colonial era. However, for several reasons there was a substantial upsurge in these following the Second World War. One reason was the return of combat veterans. Veterans knew how to fight European-style warfare. Moreover, they and their supporters felt that colonizing countries owed them a deep debt for their service, a debt to be paid partially by increased political liberties.

In some places, resistance took the form of agitation and demonstrations, but in others bitter anticolonial wars broke out. In Madagascar, for example, almost 90,000 died in a rebellion in 1947 and 1948. In Algeria, between 1954 and 1962 France fought a protracted war that left at least one quarter of a million dead (Kepel 2005). Anticolonial wars also broke out in Vietnam, Mozambique, Angola, and numerous other places.

The end of World War II also created a fundamentally different balance of world power. European nations, which held the largest number of colonies, were greatly weakened, which left the United States and the Soviet Union as the dominant superpowers. They quickly engaged in a cold war that was to last for more than 4 decades, but neither nation had a strong interest in preserving the colonial status quo. Based on the belief that they could bring former colonies into their own economic and political orbit, both the United States and the Soviet Union promoted rapid independence for colonial possessions and supplied money and weaponry to their supporters within the colonies.

Finally, international economics was also changing. In many cases colonies had been created to allow European corporations access to areas where they could operate free of competition from those based in other nations. However, in the wake of World War II, corporate ownership began to become multinational, and corporations were less tied to their nations of origin, a move that continues today. This process undercut an important economic rationale of colonialism.

By December 1960, when the United Nations declared that "all peoples have the right to self determination" and that "immediate steps shall be taken . . . to transfer all powers to the peoples of [countries that have not yet achieved independence] (UN Resolution 1514)," the process of decolonization was already well underway. At that time, recently decolonized nations included India and Pakistan (1947), Cambodia (1953), Vietnam (1954), Ghana (1957), Guinea (1958), and many others.

By the late 1970s, almost all colonies held by western European nations had achieved independence. With the formal end of the Soviet Union in 1991 and the collapse of South African apartheid in 1994, almost all areas of the world had some form of home rule. Colonized areas became independent under a variety of circumstances and with many different levels of preparedness. In some, like Ghana, the transition to independence was reasonably orderly, and there were a sizable (but still inadequate) number of individuals trained as administrators. In others, like Congo, the transition was profoundly violent, and very few colonial subjects had any experience with running government. But although there were great differences among colonies, all came to independence as relatively poor nations in a world that was increasingly divided into the wealthy and the poor rather than the independent and the colonized.

Formal independence was critical for former colonies. However, compelling connections between newly independent nations and their former colonial powers remained. In most cases, diplomatic and cultural ties between nations and their former colonies continued to be strong. In many cases, economic ties persisted as well. European and American corporations continued their operations, albeit frequently with new names, and in many places countries continued to supply the raw materials for European, American, and increasingly Asian industries. In the 1960s, the word "neocolonialism" came to express the idea that although nations were no longer colonized, many of the institutions of colonialism remained intact.

The European expansion and the era of colonization were historic processes that changed the world from a collection of relatively independent economies and societies to a complex world system. Technological and political processes since the end of colonialism have only accelerated this process. In Chapter 14 we explore some of the problems faced by independent but poor nations as well as the forces of technology, finance, and politics that are weaving an increasingly dense fabric of globalization.

BRINGING IT BACK HOME: CELEBRATING GHANA'S 50TH ANNIVERSARY

2007 marked the 50th year of independence for the West African nation of Ghana. On March 11 of that year, Niall Ferguson wrote an excoriating editorial in the British Newspaper *The Sunday Telegraph.* According to Ferguson, independence has been a disaster for Ghana. Ferguson says that at the time of independence from England, the average Britain was 39 times wealthier than the average Ghanaian. Today, the average Britain is 93 times wealthier. Today, foreign aid accounts for 16 percent of the Ghanaian national income and 73 percent of its government expenditures. Even though the average citizen is living on $1.30 per day and the United States gave Ghana $22.5 million in food aid in 2006, the government spent approximately $20 million on its 50th anniversary celebrations. According to Ferguson, Ghana's case is not exceptional. He claims that "In virtually every case . . . former British colonies in sub-Saharan Africa have faired worse under independence than they did under British rule." Ferguson lays the blame for this failure on bad government.

Ferguson's comments elicited a firestorm of protest. Kwame Ardin's (2007) reaction was typical. Writing on Ghanaweb.com, Ardin said that Ferguson's comments were "typical of hold-back racists who continue to wage a war of words against black people." Some critics argued that although Ghana had not lived up to the hopes of its people, Ferguson had ignored its successes. For example, according to Ekow Nelson and Michael Gyamerah (2007), in 1951 fewer than 4000 students were enrolled in secondary school, but by 2005 that number had risen to 1.3 million. They noted that in 1955 there was one doctor to 25,000 of population, but today there is about one doctor for each 7000 Ghanaians. However, most of Ferguson's critics responded by describing the oppression and political mismanagement faced by Africans under European rule. The catalog of crimes starts with slavery and includes divide-and-rule policies that set one ethnic group against another, the creation of states with artificial boundaries that divided members of ethnic groups from each other, the forging of economies designed to supply raw materials at extremely low prices, and the encouraging of a political and administrative style that favored extraction of wealth rather than service to people. For Ferguson's critics, African countries such as Ghana have failed to achieve prosperity because they faced almost insurmountable obstacles, most of which were caused by their experience of colonialism.

YOU DECIDE

1. It is clear that, in many cases, poor country governments have failed to bring either peace or stability to their citizens. What do you think are the key reasons why this is so?
2. Some scholars argue that although formal colonial control has ended, the structures of colonialism remain in place and informal control remains; colonialism has merely been replaced with neocolonialism. By this they mean that although nations are, in name, independent, many of the relations between colonizing nations and their former colonies are still intact. Do you believe this to be the case? Give some examples of neocolonialism and show how they operate against prosperity in poor nations.
3. Some nations, such as Botswana and Malaysia, have been economically successful since the end of colonial rule. Others, such as Rwanda and Congo, have fared extremely poorly. What factors do you think made for the success and failure of newly independent nations? How do you think these are related to global and domestic politics, economics, and culture?

CHAPTER SUMMARY

1. Although we are aware of history, we tend to think of current world conditions as similar to past conditions. This is illusion. The world as we see it is the result of historical processes that have moved wealth and power from one area of the world to another. The rise of today's wealthy nations was connected with the emergence of modern poverty.
2. In the 15th century, Europe was neither wealthy nor technologically advanced. The centers of world power lay primarily in the Middle East and Asia. However, Europe was poised on the brink of a great expansion.

3. A combination of religious faith, greed, new social arrangements, and new technologies drove European expansion. Europeans were particularly successful in the Americas, where they were aided by the diseases they carried. They met far more resistance in Asia.
4. Plunder of precious metals, the use of slave labor, and the joint stock company as well as political and military maneuvering drew wealth from around the world into Europe. European nations became prosperous, but other areas of the world were impoverished.
5. Colonialism occurred when European governments took direct control of overseas territories. This happened very early in the Americas but was a much later development elsewhere in the world.
6. Although European governments often justified colonialism by calling it a civilizing mission, governments colonized to increase their wealth and protect their trade. They used forced labor, taxation, and education programs designed to discredit local culture to compel natives to produce for European interests.
7. Anthropological knowledge was sometimes used in the process of colonialism, and some anthropologists wished to make themselves useful to colonial governments. However, anthropology did not come into being to promote colonialism, which would have gone on without it.
8. Most colonies gained their independence between the end of World War II and 1965. Civil unrest in the colonies, the emergence of the United States and the Soviet Union as superpowers, and changes in the structure of international economics played critical roles in the timing of independence.

KEY TERMS

Colonialism
Colonies
Corvée labor
Dutch East India Company
Heeren XVII
Joint stock company
Monoculture plantation
Pillage
Tirailleurs Senegalais
VOC

© Time & Life Pictures/Getty Images

We live in a world of sharp contrasts. Individuals and cultures worldwide are affected by changes in communication, technology, and the flow of wealth among nations.

CHAPTER 14

GLOBALIZATION AND CHANGE

CHAPTER OUTLINE

Global Poverty

Development

- Modernization Theory
- Human Needs Approaches
- Structural Adjustment

Multinational Corporations

Urbanization

Population Pressure

- China's One Child Policy

Environmental Changes

- Pollution
- Global Warming

Political Instability

Migration

Looking to the Future

Bringing It Back Home: How Flat Is Your World?

- You Decide

GLOBAL POVERTY

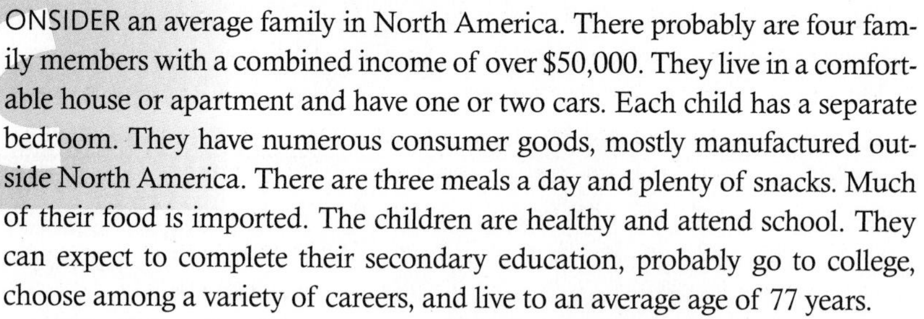

CONSIDER an average family in North America. There probably are four family members with a combined income of over $50,000. They live in a comfortable house or apartment and have one or two cars. Each child has a separate bedroom. They have numerous consumer goods, mostly manufactured outside North America. There are three meals a day and plenty of snacks. Much of their food is imported. The children are healthy and attend school. They can expect to complete their secondary education, probably go to college, choose among a variety of careers, and live to an average age of 77 years.

On the surface life seems good for this family, but there are problems as well. The competitive pressures are strong and take their toll on the health of both parents. Rising medical costs, high costs for college education, job insecurity, and debt threaten their way of life. But on the whole, theirs is an economic status and lifestyle toward which many millions of people throughout the world seem to be aspiring.

Now consider a typical "extended" family in rural Asia. The household likely comprises 10 or more people, including parents, children, and other relatives. They have a combined annual income of less than $500. They live in a one-room house as tenant farmers on a large agricultural estate owned by an absentee landlord. The adults and older children work all day on the land. None of the adults can read or write. Of the five school-age children, only two attend school regularly, and they will get only a basic primary education. There is often only one meal a day; it rarely changes and rarely is sufficient to alleviate the children's hunger pains. The house has no electricity or fresh water supply. There is much sickness but very few medical practitioners. The work is hard, the sun is hot, and the aspirations for a better life are continually being snuffed out.

Shifting to a large city along the coast of South America, we would immediately be struck by the sharp contrast in living conditions among neighborhoods. There is a modern stretch of tall buildings, wide boulevards, and gleaming beaches, but just a few hundred yards away there are squalid shanties.

It is a typical Saturday evening at an hour when families should be preparing dinner. In the apartment of a wealthy family, a servant sets the table with imported china, high-quality silverware, and fine linen. The family's eldest son is home from his university in North America, and the other two children are on vacation from their boarding schools in France and Switzerland. The father is a medical doctor with a wealthy clientele. Annual vacations abroad, imported luxuries, and fine food and clothing are commonplace amenities for this fortunate family.

And what of a poor family? They live in a dirt-floor hillside shack. The stench of open sewers fills the air. There is no dinner table being set; in fact, there is no dinner—only a few scraps of stale bread. The four children spend most of their time on the streets begging, shining shoes, or even trying to steal. They are recent immigrants to the city. The father has had part-time jobs but nothing permanent, and the family income is less than $1000 a year. The children have been in and out of school many times because they have to help out financially in any way they can. Occasionally the eldest teenage daughter seems to have some extra money, but no one asks where it comes from or how it is obtained.

The contrast between these two South American families is disturbing, but had we looked at almost any other major city in the world, we have seen similar things (although the extent of inequality might have been less pronounced).

Finally, imagine that you are in eastern Africa, where many small clusters of tiny huts dot a dry and barren land. Each cluster contains a group of extended families, all participating in and sharing the work. There is very little money because most food, shelter, and other goods are made and consumed by the people themselves. There are few roads and no schools, hospitals, electricity, or water supply. In many respects life is as difficult as for the poor family in Latin America. Yet, because it is shared by all, it is probably less psychologically troubling.

Soon a road will pass near this village. It will bring more information about the outside world, more gadgets of modern civilization. Before long, exportable tropical fruits will be grown in this region. They may even end up on the dinner table of the rich South American family. Meanwhile, radios made in southeast Asia playing music performed by African bands recorded in northern Europe will become prized possessions. Throughout the world remote villages are being linked with the rest of the world in an increasing number of ways. This process will only intensify in the coming years.

The passage you've just read, adapted from Todaro and Smith's (2003) classic textbook, *Economic Development,* is simplistic but dramatically captures some important truths. The historical processes we described in Chapter 13 have transformed the world, creating a global economic network. However, it is not a global village. The global village is a pastoral metaphor suggesting a relatively small place, a place where anyone can easily visit any part, a place where differences are minimized, a world of screen doors, broad porches, and friendly neighbors. But we live in a world of privilege and exclusion, a world of rapid change and of shocking inequality. In our world, some areas are centers: easy to get to, wealthy, powerful, and in constant communication with each other. Other places are more difficult to reach, less in contact with the rest of the world. Still others can be entered and exited only with real difficulty. In our world, the distances created by inequality often dwarf those of mere distance. For example, a technology or financial specialist working in Manhattan is likely to have close ties to colleagues, relatives, and friends living and working thousands of miles away and to communicate frequently with these people. They may have almost no social connections with members of the urban poor living within sight of their office and may almost never communicate with these people.

As the opening passages of this chapter show, our world is an enormously contradictory place. All around us, we see increasing cultural homogeneity; you can find a bottle of soda, a radio, or a CD player almost anywhere. Cell phones connect people in remote African villages to relatives in industrialized urban metropolises. The Internet lets teenagers in Houston bid on products in Hong Kong. At the same time, it is in many ways an increasingly divided world. The disparities in both quality and quantity of life are enormous. More than 1.2 billion of the world's population lives on less than $1 a day. At the same time, a meal for two at a good restaurant in any American city can easily top $100. Someone born in the late 1990s in Japan had a life expectancy of 81 years. If you were born in those same years in Malawi or Mozambique, your life expectancy would be only 37 years. Moreover, although many forces at work in the world favor cultural homogeneity, in many places people are insisting, sometimes violently, on their right to preserve their cultural identity or to create new identities intentionally separating themselves from the dominant global culture (for examples see Friedman 2003; Hefner 2002).

The end of colonial rule brought numerous challenges to the newly independent nations. They were beset by issues of poverty, the presence of multinational corporations, urbanization, population growth, problems of immigration and emigration, ecological disaster, war, and instability. A few nations, such as Singapore (formerly a British colony) and Korea (a Japanese colony from 1905 to 1945), have done extremely well. In 1981 almost 64 percent of Chinese were living on less than $1 a day. By 2001, that number had dropped to 16.6 percent and today is believed to be close to 8 percent (in constant dollars). Despite these successes, most nations remain poor.

The **gross national income (GNI)** of a nation is the total value of all its production and provides a rough estimate of national prosperity. Adjusting the GNI for price differences between nations allows us to compare countries. In the United States, in 2005 the GNI per capita, adjusted for purchasing power, was $42,000, but 80 of the 208 nations listed by the World Bank had a per capita GNI of less than $5000. For 53 of these nations, the figure was less than $2500. In 2004, about one billion people were living on less than $1 a day.

No culture has been left unchanged by history. However, the burden has fallen with particular force on the world's indigenous people. Cultures have had to adjust to extraordinary circumstances. In the face of economic and political change, some indigenous groups have simply disappeared. Many groups have managed to adapt, preserve some of their ways of life, and maintain a degree of cultural integrity. New identities have been forged as people and cultures have responded to change. In this chapter we examine some of the principal challenges resulting from globalization and consider what anthropology teaches us about the effects of global forces on cultures worldwide.

DEVELOPMENT

The decline of colonialism after World War II did not mean the end of forced cultural change, foreign intervention, or foreign influence. Nations were brought into ever closer contact, the pace of change increased as communications improved, and both individuals and groups, attracted by new opportunities or compelled to flee from violence, moved to new locations. Virtually all nations were drawn into the long conflict between the Western powers and the Soviet bloc. In wealthy nations, the Cold War was fought with military construction programs, diplomacy, and espionage. In poor nations such as Nicaragua, Congo, and Vietnam, it was fought with bullets and aircraft as well.

Under colonialism, economic plans focused on making colonies productive for their owners, but independent nations needed to be prosperous in their own right. Both Eastern and Western blocs saw this as an opportunity to spread their ideology and advance their economic systems. Both provided financial and military aid to poor nations. Their goals were to create political allies and stable trading partners as well as to secure sources of raw materials. Additionally, some international agencies, wealthy nation governments, and thousands of private organizations truly hoped to bring a better life to the world's poor.

Modernization Theory

The model of progress promoted by Western nations was called **modernization theory.** It started with the presumption that former colonies were poor because they had underdeveloped, backward economies. Modernization theorists held that poor nations could become rich by repeating the historical experience of the wealthy nations. To this end, foreign advice and financial aid were designed to alter the structural, cultural, and psychological features the theorists believed stood in the way of modernization.

New roads and factories would bring industrialization to the countryside. New farming techniques would allow peasants to cultivate cash crops. The market would replace the old mechanisms of obligation and reciprocity. The result would be increased wealth and higher standards of living.

This kind of development served the interests of both donors and elites in poor nations. It spread the influence of wealthy nations and made new markets for their products. In poor nations, money from development aid was often used to support an elite lifestyle and opened many possibilities for political patronage, not to mention bribery, graft, and other forms of corruption. However, it did little to improve conditions for most people in the recipient nations. Not only did nations fail to develop, in a great many cases their poverty increased. There were many reasons for this failure, but surely a critical reason was a problem with the theory itself. The proponents of modernization theory believed that poor nations could become wealthy by repeating the historical experience of wealthy nations. They assumed that poor nations were traditional and timeless, ignoring the roles that colonialism and exploitation had played in the history of both the rich and the poor. Poor nations could not repeat the historical experiences of the wealthy because they were products of that history. There were no places for them to colonize, even if such a course of action had been acceptable.

Human Needs Approaches

The failure of economic development plans in the 1960s led to the emergence of new ideas. These included the basic human needs approach of the 1970s and 1980s. In 1972 and 1973, the World Bank and other development agencies began to focus on filling the basic needs of the rural poor. Speaking in Nairobi in 1973, Robert McNamara, then World Bank President, identified the elimination of absolute poverty as a principal goal of development aid. McNamara described absolute poverty as:

> a condition of life so degraded by disease, illiteracy, malnutrition and squalor as to deny its victims basic human necessities and a condition of life so common as to be the lot of some 40 percent of the peoples of the developing countries (World Bank Group Archives 2003).

Proponents of the basic human needs approach argued that **development** had failed because it had focused on large-scale projects and technological change and had paid insufficient attention to improving the lives of the very poor and increasing their capacity to contribute effectively to the economy. Basic human needs projects focused on assuring poor people access to land and improved but simple farming techniques and on providing basic education, access to pure water, and basic health and sanitation facilities. The focus was on involving members of rural communities in managing and promoting these goals. Since anthropologists often had expertise in studying such communities, they came to play increasingly important roles in development aid. In 1974, the United States Agency for International Development (USAID) employed one full-time anthropologist. By 1980 this number had risen to more than 50 (Escobar 1997).

Although basic human needs projects continued, by the end of the 1980s they had lost their prominent role in development. First, although the projects did provide benefits to some communities, they failed to provide the economic growth that planners hoped for. Beyond this, donor governments did not like these projects because they had high overhead expenses and did not generate very much publicity. Recipient governments disliked them because the amount of money disbursed for them was lower than for more traditional modernization projects, and often the groups that the projects tried to help had relatively little political power. Perhaps most importantly, beginning in the 1980s, development philosophy in wealthy nations again changed.

Structural Adjustment

By the late 1970s, the failure of development programs and changing economic conditions left poor nations very deeply in debt to wealthy nations. This coincided with the rise of neoliberalism in the United States and Europe. **Neoliberalism** is a series of political and economic policies promoting free trade, individual initiative, and minimal government regulation of the economy. Neoliberals have opposed state control of industries or government subsidies to them and opposed all but minimal aid to impoverished individuals. This political philosophy led to a new approach to development called **structural adjustment.** Following neoliberal policies, before making any additional loans or grants, wealthy nations demanded that poor nations restructure their economies. They required poor nations to sell off state-owned enterprises, reduce subsidies to local businesses and industries, reduce spending on education, health, and social programs, and open their markets to free trade. Critics charge that these policies have created a spiral of deepening impoverishment that particularly affects the poorest and most vulnerable populations. Supporters argue that although such policies do cause pain, earlier policies were unsustainable. They claim that unleashing free market forces will promote industry, investment, and entrepreneurship. These will lead to increased wealth and a better standard of living for all. Although there certainly are two sides to this argument, it is clear that, thus far, structural adjustment policies have increased inequality and that poverty remains an intractable problem (Greenberg 1997; Kim, Millen, Irwin, and Gershman 2000; SAPRIN 2004).

Despite many failures and the persistence of global poverty, development efforts of both governments and private organizations have led to some notable successes. For example, in poor nations, life expectancy has increased 20 percent and literacy 25 percent in the past generation. Children are only half as likely to die before the age of 5 as they were a generation ago. The Grameen bank is another success story. The bank, a grassroots organization that offers small loans to poor women, has reached over a million families around the world and has been effective in raising the standard of living among some of the world's poorest people. The Grameen bank and its founder, the Bangladeshi economist Muhammad Yunus, won the Noble Peace Prize in 2006. However, the overall record of development projects around the world continues to be poor. Projects have been plagued by poor design, inappropriate technologies, and deleterious effects on environment, culture, and political stability. For example, aid projects helped to increase the export of shrimp in Honduras by more than 1500 percent, but the price of this growth was pollution, environmental destruction, and the impoverishment of people who lived near the shrimp farms (Stonich, Murray, and Rossart 1994).

Although the track record of development projects is mixed and the politics behind them controversial, they still have strong support and are likely to continue. Anthropologists play increasingly important roles in the planning of development. For example, Margaret Clarke has worked in projects in health care and education in Kenya, Egypt, Greece, and Turkey as well as other places. She has designed instruction for midwives and training materials for Peace Corps volunteers. She notes that economists and development planners often err because they assume that all people think alike and that they respond to the same incentives. Anthropologists, on the other hand, take a holistic approach, looking for links between different facets of society that others may miss. They think in terms of understanding the entire system rather than single elements. Anthropologists use their skills in listening and observing to understand local people's perceptions of the world and to access their knowledge, a process that makes for better, more effective project designs (Clarke 2000). Jim Igoe's work with wildlife conservation, national parks, and indigenous communities in East Africa, provides a good example. Igoe's work explores the difficulties in communication, perspective, and goals between donors and the local organizations and indigenous peoples they work with. He reports that development in general and conservation in particular are never as simple as they may seem. In working with the Maasai, Igoe found that the ideas and plans of Western-based conservation agencies were oversimplified and ignored local history. They were based primarily on long-standing Western ideas about the place of human beings in nature and the ways in which society and economy should be organized. Igoe (2004:133) writes that because these ideas resonate with Western ideas and Western history, "these simple solutions seem plausible to Westerners, but usually less plausible to the non-Western people who they target."

MULTINATIONAL CORPORATIONS

Multinational corporations (MNCs) are businesses that own enterprises in more than one nation or that seek the most profitable places to produce and market their goods and services regardless of national boundaries. MNCs bring employment opportunities as well as goods and services to people who otherwise would not have them. At the same time they create major and controversial changes in the natural, economic, social, and cultural environments.

Because MNCs control vast amounts of wealth, they are significant political forces throughout the world and are particularly problematic for poor nations. No corporation controls more than a small percentage of the economy of any rich nation. But many MNCs may have yearly budgets that are greater than those of poor nation governments. For example, in 2005, each of the world's 20 largest MNCs had gross revenues of more than $100 billion, larger than all but 47 of the 208 countries tracked by the World Bank. Exxon Mobil's 2006 *profit* of $39.1 billion was larger than the 2005 total economy of 147 of these countries (Fortune 2006; World Bank 2008). The financial power of these corporations enables them to exert enormous influence on poor nations and makes it extremely difficult for these nations to set and enforce policies that effectively regulate them.

Multinationals are also problematic because, like all capitalist corporations, their fundamental goal is to return wealth to their shareholders, the vast majority of whom live in wealthy nations. Thus, most of the profits earned by MNCs in poor nations contribute to the economy of wealthy nations. Although few poor nations remain colonies, MNCs contribute to the persistence of colonial-style relationships. Through them wealth continues to move from the poor to the rich.

An important debate over the impact of multinationals involves sweatshops. **Sweatshops** are factories where workers, particularly women and children, are employed for long hours under difficult conditions and at low pay (see Chapter 8, p. 188 for another example). Large areas of South and East Asia including China, South Korea, Indonesia, Malaysia, India, and Bangladesh might be considered a sweatshop belt. Kristoff and WuDunn (2000) estimate that this area accounts for about one quarter of the global economy. Much of the production of sweatshops is funneled into the United States in the form of cheap consumer goods. For example, in 2004 more than 3000 factories in 50 nations made the clothing sold at

The Gap, Old Navy, and Banana Republic. All three chains are owned by a single company. The company's own study found that between 10 percent and 25 percent of its factories in China, Taiwan, and Saipan use psychological coercion or verbal abuse and more than 50 percent of the factories in sub-Saharan Africa had inadequate safety practices (Merrick 2004).

In spite of the terrible conditions in sweatshops, for many of the people who work there, the alternatives are worse. Many workers are drawn from the ranks of the landless poor, and the money they earn, however small, often marks the difference between food and a roof over their head and hunger on the streets. Furthermore, over time both conditions and wages tend to improve. Finally, public protests and import restrictions aimed at sweatshops tend to backfire, causing drops in sales, throwing people out of work, and harming the very workers these actions are designed to help (Bhagwati 1996; Brown, Deardorff, and Stern 2003; Maskus 1997).

Still, those who favor taking action against sweatshops argue that conditions in sweatshops are fundamentally dehumanizing and insist that governments should apply global standards to labor conditions. They point out that sweatshops were once common in the United States and other wealthy nations. It took strong government intervention to improve factory conditions, limit child labor, and impose minimum wages. Today's poor nations are often discouraged from taking the actions that enabled wealthy nations to restrict sweatshop labor and create a strong middle class (Rothstein 2005).

In sweatshops, workers, often women and children, are employed for long hours under difficult conditions at low pay. Here boys press tin in Mumbai

Sweatshop labor is not entirely a problem of poor nations. As many as 175,000 people, most of them immigrant women, work in sweatshop conditions in the United States (Malveaux 2005), and there are hundreds of sweatshop garment factories in New York City alone (Port 2001). In many cases, sweatshop workers are the victims of labor law violations. Some of them are held against their will, victims of human trafficking as well.

The footwear corporation Nike, studied by anthropologist Robert Hackenburg, provides a good example of globalization, sweatshop labor, and both the influence and limits of public opinion. In its early years, most of Nike's manufacturing took place in New England. Today, Nike uses manufacturing facilities in more than 50 countries (Nike 2005).

In the late 1980s and early 1990s, a grim picture of Nike's employment practices began to emerge. More than 75 percent of Nike workers were women who put in

10- to 13-hour days 6 days a week. Frequently forced to work overtime, their wages were less than the subsistence level for a single adult. In some cases, workers were subject to harsh corporal punishment, including having their mouths taped shut for disobedience (Sage 1999:209).

As opposition to Nike's practices began to build, a loose coalition of organizations located in wealthy nations and concerned with labor rights, called the Anti-Nike Transnational Advocacy Network, was formed. Network members shared information, coordinated efforts to monitor working conditions at Nike factories, pressured the company to change its policies, and used the media and protests to keep Nike's labor practices in the public eye (Rothenberg-Aalami 2004; Sage 1999). University students and campus organizations played a major role in this mobilization effort (Hackenberg 2000).

At first Nike met these protests with small policy changes and advertising campaigns. However, when these methods proved ineffective, the company was forced to move toward real reform. It increased the minimum age for workers, adopted some U.S. occupational safety standards, offered its employees expanded educational programs and loan programs, and began to implement effective monitoring of the workplace. Although many problems remain, the company has made significant strides toward eliminating the worst of the abuses.

The Nike campaign shows that a well-orchestrated grassroots campaign can help to improve conditions for low-wage workers. However, it also suggests some of the limits of such a campaign. The Anti-Nike Transnational Advocacy Network was successful because Nike was extremely vulnerable to its tactics. The market for athletic footwear is highly competitive, and Nike's success is based primarily on its image. The campaign against Nike dealt a severe blow to that image, substituting images of oppressed workers for those of sports heroes. Other companies are far less vulnerable. For example, a supplier of electronic or mechanical components to other manufacturers may be virtually unknown to the public, unconcerned with its image, and face little competition. Such companies account for a high percentage of the economy, but actions against them are very difficult to organize and not likely to be effective.

Anthropologists are deeply concerned about labor abuses by MNCs (Gill 2005; Hackenberg 2000; Jamali 2007) but also are interested in the ways MNCs are changing social structures and cultural ideals. Gender relations is a field of particular interest. In some places, MNCs and close links with the world economy have given new economic power to men. In New Guinea, for example, oil revenues paid to male groups have enabled them to expand their social networks but have alienated them from earlier exchange networks and from women as well (Gilberthorpe 2007). In other places, MNCs employ large numbers of female workers because they are perceived as more easily controllable than males. Indeed, women are victims of some of the worst labor abuses. However, money earned working at MNCs gives women economic power that can improve their position relative to men in society (Freeman 2007; Reeves 2006).

Multinationals raise critical questions that must be faced by people in wealthy and in poor nations alike. Can low-wage jobs lead to prosperity? Can groups maintain cultural distinctiveness in the face of an increasingly uniform society? What are the consequences of a system that makes people wealthier and increases their access to consumer goods but, at the same time, both increases the disparity between the rich and the poor and makes people increasingly aware of that disparity?

URBANIZATION

Although many preindustrial societies had cities, their size and importance have increased dramatically in the contemporary world. In 1950, only about 16 percent of the total population of nonindustrialized nations lived in large cities. By 2000 this figure had reached 40 percent, and by 2020 it is projected to reach 50 percent (United Nations 2003). In 1950, seven of the world's 10 largest cities were located in Europe, Russia, Japan, and the United States. The average population of these cities was about 6.5 million. By 2015, eight of the world's 10 largest cities are expected to be located in poor nations, and the average population of these cities will be over 20 million inhabitants (Population Reference Bureau 2005). They truly will be megacities. Providing basic services to such large populations in places such as Lagos, Bombay, and Karachi is difficult and can only become more so.

Rural people come to cities seeking jobs and the social, material, and cultural advantages they believe are available in urban areas. They are forced out of the countryside by high population levels, inability to acquire land, environmental degradation, and, sometimes, violence. When new migrants arrive in urban areas, they often find dismal living conditions. In places such as Bogota, Casablanca, Cairo, Calcutta, and Caracas, more than half of the urban population lives in slums and squatter settlements (Todaro and Smith 2003).

Migration changes both the migrants themselves and the communities they left. New ideas and values as well as consumer goods enter the countryside through urban centers, through links between urban migrants, and through those who remain at home. Radio, television, and now websites located primarily in urban areas broadcast their messages and their advertisements to the countryside.

© Bill Bachmann/Stock, Boston, LLC

© David Frazier/Photo Researchers, Inc.

These pictures of Rio de Janeiro, Brazil, show the enormous contrasts present in megacities in the world's poor nations. Modern office and apartment buildings (left) are found a short distance from shanty towns (right).

With urbanization comes the development of a great variety of social groups based on voluntary membership. Such associations may serve as mutual aid societies, lending money to members, providing scholarships for students, arranging funerals, and taking care of marriage arrangements for urban migrants. Some develop along kinship or ethnic lines that were relevant in the traditional culture; others, such as labor unions, are based on relationships deriving from new economic contexts and have no parallel in rural society.

Urban life can be extremely difficult. Many of the urban poor are unemployed and face hunger, unsafe drinking water, inadequate sanitation facilities, and substandard shelter. Disease and early death are rampant in the slums of the world's large cities. Many of those who are employed fare little better, and most migrants to cities live in poverty for many years. In one study, Ariella Friedman and Judith Todd (1994) used a storytelling technique to study Kenyan rural women in a traditional village, poor urban women, and middle-class urban women. They showed each woman a picture and asked her to tell a story about it. The stories provided information on the ways the women perceived their lives. The researchers found that the traditional women almost always told very positive stories that usually had a happy ending. Middle-class, nontraditional urban women told stories that emphasized their own power and competence. Poor urban women told stories that generally were tragic and focused on powerlessness and vulnerability. The researchers note that many poor urban women have "lost the security and protection of the old [traditional] system without gaining the power or rewards of the new system."

The fact that urban centers continue to grow is indicative both of their appeal and of the desperate poverty of the countryside. Any solution to the problems caused by urbanization must focus on both rural and urban areas. Nations must provide adequate services, including water, sewage, education, and health care to their urban populations. However, unless life chances and opportunities also are greatly improved for rural populations, better services in the cities will only draw more migrants who will quickly overwhelm any advances made.

POPULATION PRESSURE

The rate of population growth provides a dramatic index of the increasing speed of social change. About 2 million years ago, our remote ancestors numbered perhaps 100,000. By the time the first agricultural societies were developing 10,000 years ago, world population had reached 5 to 10 million. Two thousand years ago there were about 250 million people in the world. By 1750, this number had tripled to 750 million. Then population growth really began to accelerate. Fifty years later, in 1800, there were one billion people; by 1930, there were two billion. Since then, world population has tripled, surpassing the six billion mark in the summer of 1999 (Erickson 1995; Fetto 1999). Much of this population growth took place in poor nations where, between 1950 and 2000, the population rose by some three billion (Geographical 2005). World population continues to increase and is expected to rise to more than 10 billion by 2050, with most of the increase in the world's poor nations (see Figure 14.1).

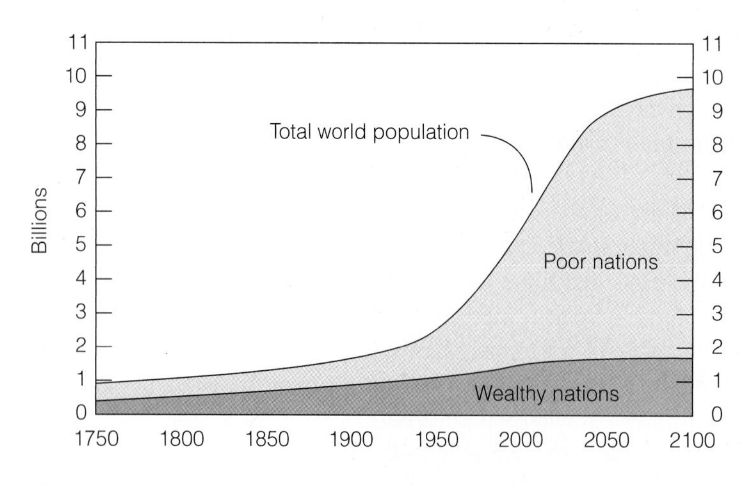

Figure 14.1

If current trends continue, world population will increase to about 10 billion by the middle of the 21st century before leveling off. The great majority of this increase will come in poor nations.

In some cases, high population levels mean that traditional subsistence strategies can no longer provide enough food. In parts of East Africa, for example, the amount of arable land per person declined 40 percent between 1965 and 1987 (World Bank 1992), and this has resulted in important cultural changes. Among the Waluguru in Tanzania, population increase resulted in land shortage, which increasingly resulted in the privatization of land. In the first half of the 20th century and before, people gained access to land through their lineage, and the lineage head was a powerful figure. Now land must be purchased, and not only has the institution of the lineage head completely disappeared, it is hardly even remembered (van Donge 1992).

In other cases, the population explosion and the search for land and wealth have pushed people onto land previously occupied only by indigenous groups. For example, between 1955 and 1993, the Agta, a foraging group in the Philippines mentioned in Chapter 8, was increasingly encroached upon by loggers and migrant farmers. By 1993, the Agta had become landless migrant workers living at the lowest rung of Philippine society (Early and Headland 1998).

China's One Child Policy

Programs to control population growth are often extremely controversial. They both affect and are affected by culture. China's attempts to control its population is a good example. In 1979, the Chinese government introduced a radical population policy limiting families to a single child (although parents were allowed to keep twins or triplets). Families faced stiff financial penalties for additional children. This policy was a key factor in reducing fertility in China from about five births per women 30 years ago to fewer than two today (Baochang et al. 2007). However, the cultural effects of the policy have been dramatic.

The most evident effect has been a skewing of births in favor of males. In 2000, for every 100 girls born, 120 boys were born, and in some poor regions of the country, there were twice male births as female births. The reason for the imbalance is a historical cultural preference for boys, but in some places this is changing. According to anthropologist Susan Greenhalgh (2005, 2007a), among the newly prosperous urban Chinese, girls now are considered as good as or even preferable to boys because girls are believed to be emotionally closer to their parents and more willing to provide support in their parents' old age. However, girls fare less well in poorer rural areas, where population control policies are less rigid and second children more common. The continued strong preference for boys is shown by the fact that, in some areas, up to 90 percent of second pregnancies are aborted if the fetus is female.

The extreme sex imbalance resulting from China's policy is creating fundamental changes in society. Wealthy men have no trouble finding mates, but it is much more difficult for the rural poor. Greenhalgh reports that

27 percent of rural men with little schooling were unmarried at age 40. The difficulty of marriage has led to the importation of women from poorer countries such as Vietnam and Myanmar, informal polyandry, the sale of young women, and a trade in kidnapped girls. Since such women are essentially captives in their husband's home, physical and emotional abuse are rife.

China's limits on family size and the emphasis it places on creating "quality children" have produced a generation of single children, the most prosperous and best educated children in the nation's history. However, they also are the subjects of intense family affection and pressure to succeed. Greenhalgh (2007b) describes them as little emperors and empresses, "talented and savvy, but also spoiled and self-centered." She wonders if, when such children grow up, they will be the sort of decisive and culturally sophisticated leaders who are able to make wise decisions on behalf of their nation.

Although China's population issues are unique to its historical and cultural circumstances, population control is problematic in other societies as well. In many places, a woman's value is measured to some degree by the number of children she bears. Religious and political authorities often take active stands against the use of birth control. Furthermore, intellectuals and governments in many poor nations are deeply suspicious of population control programs coming from wealthy nations. They note that the economies of wealthy nations have often prospered in times of population growth and suspect that the wealthy nations are promoting their own interests when they attempt to limit population in other countries. Sometimes, they accuse the promoters of population control programs of racist intentions, observing that such programs usually consist of efforts by wealthy white people to limit the population growth of poor nonwhite people (Lichtenberg 1994).

Behind these accusations lies a series of difficult political and economic issues. It is often asserted that there is a maximum population the earth can support (its "carrying capacity"), and some analysts worry that the total population is approaching that number. They argue that we must control population or face wide-scale starvation. They see population growth as a "bomb" that will destroy Western society (see Ross 1998 for a historical review of this literature). This position ignores several important factors. First, the number of people who can be supported by any given environment is critically dependent on the technologies used to support them. Estimates of carrying capacity are inaccurate because technological change is unpredictable. But, more importantly, populations cannot be considered apart from their levels of consumption. The average person in an industrialized nation consumes three times as much fresh water and 10 times as much energy as someone in a poor nation (Durning 1994). The number of people who can be supported living this lifestyle is far different than the number of people who could be supported if wealthy populations consumed at a lower level. Finally, the number of people who could be supported is critically dependent on assumptions we make about the value of the natural world. If we desire to preserve forest land, tropical rainforest, or other environments, we diminish the amount of land that is available for human population growth. Thus, the issues central to problems of population growth are primarily cultural, social, political, and moral, not scientific.

The high level of population growth and the low level of wealth and consumption in poor nations are closely related. When life expectancy at birth is low and poverty is rampant, it makes good economic sense for families to have large numbers of children. Having many children helps to assure that at least some will survive to adulthood. It increases the labor pool available to the family and improves the odds that one or more child will prosper and increase the family wealth.

As the wealth and consumption level of a population increases, the benefits of large families decline. When health conditions improve, children are more likely to survive. When jobs that pay livable salaries are available, fewer children are necessary to support a family. Additionally, increasing wealth and consumption makes raising children far more expensive, which makes large families less desirable. Clearly the best way, indeed perhaps the only way, to control population growth is to improve the life chances and increase the wealth of people in poor countries.

ENVIRONMENTAL CHANGES

Pollution

Ironically, even though the world's poor consume only a small fraction of the earth's resources, they also face some of the world's worst problems of pollution and environmental deterioration. The energy consumption of the United States alone is more than 14 times the energy consumption of the entire African continent (excluding the nation of South Africa) (Harrison and Pearce 2000). Given that consumption creates pollution, one might expect that people in the United States would live in a far dirtier environment than those in Africa. But this is not the case. Consider the city of Bamako, the capital of Mali, on any late afternoon in the dry season. Most streets are unpaved, and automobiles, trucks, carts, bicycles, and foot traffic have been stirring up dust all day. Since most of the city lacks regular trash pickup or sewage, waste from humans and animals has been churned into the air. People are beginning to cook their evening meal. Many, perhaps the majority, of the city's 1.6 million residents cook either

Although people in poor nations use only a small fraction of the world's resources, they face some of the world's worst pollution. Here, dust, car exhaust, and smoke fill a typical afternoon sky in Bamako, Mali.

on charcoal or wood fires that consume about one million tons of wood a year (Cissé 2007), and the smoke from cook fires joins the dust in the air. The combined effect of smoke and dust is like a thick, hot, dry fog. Because most houses are relatively open, lacking glass windows or doors that seal, the dust permeates the indoors as well as the outdoors. The total effect is an environment far dirtier and more hazardous than in any city of a comparable population in the wealthy world. And Bamako's population suffers. Pollution contributes to respiratory ailments, malaria, many diseases born by sewage contaminated water and air, and high childhood mortality.

Compare this with a similarly sized American city, say San Antonio, Texas, a city of about 1.4 million. In San Antonio, most streets are paved, and almost all homes have access to safe, publicly maintained water and sewage systems. Meals are cooked on appliances powered by electricity or gas. There is a huge amount of vehicular traffic, but cars and trucks are equipped with pollution-controlling devices. Although San Antonio is not one of America's wealthier cities, its population consumes many times the resources than does the population of Bamako. But almost all of San Antonio's population lives in environments that are healthier and far less polluted than Bamako.

Pollution is closely related to industrialization and globalization. Poor nations often are desperate to provide some degree of prosperity to their citizens. They have limited amounts of capital to invest and limited means of attracting investment from abroad. Less expensive production technologies are generally more polluting than more expensive, higher-technology processes. Therefore, industry in poor nations tends to be dirtier and more polluting than similar industries in wealthy nations. For example, China has experienced enormous economic growth but has relied extensively on lower-cost, more highly polluting industries. A Chinese government study estimated that at least 20 percent of the Chinese population lives in severely polluted areas. Ameliorating this problem by installing adequate pollution control in existing Chinese industries would cost $135 billion (Bremner 2006).

Multinational corporations may play an important role in pollution because their financial power allows them to circumvent national laws designed to control pollution. A good example is oil production in the Niger delta in Nigeria, where gas flaring (the burning off of the natural gas that is a by-product of oil production) releases toxins into the air as well as more carbon dioxide than the rest of Africa combined. Gas flaring has been illegal in Nigeria since the 1980s but continues today because strong and wealthy corporations, using techniques that include bribery and intimidation, are able to ignore or circumvent regulations enacted by the relatively weak government (Adetunji 2006). Gas flaring, oil spills, and other ecological problems have created an environmental disaster that has been instrumental in fomenting violence and civil unrest in the region.

Global Warming

Global warming is another important aspect of ecological change. Human activity substantially contributes to the warming of the planet (Intergovernmental Panel on Climate Change 2008; Oreskes 2004), and it is unclear what the long-term effects of this warming trend will be. For example, there are some possible benefits to global warming, particularly in northern Europe and Russia, where it may extend the growing season through increased rainfall and reduce fuel consumption for heating. However, the impacts of warming are expected to be largely negative and to fall disproportionately on the poor. Many of the world's poor live in the tropics, where the effects of climate change are expected to be particularly severe. Warming in these climates may cut the growing season and reduce crop yields. The intensity of tropical storms is also expected to increase, which could have devastating effects on areas affected by them. Wealthy nations have the resources to respond to climate change. They can build levees to control flooding, move their populations and their industries, and open new land to cultivation. Poor nations simply do not have the means at their disposal to do such things. Where survival is precarious today, climate change is likely to precipitate disaster (Intergovernmental Panel on Climate Change 2008; see Chapter 5, pp. 94–95).

POLITICAL INSTABILITY

Political instability has had dire consequences for cultures worldwide. Violent confrontation is nothing new. Traditional societies often fought with one another, and Western expansion was accompanied by great loss of life and culture. However, in the past hundred years people have unleashed more brutality on each other than at any time in earlier human history. Industrialized and wealthy societies are primarily responsible for this savagery, having created the trenches of World War I, the death camps of World War II, nuclear weapons, the purge, and the Gulag.

Although poor nations were deeply affected by Europe's wars, the era since the end of World War II has been devastating for them. In some, such as French Indochina (later Vietnam), World War II faded into wars of independence that persisted until the 1970s. In many cases, traditional people became involved in networks of warfare that drew them into competition between the great powers. Both the United States and the Soviet Union furnished guerilla movements, impoverished governments, and rebel armies with vast amounts of weaponry.

Most anthropology students are familiar with the !Kung or Ju/'hoansi foragers of southern Africa. They were featured in many films by John Marshall, and anthropological work done on their lifestyle in the 1950s and 1960s contributed heavily to our understanding of foragers. Most students are unaware that many of the Ju/'hoansi became soldiers in South Africa's war against guerillas fighting for the independence of Namibia. In 1974, the South African Defense Forces (SADF) began to recruit foraging peoples to act as trackers, and by 1981 virtually the entire foraging population of the Caprivi was supported by the military. When South Africa lost its war in 1990, almost 4000 foragers were resettled in South Africa (Gordon 1992:185–192). Today little remains of the hunting-and-gathering lifestyles documented by anthropologists in the 1950s and 1960s (Lee 2003; Marshall 2002).

The end of the Cold War brought relief to some poor nations. Wars that were fueled by great power rivalries, such as those in Namibia and El Salvador, came to a rapid end. However, in other nations rivalries that had been muted by the Cold War reemerged in new violent forms. In many places strong, centralized, and frequently repressive governments were supported by aid from the United States, the Soviet Union, and other nations. When the Cold War ended, this support diminished, and governments that relied on it often fell apart. Nations such as Yugoslavia, Somalia, Liberia, Sudan, and others disintegrated as different groups within them fought for wealth, power, and control.

One particularly horrific example is the 1994 genocide in Rwanda. Most Rwandans are either Hutu or Tutsi. Although they all speak the same language, the Hutu majority are primarily farmers, while most Tutsi are herders. The rivalry between the Hutu and Tutsi originated well before Rwanda was colonized, first by Germany and then by Belgium. However, colonial policies favored the Tutsi and exacerbated tensions between the two groups. Since 1959, there have been numerous clashes between Hutu and Tutsi, but in 1994, in a matter of weeks, Hutus murdered 800,000 to 850,000 Tutsis and their Hutu friends and supporters. Only about 130,000 Tutsis in Rwanda survived the massacre. Every level of society was involved, and in many cases women led the killings (Fenton 1996; Prunier 1995). Tutsis were massacred by their clergy in churches where they sought sanctuary: 2800 in Kibungo, 6000 in Cyahinda, 4000 in Kibeho, and more in many other places. Although most of the killing was done with machetes, technology played an important part, as the Hutu-controlled Radio Mille Collines—called "the radio that kills" by its opponents—spewed out a daily message of hate and encouragement to slaughter (Destexhe 1995). In the weeks following the genocide, a Tutsi army from neighboring Uganda took over the government, and more than two million Hutu refugees fled to neighboring countries. The refugees fueled unrest already seething in these nations, and the war spread to Congo and much of Central Africa.

MIGRATION

Widespread political, economic, and social instability combined with relatively inexpensive air travel and economic opportunity has led to a boom in international migration, particularly of people from poor nations. Today, an estimated 200 million people, 3 percent of the world's population, live outside of the countries of their birth (Martin 2007). These migrants have enormous influence both on the countries they leave and those where they settle.

When migrants leave, they often make their home communities poorer by depriving these areas of their skills and labor. High-skilled workers can earn many times their local wages through migration. It is difficult to convince people to remain in poor, unstable countries when the salaries paid for their skills may be 30 or more times higher in wealthy nations. This has led to a "brain drain" from poor nations to rich nations.

Although home communities lose members, they may gain many other benefits. Migrants provide their communities of origin with connections to the rest of the world, creating a broad network of support for community members. People in seemingly isolated villages often have connections with family and friends throughout the world. These connections bring information, ideas, products, and, perhaps most importantly, money. In 2005, the World Bank estimated that $232 billion was sent by migrants to people in their home countries. Of this sum, $162 billion was sent to poor countries. By comparison, total U.S. humanitarian aid in 2005 was about $27 billion, almost 30 percent of which was spent in Iraq and Afghanistan (Organization for Economic Cooperation and Development. 2007; World Bank 2006). In some nations, remittances from migrants constitute a substantial percentage of the national economy. For example, remittances account for 20 percent of the GNI in Honduras, 12.75 percent in the Philippines, and 21.77 percent in Lebanon.

Migrants also affect profound changes in the countries in which they arrive. Some of these effects are cultural. Cities and small towns throughout the wealthy nations are increasingly multiethnic. Immigrants bring their cultural traditions, increasing the complexity and enriching the variety of the places where they settle. Immigrants provide a pool of inexpensive labor that creates large profits for businesses in wealthy country and low prices for consumers. However, the availability of immigrant labor also suppresses wages in their host countries.

Economic immigrants come to new nations for their own profit, but they face discrimination in the places they settle. They increase their wealth, but often at the price of decreasing their social status (Haines 2007:62). Discrimination resulting in isolation and alienation has led to unrest among immigrant communities in Europe, particularly among African and Muslim immigrants in England and France. This was revealed dramatically by rioting in France in 2005 and by terrorist attacks in London that same year. Illegal immigrants are in a particularly weak position. Their status makes them extremely vulnerable to exploitation.

Immigrants frequently come to their new nations with an "ideology of return" (Brettell 2003, 2007). They understand their immigration as temporary and hope to return to their home countries. In the past, belief in return has been more common than return itself. Immigrants have remained in their new countries because maintaining communication with those left behind was difficult, because travel was expensive, and because they established social ties in their new country. The first two of these reasons are no longer true, and we do not yet know the effect this will have on return migration.

LOOKING TO THE FUTURE

Although the world is faced with grave problems, we have greater means at our disposal to solve them and to improve people's lives than ever before. Anthropology can play a critical role in this process. The anthropological methodology and perspective emphasizes understanding the meaning and experience of cultural differences. It teaches us about the dynamic elements of social organization and their interrelationships. Anthropology cannot solve all of the problems we have described. But it does have important contributions to make. With our holistic approach and our emphasis

© Charles O. Cecil/Alamy

In the 21st century, contrasts and conflicts, both within and among cultures will increase. Anthropology with its emphasis on analyzing diversity and complexity, will play an important role in increasing our understanding of these phenomena. In this photograph, Libyan women in modest dress consider the fashions on display in a shop window.

on the importance of local cultures, anthropologists can develop frameworks to analyze and understand events and processes. We can help governments, organizations, and other groups find solutions that are sensitive to local cultural traditions and respond to people's needs and aspirations. Applied anthropologists have successfully addressed some of these problems (see Paiement 2007). Perhaps above and beyond solving any particular problem, anthropology has a significant role to play in ensuring that people's stories are told and heard, and not forgotten.

Anthropology particularly offers hope for success in solving problems because it shows us that biology is not destiny. The human capacity for culture rests on biological foundations. We have culture because our brains and bodies have evolved to learn and to be dependent on it. Our biology may predispose us to behave in certain ways, but no aspect of human culture can be firmly tied to a gene. Instead, anthropologists have shown over and over that culture is enormously flexible, fantastically changeable, and almost incredibly varied. This implies that the problems we face are not the result of a fixed and unchanging human nature. War, poverty, pollution, and the other ills that we face do not exist because humans are invariably given to warfare or human nature somehow demands extreme wealth and desperate poverty. These are social facts, aspects of human culture and human society. Because of this, they can be changed. We can continue to invent new cultural forms, new designs for living.

More than a century ago, E. B. Tylor, the man often considered the founder of British anthropology, wrote that anthropology was a reformer's science. By this he meant that if we could first understand that culture was not simply a reflection of human biology, and if we could then analyze and understand culture itself, we could discover ways to improve humanity's lot. Understanding that culture is flexible and variable gives us hope for a better future. Anthropology gives us some of the analytical tools to act on that hope.

BRINGING IT BACK HOME: HOW FLAT IS YOUR WORLD?

In 2005, Thomas Friedman published the bestselling book, *The World Is Flat.* In it, he argues that free trade and recent technological innovations have enormously increased productivity and efficiency. The Internet, the fall of the Berlin Wall, outsourcing, the development of collaborative software, and other innovations have enabled individuals and corporations to compete and connect with each other across vast distances. Friedman claims that the result is a world that is "flat" in the sense that economic and social opportunities are increasingly available to all people, regardless of their geographical location. Friedman cites numerous examples to show how companies and individuals in India, China, and elsewhere use technology to engage effectively with the world and to build prosperity. He interviews Bill Gates, who says that thirty years ago, the life chances of an average American were better than those of a genius born in India or China. But today, it would be better to be a genius in India or China than an average American. Friedman does see problems, including persistent poverty in some places, AIDS, and the use of technology by terrorist organizations. However, he is an optimist, perhaps even a utopian. He believes that pursuing the correct kinds of training and making the right decisions will bring us a world of peace, prosperity, and opportunity, a world in which culture is enriched and preserved as technology allows each person his or her own voice and vehicle of expression.

John Grey is a critic of Friedman. Grey (2005) notes that Friedman ignores or minimizes numerous problems in globalization. For example, Friedman contrasts the road leading to a company in India, "pockmarked" and filled with jostling "sacred cows, horse-drawn carts and motorized rickshaws," and the sedate and luxurious corporate campus. However, he does not consider the relationship between the two. The same forces of technology and globalization that open possibilities for companies and elites may foreclose them for the poor, denying them jobs, affordable food, housing, and education. Friedman believes that complex trade and communication links between nations create peace and stability, but Grey points out that historically these have created friction and warfare as well. Nationalism fueled the growth of capitalism in Europe and the United States and is doing the same in China and India. Countries promote globalization in the hopes of prosperity but also in pursuit of international power. Finally, Friedman sees a connection between globalization, the free market, and Western-style democracy. But Grey notes that the forces of globalization and technology operate effectively in both democratic nations and nondemocratic countries such as China. Grey (2005) says that globalization does make the world smaller and may make some parts of it richer, but it does not necessarily make it more peaceful, more democratic, or flat.

YOU DECIDE

1. Is Bill Gates right that today it is better to be a genius in China or India than an average man in America? Do you think your opportunities would be greater if you were born in India or China? Do you think you will one day live in countries such as India and China?
2. Friedman hopes for a world in which culture is enriched because every individual has the ability to be creative and to reach other people through web technologies. Is his definition of culture the same as one you would find in anthropology? Does creating websites enrich culture?
3. Given Friedman and Grey's positions, do you believe that global culture will be more or less homogeneous 100 years from now? What aspects of culture do you think will be homogeneous? What do you think will remain of distinctive cultural traditions?

CHAPTER SUMMARY

1. We live in a world of extreme inequality. Although all nations suffer problems of inequality and poverty, these problems are particularly acute in poor nations and have a profound effect on many of the people that anthropologists have historically studied.
2. After World War II, development became a critical issue for former colonies and other poor nations. Economists believed that many nations were poor because they had undeveloped economies. Earlier development efforts focused on modernizing economies. More recent efforts have focused on enforcing free markets in the hope that these will create more efficient delivery of services.
3. Multinational corporations have become extremely important in poor nations. MNCs search for the most profitable places to buy, sell, and manufacture goods. Shareholders, located primarily in wealthy nations, are the primary beneficiaries of MNC activities. MNCs provide

jobs but also exercise enormous influence that frequently allows them to avoid regulation.

4. More than half of the world's largest cities are located in poor nations, and urbanization has been a major force in changing traditional cultures. Providing services to poor people in large cities is beyond the financial capacity of many nations.
5. Although historically prosperity and population increase often go together, in poor nations even high rates of economic growth have failed to keep up with rising population, and, in some cases, subsistence strategies have collapsed. The appropriate level of human population for any area is a political question involving critical assumptions about distribution of resources and the types of environment people consider desirable.
6. Even though the poor produce only a small percentage of the world's pollution, environments in poor nations frequently are more polluted than those in rich nations. Global warming is anticipated to have more dire effects in poor countries because many of these are located in ecologically fragile zones that have limited financial resources to cope with environmental change.
7. Political instability has had horrific consequences for people worldwide. Wars of independence, the Cold War, and ethnic rivalries have led to violence that has destroyed cultures and societies.
8. Very high levels of migration have created enormous flows of information and money between nations. Migrants change both the societies they leave and those in which they settle, frequently enriching both. Migrants often face discrimination, alienation, and isolation.
9. Despite the difficulties facing us, the future is not necessarily bleak. Anthropology gives us the tools to deal with a world characterized by ethnic diversity. Anthropology instructs us that humans are cultural beings. Cultures can be changed and perhaps improved. For humans, biology is never destiny.

KEY TERMS

Development
Gross national income (GNI)
Modernization theory
Multinational corporation (MNC)
Neoliberalism
Structural adjustment
Sweatshop

GLOSSARY

acephalous: lacking a government head or chief.

achieved status: a social position that a person chooses or achieves on his or her own.

adaptation: a change in the biological structure or lifeways of an individual or population by which it becomes better fitted to survive and reproduce in its environment.

affinal: related by marriage.

age grades: specialized associations, based on age, that stratify a society by seniority.

age set: a group of people of similar age and sex who move through some or all of life's stages together.

agglutinating language: a language that allows a great number of morphemes per word and has highly regular rules for combining morphemes.

agriculture: a form of food production in which fields are in permanent cultivation using plows, animals, and techniques of soil and water control.

allophone: two or more different phones that can be used to make the same phoneme in a specific language.

animism: the notion that all objects, living and nonliving, are imbued with spirits.

anthropological linguistics: the study of language and its relation to culture.

anthropology: the scientific and humanistic study of human beings.

antistructure: the socially sanctioned use of behavior that radically violates social norms; frequently found in religious ritual.

apartheid: the South African system of multiple exclusive racial groups—black, white, coloured, and Asian—that were formally recognized, segregated, treated differently in law and life, and occupied different and almost exclusive statuses within the society.

applied anthropology: the application of anthropology to the solution of human problems.

archaeology: the subdiscipline of anthropology that focuses on the reconstruction of past cultures based on their material remains.

arranged marriage: the process by which senior family members significantly control the choice of their children's spouses.

artifacts (in communications studies): communication by clothing, jewelry, tattoos, piercings, and other visible body modifications.

ascribed status: a social position into which a person is born.

assimilation model: a model of U.S. ethnicity that holds that people should abandon their cultural traditions and become wholly absorbed in mainstream American culture.

authority: the approved use of power, based on personal characters or on the holding of formal public office.

avunculocal residence: system under which a married couple lives with the husband's mother's brother.

balanced reciprocity: the giving and receiving of goods of nearly equal value with a clear obligation of a return gift within a specified time limit.

band: a small group of people related by blood or marriage, who live together and are loosely associated with a territory in which they forage.

bifurcation: a principle of classifying kin under which different kinship terms are used for the mother's side of the family and the father's side of the family.

bigman: a self-made leader who gains power through personal achievements rather than through political office.

bilateral descent: system of descent under which individuals are equally affiliated with their mother's and their father's descent groups.

bilocal residence: system under which a married couple has the choice of living with the husband's family or the wife's family.

biological (or physical) anthropology: the subdiscipline of anthropology that studies people from a biological perspective, focusing primarily on aspects of humankind that are genetically inherited.

bound morpheme: a unit of meaning that must be associated with another.

bride service: the cultural rule that a man must work for his bride's family for a variable length of time either before or after the marriage.

bridewealth: goods presented by the groom's kin to the bride's kin to legitimize a marriage.

bureaucracy: administrative hierarchy characterized by specialization of function and fixed rules.

call system: the form of communication among nonhuman primates composed of a limited number of sounds that are tied to specific stimuli in the environment.

capital: productive resources that are used with the primary goal of increasing their owner's financial wealth.

capitalism: an economic system in which people work for wages, land and capital goods are privately owned, and capital is invested for profit.

cargo system: a ritual system common in Central and South America in which wealthy people are required to hold a series of costly ceremonial offices.

caste system: a system of stratification based on birth in which movement from one stratum (caste) to another is not possible.

chiefdom: a society with social ranking in which political integration is achieved through an office of centralized leadership called the chief.

chronemics: the study of the different ways that cultures understand time and use it to communicate.

citizenship: those persons invested by the state with rights and duties, based on criteria such as residence or other group affiliations.

clan: a unilineal kinship group whose members believe themselves to be descended from a common ancestor but who cannot trace this link through known relatives.

class: a category of persons who all have about the same opportunity to obtain economic resources, power, or prestige.

class system: a form of social stratification in which the different strata form a continuum and social mobility is possible.

closed system (social stratification): a stratification system based primarily on ascription.

cognitive anthropology: a theoretical position in anthropology that focuses on the relationship between the mind and society.

collaborative ethnography: ethnography that gives priority to cultural consultants on the topic, methodology, and written results of fieldwork.

collateral kin: kin descended from a common ancestor but not in a direct ascendant or descendent line, such as cousins or siblings.

colonialism: the active possession of a foreign territory and the maintenance of political domination over that territory.

colony: a territory under the immediate political control of a nation state.

communitas: a state of perceived solidarity, equality, and unity among people sharing a religious ritual, often characterized by intense emotion.

comparative linguistics: the science of documenting the relationships between languages and grouping them into language families.

compensation: a payment demanded by an aggrieved party to compensate for damage.

composite (compound) family: an aggregate of nuclear families linked by a common spouse.

conflict theory: a perspective on social stratification that focuses on inequality as a source of conflict and change.

conjugal tie: the relationship between a husband and wife formed by marriage.

consanguineal: related by birth.

consultant: a person from whom anthropologists gather data. Also known as an informant or sometimes an interlocutor.

contagious magic: the belief that things once in contact with a person or object retain an invisible connection with that person or object.

conventionality: the notion that, in human language, words are only arbitrarily or conventionally connected to the things for which they stand.

core vocabulary: a list of 100 or 200 terms that designate things, actions, and activities likely to be named in all the world's languages.

corporate descent groups: permanent units that have an existence beyond the individuals who are members at any given time.

corvée labor: unpaid labor required by a governing authority.

cosmology: a system of beliefs that deals with fundamental questions in the religious and social order.

cultural anthropology: the study of human thought, behavior, and lifeways that are learned rather than genetically transmitted and that are typical of groups of people.

cultural construction of gender: the idea that gender characteristics are the result of historical, economic, and political forces acting within each culture.

cultural ecology: a theoretical position in anthropology that focuses on the adaptive dimension of culture.

cultural relativism: the notion that cultures should be analyzed with reference to their own histories and values rather than according to the values of another culture.

culture: the learned behaviors and symbols that allow people to live in groups; the primary means by which humans adapt to their environment; the ways of life characteristic of a particular human society.

culture and personality: a theoretical position in anthropology that held that cultures could best be understood by examining the patterns of child rearing and considering their effect on adult lives and social institutions.

culture shock: feelings of alienation and helplessness that result from rapid immersion in a new and different culture.

descent: the culturally established affiliation between a child and one or both parents.

descent group: a group of kin who are descendants of a common ancestor, extending beyond two generations.

development: the notion that life in some regions and countries is less good than it should be because these areas lack financial wealth, have small industrial plants, and have little infrastructure (roads, electric power, lines of communication, etc.) and that these countries and regions should pursue wealth through industrialization, trade, and improvements in infrastructure.

deviants: those who transgress society's rules.

diffusion: the spread of cultural elements from one culture to another.

displacement: the capacity of all human languages to describe things not happening in the present.

divination: a religious ritual performed to find hidden objects or information.

dominant culture: the culture with the greatest wealth and power in a society that consists of many subcultures.

double descent: the tracing of descent through both matrilineal and patrilineal links, each of which is used for different purposes.

dowry: required presentation of goods by the bride's kin to the family of the groom or to the couple.

Dutch East India Company: a joint stock company chartered by the Dutch government to control all Dutch trade in the Indian and Pacific oceans. Also known by its Dutch initials VOC for Verenigde Ostendische Compagnie.

ecological functionalism: a theoretical position in anthropology that focuses on the relationship between environment and society.

economic system: the norms governing production, distribution, and consumption of goods and services within a society.

economics: the study of the ways in which the choices people make combine to determine how their society uses its scarce resources to produce and distribute goods and services.

efficiency: yield per person per hour of labor invested.

egalitarian society: a society in which no individual or group has more privileged access to resources, power, or prestige than any other.

ego (kinship studies): the person from whose perspective a kinship chart is viewed.

elites: the social strata that has differential access to all culturally valued resources, whether power, wealth, or prestige, and possessively protects its control over these resources.

emic (perspective): examining societies using concepts, categories, and distinctions that are meaningful to members of that culture.

enculturation: the process of learning to be a member of a particular cultural group.

endogamy: a rule prescribing that a person must marry within a particular group.

essentialism: a view of ethnicity that holds that ethnic groups are distinguished by essential, historically rooted, and emotionally experienced cultural differences.

ethnic boundaries: the perceived cultural attributes by which ethnic groups distinguish themselves from others.

ethnic groups: categories of people who see themselves as sharing an ethnic identity that differentiates them from other groups or from the larger society as a whole.

ethnic identity: the sense of self a person experiences as a member of an ethnic group.

ethnicity: perceived differences in culture, national origin, and historical experience by which groups of people are distinguished from others in the same social environment.

ethnobotany: a focus within anthropology that examines the relationship between humans and plants in different cultures.

ethnocentrism: judging other cultures from the perspective of one's own culture. The notion that one's own culture is more beautiful, rational, and nearer to perfection than any other.

ethnography: the major research tool of cultural anthropology; includes both fieldwork among people in a society and the written results of such fieldwork.

ethnology: the attempt to find general principles or laws that govern cultural phenomena.

ethnomedicine: a focus within anthropology that examines the ways in which people in different cultures understand health and sicknesses as well as the ways they attempt to cure disease.

ethnoscience: a theoretical position in anthropology that focuses on recording and examining the ways in which members of a culture use language to classify and organize their cognitive world.

etic (perspective): examining societies using concepts, categories, and rules derived from science; an outsider's perspective.

exogamy: a rule specifying that a person must marry outside a particular group.

extended family: family based on blood relations extending over three or more generations.

factions: informal alliances within a group or society.

firm: an institution composed of kin and/or non-kin that is organized primarily for financial gain.

foraging (hunting and gathering): a food-getting strategy that does not involve food production or domestication of animals.

forensic anthropology: the application of biological anthropology to the identification of skelatalized or badly decomposed human remains.

free morpheme: a unit of meaning that may stand alone as a word.

functionalism: a theoretical position in anthropology, common in the first half of the 20th century, that focuses on finding general laws that identify different elements of society, show how they relate to each other, and demonstrate their role in maintaining social order.

fundamentalism: a proclamation of reclaimed authority over a sacred tradition that is to be reinstated as an antidote for a society that is believed to have strayed from its cultural moorings.

gender: a cultural construction that makes biological and physical differences into socially meaningful categories that seem reasonable and appropriate.

gender ideology: the totality of ideas about sex, gender, the natures of men and women, including their sexuality, and the relations between the genders.

gender role: the cultural expectations of men and women in a particular society, including the division of labor.

gender stratification: the ways in which gendered activities and attributes are differentially valued and related to the distribution of resources, prestige, and power in a society.

generalized reciprocity: giving and receiving goods with no immediate or specific return expected.

globalization: the integration of resources, labor, and capital into a global network.

glottochronology: a statistical technique that linguists have developed to estimate the date of separation of related languages.

god (deity): a named spirit who is believed to have created or to have control of some aspect of the world.

government: an interrelated set of status roles that become separate from other aspects of social organization such as kinship.

great vowel shift: a change in the pronunciation of English language that took place between 1200 and 1600.

gross national income (GNI): the total market value of all goods and services produced in a country.

haptics: the analysis and study of touch.

Heeren XVII: the Lords Seventeen, members of the board of directors of the Dutch East India Company.

hegemony: the (usually elite) construction of ideologies, beliefs, and values that attempt to justify the stratification system in a state society.

hijra: an alternative gender role in India conceptualized as neither man nor woman.

historical particularism: a theoretical position in anthropology associated with American anthropologists of the early 20th century that focuses on providing objective descriptions of cultures within their historical and environmental context.

holism: in anthropology, an approach that considers culture, history, language, and biology essential to a complete understanding of human society.

horticulture: production of plants using a simple, nonmechanized technology; fields are not used continuously.

household: a group of people united by kinship or other links who share a residence and organize production, consumption, and distribution among themselves.

human paleontology: the focus within biological anthropology that traces human evolutionary history.

Human Relations Area Files: an ethnographic database that includes cultural descriptions of more than 300 cultures.

imitative magic: the belief that imitating an action in a religious ritual will cause the action to happen in the material world.

incest taboos: prohibitions on sexual relations between relatives.

indigenous peoples: groups of people who have occupied a region for a long time but who have a minority position and usually little or no influence in the government of the nation-state that ultimately controls their land.

industrialism: the process of the mechanization of production.

informant: a person from whom anthropologists gather data. Also known as an consultant or sometimes an interlocutor.

inheritance: the transfer of property between generations.

innovation: an object or a way of thinking or behaving that is new because it is qualitatively different from existing forms.

interpretive anthropology: a theoretical position in anthropology that focuses on using humanistic methods, such as those found in the analysis of literature, to analyze culture and discover the meaning of culture to its participants.

isolating language: a language with relatively few morphemes per word and fairly simple rules for combining them.

joint stock company: a firm that is managed by a centralized board of directors but is owned by shareholders.

kindred: a unique kin network made up of all the people related to a specific individual in a bilateral kinship system.

kinesics: the study of body position, movement, facial expressions, and gaze.

kinship: a culturally defined relationship established through blood ties or marriage.

kinship system: the totality of kin relations, kin groups, and terms for classifying kin in a society.

kinship terminology: the words used to identify different categories of kin in a particular culture.

kula ring: a pattern of exchange among trading partners in the South Pacific Islands.

law: a means of social control and dispute management through the systematic application of force by those in society with the authority to do so.

leadership: the ability to direct an enterprise or action.

leveling mechanism: a practice, value, or form of social organization that evens out wealth within a society.

levirate: the custom whereby a man marries the widow of a deceased brother.

lexicon: the total stock of words in a language.

life chances: the opportunities that people have to fulfill their potential in society.

liminal: the stage of a ritual, particularly a rite of passage, in which one has passed out of an old status but has not yet entered a new one.

lineage: a group of kin whose members trace descent from a known common ancestor.

magic: a religious ritual believed to produce a mechanical effect by supernatural means. When magic is done correctly, believers think it must have the desired effect.

mana: religious power or energy that is concentrated in individuals or objects.

manhood puzzle: the question of why in almost all cultures masculinity is viewed not as a natural state but as a problematic status to be won through overcoming obstacles.

market exchange: an economic system in which goods and services are bought and sold at a money price determined primarily by the forces of supply and demand.

marriage: the customs, rules, and obligations that establish a special relationship between sexually cohabiting adults, between them and any children they take responsibility for, and between the kin of the married couple.

matriarchy: a female-dominated society in which all important public and private power is held by women.

matrilineage: a lineage formed by descent in the female line.

matrilineal descent: a rule that affiliates a person to kin of both sexes related through females only.

matrilocal residence: system under which a husband lives with his wife's family after marriage.

mediation: a form of managing disputes that uses the offices of a third party to achieve voluntary agreement between disputing parties.

messianic: focusing on the coming of an individual who will usher in a utopian world.

millenarian: one who believes that a coming catastrophe will signal the beginning of a new age and the eventual establishment of paradise.

modernization theory: a model of development that says some nations are poor because their societies are traditional. Such nations should achieve wealth by attempting to repeat the historical experience of today's wealthy nations.

monoculture plantation: an agricultural plantation specializing in the large-scale production of a single crop to be sold on the market.

monogamy: a rule that permits a person to be married to only one spouse at a time.

monotheism: belief in a single god.

morpheme: the smallest unit of language that has a meaning.

morphology: a system for creating words from sounds.

multiculturalism: the view that cultural diversity is a positive value and makes an important contribution to contemporary societies.

multinational corporation (MNC): a corporation that owns business enterprises in more than one nation. A business that is able to seek the most profitable venues to produce and market its goods and services regardless of national boundaries.

myths (sacred narratives): stories of historical events, heroes, gods, spirits, and creation that are held to be holy and true by members of a religious tradition.

nation-state: a sovereign, geographically based state that identifies itself as having a distinctive national culture and historical experience.

negative reciprocity: exchange conducted for the purpose of material advantage and the desire to get something for nothing.

neoliberalism: political and economic policies promoting free trade, individual initiative, and minimal government regulation of the economy and opposing state control or subsidy to industries and all but minimal aid to impoverished individuals.

neolocal residence: system under which a couple establishes an independent household after marriage.

nomadic pastoralism: a form of pastoralism in which the whole social group (men, women, children) and their animals move in search of pasture.

non-unilineal (cognatic) descent: a system of descent in which both the father's and the mother's lineages have equal claim to the individual.

norms: shared ideas about the way things ought to be done; rules of behavior that reflect and enforce culture.

nuclear family: a family organized around the conjugal tie (the relationship between husband and wife) and consisting of a husband, a wife, and their children.

open system: a stratification system based primarily on achievement.

organic analogy: the comparison of societies to living organisms.

participant observation: the fieldwork technique that involves gathering cultural data by observing people's behavior and participating in their lives.

pastoralism: a food-getting strategy that depends on the care of domesticated herd animals.

patriarchy: a male-dominated society in which all important public and private power is held by men.

patrilineage: a lineage formed by descent in the male line.

patrilineal descent: a rule that affiliates a person to kin of both sexes related through males only.

patrilocal residence: system under which a bride lives with her husband's family after marriage.

peasants: rural cultivators who produce for the subsistence of their households but are also integrated into larger, complex state societies.

phone: a sound made by humans and used in any language.

phoneme: the smallest significant unit of sound in a language.

phonology: the sound system of a language.

pillage: to strip an area of money, goods, or raw materials through the threat or use of physical violence.

plasticity: the ability of human individuals or cultural groups to change their behavior with relative ease.

political ideology: the shared beliefs and values that legitimize the distribution and use of power in a particular society.

political organization: the patterned ways in which power is legitimately used in a society to regulate behavior, maintain social order, make collective decisions, and deal with social disorder.

political process: the ways in which individuals and groups use power to achieve public goals.

polyandry: a rule permitting a wife to have more than one husband at a time.

polygamy: a rule allowing more than one spouse.

polygyny: a rule permitting a husband to have more than one wife at a time.

polytheism: belief in many gods.

population density: the number of people inhabiting a given area of land.

postmodernism: a theoretical position in anthropology that focuses on issues of power and voice. Postmodernists suggest that anthropological accounts are partial truths reflecting the backgrounds, training, and social positions of their authors.

potlatch: a form of redistribution involving competitive feasting practiced among Northwest Coast Native Americans.

power: the ability to impose one's will on others.

prayer: any communication between people and spirits or gods in which people praise, plead, or request without assurance of results.

prestige: social honor or respect.

priest: one who is formally elected or appointed to a full-time religious office.

primatology: the focus within biological anthropology that is concerned with the biology and behavior of nonhuman primates.

private/public dichotomy: a gender system in which women's status is lowered by their almost exclusive cultural identification with the home and children, whereas men are identified with public, prestigious economic, and political roles.

productive resources: material goods, natural resources, or information used to create other goods or information.

productivity (food production): yield per person per unit of land.

productivity (linguistics): the idea that humans can combine words and sounds into new, meaningful utterances they have never before heard.

prophets: persons who create new religious ideas or call for a purification of existing religious practices.

proxemics: the study of the cultural use of interpersonal space.

racism: the belief that some human populations are superior to others because of inherited, genetically transmitted characteristics.

rank society: a society characterized by institutionalized differences in prestige but no important restrictions on access to basic resources.

rebellion: the attempt of a group within society to force a redistribution of resources and power.

reciprocity: a mutual give-and-take among people of equal status.

redistribution: exchange in which goods are collected and then distributed to members of a group.

reincorporation: the third phase of a rite of passage during which participants are returned to their community with a new status.

religion: a social institution characterized by sacred stories; symbols, and symbolism; the proposed existence of immeasurable beings, powers, states, places, and qualities; rituals and means of addressing the supernatural; specific practitioners; and change.

respondent: a person from whom anthropologists collect data. Also known as informant, consultant, or sometimes interlocutor.

revitalization movement: a movement that proposes that society can be improved through the adoption of a set of new religious beliefs.

revolution: an attempt to overthrow an existing form of political organization.

rite of intensification: a ritual structured to reinforce the values and norms of a community and to strengthen group identity.

rite of passage: a ritual that moves an individual from one social status to another.

ritual: a patterned act that involves the manipulation of religious symbols.

sacrifice: an offering made to increase the efficacy of a prayer or the religious purity of an individual.

Sapir Whorf hypothesis: the hypothesis that perceptions and understandings of time, space, and matter are conditioned by the structure of a language.

secret societies: West African societies whose membership is secret or whose rituals are known only to society members. Their most significant function is the initiation of boys and girls into adulthood.

sedentary: settled, living in one place.

semantics: the subsystem of a language that relates words to meaning.

separation: the first stage of a rite of passage in which individuals are removed from their community or status.

sex: the biological difference between male and female.

shaman: an individual socially recognized as being able to mediate between the world of humanity and the world of gods or spirits but who is not a recognized official of any religious organization.

social complexity: the number of groups and their interrelationships in a society.

social constructionism: a view of ethnicity that holds that ethnic groups emerge and change based on specific historical conditions.

social differentiation: the relative access individuals and groups have to basic material resources, wealth, power, and prestige.

social mobility: movement from one social class to another.

social stratification: a system where two or more categories of people are ranked high or low in relation to each other and have differential access to wealth and status.

society: a group of people who depend on one another for survival or well-being as well as the relationships among such people, including their status and roles.

sociolinguistics: the study of the relationship between language and culture and the ways language is used in varying social contexts.

sorcery: the conscious and intentional use of magic.

sororate: the custom whereby, when a man's wife dies, her sister is given to him as a wife.

state: characterized by centralized governments, differentiated from other social institutions, with control over use of legitimate force, market exchanges, and social inequalities.

stratified society: a society characterized by formal, permanent social and economic inequality in which some people are denied access to basic resources.

structural adjustment: a development policy promoted by Western nations, particularly the United States, that requires poor nations to pursue free market reforms in order to get new loans from the International Monetary Fund and the World Bank.

subculture: a group within a society that shares norms and values significantly different from those of the dominant culture.

subsistence strategies: the pattern of behavior used by a society to obtain food in a particular environment.

succession: the transfer of office or social position between generations.

sweatshop: generally a pejorative term for a factory with working conditions that may include low wages, long hours, inadequate ventilation, and physical, mental, or sexual abuse.

swidden (slash and burn) cultivation: a form of cultivation in which a field is cleared by felling the trees and burning the brush.

symbol: something that stands for something else. Central to culture.

symbolic anthropology: a theoretical position in anthropology that focuses on understanding cultures by discovering and analyzing the symbols that are most important to their members.

syncretism: the merging of elements of two or more religious traditions to produce a new religion.

syntax: a system of rules for combining words into meaningful sentences.

Tirailleurs Senegalais: Senegalese Riflemen. An army that existed from 1857 to 1960 composed largely of soldiers from French African colonies led by officers from metropolitan France.

totemism: religious practices centered around animals, plants, or other aspects of the natural world held to be ancestral or to have other intimate relationships with members of a group.

transhumant pastoralism: a form of pastoralism in which herd animals are moved regularly throughout the year to different areas as pasture becomes available.

tribe: a culturally distinct population whose members consider themselves descended from the same ancestor.

unilineal descent: a rule specifying that membership in a descent group is based on links through either the maternal line or the paternal line, but not both.

universal grammar: a basic set of principles, conditions, and rules that form the foundation of all languages.

values: shared ideas about what is true, right, and beautiful.

VOC: see Dutch East India Company.

war: a formally organized and culturally recognized pattern of collective violence directed toward other societies or between segments within a larger society.

wealth: the accumulation of material resources or access to the means of producing these resources.

witchcraft: the ability to harm others by harboring malevolent thoughts about them; the practice of sorcery.

REFERENCES

Adams, Kathleen M. 1995. "Making-Up the Toraja? The Appropriation of Tourism, Anthropology, and Museums for Politics in Upland Sulawesi, Indonesia." *Ethnology* 34:143–152.

Adetunji, Jimoh I. 2006. "Nigeria: An End to Gas Flaring." *E Magazine: The Environmental Magazine* 17(4):38–39.

Allen, Theodore W. 1997. *The Invention of the White Race* (Vols. 1 and 2). London: Verso.

Allitt, Patrick N. 2002. *Victorian Britain.* Chantilly, VA: Teaching Co.

Alonso, Ana Maria. 1994. "The Politics of Space, Time and Substance: State Formation, Nationalism, and Ethnicity." In B. Siegel (Ed.), *Annual Review of Anthropology* (Vol. 23, pp. 379–405). Stanford, CA: Stanford University Press.

American Anthropological Association. 1998. *Statement on Race.* Available at http://www.aaanet.org/stmts/racepp.htm.

American Anthropological Association. 1998. *Code of Ethics of the American Anthropological Association.* Available at http://www.aaanet.org/committees/ethics/ethcode.htm.

American Anthropological Association. 2007. *"RACE: Are We So Different."* Available at http://www.understandingRACE.org.

Ammon, Paul R., and Mary S. Ammon. 1971. "Effects of Training Black Preschool Children in Vocabulary Versus Sentence Construction." *Journal of Educational Psychology* 62(5):421–426.

Anagnost, Ana. 1989. "Transformations of Gender in Modern China." In S. Morgen (Ed.), *Gender in Anthropology: Critical Reviews for Research and Teaching* (pp. 313–342). Washington DC: American Anthropological Association.

Anderson, Benedict. 1991. *Imagined Communities: Reflections on the Origin and Spread of Nationalism.* New York: Verso.

Anderson, Elijah. 1999. *Code of the Streets.* New York: W.W. Norton.

Andrews, George Reid. 1992. "Racial Inequality in Brazil and the United States: A Statistical Comparison." *Journal of Social History* 26(2):229–263.

Archibold, Randal C. 2006. "Border Fence Must Skirt Objections From Arizona Tribe." *New York Times,* September 20, p. A24.

Ardin, Kwame. 2007. *Ghana's 50th Anniversary: A Response to a Racist Report.* Available at http://www.ghanaweb.com/GhanaHomePage/features/artikel.php?ID=121006.

Asad, Talal. 2007. *On Suicide Bombing.* New York: Columbia University Press.

Associated Press. 2003. *'Our Lady' Controversy Still Chills Santa Fe Museums.* Available at http://Firstamendmentcenter.org/news.aspx?id=11497.

Atran, Scott. 2003. "Genesis of Suicide Terrorism." *Science* 299(5612):1534–1539.

Atran, Scott. 2007. "The Nature of Belief." *Science* 317(5837):456.

Augusto dos Santos, Salas. 2002. "Historical Roots of the 'Whitening' of Brazil." Trans. by Laurence Hallewell. *Latin American Perspectives* 29(1):61–82.

Bailey, Stanley R., and Edward E. Telles. 2006. "Multiracial Versus Collective Black Categories: Examining Census Classification Debates in Brazil." *Ethnicities* 6(1):74–101.

Bajaj, Vikas, and Ron Nixon. 2006. "Subprime Loans Going from Boon to Housing Bane." *New York Times,* December 6, p. C1.

Balikci, Asen. 1970. *The Netsilik Eskimo.* Prospect Heights, IL: Waveland.

Barfield, Thomas J. 1993. *The Nomadic Alternative.* Englewood Cliffs, NJ: Prentice Hall.

Barnes, Virginia Lee, and Janice Boddy. 1995. *Aman: The Story of a Somali Girl.* New York: Vintage.

Barnes-Dean, Virginia Lee. 1989. "Clitoridectomy and Infibulation." *Cultural Survival Quarterly* 9(2):26–30.

Barnett, Homer. 1953. *Innovation: The Basis of Cultural Change.* New York: McGraw-Hill.

Barth, Fredrik. 1998. *Ethnic Groups and Boundaries: The Social Organization of Culture Difference.* Prospect Heights, IL: Waveland. (Originally published 1969.)

Basso, Keith. 1979. *Portraits of "The Whitemen."* New York: Cambridge University Press.

Benedict, Ruth. 1923. "The Concept of the Guardian Spirit in North America," Thesis. Ph.D. Columbia University, New York. *Memoirs of the American Anthropological Association* 29:1–97.

Benedict, Ruth. 1934. "Anthropology and the Abnormal." *Journal of General Psychology* 10:791–808.

Benson, Janet E. 1999. "Undocumented Immigrants and the Meatpacking Industry in the Midwest." In D. W. Haines and K. E. Rosenblum (Eds.), *Illegal Immigration in America: A Reference Handbook* (pp. 172–192). Westport, CT: Greenwood.

Berdan, Frances F. 1982. *The Aztecs of Central Mexico: An Imperial Society.* New York: Holt, Rinehart, and Winston.

Bereiter, Carl, and Siegfried Engelmann. 1966. *Teaching Disadvantaged Children in Preschool.* Englewood Cliffs: Prentice Hall.

Berreman, Gerald D. 1981. *Social Inequality: Comparative and Developmental Approaches.* New York: Academic Press.

Berreman, Gerald D. 1988. "Race, Caste, and Other Invidious Distinctions in Social Stratification." In J. Cole (Ed.), *Anthropology for the Nineties: Introductory Readings* (pp. 485–518). New York: Free Press.

Besnier, Niko. 1996. "Polynesian Gender Liminality Through Time and Space." In G. Herdt (Ed.), *Third Sex, Third Gender: Beyond Sexual Dimorphism in Culture and History* (pp. 285–328). New York: Zone.

Beteille, Andre. 1998. *Society and Politics in India: Essays in a Comparative Perspective.* New Delhi: Oxford India.

Bhagwati, Jagdish. 1996. "The Demand to Reduce Domestic Diversity Among Trading Nations." In Jagdish Bhagwati and R. E. Hudec (Eds.), *Fair Trade and Harmonization.* Cambridge: MIT Press.

Bickerton, Derek. 1998. "Catastrophic Evolution: The Case for a Single Step from Protolanguage to Full Human Language." In James Hurford, M. Studdert-Kennedy, and C. Knight (Eds.), *The Evolutionary Emergence of Language: Social Function and the Origins of Linguistic Form* (pp. 341–358). Cambridge: Cambridge University Press.

Blackwood, Evelyn. 1998. *Female Desires: Same-sex Relations and Transgender Practices Across Cultures.* New York: Columbia University Press.

Bodley, John H. 1999. *Victims of Progress* (4th ed.). Mountain View, CA: Mayfield.

Bodley, John H. 2000. *Cultural Anthropology: Tribes, States, and the Global System* (3rd ed.). Mountain View, CA: Mayfield.

Boellstorff, Tom. 2004. "Playing back the Nation: *Waria,* Indonesian transvestites." *Cultural Anthropology* 19:159–195.

Bonvillain, Nancy. 1997. *Language, Culture, and Communication* (2nd ed.). Englewood Cliffs, NJ: Prentice Hall.

Borgerhoff Mulder, Monique. 1995. "Bridewealth and Its Correlates: Quantifying Changes over Time." *Current Anthropology* 36:573–603.

Bornstein, Avram S. 2002. *Crossing the Green Line Between the West Bank and Israel.* Philadelphia: University of Pennsylvania Press.

Borofsky, Robert. 1994. "On the Knowledge and Knowing of Cultural Activities." In R. Borofsky (Ed.), *Assessing Cultural Anthropology* (pp. 331–347). New York: McGraw-Hill.

Borofsky, Robert. 2005. *Yanomami: The Fierce Controversy and What We Might Learn From It.* Berkeley, CA: University of California.

Bowen, John Richard. 2007. *Why the French Don't Like Headscarves: Islam, the State, and Public Space.* Princeton: Princeton University Press.

Bowerman, M. 1996. "Learning How to Structure Space for Language: A Cross-Linguistic Perspective." In P. Bloom, M. A. Peterson, L. Nadel, and M. F. Garrett (Eds.), *Language and Space* (pp. 385–436). Cambridge, MA: MIT Press.

Bowles, Samuel, Herbert Gintis, and Melissa Osborne Groves (Eds.). 2005. *Unequal Changes: Family Background and Economic Success.* Princeton: Princeton University Press.

Boxer, C. R. 1965. *The Dutch Seaborne Empire 1600–1800.* New York: Knopf.

Boyd-Bowman, Peter. 1975. "A Sample of Sixteenth Century 'Caribbean' Spanish Phonology." In William Milan, John Staczek, and Juan Zamora (Eds.), *1974 Colloquium on Spanish and Portuguese Linguistics* (pp. 1–11). Washington: Georgetown University Press.

Boynton, Robert S. 2006. "The Plot Against Equality," (book review of *The Trouble With Diversity: How We Learned to Love Identity and Ignore Inequality,* Walter Benn Michaels). *The Nation,* December 25, pp. 23 ff.

Bracey, Dorothy. 2006. *Exploring Law and Culture.* Long Grove, IL: Waveland.

Bracken, Christopher. 1997. *The Potlatch Papers: A Colonial Case History.* Chicago: University of Chicago Press.

Bradsher, Keith. 2008. "A Drought in Australia, A Global Shortage of Rice." *The New York Times,* April 17.

Brain, James L. 1989. "An Anthropological Perspective on the Witchcraze." In Jean R. Brink, A. P. Coudert, and M. C. Horowitz (Eds.), *The Politics of Gender in Early Modern Europe* (pp. 15–27). Kirksville, MO: Sixteenth Century Journal Publishers.

Brandes, Stanley. 1981. "Like Wounded Stags: Male Sexual Ideology in an

Andalusian Town." In S. B. Ortner and H. Whitehead (Eds.), *Sexual Meanings: The Cultural Construction of Gender and Sexuality* (pp. 216–239). Cambridge: Cambridge University Press.

Bremner, Brian. 2006. "What's It Going to Cost to Clean Up China?" *Business Week.* Available at http://www.businessweek.com/globalbiz/content/sep2006/gb20060927_774622.htm?chan=top+news_top+news+index_global+business.

Brettell, Caroline B. 2003. *Anthropology and Migration: Essays on Transnationalism, Ethnicity, and Identity.* Walnut Creek, CA: Altamira.

Brettell, Caroline B. 2007. "Adjustment of Status, Remittances, and Return: Some Observations on 21st Century Migration Processes." *City and Society* 19(1):47–59.

Breusers, Mark. 1999. *On the Move: Mobility, Land Use and Livelihood Practices on the Central Plateau in Burkina Faso.* Miinster, Hamburg and London: LIT Verlag.

Briggs, Jean L. 1991. "Expecting the Unexpected: Canadian Inuit Training for an Experimental Lifestyle." *Ethos* 19(3):259–287.

Brookfield, Harold C. 1988. "The New Great Age of Clearance and Beyond." In Julie Sloan Denslow and Christine Padoch (Eds.), *People of the Tropical Forest* (pp. 209–224). Berkeley, CA: University of California Press.

Brosius, Peter J. 1999. "Green Dots, Pink Hearts: Displacing Politics from the Malaysian Rain Forest." *American Anthropologist* 101:36–57.

Brown, Drusilla, Alan Deardorff, and Robert Stern. 2003. "The Effects of Multinational Production on Wages and Working Conditions in Developing Countries." National Bureau of Economic Research, Working Paper 9669. Cambridge, MA: National Bureau of Economic Research. Available at http://www.nber.org/papers/w9669.

Brown, Judith. 1965. "A Cross Cultural Study of Female Initiation Rites." *American Anthropologist* 65:837–855.

Brown, Judith. 1975. "Iroquois Women: An Ethnohistoric Note." In R. R. Reiter (Ed.), *Toward an Anthropology of Women* (pp. 235–251). New York: Monthly Review Press.

Brown, Karen McCarthy. 1991. *Mama Lola: A Vodou Priestess in Brooklyn.* Berkeley, CA: University of California Press.

Brumfiel, Elizabeth. 1991. "Weaving and Cooking: Women's Production in Aztec Mexico." In J. M. Gero and M. W. Conkey (Eds.), *Engendering Archaeology: Women and Prehistory* (pp. 224–251). Cambridge, MA: Basil Blackwell.

Brumfiel, Elizabeth M. 2006. "Cloth, Gender, Continuity, and Change: Fabricating Unity in Anthropology." *American Anthropologist* 108(4): 862–877.

Burton, John W. 1992. "Representing Africa: Colonial Anthropology Revisited." *Journal of Asian and African Studies* 27:181–201.

Burton, Thomas G. 1993. *Serpent-handling Believers.* Knoxville, TN: University of Tennessee Press.

Buruma, Ian. 2006. *Murder in Amsterdam: The Death of Theo van Gogh and the Limits of Tolerance.* New York: Penguin.

Cagan, Jonathan and Craig M. Vogel. 2002. *Creating Breakthrough Products: Innovation from Product Planning to Program Approval.* Upper Saddle River: Prentice Hall.

Calman, Neil, Charmaine Ruddock, Maxine Golub, and Lan Le. 2005. *Separate and Unequal: Medical Apartheid in New York City.* New York: Institute for Urban Family Health.

Canadian Broadcasting Company. 1982. *Ear Pull Hoopla.* Broadcast March 21, 1982. Available at http://archives.radio-canada.ca/IDC-1-41-1194-6705/sports/arcticgames/clip4.

Cancian, Frank. 1989. "Economic Behavior in Peasant Communities." In Stuart Plattner (Ed.), *Economic Anthropology* (pp. 127–170). Stanford, CA: Stanford University Press.

Cannon, Walter B. 1942. "The 'Voodoo' Death." *American Anthropologist* 44:169–180.

Carneiro, Robert. 1970. "A Theory of the Origin of the State." *Science* 169:733–738.

Carneiro, Robert. 1981. "The Chiefdom: Precursor of the State." In Grant Jones and Robert Kautz (Eds.), *The Transition to Statehood in the New World* (pp. 37–79). Cambridge: Cambridge University Press.

Carroll, Joseph. 2005. "Who Supports Marijuana Legalization?" *Gallup Poll Tuesday Briefing,* November 1.

Cashdan, Elizabeth. 1989. "Hunters and Gatherers: Economic Behavior in Bands." In S. Plattner (Ed.), *Economic Anthropology* (pp. 21–48). Stanford, CA: Stanford University Press.

Cerroni-Long, E. L. 1993. "Teaching Ethnicity in the USA: An Anthropological Model." *Journal of Ethno-Development* 2(1):106–112.

Cerroni-Long, E. L. 1995. "Introduction." In E. L. Cerroni-Long (Ed.), *Insider Anthropology* (Napa Bulletin, Vol. 16). Washington, DC: American Anthropological Association.

Chagnon, Napoleon. 1997. *Yanomamo* (5th ed.). Fort Worth, TX: Harcourt Brace Jovanovich.

Chance, John K., and William B. Taylor. 1985. "Cofradias and Cargos: An Historical Perspective on the Mesoamerican Civil-Religious Hierarchy." *American Ethnologist* 12(1):1–26.

Chance, Norman. 1990. *The Inupiat and Arctic Alaska: An Ethnography of Development.* Fort Worth, TX: Holt, Rinehart and Winston.

Chavez, Leo R. 1998. *Shadowed Lives: Undocumented Immigrants in American Society.* Belmont, CA: Wadsworth.

Checker, Melissa. 2005. *Polluted Promises: Environmental Racism and the Search for*

Justice in a Southern Town. New York: New York University Press.
Chelala, Cesar. 2006. "Chronically Hungry Children of America." *The Japan Times,* September 18.
Chibnik, Michael. 2005. "Experimental Economics in Anthropology: A Critical Assessment." *American Ethnologist* 32(2):198–209.
Chomsky, Noam. 1965. *Syntactic Structures.* London: Mouton.
Chomsky, Noam. 1975. *The Logical Structure of Linguistic Theory.* New York: Plenum Press.
Cissé, Almahady. 2007. "Mali: Wood—The Gift That Can't Keep On Giving." *Inter Press Service (Johannesburg),* April 13. Available at http://ipsnews.net/news.asp?idnews=37339.
Clark, Lauren and Ann Kingsolver. "Briefing Paper on Informed Consent." *AAA Committee on Ethics.* Available at http://www.aaanet.org/committees/ethics/bp5.htm.
Clarke, Mari H. 2000. "On the Road Again: International Development Consulting." In Paula Sabloff (Ed.), *Careers in Anthropology: Profiles of Practitioner Anthropologists* (pp. 71–74). Washington, DC: National Association for the Practice of Anthropology.
Clendinnen, Inga. 1991. *Aztecs: An Interpretation.* Cambridge: Cambridge University Press.
Cleveland, A. A., J. Craven, and M. Dadfelser. 1979. *Universals of Culture.* New York: Global Perspectives in Education.
Cohen, Yehudi. 1971. *Man in Adaptation: The Institutional Framework.* Chicago: Aldine.
Coleman, Michael C. 1999. "The Responses of American Indian Children and Irish Children to the School, 1850s–1920s: A Comparative Study in Cross-Cultural Education." *American Indian Quarterly* 23(3/4):83–112.
Condon, Richard G., with Julia Ogina and the Holman Elders. 1996. *The Northern Copper Inuit: A History.* Toronto: University of Toronto Press.
Conklin, Beth A. 1995. "'Thus Are Our Bodies, Thus Was Our Custom': Mortuary Cannibalism in an Amazonian Society." *American Ethnologist* 22(1):75–101.
Connolly, Bob, and Robin Anderson. 1987. *First Contact: New Guinea's Highlanders Encounter the Outside World.* New York: Penguin.
Conway-Long, Don. 1994. "Ethnographies and Masculinities." In Harry Brod and Michael Kaufman (Eds.), *Theorizing Masculinities* (pp. 61–81). Thousand Oaks, CA: Sage.
Coquery-Vidrovitch, Catherine. 1988. *Africa: Endurance and Change South of the Sahara.* Berkeley, CA: University of California Press.
Corak, Miles. 2004. *Generational Income Mobility in North America and Europe.* Cambridge, UK: Cambridge University Press.
Costa, LeeRay, and Andrew Matzner. 2007. *Male Bodies, Women's Souls: Personal Narratives of Thailand's Transgendered Youth.* Binghamton, NY: Haworth Press.
Covington, Dennis. 1995. *Salvation on Sand Mountain: Snake Handling and Redemption in Southern Appalachia.* Reading, MA: Addison-Wesley.
Crespin, Pamela. 2005. "The Global Transformation of Work." *Anthropology News* 46(3):20–21.
Cunningham, Lawrence S., John Kelsay, R. Maurice Barineau, and Heather Jo McVoy. 1995. *The Sacred Quest: An Invitation to the Study of Religion* (2nd ed.). Englewood Cliffs, NJ: Prentice Hall.
Curtis, Lewis P. 1968. *Anglo-Saxons and Celts: A Study of Anti-Irish Prejudice in Victorian England.* Bridgeport: University of Bridgeport.

Dalton, George. 1961. "Economic Theory and Primitive Society." *American Anthropologist* 63:1–25.
Danfulani, Umar Habila Dadem. 1999. "Exorcising Witchcraft: The Return of the Gods in New Religious Movements on the Jos Plateau and the Benue Regions of Nigeria." *African Affairs* 98(391):167–193.
Danher, Kevin, and Michael Shellenberger (Eds.). 1995. *Fighting for the Soul of Brazil.* New York: Monthly Review Press.
Darian-Smith, Eve. 2004. *New Capitalists: Law, Politics and Identity Surrounding Casino Gaming on Native American Land.* Belmont: Wadsworth.
Das, Raju. 1998. "The Green Revolution, Agrarian Productivity and Labor." *International Journal of Urban and Regional Research* 22(1):122–135.
Dawkins, Richard. 2006. *The God Delusion.* London: Bantam Press.
De Vos, George A., and Hiroshi Wagatsuma. 1966. *Japan's Invisible Race: Case Studies in Culture and Personality.* Berkeley, CA: University of California Press.
De Vos, George, and Lola Romanucci-Ross. 1995. "Ethnic Identity: A Psychocultural Perspective." In Lola Romanucci-Ross and George A. De Vos (Eds.), *Ethnic Identity: Creation, Conflict, and Accommodation* (3rd ed., pp. 349–380). London: Sage.
Destexhe, Alain. 1995. *Rwanda and Genocide in the Twentieth Century* (Alison Marschner, Trans.). New York: New York University Press.
di Leonardo, Micaela. 1984. *The Varieties of Ethnic Experience: Kinship, Class, and Gender among California Italian-Americans.* Ithaca, NY: Cornell University Press.
di Leonardo, Micaela. 1998. *Exotics at Home: Anthropologies, Others, American Modernity.* Chicago: University of Chicago Press.
di Leonardo, Micaela. 2003. "Margaret Mead and the Culture of Forgetting." *American Anthropologist* 105(3):592–595.
Diamond, Jared. 1992. "The Arrow of Disease." *Discover* 13(10):64–73.

Diamond, Jared. 1998. *Guns, Germs, and Steel: The Fate of Human Societies.* New York: W.W. Norton.

Divale, William Tulio, and Marvin Harris. 1976. "Population, Warfare and the Male Supremacist Complex." *American Anthropologist* 78:521–538.

Dollard, John. 1937. *Caste and Class in a Southern Town.* New Haven, CT: Yale University Press.

Dominguez, Virginia. 1986. *White by Definition.* New Brunswick, NJ: Rutgers University Press.

Dozon, Jean-Pierre. 1985. "Les Bété: une creation coloniale." In J. L. Amselle and E. M'bokolo (Eds.), *Au Coeur de l'ethnie* (pp. 49–85). Paris: Editions La Decouverte.

Duncan, David Ewing. 1995. *Hernando de Soto: A Savage Quest in the Americas.* New York: Crown.

Duncan, David James. 2000. "Salmon's Second Coming." *Sierra* March/April:30–41.

Durkheim, Émile. 1961. *The Elementary Forms of the Religious Life.* New York: Collier. (Originally published 1915.)

Durning, Alan Thein. 1994. "The Conundrum of Consumption." In L. A. Mazur (Ed.), *Beyond the Numbers: A Reader on Population, Consumption, and the Environment* (pp. 40–47). Washington, DC: Island Press.

Durrenberger, E. Paul. 2001. "Explorations of Class and Consciousness in the U.S." *Journal of Anthropological Research* 57(1):41–60.

Earle, Timothy K. 1987. "Chiefdoms in Archaeological and Ethnological Perspective." *Annual Reviews in Anthropology* 16:279–308.

Early, John D., and Thomas N. Headland. 1998. *Population Dynamics of a Philippine Rain Forest People: The San Ildefonso Agta.* Gainesville, FL: University Press of Florida.

Eckholm, Eric. 2007. "Boys Cast Out by Polygamists Find New Help." *New York Times,* September 9.

Economist, The. 2005. "Mind the Gap." *The Economist,* June 9.

Eggan, Fred. 1950. *The Social Organization of Western Pueblos.* Chicago: University of Chicago Press.

El Saadawi, Nawal. 1980. *The Hidden Face of Eve.* London: Zed Books.

Elkin, A. P. 1967. "The Nature of Australian Totemism." In J. Middleton (Ed.), *Gods and Rituals* (pp. 159–176). Garden City, NY: Natural History Press.

Ember, Carol. 1983. "The Relative Decline in Women's Contribution to Agriculture with Intensification." *American Anthropologist* 85(2): 285–304.

Ember, Carol R., and Melvin Ember. 2005. "Explaining Corporal Punishment of Children: A Cross-Cultural Study." *American Anthropologist* 107(4):609–619.

Ember, Melvin, and Carol R. Ember. 1971. "The Conditions Favoring Matrilocal vs. Patrilocal Residence." *American Anthropologist* 73:571–594.

Engelmann, Siegfried, and Therese Engelmann. 1966. *Give Your Child a Superior Mind: A Program for the Preschool Child.* New York: Simon and Schuster.

Ensminger, Jean. 2002. "Experimental Economics: A Powerful New Method for Theory Testing in Anthropology." In Jean Ensminger (Ed.), *Theory in Economic Anthropology* (pp. 59–78). Walnut Creek: Altamira.

Erickson, Jon. 1995. *The Human Volcano: Population Growth as Geologic Force.* New York: Facts on File.

Escobar, Arturo. 1997. "The Making and Unmaking of the Third World Through Development." In M. Rahnema and V. Bawtree (Eds.), *The Post-Development Reader* (pp. 263–273). Atlantic Highlands, NJ: Zed Books.

Estioko-Griffin, Agnes. 1986. "Daughters of the Forest." *Natural History* 5:37–42.

Evans, Peter. 2000. "Fighting Marginalization With Transnational Networks: Counter Hegemonic Globalization." *Contemporary Sociology* 29:230–241.

Evans-Pritchard, E. E. 1958. *Witchcraft, Oracles, and Magic among the Azande.* Oxford: Clarendon Press. (Originally published 1937.)

Evans-Pritchard, E. E. 1968. *The Nuer.* Oxford: Clarendon Press. (Originally published 1940.)

Fábrega, Horacio. 1997. *Evolution of Sickness and Healing.* Berkeley, CA: University of California Press.

Feinberg, Richard. 1986. "Market Economy and Changing Sex-Roles on a Polynesian Atoll." *Ethnology* 25:271–282.

Feinberg, Richard. 1994. "Contested Worlds: Politics of Culture and the Politics of Anthropology." *Anthropology and Humanism* 19:20–35.

Fenton, James. 1996. "A Short History of Anti-Hamitism." *New York Review of Books* 43(3):7–9.

Ferguson, Niall. 2007. "Wearing a Red Nose for Africa's Corrupt Clowns Is a Bad Joke." *The Sunday Telegraph,* March 11.

Ferguson, R. Brian. 1992. "A Savage Encounter: Western Contact and the Yanomamo War Complex." In R. B. Ferguson and N. L. Whitehead (Eds.), *War in the Tribal Zone: Expanding States and Indigenous Warfare* (pp. 199–227). Santa Fe, NM: School of American Research Press.

Ferraro, Gary P. 1994. *The Cultural Dimension of International Business* (2nd ed.). Englewood Cliffs, NJ: Prentice-Hall.

Fetto, John. 1999. "Six Billion Served." *American Demographics* June:14.

Fisher, Roger, and William Ury. 1981. *Getting to Yes: Negotiating Agreement Without Giving In.* New York: Penguin.

Fix, Michael, and Jeffrey Passel. 1994. *Immigration and Immigrants: Setting the Record Straight.* Washington, DC: Urban Institute.

Flamm, Bruce L. 2002. "Faith Healing by Prayer: Review of Cha, KY, Wirth, DP, Lobo, RA. Does Prayer Influence the Success of In Vitro Fertilization-Embryo Transfer?" *The Scientific Review of Alternative Medicine* 6(1):47–50.

Flood, Merielle K. 1994. "Changing Gender Relations in Zinacantan, Mexico." *Research in Economic Anthropology* 15:145–173.

Fluehr-Lobban, Carolyn. 2005. "Cultural Relativism and Universal Rights in Islamic Law." *Anthropology News* 46(9):23.

Foner, Eric. 1988. *Reconstruction: America's Unfinished Revolution 1863–1877.* New York: Harper.

Forbes. 2007. *NPB Team Valuation, #8, The Miami Heat.* Available at http://www.forbes.com/lists/2006/32/biz_06nba_Miami-Heat_329036.html.

Fortune. 2006. *Global 500.* Available at http://money.cnn.com/magazines/fortune/global500/2005/.

Foster, Robert J. 1991. "Making National Cultures in the Global Ecumene." *Annual Reviews of Anthropology* 20:235–260.

Frank, Robert, and Phillip J. Cook. 1996. *The Winner-Take-All Society: Why the Few at the Top Get So Much More than the Rest of Us.* New York: Penguin.

Frank, Thomas. 2004. *What's the Matter with Kansas? How Conservatives Won the Heart of America.* New York: Henry Holt.

Frankenberg, Ruth. 1993. *White Women, Race Matters: The Social Construction of Whiteness.* Minneapolis: University of Minnesota Press.

Freeman, Carla. 2007. "The 'Reputation' of Neoliberalism." *American Ethnologist* 34(2):252–267.

Freyre, Gilberto. 1946. *The Masters and the Slaves: A Study in the Development of Brazilian Civilization.* New York: Knopf.

Fried, Morton. 1967. *The Evolution of Political Society.* New York: Random House.

Friedl, Ernestine. 1975. *Women and Men: An Anthropologist's View.* New York: Holt, Rinehart and Winston.

Friedman, Ariella, and Judith Todd. 1994. "Kenyan Women Tell a Story: Interpersonal Power of Women in Three Subcultures in Kenya." *Sex Roles* 31:533–546.

Friedman, Jonathan. 1992. "The Past in the Future: History and the Politics of Identity." *American Anthropologist* 94:837–859.

Friedman, Jonathan (Ed.). 2003. *Globalization, the State, and Violence.* Walnut Creek, CA: AltaMira.

Friedman, Thomas. 2005. *The World Is Flat.* New York: Farrar, Straus and Giroux.

Fry, Douglas P., and Kaj Bjorkqvist (Eds.). 1997. *Cultural Variation and Conflict Resolution: Alternatives to Violence.* Mahwah, NJ: Erlbaum.

Fuller, Christopher J. (Ed.). 1995. *Caste Today.* Delhi: Oxford University Press.

Galaty, John. 1986. "Introduction." In T. Saitoti (Ed.), *The Worlds of a Maasai Warrior: An Autobiography of Tepilit Ole Saitoti.* Berkeley: University of California Press.

Geertz, Clifford. 1963. *Agricultural Involution: The Process of Ecological Change in Indonesia.* Berkeley, CA: University of California Press.

Geertz, Clifford. 1973a. "Deep Play: Notes on the Balinese Cockfight." In C. Geertz (Ed.), *The Interpretation of Cultures* (pp. 412–453). New York: Basic Books.

Geertz, Clifford (Ed.). 1973b. *The Interpretation of Cultures.* New York: Basic Books.

Geertz, Clifford. 2001. "The Visit." *New York Review of Books* 48(16).

Geertz, Clifford. 2008. "Deep Play: Notes on a Balinese Cockfight." In R. Jon McGee and Richard L. Warms (Eds.), *Anthropological Theory: An Introductory History.* Boston: McGraw Hill.

Geographical. 2005. "The Fertile Century." *Geographical* 77(3):50–51.

Ghosh, Anjan. 1991. "The Structure of Structure, or Appropriation of Anthropological Theory." *Review* 14(1):55–77.

Gibbs, James L., Jr. 1988. "The Kpelle Moot: A Therapeutic Model for the Informal Settlement of Disputes." In J. B. Cole (Ed.), *Anthropology of the Nineties* (pp. 347–359). New York: Free Press.

Gibbs, W. Wayt. 2002. "Saving Dying Languages." *Scientific American* 287:78–86.

Gibson, Margaret A. 1997. "Ethnicity and School Performance: Complicating the Immigrant/Involuntary Minority Typology." *Anthropology and Education Quarterly* 28(3):431–454.

Gibson, Margaret A., and John Ogbu. 1991. *Minority Status and Schooling: A Comparative Study of Immigrant and Involuntary Minorities.* New York: Garland.

Gilbert, Matthew. 2007. "Farewell, Sweet Ice." *The Nation,* May 7, pp. 26–27.

Gilberthorpe, Emma. 2007. "Fasu Solidarity: A Case Study of Kin Networks, Land Tenure, and Oil Extraction in Kutubu, Papua New Guinea." *American Anthropologist* 109(1):101–112.

Gill, Lesley. 2005. "Empire, Ethnography and Engagement." *Anthropology Newsletter* January:12.

Gill, Lesley. 2005. "Labor and Human Rights: The 'Real Thing' in Colombia." *Transforming Anthropology* 13(2):110–115.

Gilliland, Mary. 1995. "Nationalism and Ethnogenesis in the Former Yugoslavia." In Lola Romanucci-Ross and George A. De Vos (Eds.), *Ethnic Identity: Creation, Conflict, and Accommodation* (3rd ed., pp. 197–221). London: Sage.

Gilmore, David D. 1990. *Manhood in the Making: Cultural Concepts of Mas-*

culinity. New Haven, CT: Yale University Press.

Gilmore, David D. 1996. "Above and Below: Toward a Social Geometry of Gender." *American Anthropologist* 98:54–66.

Ginsburg, Faye. 1989. *Contested Lives: The Abortion Debate in an American Community.* Berkeley, CA: University of California Press.

Gjerde, Jon. 1998. *Major Problems in American Immigration and Ethnic History.* Boston: Houghton Mifflin.

Glazer, Nathan, and Daniel P. Moynihan. 1970. *Beyond the Melting Pot* (2nd ed.). Cambridge, MA: MIT.

Glick-Schiller, Nina, Linda Basch, and Christina Szanton-Blanc (Eds.). 1992. *Towards a Transnational Perspective on Migration: Race, Class, Ethnicity and Nationalism Reconsidered.* New York: New York Academy of Sciences.

Gmelch, George. 2000. "Baseball Magic." In James Spradley and David McCurdy (Eds.), *Conformity and Conflict* (pp. 322–331). Boston: Allyn and Bacon.

Godelier, Maurice. 1993. "L'Occident, miroir brisé: une evaluation partielle de l'anthropologie sociale assortie de quelques perspectives." *Annales* 48:1183–1207.

Goldschmidt, Walter R. 1986. *The Sebei: A Study in Adaptation.* New York: Holt, Reinhart and Winston.

Goldstein, Donna. 1999. "'Interracial' Sex and Racial Democracy in Brazil: Twin Concepts?" *American Anthropologist* 101:563–578.

Goodale, J. 1971. *Tiwi Wives.* Seattle, WA: University of Washington Press.

Goody, Jack. 1995. *The Expansive Moment: Anthropology in Britain and Africa 1918–1970.* Cambridge: Cambridge University Press.

Gordon, Peter. 2004. "Numerical Cognition Without Words: Evidence from Amazonia." *Science* 306(5695):496–499.

Gordon, Robert J. 1992. *The Bushman Myth: The Making of a Namibian Underclass.* Boulder, CO: Westview Press.

Gore, Al. 2006. *An Inconvenient Truth: The Planetary Emergency of Global Warming and What We Can Do About It.* New York: Melcher Media/ Rodale. Also available on DVD. Hollywood, CA: Paramount.

Graham, Laura R. 2006. "Anthropologists Are Obligated to Promote Human Rights and Social Justice: Especially Among Vulnerable Communities." *Anthropology News* 47(7):4–5.

Graham, Laura, Alexandra Jaffe, Bonnie Urciuoli, and David Valentine. 2007. "Why Anthropologists Should Oppose English Only Legislation in the U.S." *Anthropology News* 48(1):32–33.

Graham, Sharon. 2006. *Challenging Gender Norms: The Five Genders of Indonesia.* Belmont, CA: Wadsworth.

Greenberg, James B. 1997. "A Political Ecology of Structural-Adjustment Policies: The Case of the Dominican Republic." *Culture & Agriculture* 19(3):85–93.

Greenhalgh, Susan. 2005. "Globalization and Population Governance in China." In Aihwa Ong and Stephen J. Collier (Eds.), *Global Assemblages: Technology, Politics, and Ethics as Anthropological Problems* (pp. 354–372). Malden, MA.

Greenhalgh, Susan. 2007a. *Just One Child: Science and Policy in Deng's China.* Berkeley: University of California Press.

Greenhalgh, Susan. 2007b. "China's Future With Fewer Females." *China From the Inside.* Washington, DC: Public Broadcasting Service. Available at http://www.pbs.org/kqed/chinainside/women/population.html.

Grey, John. 2005. "The World Is Round." *New York Review of Books.* 52(13).

Grosfoguel, Ramon. 2003. *Colonial Subjects: Puerto Ricans in a Global Perspective.* Berkeley: University of California Press.

Gruenbaum, Ellen. 2001. *The Female Circumcision Controversy: An Anthropological Perspective.* Philadelphia, PA: University of Pennsylvania Press.

Gu Baochang, Wang Feng, Guo Zhigang, Zhang Erli. 2007. "China's Local and National Fertility Policies at the End of the Twentieth Century." *Population and Development Review* 33(1):129–148.

Guillermoprieto, Alma. 2006. "A New Bolivia?" *New York Review of Books* 53(13):36.

Gutmann, Matthew C. 1996. *The Meanings of Macho: Being a Man in Mexico City.* Berkeley, CA: University of California Press.

Hackenberg, Robert. 2000. "Advancing Applied Anthropology: Joe Hill in Cyberspace: Steps Toward Creating 'One Big Union.'" *Human Organization* 59(3):365–369.

Hacker, Jacob. 2002a. *The Divided Welfare State: The Battle Over Public and Private Social Benefits in the United States.* New York: Cambridge.

Hacker, Jacob. 2002b. *The Great Risk Shift: The Assault on American Jobs, Families, Health Care, and Retirement and How You Can Fight Back.* New York: Oxford University Press.

Hadden, Jeffrey K., and Anson Shupe. 1989. "Is There Such a Thing as Global Fundamentalism?" In Jeffrey K. Hadden and Anson Shupe (Eds.), *Secularization and Fundamentalism Reconsidered* (pp. 109–122). New York: Paragon House.

Haines, David. 2007. "Labor, Migration, and Anthropology: Reflections From the Work of Philip L. Martin." *City and Society* 19(1):60–71.

Hale, Sondra. 1989. "The Politics of Gender in the Middle East." In S. Morgen (Ed.), *Gender and Anthropology: Critical Reviews for Research and Teaching* (pp. 246–267). Washington, DC: American Anthropological Association.

Hall, Edward T. 1959. *The Silent Language.* Greenwich, CT: Fawcett.

Hall, Edward T. 1966. *The Hidden Dimension.* New York: Doubleday.

Hall, Edward T. 1968. "Proxemics." *Current Anthropology* 9:83–109.

Hall, Edward T. 1983. *The Dance of Life: The Other Dimension of Time.* New York: Anchor/Doubleday.

Halperin, Rhoda H. 1990. *The Livelihood of Kin: Making Ends Meet "The Kentucky Way."* Austin, TX: University of Texas Press.

Handler, Richard. 1988. *Nationalism and the Politics of Culture in Quebec.* Madison, WI: University of Wisconsin Press.

Hansen, Edward C. 1995. "The Great Bambi War: Tocquevillians versus Keynesians in an Upstate New York County." In J. Schneider and R. Rapp (Eds.), *Articulating Hidden Histories: Exploring the Influence of Eric R. Wolf* (pp. 142–155). Berkeley, CA: University of California Press.

Harries, Patrick. 1987. "The Roots of Ethnicity: Discourse and the Politics of Language Construction in South-East Africa." *African Affairs* 87:25–52.

Harris, Marvin. 1966. "The Cultural Ecology of India's Sacred Cattle." *Current Anthropology* 7:51–66.

Harris, Marvin. 1989. *Our Kind: Who We Are, Where We Came From, Where We Are Going.* New York: Harper Perennial.

Harrison, Faye V. 1998. "Introduction: Expanding the Discourse on 'Race.'" *American Anthropologist* 100:609–631.

Harrison, Paul and Fred Pearce. 2000. *AAAS Atlas of Population and Environment.* Victoria Dompka Markham (Ed.). American Association for the Advancement of Science and the University of California Press. Available at http://atlas.aaas.org/.

Hart, C. W. M. 1967. "Contrasts between Pre-Pubertal and Post-Pubertal Education." In R. Endelman (Ed.), *Personality and Social Life* (pp. 275–290). New York: Random House.

Hart, C. W. M., and Arnold R. Pilling. 1960. *The Tiwi of Northern Australia.* New York: Holt, Rinehart and Winston.

Hartigan, John. 1997. "Establishing the Fact of Whiteness." *American Anthropologist* 99:495–505.

Hefner, Robert. 2002. "Global Violence and Indonesian Muslim Politics." *American Anthropologist* 104(3): 754–765.

Henrich, Joseph, et al. 2004. *Foundations of Human Sociality: Economic Experiments and Ethnographic Evidence From 15 Small-Scale Societies.* Oxford: Oxford University Press.

Henrich, Joseph, et al. 2004. "Overview and Synthesis." In Joseph Henrich et al. (Eds.), *Foundations of Human Sociality: Economic Experiments and Ethnographic Evidence From 15 Small-Scale Societies.* Oxford: Oxford University Press.

Herdt, Gilbert H. 1981. *Guardians of the Flutes: Idioms of Masculinity.* New York: McGraw-Hill.

Herdt, Gilbert H. 1987. *The Sambia.* New York: Holt, Rinehart and Winston.

Herdt, Gilbert H. (Ed.). 1996. *Third Sex, Third Gender: Beyond Sexual Dimorphism in Culture and History.* New York: Zone.

Herrenstein, Richard J., and Charles A. Murray. 1994. *The Bell Curve: Intelligence and Class Structure in American Life.* New York: Free Press.

Hester, Marianne. 1988. "Who Were the Witches?" *Studies in Sexual Politics* 26–27:1–22.

Hill, Jane H. 1998. "Language, Race, and White Public Space." *American Anthropologist* 100:680–689.

Hirschfeld, Lawrence A. 1996. *Race in the Making.* Cambridge, MA: MIT Press/Bradford Books.

Hobsbawm, Eric, and Terence Ranger (Eds.). 1983. *The Invention of Tradition.* Cambridge: Cambridge University Press.

Hochschild, Adam. 1998. *King Leopold's Ghost.* New York: Houghton Mifflin.

Hoebel, E. Adamson. 1960. *The Cheyennes: Indians of the Great Plains.* New York: Holt.

Hoebel, E. Adamson. 1974. *The Law of Primitive Man.* New York: Henry Holt.

Hoffer, Carol P. 1974. "Madam Yoko: Ruler of the Kpa Mende Confederacy." In M. Z. Rosaldo and L. Lamphere (Eds.), *Women, Culture and Society* (pp. 173–188). Stanford, CA: Stanford University Press.

Holthouse, David. 2005. "Arizona Showdown." *Southern Poverty Law Center Intelligence Report,* Summer.

Hopkins, Nicholas. 1987. "Mechanized Irrigation in Upper Egypt: The Role of Technology and the State in Agriculture." In B. Turner II and S. B. Brush (Eds.), *Comparative Farming Systems* (pp. 223–247). New York: Guilford.

Horowitz, Irving L. (Ed.). 1967. *The Rise and Fall of Project Camelot.* Cambridge, MA: MIT Press.

Horsley, Richard A. 1979. "Who Were the Witches? The Social Roles of the Accused in the European Witch Trials." *Journal of Interdisciplinary History* 9:689–715.

Hua, Cai. 2001. *A Society Without Fathers or Husbands: The Na of China.* Cambridge, MA: Zone Books.

Human Rights Watch. 2001. *Human Rights in Saudi Arabia: A Deafening Silence.* Available at http://hrw.org/backgrounder/mena/saudi/.

Human Rights Watch. 2004 "'Political Shari'a'? Human Rights and Islamic Law in Northern Nigeria." *Human Rights Watch* 16(9)A.

Igoe, Jim. 2004. *Conservation and Globalization: A Study of the National Parks and Indigenous Communities from East Africa to South Dakota.* Belmont, CA: Thomson/Wadsworth.

Intergovernmental Panel on Climate Change. 2007. *IPVV Fourth Assessment Report: Climate Change 2007: Synthesis Report.* Available at http://www.ipcc-wg2.org/.

Investment Company Institute. 2005. *Equity Ownership in America.* Washington, DC: Investment Company Institute.

Ireland, Doug. 2005. "Why is France Burning?" *The Nation,* November 28.

Isaacman, Allen. 1996. *Cotton Is the Mother of Poverty: Peasants, Work, and Rural Struggle in Colonial Mozambique (1938–1961).* Portsmouth, NH: Heinemann.

Ishemo, Shubi L. 1995. "Cultural Response to Forced Labour and Commodity Production in Portugal's African Colonies." *Social Identities* 1(1):95–110.

Jamali, Hafeez. 2007. "Anthropologists Should Shed Light on the Violence in Balochistan Province, Pakistan." *Anthropology News* 48(5):37–38.

Jones, Delmos J. 1995. "Anthropology and the Oppressed: A Reflection on 'Native' Anthropology." In E. L. Cerroni-Long (Ed.), *Insider Anthropology* (Napa Bulletin, Vol. 16, pp. 58–70). Washington, DC: American Anthropological Association.

Judt, Tony. 2005. *Postwar: A History of Europe Since 1945.* New York: Penguin.

Kaplan, Flora E. S. (Ed.). 1997. *Queens, Queen Mothers, Priestesses, and Power: Case Studies in African Gender.* New York: New York Academy of the Sciences.

Karlen, Arno. 1995. *Man and Microbes: Disease and Plagues in History and Modern Times.* New York: G. P. Putnam's Sons.

Kelly, Gail P. 1986. "Learning to Be Marginal: Schooling in Interwar French West Africa." *Journal of Asian and African Studies* 21:171–184.

Kepel, Gilles. 2005. *The Roots of Radical Islam.* London: Saqi.

Kilbride, Philip L. 1994. *Plural Marriage for Our Times: A Reinvented Option?* Westport, CT: Bergin and Garvey.

Kilbride, Philip L. 2004. "Plural and Same Sex Marriage." *Anthropology News* 45(5):17.

Kilbride, Philip L. 2006. "African Polygyny: Family Values and Contemporary Changes." In Aaron Podolefsky and Peter J. Brown (Eds.), *Applying Cultural Anthropology: An Introductory Reader* (5th ed., pp. 201–208). Mountain View, CA: Mayfield.

Kim, Jim Yong, Joyce V. Millen, Alec Irwin, and John Gershman. 2000. *Dying for Growth: Global Inequality and the Health of the Poor.* Monroe, ME: Common Courage Press.

Klein, Laura F. 1976. "'She's One of Us, You Know': The Public Life of Tlingit Women: Traditional, Historical, and Contemporary Perspectives." *Western Canadian Journal of Anthropology* 6(3):164–183.

Klein, Laura F. 1995. "Mother as Clanswoman: Rank and Gender in Tlingit Society." In L. F. Klein and L. A. Ackerman (Eds.), *Women and Power in Native North America* (pp. 28–45). Norman, OK: University of Oklahoma Press.

Klein, Laura F., and Lillian A. Ackerman (Eds.). 1995. *Woman and Power in Native North America.* Norman, OK: University of Oklahoma Press.

Kluckhohn, Clyde. 1959. "The Philosophy of the Navaho Indians." In M. H. Fried (Ed.), *Readings in Anthropology* (Vol. 2). New York: Crowell.

Kofinas, Gary. 2007. *Subsistence Hunting in a Global Economy.* Retrieved June 12, 2007. Available at http://arcticcircle.uconn.edu/NatResources/subsistglobal.html.

Kohn, Hans. 1958. "Reflections on Colonialism." In R. Strausz-Hupe and H. W. Hazard (Eds.), *The Idea of Colonialism* (pp. 2–16). New York: Praeger.

Kottak, Conrad P. 1992. *Assault on Paradise: Social Change in a Brazilian Village* (2nd ed.). New York: McGraw-Hill.

Krakauer, Jon. 2003. *Under the Banner of Heaven: A Story of Violent Faith.* New York: Doubleday.

Krauss, Michael E. 1992. "The World's Languages in Crisis." *Language* 68(1): 6–10.

Kristoff, Nicholas, and Sheryl WuDunn. 2000. "The Cheers for Sweatshops." *New York Times,* September 24.

Kulick, Don. 1998. *Travesti: Sex, Gender, and Culture Among Brazilian Transgendered Prostitutes.* Chicago: University of Chicago Press.

Labov, William. 1972. *Language in the Inner City.* Philadelphia: University of Pennsylvania Press.

Labov, William, Sharon Ash, and Charles Boburg. 2005. *Atlas of North American English: Phonetics, Phonology and Sound Change.* Berlin: Mouton de Gruyter.

Lamphere, Louise (Ed.). 1992. *Structuring Diversity: Ethnographic Perspectives on the New Immigration.* Chicago: University of Chicago Press.

Lamphere, Louise. 1997. "The Domestic Sphere of Women and the Public World of Men: The Strengths and Limitations of an Anthropological Dichotomy." In C. B. Brettell and C. F. Sargent (Eds.), *Gender in Cross Cultural Perspective* (2nd ed., pp. 82–91). Upper Saddle River, NJ: Prentice Hall.

Lamphere, Louise. 2005. "The Domestic Sphere of Women and the Public World of Men: The Strength and Limitations of an Anthropological Dichotomy." In Caroline B. Brettell and Carolyn F. Sargent (Eds.), *Gender in Cross-Cultural Perspective* (4th ed., pp. 86–94). Upper Saddle River, NJ: Pearson/Prentice Hall.

Lapidus, Ira M. 1988. *A History of Islamic Societies.* Cambridge: Cambridge University Press.

Lareau, Annette. 2003. *Unequal Childhoods: Class, Race, and Family Life.* Berkeley, CA: University of California.

Lassiter, Luke Eric. 2004. "Collaborative Ethnography." *AnthroNotes* 25(1):1–9.

Leacock, Eleanor Burke. 1981. *Myths of Male Dominance.* New York: Monthly Review Press.

Leathers, Dale G. 1997. *Successful Nonverbal Communication* (3rd ed.). Boston: Allyn and Bacon.

LeDuff, Charlie. 2006a. "American Album: As the Jobs Go South, the Hope Goes with Them." *New York Times,* October 30, p. A16.

LeDuff, Charlie. 2006b. "Dreams in the Dark at the Drive-Through Window." *New York Times,* November 27, p. A12.

Lee, Richard B. 1984. *The Dobe !Kung.* New York: Holt, Rinehart and Winston.

Lee, Richard B. 2000. "Indigenism and Its Discontents: Anthropology and the Small Peoples at the Millennium." Keynote address at the annual meeting of the American Ethnological Society, Tampa, Florida, March 2000.

Lee, Richard B. 2003. *The Dobe Ju/'hoansi* (3rd ed.). Belmont, CA: Wadsworth.

Lefever, Harry G. 1996. "When the Saints Go Riding In: Santeria in Cuba and the United States." *Journal for the Scientific Study of Religion* 35:318–330.

Lemert, Edwin M. 1997. *The Trouble with Evil: Social Control at the Edge of Morality.* Albany, NY: State University of New York Press.

Lepowsky, Maria. 1993. *Fruit of the Motherland: Gender in an Egalitarian Society.* New York: Columbia University Press.

Lesser, Alexander. 1933. *The Pawnee Ghost Dance Hand Game: Ghost Dance Revival and Ethnic Identity.* Lincoln, NE: University of Nebraska.

Levine, Mary Ann, and Rita Wright. 1999. "COSWA Corner." *Society for American Archaeology Bulletin* 17(2).

Levinson, David. 1989. "Family Violence in Cross-Cultural Perspective." *Frontiers of Anthropology* (Vol. 1). Newbury Park, CA: Sage.

Levinson, David. 1996. *Religion: A Crosscultural Dictionary.* New York: Oxford University Press.

Lévi-Strauss, Claude. 1969. *The Elementary Structures of Kinship.* Boston: Beacon Press. (Originally published 1949.)

Lewchuk, Wayne A. 1993. "Men and Monotony: Fraternalism as a Managerial Strategy at the Ford Motor Company." *Journal of Economic History* 53(4):824–856.

Lewis, Richard D. 1996. *When Cultures Collide: Managing Successfully Across Cultures.* London: Nicholas Brealey.

Lewis, Rupert. 1998. "Marcus Garvey and the Early Rastafarians: Continuity and Discontinuity." In Nathaniel Murrell, William Spencer, and Adrian McFarlane (Eds.), *Chanting Down Babylon: The Rastafari Reader* (pp. 145–158). Philadelphia: Temple University Press.

Lewis, Tom. 1991. *Empire of the Air: The Men Who Made Radio.* New York: Harper Perennial.

Lexington. 2005. "Minding About the Gap." *The Economist,* June 9.

Lichtenberg, Judith. 1994. "Population Policy and the Clash of Cultures." In L. A. Mazur (Ed.), *Beyond the Numbers: A Reader on Population, Consumption, and Environment* (pp. 273–280). Washington, DC: Island Press.

Lindstrom, Lamont. 1993. *Cargo Cult: Strange Stories of Desire from Melanesia and Beyond.* Honolulu, HI: University of Hawaii Press.

Lockwood, Victoria. 2005. "The Impact of Development on Women: The Interplay of Material Conditions and Gender Ideology." In Caroline B. Brettell and Carolyn F. Sargent (Eds.), *Gender in Cross Cultural Perspective* (4th ed.) (pp. 500–514). Upper Saddle River, NJ: Prentice Hall.

Lopez, Ian Haney. 2006. *White by Law: The Legal Construction of Race* (Revised and updated 10th anniversary ed.). New York: New York University Press.

Lovejoy, Paul E. 1983. *Transformations in Slavery: A History of Slavery in Africa.* Cambridge: Cambridge University Press.

Luce, Edward. 2007. *In Spite of the Gods: The Strange Rise of Modern India.* New York: Doubleday.

Luker, Kristin. 1996. *Dubious Conceptions: The Politics of Teenage Pregnancy.* Cambridge, MA: Harvard University Press.

Lutkehaus, Nancy C., and Paul B. Roscoe (Eds.). 1995. *Gender Rituals: Female Initiation in Melanesia.* New York: Routledge.

Lynch, Owen K. 1969. *The Politics of Untouchability.* New York: Columbia University Press.

Lyon-Callo, Vincent. 2004. *Inequality, Poverty, and Neoliberal Governance: Activist Ethnography in the Homeless Sheltering Industry.* Toronto: Broadview Press.

MacCormack, Carol P. Hoffer. 1974. "Madam Yoko: Ruler of the Kpa Mende Confederacy." In Michele Z. Rosaldo and Louise Lamphere (Eds.), *Woman, Culture and Society* (pp. 171–187). Stanford: Stanford University Press.

Malinowski, Bronislaw. 1929a. "Practical Anthropology." *Africa* 2:22–38.

Malinowski, Bronislaw. 1929b. *The Sexual Life of Savages.* New York: Harcourt, Brace and World.

Malinowski, Bronislaw. 1935. *Coral Gardens and Their Magic.* New York: American Book Company.

Malinowski, Bronislaw. 1948. *Magic, Science, and Religion and other Essays.* New York: Free Press.

Malinowski, Bronislaw. 1984. *Argonauts of the Western Pacific.* Prospect Heights, IL: Waveland. (Originally published 1922.)

Malinowski, Bronislaw. 1992. *Magic, Science, and Religion.* Prospect Heights, IL: Waveland. (Originally published 1954.)

Malveaux, Julianne. 2005. "Sweatshops Aren't History Just Yet." *USA Today,* March 18.

Marcus, George E., and Michael M. J. Fischer. 1986. *Anthropology as Culture Critique: An Experimental Moment in the Human Sciences.* Chicago: University of Chicago Press.

Marlowe, Frank W. 2004. "Marital Residence Among Foragers." *Current Anthropology* 45(2):277–284.

Marshall, Donald. 1971. "Sexual Behavior on Mangaia." In D. S. Marshall and R. C. Suggs (Eds.), *Human Sexual Behavior: Variations in the Ethnographic Spectrum* (pp. 163–172). New York: Basic Books.

Marshall, John. 2002. *A Kalahari Family* (330 mins). Watertown, MA: Documentary Educational Resources.

Marshall, Mac. 1979. *Weekend Warriors.* Palo Alto, CA: Mayfield.

Martin, Andrew. 2008. "Largest Recall of Ground Beef Is Ordered." *New York Times,* February 18.

Martin, Emily. 1987. *The Woman in the Body.* New York: Beacon Press.

Martin, M. K., and Barbara Voorhies. 1975. *Female of the Species.* New York: Columbia University Press.

Martin, Philip. 2007. "Managing Labor Migration in the 21st Century." *City and Society* 19(1):5–18.

Marx, Anthony. 1998. *Making Race and Nation: A Comparison of South Africa, the United States and Brazil.* Cambridge: Cambridge University Press.

Maskus, Keith. 1997. "Should Core Labor Standards be Imposed Through International Trade Policy?" *World Bank Working Paper 1817.* Washington, DC: World Bank. Available at http://www.worldbank.org/research/trade/wp1817.html.

Mateu-Gelabert, Pedro, and Howard Lune. 2003. "School Violence: The Bidirectional Conflict Flow Between Neighborhood and School." *City & Community* 2(4):353–368.

Mateu-Gelabert, Pedro, and Howard Lune. 2007. "Street Codes in High School: School as an Educational Deterrent." *City & Community* 6(3):173–191.

Matory, J. Lorand. 1994. *Sex and the Empire That Is No More: Gender and the Politics of Metaphor in Oyo Yoruba Religion.* Minneapolis: University of Minnesota Press.

Matsumoto, David, and Tsutomu Kudoh. 1993. "American-Japanese Cultural Differences in Attributions of Personality Based on Smiles." *Journal of Nonverbal Communication* 17(4):231–243.

Matthews, Richard. 1997. "The Ebonic Plague Will Kill America Yet." *Atlanta Journal and Constitution,* January 23, p. A18.

Matthiessen, Peter. 2007. "Alaska: Big Oil and the Whales." *New York Review of Books* November 22:57–64.

Matzner, Andrew. 2001. *'O Au No Keia: Voices from Hawai'i's Mahu and Transgender Communities.* Philadelphia, PA: XLibris.

Mauss, Marcel. 1990. *The Gift: Form and Reason of Exchange in Archaic Societies* (W. D. Halls, Trans.). New York: W.W. Norton. (Originally published 1924.)

Maybury-Lewis, David. 1993. "A Special Sort of Pleading: Anthropology at the Service of Ethnic Groups." In W. A. Haviland and R. J. Gordon (Eds.), *Talking About People: Readings in Contemporary Cultural Anthropology* (pp. 16–24). Mountain View, CA: Mayfield.

Maybury-Lewis, David. 1997. *Indigenous Peoples, Ethnic Groups, and the State.* Boston: Allyn and Bacon.

McGee, R. Jon. 1990. *Life, Ritual, and Religion Among the Lacandon Maya.* Belmont, CA: Wadsworth.

McIntosh, Peggy. 1999. "White Privilege: Unpacking the Invisible Knapsack." In A. Podolefsky and P. J. Brown (Eds.), *Applying Cultural Anthropology: An Introductory Reader* (4th ed., pp. 134–137). Mountain View, CA: Mayfield.

Mead, Margaret. 1963. *Sex and Temperament in Three Primitive Societies.* New York: Dell. (Originally published 1935.)

Mead, Margaret. 1971. *Coming of Age in Samoa.* New York: Morrow. (Originally published 1928.)

Meier, Matt S., and Feliciano Ribera. 1993. *Mexican Americans/American Mexicans: From Conquistadors to Chicanos.* New York: Hill & Wang.

Melendez, Edwin. 1993. *Colonial Subjects: Critical Perspectives on Contemporary Puerto Ricans.* Boston: South End Press.

Merrick, Amy. 2004. "Gap Offers Unusual Look at Factory Conditions." *Wall Street Journal,* May 12.

Merry, Sally E. 1981. *Urban Danger: Life in a Neighborhood of Strangers.* Philadelphia: Temple University Press.

Merry, Sally E. 1991. "Law and Colonialism." *Law and Society Review* 25:891–922.

Merry, Sally E. 2000. *Colonizing Hawai'i: The Cultural Power of Law.* Princeton, NJ: Princeton University Press.

Messenger, John C. 1971. "Sex and Repression in an Irish Folk Community." In D. S. Marshall and R. C. Suggs (Eds.), *Human Sexual Behavior: Variations in the Ethnographic Spectrum* (pp. 3–37). New York: Basic Books.

Meyer, Stephen. 2004. "The Degradation of Work Revisited: Workers and Technology in the American Auto

Industry, 1900–2000." *Automobile in American Life and Society.* Available at: http://www.autolife.umd.umich.edu/Labor/L_Overview/L_Overview3.htm.

Mintz, Sidney W. 1985. *Sweetness and Power: The Place of Sugar in Modern History.* New York: Penguin.

Mishra, Pankaj. 2006. "The Myth of the New India." *New York Times,* July 6.

Moberg, David. 2006. Maytag Moves to Mexico. In D. Stanley Eitzen and Maxine Baca Zinn (Eds.), *Globalization: The Transformation of Social Worlds* (pp. 92–96). Belmont, CA: Wadsworth.

Monaghan, Leila. 1997. "Ebonics Discussion Continues." *Anthropology Newsletter* 38(2):44–45.

Montagu, Ashley. 1978. *Touching: The Human Significance of the Skin* (2nd ed.). New York: Harper and Row.

Mooney, James. 1973. *The Ghost-Dance Religion and the Sioux Outbreak of 1890.* Glorieta, NM: Rio Grande Press. (Originally published 1896.)

Moore, Kathleen M. 2000. "U.S. Immigration Reform and the Meaning of Responsibility." *Studies in Law, Politics, and Society* 20:125–155.

Moore, Sally Falk. 1978. *Law as Process: An Anthropological Approach.* London: Routledge and Kegan Paul.

Morgan, Marcyliena. 2004. "Speech Community." In Alassandro Duranti (Ed.), *A Companion to Linguistic Anthropology* (pp. 3–33). Malden, MA: Blackwell.

Moser, Caroline. 1993. *Gender Planning and Development: Theory, Practice, and Training.* New York: Routledge.

Murdock, George Peter. 1949. *Social Structure.* New York: Free Press.

Murphy, Joseph M. 1989. *Santeria: An African Religion in America.* Boston: Beacon Press.

Murphy, Robert. 1964. "Social Distance and the Veil." *American Anthropologist* 66:1257–1273.

Murphy, Yolanda, and Robert Murphy. 1974. *Women of the Forest.* New York: Columbia University Press.

Myerhoff, Barbara G. 1974. *Peyote Hunt: The Sacred Journey of the Huichol Indians.* Ithaca: Cornell University Press.

Myerhoff, Barbara. 1978. *Number Our Days.* New York: Simon and Schuster.

Myers, Steven Lee, Andrew C. Revkin, Simon Romero, and Clifford Krauss. 2005. "Old Ways of Life Are Fading as the Arctic Thaws." *New York Times,* October 20, p. A1.

Nader, Laura. 2006. "Human Rights and Moral Imperialism: A Double-Edged Story." *Anthropology News* 47(7):6.

Nagashima, Kenji, and James A. Schellenberg. 1997. "Situational Differences in Intentional Smiling: A Cross-Cultural Exploration." *Journal of Social Psychology* 137:297–301.

Nagengast, Carole. 1994. "Violence, Terror, and the Crisis of the State." In B. J. Siegel (Ed.), *Annual Review of Anthropology* (Vol. 23, pp. 109–136). Stanford, CA: Stanford University Press.

Nanda, Serena. 1999. *Neither Man nor Woman: The Hijras of India* (2nd ed.). Belmont, CA: Wadsworth.

Nanda, Serena. 2000a. "Arranging a Marriage in India." In P. R. DeVita (Ed.), *Stumbling Towards Truth: Anthropologists at Work* (pp. 196–204). Prospect Heights, IL: Waveland.

Nanda, Serena. 2000b. *Gender Diversity: Crosscultural Variations.* Prospect Heights, IL: Waveland.

Nanda, Serena. 2004. "South African Museums and the Creation of a New National Identity." *American Anthropologist* 106(2):379–384.

Narasimhan, Sakuntala. 1990. *Sati: Widow Burning in India.* New York: Anchor/Doubleday.

Narayan, Kirin. 1993. "How Native Is a 'Native' Anthropologist?" *American Anthropologist* 95:671–686.

Nash, June. 1970. *In the Eyes of the Ancestors: Belief and Behavior in a Mayan Community.* New Haven: Yale University Press.

Nash, June. 1993. "Introduction: Traditional Arts and Changing Markets in Middle America." In June Nash and Helen Safa (Eds.), *Crafts in the World Market* (pp. 1–24). Albany: State University of New York Press.

Nash, June. 1994. "Global Integration and Subsistence Insecurity." *American Anthropologist* 96:7–30.

Nash, Maning. 1961. "The Social Context of Economic Choice in a Small Society." *Man* 219:186–191.

Neckerman, Kathryn M. (Ed.). 2004. *Social Inequality.* New York: The Russell Sage Foundation.

Nelson, Edward William. 1983. *The Eskimo About Bering Strait.* Washington: The Smithsonian Institution Press.

Nelson, Ekow and Michael Gyamerah. 2007. *Independence or 'aid-dependence'?* Available at http://www.ghanaweb.com/GhanaHomePage/features/artikel.php?ID=121437.

Netting, Robert. 1977. *Cultural Ecology.* Menlo Park, CA: Cummings.

New York Times. 2005. *Class Matters.* New York: New York Times.

New York Times. 2005. *Graphic: How Class Works.* Available at http://www.nytimes.com/packages/html/national/20050515_CLASS_GRAPHIC/index_03.html.

New York Times. 2006. "Racial Disparities Persist." *New York Times* November 14, p. A22.

Newman, Katherine S. 1999. *Falling from Grace: Downward Mobility in an Age of Affluence* (2nd ed.). Berkeley: University of California.

Newman, Katherine S. 2006. *Chutes and Ladders: Navigating the Low-Wage Labor Market.* New York: Russell Sage Foundation/Harvard University Press.

Newman, Katherine, and Victor Chen. 2007. *The Missing Class: Portraits of the Near Poor in America.* Boston: Beacon.

Newson, L. 1999. "Disease and Immunity in the Pre-Spanish Philippines." *Social Science and Medicine* 48: 1833–1850.

Ngai, Pun. 2005. *Made in China: Women Factory Workers in a Global Workplace.* Durham: Duke University Press.

Nicolaisen, Ida. 2006. "Anthropology Should Actively Promote Human Rights." *Anthropology News* 47(7):6.

Nielsen, Joyce McCarl. 1990. *Sex and Gender in Society: Perspectives on Stratification* (2nd ed.). Prospect Heights, IL: Waveland.

Nike. 2005. *Disclosure List.* Available at http://www.nike.com/nikebiz/gc/mp/pdf/disclosure_list_2005-06.pdf.

Nisbett, Richard E. 2007. "All Brains are the Same Color." *New York Times,* December 9, Section 4 (Science), p. 11.

Norbeck, Edward. 1974. *Religion in Human Life: Anthropological Views.* Prospect Heights, IL: Waveland.

Norgren, Jill. 1996. *The Cherokee Cases: The Confrontation of Law and Politics.* New York: McGraw-Hill.

Norgren, Jill, and Serena Nanda. 1996. *American Cultural Pluralism and Law* (2nd ed.). New York: Praeger.

Norgren, Jill, and Serena Nanda. 2006. *American Cultural Pluralism and Law* (3rd ed.). Westport, CT: Praeger.

Offiong, Daniel A. 1983. "Witchcraft Among the Ibibio of Nigeria." *African Studies Review* 26:107–124.

Ogbu, John. 1978. "African Bridewealth and Women's Status." *American Ethnologist* 5:241–260.

O'Kelly, Charlotte G., and Larry S. Carney. 1986. *Women and Men in Society: Cross-Cultural Perspectives on Gender Stratification.* Belmont: Wadsworth.

Oliver, Mary Beth. 2003. "Race and Crime in the Media: Research From a Media Effects Tradition." In A. Valdivia (Ed.), *A Companion to Media Studies* (pp. 421–436). London: Blackwell Publishing.

Ong, Aihwa. 1989. "Center, Periphery, and Hierarchy: Gender in Southeast Asia." In S. Morgen (Ed.), *Gender and Anthropology: Critical Reviews for Research and Teaching* (pp. 294–303). Washington, DC: American Anthropological Association.

Oreskes, Naomi. 2004. "The Scientific Consensus on Climate Change." *Science* 306(5702):1686.

Organization for Economic Cooperation and Development. 2007. *United States Donor Information.* Available at http://www.oecd.org/dataoecd/42/30/40039096.gif.

Oriard, Michael. 1993. *Reading Football: How the Popular Press Created an American Spectacle.* Chapel Hill: University of North Carolina Press.

Ottley, Bruce L., and Jean G. Zorn. 1983. "Criminal Law in Papua New Guinea: Code, Custom and the Courts in Conflict." *American Journal of Comparative Law* 31:251–300.

Page, Tim. 2007. "Parallel Play: A Life of Restless Isolation Explained." *The New Yorker,* August 20.

Paiement, Jason J. 2007. "Anthropology and Development." *National Association for the Practice of Anthropology Bulletin* 27(1):196–223.

Palkovich, Anna M. 1994. "Historic Epidemics of the American Pueblos." In C. S. Larsen and G. R. Milner (Eds.), *In the Wake of Contact: Biological Responses to Conquest* (pp. 87–95). New York: Wiley.

Paredes, Anthony J. (Ed.). 2006. Introduction to In Focus: The Impact of the Hurricanes of 2005 on New Orleans and the Gulf Coast of the United States. *American Anthropologist* 108(4):637–642.

Patterson, Orlando. 2006. "A Poverty of the Mind." *New York Times,* March 26.

Peacock, James, et al. 2007. "AAA Commission on the Engagement of Anthropology With the US Security and Intelligence Communities Final Report November 4, 2007." Washington, DC: American Anthropological Association.

Peacock, Nadine R. 1991. "Rethinking the Sexual Division of Labor: Reproduction and Women's Work among the Efe." In M. di Leonardo (Ed.), *Gender and the Crossroads of Knowledge: Feminist Anthropology in the Postmodern Era* (pp. 339–360). Berkeley, CA: University of California Press.

Pear, Robert. 2006. "Married and Single Parents Spending More Time With Children, Study Finds." *New York Times,* October 17.

Peoples, James G. 1990. "The Evolution of Complex Stratification in Eastern Micronesia." *Micronesia Suppl.* 2:291–302.

Peregrine, Peter N., Carol R. Ember, and Melvin Ember. 2004. "Universal Patterns in Cultural Evolution: An Empirical Analysis Using Guttman Scaling." *American Anthropologist* 106(1):145–149.

Peyrefitte, Alain. 1992. *The Immobile Empire* (Jon Rothschild, Trans.). New York: Knopf.

Pinker, Steven. 1994. *The Language Instinct.* New York: William Morrow.

Pitts, Leonard. 2007. "At Large, Replying to Those E-mails about Vick." *Miami Herald,* Sept. 12.

Plattner, Stuart. 1989. "Marxism." In S. Plattner (Ed.), *Economic Anthropology* (pp. 379–396). Stanford, CA: Stanford University Press.

Polyani, Karl. 1944. *The Great Transformation.* New York: Holt, Rinehart and Winston.

Population Reference Bureau. 2005. *2005 World Population Data Sheet.* Washington, DC: Population Reference Bureau. Available at http://www.prb.org/pdf05/05WorldDataSheet_Eng.pdf.

Port, Bob. 2001. "Sweat and Tears Still in Fashion in City." *New York Daily News,* July 8.

Potash, Betty. 1989. "Gender Relations in Sub-Saharan Africa." In S. Morgen (Ed.), *Gender and Anthropology: Critical Reviews for Research and Teaching* (pp. 189–227). Washington, DC: American Anthropological Association.

Prah, Kwesi K. 1990. "Anthropologists, Colonial Administrators, and the Lotuko of Eastern Equatoria, Sudan: 1952–1953." *African Journal of Sociology* 3(2):70–86.

Press, Eyal. 2007. "The Missing Class." *The Nation,* July 26.

Prunier, Gerard. 1995. *The Rwanda Crisis: History of a Genocide.* New York: Columbia University Press.

Radcliffe-Brown, A. R. 1965. *Structure and Function in Primitive Society.* New York: Free Press. (Originally published 1952.)

Ramet, Sabrina P. 1996. *Balkan Babel: Politics, Culture, and Religion in Yugoslavia* (2nd ed.). Boulder, CO: Westview.

Rasmusen Reports. 2006. *85% Support English as Official Language of U.S.* Friday, June 9. Available at http://www.rasmussenreports.com/public_content/politics/current_events/general_current_events/85_support_english_as_official_language_of_u_s.

Rasmussen, Susan. 2005. "Pastoral Nomadism and Gender: Status, Prestige, Economic Contribution, and Division of Labor among the Tuareg of Niger." In Caroline B. Brettell and Carolyn F. Sargent (Eds.), *Gender in Cross Cultural Perspective* (4th ed., pp. 155–168). Upper Saddle River, NJ: Pearson/Prentice Hall.

Reed, Jr., Adolph. 2006. "Undone by Neoliberalism." *The Nation,* September 18, 2006, p. 26.

Reeves, Glenn. 2006. "Pursuing Opportunity 'Away From Home': Encountering New Challenges and Relationships." *Anthropology News* 47(9):8–9.

Reichmann, Rebecca. 1995. "Brazil's Denial of Race." *NACLA Report on the Americas* 28(6):35–43.

Renfrew, Colin, April McMahon, and Larry Trask (Eds.). 2000. *Time Depth in Historical Linguistics* (Vols. 1 and 2). Cambridge: The McDonald Institute for Archaeological Research.

Rhode, D. L., S. Olson, and J. T. Chang. 2004. "Modelling the Recent Common Ancestry of All Living Humans." *Nature* 431(7008):562–566.

Richards, Audrey I. 1956. *Chisungu: A Girl's Initiation Ceremony among the Bemba of Northern Rhodesia.* New York: Grove Press.

Ricklefs, Merle C. 1990. "Balance and Military Innovation in 17th Century Java." *History Today* 40(11):40–47.

Ricklefs, Merle C. 1993. *A History of Modern Indonesia since c. 1300* (2nd ed.). Stanford, CA: Stanford University Press.

Rivers, W. H. R. 1906. *The Todas.* London: Macmillan.

Roberts, Alan H., D. G. Kewman, L. Mercier, and M. Hovell. 1993. "The Power of Nonspecific Effects in Healing: Implications for Psychosocial and Biological Treatments." *Clinical Psychology Review* 13:375–391.

Roberts, Sam. 2006. "It's Official: To Be Married Means to Be Outnumbered." *New York Times,* October 15.

Rohde, David. 2007. "Army Enlists Anthropologists in War Zones." *The New York Times,* October 5.

Roland, Edna. 2001. The Economics of Racism: People of African Descent in Brazil. Paper prepared for the International Council on Human Rights Policy Seminar on the Economics of Racism, November 24–25, Geneva.

Rosaldo, Michelle Z., and Louise Lamphere. 1974. "Introduction." In M. Z. Rosaldo and L. Lamphere (Eds.), *Women, Culture and Society* (pp. 1–16). Stanford, CA: Stanford University Press.

Roscoe, Paul B. 1995. "Initiation in Cross-Cultural Perspective." In Nancy C. Lutkehaus and Paul B. Roscoe (Eds.), *Gender Rituals: Female Initiation in Melanesia* (pp. 219–238). New York: Routledge.

Roscoe, Paul. 2003. "Margaret Mead, Reo Fortune, and Mountain Arapesh Warfare." *American Anthropologist* 105(3):581–591.

Roscoe, Will. 1991. *The Zuni Man-Woman.* Albuquerque: University of New Mexico Press.

Roscoe, Will. 1995. "Strange Craft, Strange History, Strange Folks: Cultural Amnesia and the Case of Lesbian and Gay Studies." *American Anthropologist* 97:448–452.

Rosman, Abraham, and Paula G. Rubel. 1971. *Feasting with Mine Enemy: Rank and Exchange among Northwest Coast Societies.* Prospect Heights, IL: Waveland.

Ross, Eric B., 1998. *The Malthus Factor: Poverty, Politics and Population in Capitalist Development.* New York: St. Martin's Press.

Rothenberg-Aalami, Jessica. 2004. "Coming Full Circle? Forging Missing Links Along Nike's Integrated Production Networks." *Global Networks* 4(4):335–354.

Rothstein, Richard. 2005. "Defending Sweatshops: Too Much Logic, Too Little Evidence." *Dissent* 52(2):41–47.

Ryan, John Paul (Ed.). 1999. "Immigration: A Dialogue on Policy, Law, and Values." *Focus on Law Studies* 14(2):1–16.

Sacks, Karen Brodkin. 1982. *Sisters and Wives.* Westport, CT: Greenwood.

Sacks, Oliver. 1995. *An Anthropologist on Mars: Seven Paradoxical Tales.* New York: Knopf.

Sage, George H. 1999. "Justice Do It! The Nike Transnational Advocacy Network: Organization, Collective Actions, and Outcomes." *Sociology of Sport Journal* 16:206–235.

Sahlins, Marshall. 1961. "The Segmentary Lineage: An Organization of Predatory Expansion." *American Anthropologist* 63:332–345.

Sahlins, Marshall. 1971. "Poor Man, Rich Man, Big Man, Chief." In J. P. Spradley and D. W. McCurdy (Eds.), *Conformity and Conflict* (pp. 362–376). Boston: Little, Brown.

Sahlins, Marshall. 1972. *Stone Age Economics.* Chicago: Aldine.

Said, Edward W. 1978. *Orientalism.* New York: Random House.

Salzman, Philip C. 2000. *Black Tents of Baluchistan.* Washington, DC: Smithsonian.

Salzmann, Zdenek. 1993. *Language, Culture and Society.* Boulder, CO: Westview Press.

Sanchez, Rene. 1997. "Ebonics Debate Comes to Capitol Hill; 'Political Correctness Gone Out of Control,' Sen. Faircloth Says." *Washington Post,* January 24, p. A15.

Sánchez-Eppler, Benigno. 1992. "Telling Anthropology: Zora Neale Hurston and Gilberto Freyre Disciplined in Their Field-Home-Work." *American Literary History* 4:464–488.

Sanday, Peggy Reeves. 1981. *Female Power and Male Dominance.* New York: Cambridge University Press.

Sanday, Peggy Reeves. 1992. *Fraternity Gang Rape: Sex, Brotherhood, and Privilege on Campus.* New York: New York University Press.

SAPRI. 2004. *Structural Adjustment: The Policy Roots of Economic Crisis, Poverty and Inequality.* London: Zed Books.

SAPRIN. 2004. *Structural Adjustment: The SAPRI Report.* London: Zed Books.

Scaglion, Richard. 1981. "Homicide Compensation in Papua New Guinea: Problems and Prospects." In *Law Reform Commission of Papua New Guinea Monograph 1.* New Guinea: Office of Information.

Scammell, G. V. 1989. *The First Imperial Age.* London: HarperCollins Academic.

Schensul, Stephen L. 1997. "The Anthropologist in Medicine: Critical Perspectives on Cancer and Street Addicts." *Reviews in Anthropology* 26(1):57–69.

Schepartz, L. A. 1993. "Language and Modern Human Origins." *Yearbook of Physical Anthropology* 36:91–96.

Schlegel, Alice, and Herbert Barry III. 1991. *Adolescence: An Anthropological Inquiry.* New York: Free Press (Macmillan).

Schlosser, Eric. 2005. *Fast Food Nation: The Dark Side of the All-American Meal.* New York: Harper Perennial.

Schneider, Harold K. 1973. "The Subsistence Role of Cattle among the Pokot in East Africa." In E. P. Skinner (Ed.), *Peoples and Cultures of Africa.* Garden City, NY: Natural History Press.

Schneider, Jane. 2002. "World Markets: Anthropological Perspectives." In Jeremy MacClancy, (Ed.), *Exotic No More: Anthropology on the Front Lines.* Chicago: University of Chicago Press.

Scott, James. 1992. *Domination and the Arts of Resistance: Hidden Transcripts.* New Haven, CT: Yale University Press.

Scott, Janny. 2005. "Life at the Top in America Isn't Just Better, It's Longer." *New York Times,* May 16.

Scott, Janny, and David Leonhardt. 2005. "Class in America: Shadowy Lines That Still Divide." *New York Times,* May 15.

Seddon, Judith S. 1993. "Possible or Impossible?: A Tale of Two Worlds in One Country." *Yale Journal of Law and Feminism* 5(2):265–288.

Seitlyn, David. 1993. "Spiders In and Out of Court, or 'The Long Legs & the Law': Styles of Spider Divination in Their Sociological Contexts." *Africa* 63:219–240.

Service, Elman. 1962. *Primitive Social Organization.* New York: Random House.

Service, Elman. 1971. *Profiles in Ethnology.* New York: Harper and Row.

Shanklin, Eugenia. 1994. *Anthropology and Race.* Belmont, CA: Wadsworth.

Sheehan, John. 1982. *The Enchanted Ring: The Untold Story of Penicillin.* Cambridge, MA: MIT Press.

Sheriff, Robin E. 2001. *Dreaming Equality: Color, Race and Racism in Urban Brazil.* East Brunswick, NJ: Rutgers University Press. 2001.

Shostak, Marjorie. 1983. *Nisa: The Life and Words of a !Kung Woman.* New York: Random House.

Simeone,William E. 1995. *Rifles, Blankets, and Beads: Identity, History, and the Northern Athapaskan Potlatch.* Norman, OK: University of Oklahoma Press.

Simmons, Tavia, and Grace O'Neill. 2001. "Households and Families 2000." Census 2000 Brief. Washington: U.S. Census. Available at http://www.census.gov/prod/2001pubs/c2kbr01-8.pdf.

Sinclair, Upton. 1906. *The Jungle.* New York: Doubleday.

Smedley, Audrey. 1998. "'Race' and the Construction of Human Identity." *American Anthropologist* 100:690–702.

Smith, Roberta. 2005. "From a Mushroom Cloud, a Burst of Art Reflecting Japan's Psyche." *New York Times,* April 8, p. E33.

Southern Baptist Convention. 2006. Resolution 5 of the SBC Meeting, 2006, June 13–14: "On Alcohol Use in America." Available at http://www.sbc.net/resolutions/amResolution.asp?ID=1156.

Sponsel, Leslie E. (Ed.). 1995. *Indigenous Peoples and the Future of Amazonia: An Ecological Anthropology of an Endangered World.* Tucson: University of Arizona Press.

Spradley, James. 1988. *You Owe Yourself a Drunk.* Boston: Little, Brown.

Stannard, David E. 2005. *Honor Killing: Race, Rape, and Clarence Darrow's Spectacular Last Case.* New York: Penguin.

Stearns, M. L. 1975. "Life Cycle Rituals of the Modern Haida." In D. B. Carlisle (Ed.), *Contributions to Canadian Ethnology* (pp. 129–169). Ottawa: National Museum of Man.

Steiner, Christopher B. 2002. "Art/Anthropology/Museums: Revulsions and Revolutions. In Jeremy MacClancy (Ed.), *Exotic No More: Anthropology on the Front Lines* (pp. 400–417). Chicago: University of Chicago Press.

Stepick, Alex. 1998. *Pride Against Prejudice: Haitians in the U.S.* Boston: Allyn and Bacon Publishers.

Stern, Pamela R. 1999. "Learning to Be Smart: An Exploration of the Culture of Intelligence in a Canadian Inuit Community." *American Anthropologist* 101:502–514.

Sternberg, Esther. 2002. "Walter B. Cannon and 'Voodoo' Death: A Perspective from 60 Years On." *American Journal of Public Health* 92: 1564–1566.

Stolberg, Sheryl Gay. 1999. "Black Mother's Mortality Rate is Under Scrutiny." *New York Times,* August 8, p. A1.

Stolcke, Verena. 1995. "Talking Culture: New Boundaries, New Rhetorics of Exclusion in Europe." *Current Anthropology* 36:1–7.

Stone, Linda, and Caroline James. 2005. "Dowry, Bride-Burning, and Female Power in India." In C. B. Brettell and C. F. Sargent (Eds.), *Gender in Cross-Cultural Perspective* (4th ed., pp. 312–320). Upper Saddle River, NJ: Prentice Hall.

Stonich, Susan C., Douglas L. Murray, and Peter R. Rossart. 1994. "Enduring Crises: The Human and Environmental Consequences of Nontraditional Export Growth in Central America." *Research in Economic Anthropology* 15:239–274.

Strathern, Marilyn. 1995. *Women in Between: Female Roles in a Male World: Mount Hagen, New Guinea.* Latham, MD: Rowman and Littlefield.

Stull, Donald D., and Michael J. Broadway. 2004. *Slaughterhouse Blues: The Meat and Poultry Industry in North America.* Belmont, CA: Wadsworth.

Stull, Donald D., Michael J. Broadway, and Ken C. Erickson. 1992. "The Price of a Good Steak: Beef Packing and Its Consequences for Garden City, Kansas." In L. Lamphere (Ed.), *Structuring Diversity: Ethnographic Perspectives on the New Immigration* (pp. 35–64). Chicago: University of Chicago Press.

Tang, Tiffany. 2007. "The Major-Career Connection." *Business Today Online Journal,* Wednesday, February 28.

Tessman, Irwin, and Jack Tessman. 2000. "Efficacy of Prayer: A Critical Examination of Claims." *Skeptical Inquirer* 24(2):31–33.

Tiger, Lionel, and Heather T. Fowler (Eds.). 1978. *Female Hierarchies.* Chicago: Beresford.

Todaro, Michael, and Stephen C. Smith. 2003. *Economic Development* (8th ed.). Harlow, UK: Pearson Addison Wesley.

Turnbull, Colin. 1968. "The Importance of Flux in Two Hunting Societies." In R. B. Lee and I. DeVore (Eds.), *Man the Hunter* (pp. 132–137). Chicago: Aldine.

Turner, Victor. 1967. *The Forest of Symbols: Aspects of Ndembu Ritual.* Ithaca: Cornell University Press.

Turner, Victor. 1969. *The Ritual Process: Structure and Antistructure.* Chicago: Aldine.

Tylor, Edward Burnett. 2008. "The Science of Culture." In R. Jon McGee and Richard L. Warms (Eds.), *Anthropological Theory: An Introductory Reader* (pp. 28–41). Boston: McGraw Hill.

Uchendu, Victor Chikezie. 1965. *The Igbo of Southeastern Nigeria.* New York: Holt, Rinehart and Winston.

Uchitelle, Louis. 2006. "Very Rich are Leaving the Merely Rich Behind." *New York Times,* November 27, p. A1.

Uchitelle, Louis. 2007. "Is There (Middle Class) Life After Maytag?" *New York Times,* August 26, p. A1.

UK National Archives. *Service Records for the First World War.* Available at http://www.nationalarchives.gov.uk/pathways/firstworldwar/service_records/sr_soldiers.htm.

United Nations. 2003. *The 2003 Revision and World Urbanization Prospects.* Available at http://esa.un.org/unup.

United States Bureau of Labor Statistics. 2005. *A Profile of the Working Poor, 2003.* U.S. Department of Labor. U.S. Bureau of Labor Statistics. Report 983.

United States Census Bureau. 2003. *Detailed Income Tabulations from the CPS.* Available at http://www.census.gov/hhes/www/income/dinctabs.html.

University of Virginia. 2006. *Choosing and Using Your Major.* Publication of University of Virginia, Office of Career Services. Available at http://www.career.virginia.edu/students/resources/handouts/choosing_a_major.pdf.

U.S. Census Bureau. 2008. *Statistical Abstract.* Available at http://www.census.gov/compendia/statab/.

Van Biema, David, and Jeff Chu. 2006. "Does God Want You To Be Rich?" *Time,* September 18.

van Donge, Jan Kees. 1992. "Agricultural Decline in Tanzania: The Case of the Uluguru Mountains." *African Affairs* 91:73–94.

van Gennep, Arnold. 1960. *The Rites of Passage.* Chicago: University of Chicago Press.

Vayda, Andrew P. 1976. *War in Ecological Perspective.* New York: Plenum.

Victor, David A. 1992. *International Business Communication.* New York: Harper Collins.

Vincent, Susan. 1998. "The Family in the Household: Women, Relationships, and Economic History in Peru." *Research in Economic Anthropology* 19:179–187.

Viswanathan, Gauri. 1988. "Currying Favor: The Politics of British Educational and Cultural Policy in India 1813–1854." *Social Text* 19–20(Fall): 85–104.

Walker, Anthony R. 1986. *The Toda of South India: A New Look.* Delhi: Hindustan Publishing Corporation.

Wallace, Anthony. 1970. *Death and Rebirth of the Seneca.* New York: Knopf.

Wallace, Anthony. 1999. *Jefferson and the Indians: The Tragic Fate of "The First Americans."* Cambridge, MA: Harvard University Press.

Wallerstein, Immanuel. 1995. *Historical Capitalism.* London: Verso.

Walley, Christine J. 1997. "Searching for 'Voices': Feminism, Anthropology, and the Global Debate over Female Genital Operations." *Cultural Anthropology* 12:405–438.

Warren, Kay B., and Susan C. Bourque. 1989. "Women, Technology, and Development Ideologies: Frameworks and Findings." In S. Morgen (Ed.), *Gender and Anthropology: Critical Reviews for Research and Teaching* (pp. 382–410). Washington, DC: American Anthropological Association.

Waters, Tony. 2006. "Who Stole Culture From Anthropology." *Anthropology News* 47(9):28–28.

Weiner, Annette B. 1976. *Women of Value, Men of Renown: New Perspectives on Trobriand Exchange.* Austin: University of Texas Press.

Wesch, Michael. 2007. "An In-Depth Look at the Cyber-Phenomenon of Our Time: Web 2.0 (Interview With Virginia Buege)." *The Lawlor Review* 15(2):10–16.

White, Benjamin. 1980. "Rural Household Studies in Anthropological Perspective." In H. Binswanger, R. Evenson, C. Florencio, and B. White (Eds.), *Rural Household Studies in Asia* (pp. 3–25). Singapore: Singapore University Press.

White, Geoffrey M. 1997. "Introduction: Public History and National Narrative." *Museum Anthropology* 21(1):3–6.

White, Jenny B. 1994. *Money Makes Us Relatives.* Austin, TX: University of Texas Press.

Whitehead, Harriet. 1981. "The Bow and the Burden Strap: A New Look at Institutionalized Homosexuality in Native North America." In S. B. Ortner and H. Whitehead (Eds.), *Sexual Meanings: The Cultural Construction of Gender and Sexuality* (pp. 80–115). Cambridge: Cambridge University Press.

Whiting, John, Richard Kluckhohn, and Albert Anthony. 1967. "The Function of Male Initiation Ceremonies at Puberty." In R. Endelman (Ed.), *Personality and Social Life* (pp. 294–308). New York: Random House.

Whorf, Benjamin L. 1941. "The Relation of Habitual Thought and Behavior to Language." In Leslie Spier (Ed.), *Language, Culture and Personality* (pp. 75–93). Menasha, WI: Sapir Memorial Publication Fund.

Wikan, Unni. 1977. "Man Becomes Woman: Transsexualism in Oman as a Key to Gender Roles." *Man* (new series) 12:304–319.

Wilk, Richard (Ed.). 2006. *Fast Food/Slow Food: The Cultural Economy of the Global Food System.* Lanham, MD: Altamira Press.

Wilkie, David S. 1988. "Hunters and Farmers of the African Forest." In J. S. Denslow and C. Padoch (Eds.), *People of the Tropical Rain Forest* (pp. 111–126). Berkeley, CA: University of California Press.

Williams, Trevor. 1984. *Howard Florey: Penicillin and After.* Oxford: Oxford University Press.

Williams, Walter. 1986. *The Spirit and the Flesh* (2nd ed.). Boston: Beacon Press.

Williams, Walter. 1996. "Amazons of America: Female Gender Variance." In Caroline B. Brettell and Carolyn F. Sargent (Eds.), *Gender in Cross-Cultural Perspective* (2nd ed., pp. 202–213). Upper Saddle River, NJ: Prentice Hall.

Wissler, C. 1916. "Aboriginal Maize Culture as a Typical Culture-Complex." *American Journal of Sociology* 21(5):656–661.

Wolf, Eric R. 1982. *Europe and the People Without History.* Berkeley, CA: University of California Press.

Wong, Bernard. 1988. *Ethnicity and Entrepreneurship: The New Chinese Immigrants in the San Francisco Bay Area.* Needham Heights, MA: Allyn and Bacon.

Woodburn, James. 1968. "An Introduction to Hadza Ecology." In R. B. Lee and I. DeVore (Eds.), *Man the Hunter* (pp. 49–55). Chicago: Aldine.

Woodburn, James. 1998. "Sharing Is Not a Form of Exchange: An Analysis of Property-Sharing in Immediate Return Hunter-Gatherer Societies." In C. M. Hann (Ed.), *Property Relations: Renewing the Anthropological Tradition* (pp. 48–63). Cambridge: Cambridge University Press.

World Bank. 1992. *Development and the Environment: World Development Report 1992.* New York: Oxford University Press.

World Bank. 2006. *Global Economic Prospects. Economic Implications of Remittances and Migration.* Washington, DC: World Bank. Available at http://go.worldbank.org/0ZRERMGA00.

World Bank. 2008. *World Development Indicators Database.* Washington, DC: World Bank. Available at http://siteresources.worldbank.org/DATASTATISTICS/Resources/GNI.pdf.

World Bank Group Archives. 2003. *Robert Strange McNamara.* Washington, DC: World Bank. Available at http://go.worldbank.org/44V9497H50.

Worthman, Carol M. 1995. "Hormones, Sex, and Gender." In William Durham, E. Valentine Daniel, and Bambi Schieffelin (Eds.), *Annual Review of Anthropology* (Vol. 24, pp. 593–618). Stanford, CA: Stanford University Press.

Yardley, Jim. 2004. "Rural Exodus for Work Fractures Chinese Family." *New York Times,* December 21.

Zaloom, Caitlin. 2006. *Out of the Pits: Trading and Technology From Chicago to London.* Chicago: University of Chicago Press.

Zeegers, Maurice, Frans van Poppel, Robert Vlietinck, Liesbeth Spruijt, and Harry Ostrer. 2004. "Founder Mutations Among the Dutch." *European Journal of Human Genetics* 12:591–600.

PHOTO CREDITS

Front Matter
vi: © Jean Pierre Dutilleux **vii:** © Judith Pearson **viii:** Colorado University **ix:** © Judith Pearson **x:** © Diane Greene Lent **xi:** © Joan Gregg **xii:** © Bob Burch/Bruce Coleman, Inc. **xiii:** © Bill Bachmann/Stock, Boston, LLC

Chapter 1
1: © Jean Pierre Dutilleux
6: © Margaret Bourke-White/Time & Life Pictures/Getty Images
11: Jerry Melbye

Chapter 2
21: © adrian arbib/Alamy **26:** © Bryan and Cherry Alexander Photography
33: © Adam G. Sylvester/Photo Researchers, Inc. **37:** © Barry Kass/Anthro-Photo, Inc.

Chapter 3
43: © Kurt Scholz/SuperStock
50: London School of Economics Archives, Malinowski/3/18/2
53: © Judith Pearson **59:** © Doranne Jacobson

Chapter 4
69: Serena Nanda **73:** Colorado University **77:** © Reuters/Corbis
84: © Jeff Greenberg/PhotoEdit
87: © Frederick Atwood

Chapter 5
93: © Bryan and Cherry Alexander Photography **100:** © Jane Hoffer
104: © F. Jack Jackson/Bruce Coleman, Inc. **107:** © Robert Caputo/Stock, Stock, Boston, LLC

Chapter 6
115: © Joan Gregg **121:** © Jialiang Gao/www.peace-on-earth.org
124: © Jeff Greenberg/PhotoEdit, Inc.
128: Alaska State Library Elbridge W. Merrill Photograph Collection
131: © Jonathan Kim/Getty Images
135: © Catherine Li, 2008

Chapter 7
141: Chander Dembla **151:** © Judith Pearson **153:** Jean Zorn
155: © Jonathan Nourak/PhotoEdit

Chapter 8
169: © Serena Nanda **176:** © Joan Gregg **182:** © Jean Pierre Dutilleux
190: © Welsh/Getty Images

Chapter 9
193: © AFP/Getty **197:** © Diane Greene Lent **203:** © Irven DeVore/AnthroPhoto, Inc. **209:** © Serena Nanda

Chapter 10
217: © Joan Gregg **227:** © Nubar Alexanian/Stock, Boston, LLC
232: © Associated Press

Chapter 11
239: Cultural Survival **246:** © Joan Gregg **252:** © AFP

Chapter 12
263: © Judith Pearson **269:** © Bob Burch/Bruce Coleman, Inc.
276: © Serena Nanda **281:** © Associated Press

Chapter 13
287: © Richard Warms **293:** Muséum de Rouen, France **303:** Anti-Slavery International Reg Charity 1039160
306: National Archives Photo No. 306-RNT-57-18116

Chapter 14
311: © Time & Life Pictures/Getty Images **320:** © Ray Dennis/Alamy
323 left: © Bill Bachmann/Stock, Boston, LLC **323 right:** © David Frazier/Photo Researchers, Inc.
328: © Margot Haag/Peter Arnold Inc.
333: © Charles O. Cecil/Alamy

INDEX

Note: Glossary words are indicated with an italic *g;* figures with an italic *f;* maps with an italic *m.*

AAEV. *See* African American English Vernacular
Aboriginals, 97, 272
Abortion rights, 189
Acephalous, 207*g*
Achieved status, 223*g*
Adams, Kathleen, 63
Adaptation
  cultural, 96
  defined, 35*g*
  models, 258–260
  nuclear families, 154–156
Africa. *See also specific countries*
  art, 293
  Azande of, 277
  Bemba of, 179
  bridewealth in, 152
  Caprivi of, 330
  colonization, 288–290, 302–303
  decolonization, 305, 307
  female circumcision, 176
  foraging in, 99
  formal associations, 196
  gender relations, 183
  generational ties, 184
  Ituri of, 99
  Kpelle of, 204
  Lese of, 100
  Maasai of, 21, 100, 318–319
  Mbuti of, 99
  Ndembu of, 29
  Nuer of, 144, 159–160, 202*f,* 273
  partitioning of, 300
  political instability, 330–331
  poverty in, 313
  puberty rites, 29
  religions, 282
  subsistence strategies in, 324–325
  Tuareg of, 83–84
African American English Vernacular (AAEV)
  analysis, 71–72
  disadvantages, 82
  interview, 70–71
  roots of, 71–72
  Sapir-Whorf hypothesis, 82
  stigmatization, 81
  study of, 71–72
African Americans
  health status, 245
  language, 70–73
  racial classification, 257
  religious practices, 282
  U.S. social hierarchy and, 260
Age grades, 202–203, 202*g*
Age sets, 202*g*
Agglutinating languages, 77*g*
Agriculture. *See also* Pastoralism
  in complex societies, 121–122
  gender relations, 185–187
  globalization and, 234
  landowners, 122
  monoculture plantations, 291*g,* 293
  peasants, 106–108
  production focus, 105–106
  sugar production, 293–294
  technological changes, 38, 96–97
Agriculture industrialism
  beef industry, 109–111
  defined, 98*g*
  economic effects of, 109
  production focus, 108
  women's status and, 186–187
Agta of the Philippines, 182
Alliance theory, 146
Alliances, informal systems of, 196
Allophones, 76*g*
Amangkurat II, 295–296
Amatenango of Mexico, 129–130
Ambilineal, 162
American Anthropological Association
  military/anthropologists' engagement, 61
  statement of ethics, 60, 62
American dream, 218–220
American(s). *See also* United States
  drug use, 34
  families, 31, 154–156
  football, 29–30
  human rights views, 64
  life chances, 225–226
  material comfort, 228
  prestige source, 222
Andalusia, 176–177, 177*m*
Anderson, Benedict, 249
Animals
  language, 73
  products, 120
  rituals, 269
Animism, 265*g*
Anthropological linguistics. *See* Linguistics
Anthropologist(s)
  British, 304–305
  development role, 318–319
  fieldwork by, 45
  French, 304–305
  holistic approach, 6–7
  human rights and, 64–65
  military use of, 61
  MNCs, concerns about, 321–322
  native, 62–64
  postmodernists, 56–57
  real world tasks, 11, 17
  women, 55–56
Anthropology. *See also* Cultural anthropology
  careers in, 13–14
  defined, 4*g*
  future of, 332–334
  history, 46–50
  knowledge from, 15–16
  specialization, 7–11
Anti-Nike Transnational Advocacy Network, 321
Antistructure, 271*g*
Anxiety reduction, 266–267
Apache. *See* Western Apache
Apartheid, 243*g,* 307
Applied anthropology, 11, 333
Arapesh of New Guinea
  location, 173*m*
  studies of, 173
  women exchange, 147
Archaeology, 9
Ardin, Kwame, 308

Ariki of Polynesia, 207
Arison, Mickey, 132
Aristotle, 25
Arranged marriage, 150
Art, 282–283, 293
Artifacts, 83*g*, 84
Asante state
 hegemony in, 211
 social stratification, 194, 199
 wealth, 194–195
Asantehene, 193
Asaro Valley people, 274
Ascribed status, 223*g*
Ashanti of Ghana, 194–195, 194*m*
Asia
 agricultural changes, 38
 decolonization, 305
 extended families in, 312
Asians
 gender relations, 183
 in Hawaii, 241
 immigrants, 257, 259
Asperger's syndrome, 22–23
Assimilation, 258*g*
Atahuallpa, 292
Atran, Scott, 7
Australia, 97, 272
Australia, Tiwi of, 182
Authority. *See also* Power
 defined, 195*g*
 social integration of, 197–198
Autism, culture of, 22–24
Automobile industry, 124
Avunculocal residence, 154*g*
Azande of East Africa, 277
Aztecs, 272, 298

Balanced reciprocity, 125*g*, 126
Baluchistan, 101*m*
Bamako, Mali, 327–328
Bamana language, 28
Bands
 defined, 198*g*
 economy, 200
 organization of, 200–201
Barbados, sugar production, 293–294
Baseball players, 274
Basic human needs policies, 316–317
Batavia, Chinese in, 296
Beef, 32, 109–111
The Bell Curve (Herrenstein, Murray), 244
Belgium colonies, 302–303
Beliefs. *See also* Religion
 common, 16
 in supernatural beings, 269–270
Belmonte, Thomas, 45, 52
Bemba of Africa, 179
Benedict, Ruth, 11, 49
Bifurcation, 164*g*
Bigman, 203–204, 203*g*
Bilateral descent, 162*g*
Bilateral kinship systems, 162
Bill of Rights, 283
Bilocal residence, 154*g*
bin Laden, Osama, 39
Biological anthropology. *See* Physical anthropology
Blended families, 156
Boas, Franz, 47, 55
 contributions of, 11
 potlatch, 128–129
 racial equality, 246
Bolivia, Indian ethnicity, 251
The Bone Lady (Manheim), 10
Bound morphemes, 76*g*
Bourgois, Philippe, 261
Brahmins, 231
Brandes, Stanley, 176–177
Brazil
 racial classification in, 245–247
 Travesti of, 171
 urbanization, 323
Bride service, 152*g*
Bridewealth, 152*g*
Brooklyn Museum of Art, 282–283
Browning, Michael, 10–11
Burakumin, 243
Bureaucracy, 208
Bush, George W., 225

Cagan, Jonathan, 137
Call systems, 73*g*
Camars, 233
Canada, ethnic subcultures, 251
Cannon, Walter, 266–267
Capital, 132*g*
Capitalism
 attributes, 132
 Chinese, 230
 defined, 132*g*
 global effects of, 134
 labor as resource, 132
 nationalism and, 335
 resistance to, 134–136
 social classes and, 134
 Turkish example, 133–134
Caprivi of South Africa, 330
Cargo cults, 264–265
Cargo systems, 130
Carnegie, Andrew, 235–236
Carneiro, Robert, 210
Caste systems
 changes in, 233–235
 defined, 230*g*
 economics, 231–232
 justification for, 232–233
 occupations, 222, 234
 rankings in, 230–231
Catholicism, 282–283
Censorship, 282–283
Central effect, 82
Ch'ien Lung, 291
Chagnon, Napoleon, 63, 205–206
Checker, Melissa, 226
Cheyenne Indians, 97
Chiefdoms
 defined, 199*g*
 political organization, 206–208
 tribes *versus*, 206
Child care
 Inuit, 25–26
 nuclear families, 155
 practices, 181
 women's share of, 155
Children
 enculturation of, 25–26
 language learning, 74
 in matrilineal societies, 160–161
 in patrilineal societies, 159
 rights of passage, 171
China
 average income, 314
 class stratification in, 229–230
 Dagongmei in, 188
 globalization and, 335
 historical wealth, 290–291
 life changes, 334
 location, 229*m*
 Na of, 142–143
 one child policy, 325–327
 pollution and, 329
 social prestige in, 222–223
 women in, 325
Chinese
 in Batavia, 296
 cultural values, 259
 footbinding, 176
 language, 89
Chinese Exclusion Act, 259
Chomsky, Noam, 74
Christianity
 in America, 14–15
 Muslim conflict with, 252
 prosperity theology, 264–265
 rituals, 268
 sacrifice, 273
Chronemics, 84*g*
Chuuk, Micronesia, 178
Citizenship, 208
Clans, 159*g*
Clarke, Margaret, 318
Class, 219*g*
Class systems
 American, 224–228
 capitalism and, 134
 Chinese, 229–230
 defined, 219*g*
 Indian, 231–235
 material basis, 225–227
 open/closed, 223–224
 subcultures and, 227–228
 urban, 323–324
Climate change. *See* Global warming
Closed stratification systems. *See* Caste systems
Closed systems, 223*g*
Cognatic systems. *See* Non-unilineal societies

Cognitive anthropology, 28*g*
Collaborative ethnography, 57–58
Collateral kin, 163–164*g*
Collaterality, 163*g*
Collier, John, 256
Colonialism. *See also* European expansion
  anthropology and, 304–304
  armies, 288–290
  British, 292–293
  defined, 297*g*
  end of, 305–308
  era of, 297–305
  forced labor and, 302–303
  holdings in 1900, 299*m*
  indigenous peoples, 254–255
  industrialization and, 299–300
  mercantilism and, 300
  post-World War II, 307
  Spanish, 292–293
  wealth creation by, 296
Colonies
  by country map, 299*f*
  defined, 297*g*
  education in, 303–304
  New World, 297–299
  political relations, 300–301
  profits, 300–302
  types of, 297
Coming of Age in Samoa (Mead), 27
Communication. *See also* Language(s)
  chronemics, 84–85
  haptics, 84
  interpersonal space, 84
  kinesics, 85
  nonverbal, 83–85
  proxemics, 85
  technological changes, 311
Communitas, 271*g*
Comparative linguistics, 88*g*
Compensation, 204
Competitive feasting, 128–129
Complex societies
  agriculture in, 121–122
  characterization, 109
  specialization, 123–124
Composite families, 156
Conflict management
  in bands, 201
  ethnic, 252–253
  process, 199
  systematic application, 200
  in tribes, 204
Congo, 302–303, 307
Conjugal tie, 154*g*
Consanguineal, 154*g*
Consultants, 52*g*
Contact cultures, 84
Contagious magic, 274*g*
Conventionality, 74*g*
Core vocabulary, 88*g*
Cortés, Hernán, 298
Corvée labor, 302
Cosmology, 266*g*
Cote d'Ivoire, 269
Creating Breakthrough Products (Cagan, Vogel), 137
Creole, 87–88
Croatia, 252–253
Cross Cultural Survey. See Human Relations Area Files (HRAF)
Cross-cousin marriage, 147
Cuba, Santeria in, 282
Cultivation, 97
Cultural anthropology. *See also* Ethnography; Fieldwork
  colonialism and, 304–304
  defined, 7*g*
  future of, 332–334
  homelessness and, 17–18
  in liberal arts programs, 13
  race and, 12–13
  specialization, 7–11
Cultural assimilation, 255
Cultural constructions, 173*g*, 172–173
Cultural deficit theorists, 71–72
Cultural ecology, 36*g*
Cultural relativism, 5–6, 5*g*, 48*g*
Culture and personality theorists, 27*g*
Culture shock, 52*g*
Culture(s)
  adaptation, 12–13, 35–36, 96
  anthropologist's view, 7
  aspects, relationships among, 31–32
  autism, 22–24
  biology and, 333
  changes, 36–39
  characteristics, 23–24
  common beliefs, 16
  conflicts in, 31
  contact, 84
  as critical idea, 40–41
  cultural comparisons, 54–55
  defined, 5*g*
  dominant, 33–34
  food choices, 112
  football, 28–29
  function of, 7
  gender relations, 172–173
  genetic aspects, 41
  historical development, 47–48
  homogenization, 39
  importance of, 39–40
  inner-city, 260–261
  language and, 78–83
  learned behaviors in, 24–27
  M-time, 84–85
  mainstream, 251
  marriage rules, 145–151
  noncontact, 84
  organic analogy, 30–31
  oriental, 56–57
  P-time, 84–85
  racial construct, 243–245
  sexual behavior, 173–177
  shared norms in, 32–35
  shared values in, 32–35
  social class and, 227–228
  survival, 239, 256
  symbol use, 27–30

Dagongmei, 188
Dalits, 231
Darrow, Clarence, 240–242
Darwin, Charles, 46, 304
Data, ethnographic, 54–55
Dead Men Do Tell Tales (Maples, *et al.*), 11
Decolonization
  Americas, 305
  challenges following, 314
  development and, 315
  reasons for, 306–307
Deity. *See* Gods
Descent, 158*g*, 162
Descent groups
  define, 158*g*
  double descent, 162
  matrilineal, 160–162
  patrilineal, 159–162
  unilineal, 158–162
Descent rules, 158
Descriptive Sociology, 54
Development
  climate change and, 329
  human needs approaches, 316–317
  migration and, 331–332
  modernization theory, 315–316
  political instability and, 330–331
  pollution and, 327–329
  post-World War II, 315
  structural adjustment, 317–319
  urbanization, 322–324
Deviants, 199*g*
Dialects, 80
Dictator game, 116
Diets, beef taboos, 32
Diffusion, 38*g*, 39
Displacement, 75*g*
Distribution systems
  capitalism, 131–134
  market exchange, 130–131
  reciprocity, 125–127
  redistribution, 127–130
Divale, William, 205–206
Divination, 274*g*
Divorce, impact of, 156
Dogon, 48
Dominant culture, 33–34, 33*g*
Double descent, 162*g*
Dutch East India Company (VOC)
  brutality of, 295–296
  characterization, 294
  charter, 294
  dividends, 294–295
  legacy of, 296–297
  principal holdings, 295*m*

East India Company, 292–293
Ebonics. *See* African American English Vernacular (AAEV)
Ecological functionalists, 31*g*
Economic Development (Todaro, Smith), 313
"Economic men" theory, 116–117
Economic systems
  agriculture, 105–109
  defined, 117*g*
  foraging, 97, 99
  horticulture, 102–105
  inequality in, 312
  nation-states, 209
  state societies, 199
Economics
  caste systems, 232
  colonial, 300–304
  defined, 117*g*
  distribution, 125–136
  "economic men" theory, 116–117
  human behavior and, 118–119
  immigration and, 257–259
  labor organization in, 122–125
  migration, 331–322
  pre-industrial, 120–121
  resource allocation, 119–122
  slavery, 293–294
  specialization, 123–124
  women's status, 187
Education, 260–261, 303–304
Efficiency productivity, 98*g*
Egalitarian societies, 198*g*
Egypt, 107*m*
Egypt, peasant agriculture, 106–108
Elites, 14, 198*g*
Emic ethnography, 8
Enculturation, 23*g*
Endogamy, 147
Engaged ethnography, 57–58
English
  changes in, 86
  only campaign, 90
  standard, 82
Ensminger, Jean, 116
Environment
  development and, 327–329
  global warming, 329
  human adaptation, 96–98
  subsistence strategies and, 97–98
Essentialism, 248*g*
Ethics, 60–62
Ethnic boundaries, 248*g*, 256
Ethnic identity, 248*g*
Ethnic stratification, 248–249, 253–256
Ethnicity
  adaptation models, 258–260
  in colonies, 302
  conflicts, 252–253
  defined, 248*g*
  educational achievements, 260–261
  immigration and, 256–260
  importance, 249
  nation-states and, 249–260
  power shaping, 251
Ethnobotany, 28*g*
Ethnocentrism
  defined, 5*g*, 47*g*
  humanness of, 5–6
  in West, 68
Ethnography
  collaborative, 57–58
  critical issues in, 55–56
  cross-cultural comparisons, 54–55
  data, 54–55
  defined, 8*g*
  engaged, 57–58
  gender issues, 172–173
  history, 49
  new product, 137
  types of, 8
Ethnology, 8*g*, 54
Ethnomedicine, 28*g*
Ethnoscience, 28*g*
Etic ethnography, 8
European expansion. *See also specific countries*
  in Africa, 287–290
  forced labor during, 293–294
  gender stratification and, 180
  impact of, 308
  joint stock companies and, 294–299
  methods, 292–297
  motives, 291–292
  pillage during, 292–293
European(s)
  diseases spread by, 292, 298
  ethnic conflict in, 252–253
  human rights views, 64
  immigrants from, 257–258
  power expansion, 279
  technological mastery, 290–291
  witchcraft, 277–278
Evolution, 46, 304
Evolutionary anthropology, 46
Exchange of goods, 152–153
Exogamy, 146–147
Extended families
  Asian, 312
  characterization, 156
  defined, 154*g*
  matrilineal, 156–157
  patrilineal, 156

Factions, 196*g*
Falling from Grace: Downward Mobility in the Age of Affluence (Newman), 226
Families. *See also* Extended families; Kinship systems
  American, 31, 154–156
  average, 312
  basic types, 154–157
  composite, 156
  concept of, 145
  defined, 145*g*, 154*g*
  neolocal residence and, 154
  nuclear, 154
  poor, 312–313
Female circumcision. *See* Genital mutilation
Feminist anthropology, 55–56
Ferguson, Niall, 308
Fertility rites, 178–179
Fieldwork
  colonialism and, 304–305
  ethics, 60–62
  experience, 45
  in one's own society, 58–60
  participant observation approach, 47
  techniques, 50–55
Firms, 132*g*
FLDS. *See* Fundamentalist Church of Jesus Christ of Latter Day Saints
Fleming, Alexander, 37
Fontanta del Re, 44–45, 52
Food
  biological need for, 25
  choices, culture and, 112
  production, 121–122
  taboos, 32
  taro production, 185
  women's contribution to, 182, 185–186
Football, 29–30
Footbinding, 176
Foraging societies
  conscription of, 330
  defined, 97*g*
  in extreme environments, 99–100
  gender relations in, 182–183, 182–185
  !Kung or Ju/'hoansi, 330
  lifestyle requirements, 120
  male dominance in, 180–181
  power and authority in, 198–199
  production focus, 99
Forced labor, 293–294
Forensic anthropology, 10–11
France
  African army, 288–290
  anthropologists, 304–305
  colonialism, 300–301, 303–304
  immigration to, 259
Free French forces, 288–289
Free morphemes, 76*g*
Freud, Sigmund, 146
Freyre, Gilberto, 246–247
Friedl, Ernestine, 180–181
Friedman, Ariella, 323
Friedman, Thomas, 334
Functionalism, 220, 220*g*
Functionalists, 31*g*
Fundamentalism, 278–279, 278*g*
Fundamentalist Church of Jesus Christ of Latter Day Saints (FLDS), 164–164

Gandhi, Mahatma, 222
Ganja. *See* Marijuana
Garage sales, 135*f*
Gates, Bill, 119, 334
Geertz, Clifford, 29

Gender. *See also* Sex
  cultural constructions, 172–173
  defined, 172*g*
  egalitarianism, 183
  imbalances, 325–326
  nature of, 172–173
  stratification, 176, 180–181
Gender differences. *See also* Men; Women
  labor division, 122–123
  sexual maturity, 174–175
Gender ideology, 173–177, 173*g*
Gender relations
  in agriculture societies, 185–187
  complexity, 181–189
  in foraging societies, 182–183, 182–185
  global economy and, 187–189
  in horticultural societies, 183–185
  in pastoral societies, 185–186
  stratification, 181
Gender roles, 170–171, 171*g*
Genders, 78*g*
General Motors, 132, 194, 196
Generalized reciprocity, 125*g*
Generation, 163*g*
Genetics, 10
Genital mutilation, 189–191
George II (England), 291
German colonies, 185, 301
Ghana
  Ashanti of, 194–195, 194*m*
  decolonization, 307
  first president, 306
  independence anniversary, 308–309
Ghana, Asante kingdom, 193
Ghost Dance, 279–280
Gibbs, James, 204
Gilbert, Matthew, 95
Gilmore, David, 178–179
Giuliani, Rudolph, 282
Glassman, Robert, 218
Global warming, 94–96, 329
Globalization
  complex linkages, 111
  defined, 109*g*
  gender relations and, 187–189
  impact of, 15
  MNCs, 319–322
  pollution and, 328–329
  problems of, 334–335
  social stratification and, 234
Glottochronology, 88*g*
GNI. *See* Gross national income
Gods
  addressing, 270–274
  African, 282
  belief in, 269–270
  defined, 269*g*
  power of, 282
Government, 208*g*
Graham, Laura R., 64
Grameen bank, 318
Grammar, 78, 86
Grandin, Temple, 22–23
Great vowel shift, 86*g*
Greek drama, 16–17
Green Revolution, 38
Greenhalgh, Susan, 325–326
Grey, John, 334–335
Gross national income (GNI), 314
Gwich'in, 95
Gyamerah, Michael, 308

Hackenburg, Robert, 320
Hadd punishments, 64–65
Haddon, Alfred Cort, 49
Hadza of Tanzania, 117
Haile Selassi I, 280
Hall, Edward, 84
Haoles, 241
Haptics, 84*g*
Harijans, 231
Harris, Marvin, 32, 205–206
Hawaii, Massie case in, 240–242
Health status, racial aspects, 246
Heeren XVII, 294*g*
Hegemony, 211
Hijabs, 176
Hijras of India
  defined, 170*g*
  identity, 170–171
  performances, 170
Hinduism
  caste system, 222, 231–232
  dietary taboos, 32
  rituals, 268–269, 271
  women and, 77
Historical particularism, 34*g*
Hoansi foragers, 330
Holi, 271
Holism, 6–7, 6*g*
Homelessness, 17–18
Homo sapiens, 12, 73
Homosexual relationships, 174–175
Honor killings, 240
Hopi Indians
  beliefs, 268
  descent lineage, 161–162
  horticultural traditions, 103
  location, 161*m*
  women's power, 196
Horticulture societies
  environments, 103
  gender relations in, 183–185
  Lua' example, 103–105
  lifestyle requirements, 120–121
  male dominance in, 181
  power and authority in, 199
  production focus, 102
  redistribution in, 127
  traditional, 102
Households
  Asian, 312
  defined, 122*g*
  families *versus,* 154
Howell, Leonard, 280
HRAF. *See Human Relations Area Files*
Hsu, Francis, 58
Hubris, 16–17
Human needs approaches, 316–317
Human paleontology, 10
Human Relations Area Files (HRAF), 54–55
Human rights, 64–65
Human Rights Watch, 64
Human(s)
  biological diversity, 35
  as biological organisms, 10
  economic needs, 118–119
  environmental adaptation, 96–98
  ethnocentrism of, 5
  language capacity, 8, 73–74
  remains, trafficking in, 293
Hurricane Katrina, 226, 245
Hurston, Zora Neale, 58
Hutu people, 330–331

Ibo of Nigeria, 269
Ida, Horace, 240
Ideologies, 173–177, 196
Igoe, Jim, 318–319
IMF. *See* International Monetary Fund
Imitative magic, 273*g*
Immigration
  economics, 257–259, 322
  ethnicity and, 256–260
  U.S. policy and, 212–213
Inca Empire, 210
Incest taboos, 145–146
India
  British educational system in, 304
  British exploitation, 292–293
  globalization and, 234–235, 335
  Hijras of, 170–171
  Kashmir conflict, 253
  life changes, 334
  location, 231*m*
  marriages in, 150–51, 153–154
  sati in, 176
  Toda of, 150
Indigenous peoples
  colonial agenda, 254–255
  cultural adaptation, 315
  defined, 253–256
  economic incorporation of, 254
  self-sufficiency of, 253–254
  UN and, 255
Indonesia
  agriculture production in, 106
  Dutch rule, 295
  Mentawai of, 263
Industrial Revolution, 97–98, 300–301
Industrial societies. *See* Complex societies
Industrialization
  agriculture (*See* Agriculture industrialism)
  colonialism and, 299–300
  labor, 124
  pollution and, 328–329

population pressures, 326–327
specialization in, 124
Inequality
in China, 229
economic, 312–314
income, 225, 229–230
protest against, 217
in South America, 312
theories of, 220–221
Infanticide, 205–206
Informants, 52*g*
Informed consent, 60
Inheritance, 157*g*
Inis Beag, Irish of, 175
Innovation, 37–39, 37*g*
International Monetary Fund (IMF), 255
International Phonetic Alphabet (IPA), 75
Internet, 314
Interpretive anthropology, 29*g*
Intimate distance, 85
Inuits
child-rearing practices, 25–26
environmental threats to, 94–96
foraging strategies, 94
political organization, 201
sexual behavior, 173–174
subsistence strategies, 97
territory, 25*m*
Inupiaq of Alaska, 269
Involuntary minorities, 260
IPA. *See* International Phonetic Alphabet
Iran, 101–102, 101*m*
Irish of Inis Beag, 175
Irish, as race, 242
Iroquois Indians, 183
Islam. *See* Muslims
Ituri of Central Africa, 99

Jamaica, 280–281, 280*m*
Japan, 243, 314
Jati, 234
Javanese kingdom, 295–296
Jeffs, Warren, 164
Joint stock companies
defined, 291*g*
Dutch, 294–297
origins, 294
Joking, 78–79
Jones, Delmos, 59–60
Ju/'hoansi of Kalahari Desert, 182

Kahahawai, Joe, 240
Kareve drinking, 185
Keller, Albert, 54
Kelley, John, 241
Kenya, 100*m*
Kenyatta, Jomo, 58
Kerry, John, 260
Kilbride, Philip, 165
Kimball, Solon T., 58
Kindreds, 162*g*
Kinesics, 85*g*
Kingsley, Charles, 242
Kinship
in band societies, 201
collateral, 163–164
defined, 157*g*
networks of, 162
Kinship ideology. *See* Descent rules
Kinship systems
bilateral, 162
chiefdoms, 207
classification, 163–164
defined, 157*g*
descent rules, 158
functions, 157
inheritance, 157
origins, 158
rites of passage and, 178
succession, 157
tribes, 202
unilineal descent groups, 158–162
Kinship terminology, 162*g*
Kiowa Indians, 57–58
Kipling, Rudyard, 300
Kipsigis, 152
Kluckhohn, Clyde, 127
Korea, average income, 314
Kottak, Conrad, 246
Kpelle of West Africa, 204
Krishna, 268–269
Kshatriyas, 231, 233
Kula ring, 126*g*
Kula trade, 126*f*
!Kung or Ju/'hoansi, 330

Labor
American dream, 218–220
capitalism and, 132–133
in complex societies, 121
corvée, 302
factory, 124
food production, 121–122
gender divisions, 122–123
immigrant, 212
organizing, 122–125
sweatshop, 320–321
value of, 132–133
women and, 186–189
Labov, William, 71–72, 81
Lacondon Maya, 28, 121
Lafferty, Daniel, 164
Lafferty, Ronald, 164
Land ownership, 120–121, 122
Language in the Inner City (Labov), 71
Language(s). *See also* Communication
Bamana, 28
changes, 86–89
Chinese, 89
components, 69
cross-culture contact, 87–88
cultural aspects, 23, 28, 78–83
dialects, 80
disappearance, 89
ebonics, 70–73
ethnicity and, 256
function, 8
genders, 78
grammar, 78, 86
human capacity for, 73–74
joking, 78–79
learning, 74
morpheme use, 77
origins, 73
relationships among, 88–89
Sapir-Whorf hypothesis, 82–83
social stratification and, 80–82
speech forms, 80
structure, 75–78
vocabulary building, 77
Lassiter, Erik, 57–58
Latinos, 260
Leadership
bands, 201
chiefdoms, 206
defined, 198*g*
Learning
Inuit, 25–26
language, 74
universality of, 24–25
Leopold II of Belgium, 302–303
Lese of Central Africa, 99
Leveling mechanism, 129*g*
Levirate rules, 148
Lexicon, 77*g*
Libyan, modest dress, 333
Life chances, 225–226, 334
Life expectancy, 314
Lifestyles
foraging societies, 120
horticulture societies, 120–121
money and, 227–228
multiple-livelihood, 136
pastoral societies, 120
urban, 323
Liminals
defined, 270*g*
forms, 271
in rites of passage, 270–271
structural dissolution, 271–272
Lineages. *See also* Kinship systems
clans and, 159
defined, 158*g*
female, 159–162
male, 158–160
membership, 159–160
Lineality, collaterally *versus,* 163*g*
Linguistics
comparative, 88*g*
homogenization, 88–89
purpose of, 8
Lopez, Alma, 283
Lua' of Northwestern Thailand, 103–105, 104*m*
Lyon-Callo, Vincent, 17–18

Maasai of East Africa
age grades, 202–203
cattle culture, 100
economic development, 318–319
initiation ritual, 21
Machiguenga of Peruvan Amazon, 117
Magic
contagious, 274
defined, 273*g*
imitative, 273–274
universality, 272–273
Magical death, 266
Mahu of Polynesia, 171
Malawi, life expectancy, 314
Mali, pollution in, 327–328
Malinowski, Bronislaw, 4, 31
fieldwork, 49–50
incest taboo theory, 146
myths, 268
reciprocity, 126
Mana, 270*g*
Manahune of Polynesia, 207
Mangaia, Polynesians of, 175
Mangu, 277
Manheim, Mary, 10
Manhood puzzle, 178*g*
Maples, William, 10
Maratram Dynasty, 295
Marijuana, religious use, 281
Maring, Tim, 274
Market exchange
defined, 130
factors, 130–131
principles, 131
variety in, 130–131
Markets
creation of, 115
globalization, 111
specialization, 115
Marriage(s)
arranged, 150
in China, 142–143
clan's role in, 159
defined, 144, 144*g*
dowries, 153–154
endogamous, 147
exchange of goods in, 151–154
exogamous, 146–147
function, 143–144
great communities interest in, 151
incest taboos, 145–146
in India, 150–154
mate selection, 150–151
preferential, 147–148
rights in, 151–154
rules, 145–151
spouse number, 148–150
Marshall, Donald, 175
Marshall, John, 330
Marx, Karl, 32, 221–223
Massie, Thalia, 240–242
Matrilineages
across villages, 161–162
defined, 159*g*
extended families in, 156–157
father's role in, 160–161
membership links, 160*f*
warfare and, 205
Matrilocal residence, 154*g*
Mauss, Marcel, 125
Maya of Mexico, 276
Maytag, 218–219
Mbuti of Central Africa, 99
McNamara, Robert, 316
Mead, Margaret, 49
cultural relativistism and, 58–59
gender relations, 172–173
impact on child rearing, 27
political role, 55
World War II role, 11
Meaning, search for, 266
Media, 37–39
Mediation, 204
Medicine, 275–276
Medlpa of New Guinea, 153
Melanesia
bigman, 203
cargo cults, 266
rituals, 264
Melbye, Jerry, 11
Men
control over women, 176
dominance, 180–181, 185–187
in horticulture societies, 183–184
marriage responsibilities, 144
in pastoral societies, 186
in patrilineal groups, 159, 160–161
rites of passage, 178–179
San Blas, 176–177
solidarity of, 205
Menarche, 179
Mende of Sierra Leone, 196
Men's houses, 182
Mentawai of Indonesia, 263
Messenger, John, 175
Messianic religions, 281–282
Mexico
Aztecs of, 272, 298
factory labor in, 124
labor from, 212
leveling mechanism, 129
Maya of, 276
Spanish conquest of, 298–299
Zinacantan, 187
Middle East. *See also specific countries*
agriculture production in, 106–108
cultures, 56–57
immigrants from, 257
Migration, 322, 331–332
Military
anthropologists in, 61
colonial, 288–290, 303
Millenarian religions, 281–282
Miner, Horace, 4
Mission civilisatrice, 300
MNCs. *See* Multinational corporations
Modernization theory
defined, 315*g*
failure of, 316
foreign aid and, 315–316
Monochronic time (M-time), 84
Monoculture plantations, 291*g*, 293
Monogamy, 148*g*, 156
Monotheism, 269*g*
Montezuma, 298
Moon, John, 218
Morales, Evo, 251
Morgan, Louis Henry, 46
Mormons, 164–165
Morphemes
defined, 76*g*
types, 76
use, differences in, 77
Morphology, 75*g*
Mozambique, 302, 314
Mudyi tree, 29
Mulattos, 246
Multiculturalism, 15, 258*g*
Multinational corporations (MNCs)
anthropologists' concerns, 321–322
cultural changes and, 321–322
defined, 319
low wages paid by, 322
political force of, 319
pollution and, 329
profits, 319
sweatshops, 319–322
Multiple-livelihood strategy, 136
Mundugamor of New Guinea, 173
Mundurucu of South America, 183–184
Murdock, George, 16, 54
Musha farmers, 106–108
Muslims
Christian conflict with, 252
empires, 290–291
Hadd punishments, 64–65
hijab use, 176
sacrifice, 273
Myerhoff, Barbara, 59
Myths, 267–268, 267*g*

Na of southwest China, 142–143, 142*m*
Nacirema culture, 2–7
Nader, Laura, 64
Namibia, Ju/'hoansi of, 182
Nash, June, 129
Nash, Manning, 129
Nation-states
construction of, 250–251
defined, 249
ethnicity and, 249–260
GNI, 314
identity intensity and, 209
immigration and, 212–213
importance of, 250*m*

political instability, 330–331
spatial dimension of, 250*f*
threats to, 251
wealthy, 316
Native American(s). *See also specific tribes*
cultural assimilation, 255–256
dying-off of, 298–299
European conquest of, 298
gender relations, 183–185
Ghost Dance, 279–280
potlatch, 128–129
secret societies, 203
shamans, 275
suppression of, 251
two-spirit concept, 171
Native anthropologists, 62–64
Nativistic religions, 279
Ndembu of East Africa, 29
Negative reciprocity
defined, 126*g*
Navajo example, 127
Nelson, Ekow, 308
Neocolonialism, 307
Neoliberalism, 317*g*
Neolocal residence, 154*g*
Netherlands, 294–297
New Guinea
Arapesh of, 147
Asaro Valley people, 274
cargo cults, 264–265
gender studies in, 173
location, 203*m*
Medlpa of, 153
oil revenues, 321
rites of passage, 178
Sambia of, 174
Newman, Katherine, 226, 228
Nicolaisen, Ida, 64
Niger, Wodaabe of, 151
Nigeria
Ibo of, 269
Yako of, 162
Yoruba of, 196
Nike campaign, 320–321
Nomadic pastoralism, 100*g*
Non-unilineal societies, 162*g*
Noncontact cultures, 84
Nonverbal communication, 83–85
Norms, 32*g*, 34–35
North America
average family in, 312
colonization of, 297
decolonization, 305
Tlingit of, 182–183
Northern city shift, 86
Nuclear families, 154*g*
Nuer of East Africa
cattle sacrifice, 273
descent lineage, 159–160
marriage bond, 144
organization, 202*f*
Nukumanu of Polynesia, 184–185
O'Neal, Shaquille, 132
Occupations, 222–224
Ofili, Chris, 282–283
Ogbu, John, 260
Oil revenues, 321
Oman, xanith of, 171
One child policy, 325–327
Open systems, 223*g*
Order, search for, 266
Organic analogy, 30*g*
Orichas, 282
Orientalism (Said), 56
Osei Tutu II, 193

Pacific Northwest, 129*m*
Page, Tim, 23
Paleontology, 10
Parallel-cousin marriage
defined, 147
relationship graft, 148*f*
types of, 148
Parda, 246
Participant observations, 47*g*
Pastoralism
defined, 98*g*
gender relations and, 185–187
lifestyle requirements, 120
management requirements, 101–102
production focus, 100
types, 100
Patrilineages
across villages, 159–160
defined, 158*g*
membership links, 159*f*
warfare and, 205
Patrilineal extended families, 156
Patrilocal residence, 154*g*
Patrilocality, 157, 205
Peasants, 107, 122
Penicillin, 37–38
Personal distance, 85
Peru
colonization of, 292
location, 210*m*
pre-Columbian, 210
Philippines, 64, 182
Phonemes, 76*g*
Phones, 75*g*
Physical anthropology, 10–11
Pidgins, 87
Pillage, 292–293, 292*g*
Pinker, Steven, 74
Pitts, Leonard, 14
Pizarro, Francisco, 292
Plains Indians, 279
Plasticity, 36*g*
Plunkett, Roy, 37
Plural Marriage for Our Times (Kilbride), 165
Polyandry
defined, 148*g*
fraternal aspects, 149
Toda example, 150
Political ideology, 196*g*
Political instability, 330–331
Political organization
associations, 203
authority in, 195–196
band societies, 200–201
chiefdoms, 206–208
conflict management, 199–200
cultural values and, 194
defined, 195*g*
development, 196–197
factions, 196
power in, 195–196
social complexity and, 197–199
social control, 199–200
state societies, 208–211
tribal societies, 201–206
types, 200–211
Political process
colonial, 300–301
conflict and, 197
defined, 196*g*
function, 196
MNCs, 319
protests, 197
Pollution
African, 327–328
American, 328
China and, 329
globalization and, 328–329
industrialization and, 328–329
MNCs and, 329
Polychronic time (P-time), 84
Polygamy, 148*g*, 164–165
Polygyny, 148*g*, 149
Polynesia
chiefdoms in, 207
Mahu of, 171
Mangaia of, 175
Nukumanu of, 184
Polytheism, 269*g*
Population density
Chinese policy, 325–327
current trends, 324*f*
defined, 98*g*
growth rate, 324
poverty and, 326–327
subsistence strategies and, 324–325
wealth and, 326–327
Poro society, 203
Portuguese colonies, 302
Postindustrial societies. *See* Complex societies
Postmodernism, 56–57
Postmodernists, 35*g*
Potlatch, 128–129
Poverty
development and, 315–319
global, 312
MCN sweatshops, 319–322
population density and, 326–327
rural, Chinese, 230
urban, 323

Powdermaker, Hortense, 58
Power. *See also* Authority
in America, 14
in Asante state, 194
defined, 195*g*, 221*g*
innovation and, 38
religious symbols, 268
social integration of, 197–198
supernatural beings, 260
Prayer, 272–273, 273*g*
Preferential marriages, 147–148
Prester John, 291
Prestige, 118*g*, 222–223, 222*g*
Preta, 246
Priests, 276*g*
Primary innovations, 37
Primatology, 10
Private/public dichotomy, 180*g*
Product anthropology, 137
Productive resources, 119*g*
access to, 120
European expansion and, 184–185
foraging societies, 120
horticulture societies, 120–121
land, 121–122
pastoralists, 120
Productivity, 75*g*, 98
Project Camelot, 60–61
Prophets, 278*g*, 280–281
Prosperity theology, 264–265
Protestants, 14–15
Proxemics, 85*g*
Pun Ngai, 188
Putnam County, New York, 135–136

Raatira of Polynesia, 207
Race
anthropologists' view, 12–13
Brazilian concept, 245–247
classification, 12
cultural construction of, 242–245
Japanese concept, 243
Racial stratification systems
American, 243–245
Brazilian, 245–247
South African, 243
Racism, 48*g*, 240–242
Radcliffe-Brown, A. R., 31
Radha, 268–269
Rank societies, 198*g*, 207
Rastafarians, 280–282
Rayonnement, 300
Rebellion, 197*g*
Reciprocity, 125–126, 125*g*
Redistribution
cargo systems, 130
defined, 127*g*
horticultural importance, 127
leveling mechanism, 129
potlatch example, 128–129
Reincorporation, 271*g*
Relative age, 163*g*
Religion. *See also specific faiths*
Bill of Rights and, 283
cargo cults, 264–265
characteristics, 265, 267–278
criminalization of, 251
defined, 265*g*
functions of, 266–267, 278
fundamentalism, 278–279
narratives, 267–268
population control and, 326
practitioners, 275–278
prayer, 272–274
prophecy and, 278
revitalization movements, 279–282
rituals, 270–274
social change and, 278–282
supernatural beings, 269–270
symbols, 268–260
treatment of women, 176–177
Residence, rules of, 157
Resource allocation, 119–122
Respondents, 52*g*
Revitalization movements
defined, 279*g*
Ghost Dance, 279–280
messianic, 281–282
millenarian, 281–282
vitalistic prophecies, 280–281
Revolution
defined, 197*g*
green, 38
industrial, 97–98, 300–301
Rio de Janeiro, 323
Rites of intensification, 272
Rites of passage
defined, 177*g*
female, 179, 190
liminals in, 270–271
male, 178–179
phases, 271
Rituals
animal, 269
body, 2–3
cargo cults, 274
divination, 274
genital, 189–190
magic, 273–274
marriage, 151
potlatch, 128–129
prayer, 273
puberty, 29
religious, 270–274
sacrifice, 273
shrine, 2
universal, 270–272
Roberts, Oral, 264–265
Rules
descent, 158
grammar, 78
levirate, 148
marriage, 145–151
residence, 157
sororate, 148
syntax, 77
Rwanda, political instability in, 330–331

Sacks, Oliver, 22
Sacred narratives. *See* Myths
Sacrifice, 272–273, 273*g*
SADF. *See* South African Defense Forces
Sahara, Tuareg of, 83–44, 186
Said, Edward, 56
Sambia of New Guinea, 174
San Antonio, Texas, 328
San Blas men, 176–177
Sanday, Peggy, 181
Santeria, 282
Sapir, Edward, 82
Sapir-Whorf hypothesis, 82
Sarara, 246
Sati, 176
Saudi Arabia, Hadd punishments in, 64–65
Schizophrenia, 32
Secret societies, 196, 203*g*
Sedentary, 97*g*
Selfish gene, 41
Seligman, Charles, 49
Semantics, 75*g*
Separation, 271*g*
Serial monogamy, 156
Service, Elman, 198
Sex, 172*g*. *See also* Gender
Sexual behavior
erotic, 173–174
foreplay, 174
regulation of, 143–144
variation in, 173–177
Shamans
defined, 275*g*
in modern world, 275–276
techniques, 275
Shudras, 231
Side effects, 82
Sierra Leone
Mende of, 196
Sande of, 184, 196, 203
Sinclair, Upton, 110
Sioux Indians, 280
Slash and burn. *See* Swidden cultivation
Slavery
demand for, 293
monoculture plantations and, 293–294
native populations, 302
Smith, Joseph, 164–165
Social classes. *See* Class systems
Social complexity, 197*g*
Social constructionists, 249
Social control
mechanisms of, 200
religion and, 266–267
tribes, 204
Social differentiation, 198*g*
Social distance, 85

Social group(s)
bands, 201
loosely defined, 30
marriage role, 144
Social mobility
in caste systems, 233–234
defined, 219*g*
downward, 224, 226–227
as life chance, 224
Social relationships
capitalism, 133
culture and, 31–32
gender, 181–189
homosexual, 174–175
in United States, 84
Social stratification
achievement, 223
American dream and, 218–219
Asante state, 194–195
aspiration, 223
basic perspectives on, 220–221
in China, 229–230
conflict theory of, 221
control in, 199
defined, 219
ethnically-based, 248–249, 253–256
functional theory of, 220–221
globalization and, 234–235
language and, 80–82
main dimensions, 221–223
racially-based, 243–247
states, societies and, 210–211
status differentiation, 223
Social structure, 30
Societies
complex (*See* Complex societies)
contact cultures, 84
defined, 5*g*
globalization of, 7
industrial, 109
interconnection, 16
non-unilineal, 162
noncontact cultures, 84
postindustrial, 109
power and authority in, 198–199
Sociolinguistics, 79*g*
Sorcery, 277*g*
Sororate rules, 148
South Africa, 307
South African Defense Forces (SADF), 330
South America
agricultural changes, 38
colonization of, 297
decolonization, 305
Indian ethnicity in, 251
Mundurucu of, 183–184
poverty in, 312–313
Yanomamo of, 63
Spanish colonialism, 292–293
Specialization, 115, 123–124
Speech forms, 80
Spencer, Herbert, 46, 54, 304
Spouses, number of, 148–150
Spradley, James, 57
SSAE. *See* Standard Spoken American English
Standard Spoken American English (SSAE), 82
State societies. *See also* Nation-states
administrations of, 209
characterization, 208–209
defined, 208
economic systems, 199
origins, 209–210
social stratification and, 210–211
Status systems, 223
Stereotypes, 244
Stratified societies, 198*g*, 199
Structural adjustment
anthropologist's role, 318–319
defined, 317*g*
successes, 318
Subartic groups, 171
Subculture(s)
defined, 33*g*
protection of, 34
religious, 251
social classes as, 227–228
Subsistence strategies
defined, 96*g*
historical changes, 96–97
Inuit, 94
population and, 324–325
social structure and, 30
types, 98–112
Succession, 157*g*
Sugar production, 293–294
Sumner, William Graham, 54
Supernatural beings. *See* Gods
Sweatshops
actions against, 320–321
defined, 319*g*
global bands and, 319–320
locations, 319
Nike campaign, 320–321
Swidden cultivation, 103
Symbolic anthropologists, 29*g*
Symbolic representation, 268–269
Symbols
ability to use, 75
cultural use of, 27–30
defined, 23*g*
function, 28–29
religious, 268–260
words as, 74
Syncretism, 282*g*
Syntax
aspects, 78
defined, 75*g*
rules, 77

Tafari, Ras (Duke), 280
Tahiti, 173, 207
Tanzania, 117, 202–203
Taro production, 185
Taxation
colonial, 300–301, 303
nation-states, 209
Tchambuli of New Guinea, 173
Technology
changes, 38
communication, 311
energy use and, 96
European advances, 290–291
Thailand, Lua' of, 103–105
Tirailleurs Senegalais
creation, 288
description, 287
units outside Africa, 303
Tito, Josip, 252–253
Tiwi of Australia, 182
Tlingit of North America
gender egalitarianism, 183
location, 182*m*
women's role, 182–183
Toda of South India, 150
Todd, Judith, 323
Tohono O'odham Reservation, 212–213
Totemism, 272*g*
Traits, 12
Transhumant pastoralism, 100*g*
Travesti of Brazil, 171
Tribes
age sets, 202–203
chiefdoms *versus,* 206
defined, 199
economy, 201–202
kinship, 202
political organization, 202
social control, 204
warfare in, 204–206
Trobriand Islands
chief's power, 208
kula exchanges, 184
location, 49*m*
Malinowski's work in, 49
Trobrianders, 174
Tuareg of Central Sahara, 83–84, 186
Tudjman, Franjo, 253
Turkey
business in, 133–134
capitalism in, 133
location, 133*m*
social organization, 133–134
Turner, Victor, 271
Tutsi people, 330–331
Tylor, Edward Burnett, 46, 333–334

U.S. ENGLISH Inc., 90
Ultimatum games, 116–117, 127
Unilineal descent, 158–162, 158*g*
United Kingdom
anthropologists, 304–305
colonialism, 292–293
Industrial Revolution in, 300–301
United Nations Declaration on Rights of Indigenous Peoples, 255

United Nations Universal Declaration of Human Rights, 190
United States. *See also* American(s)
abortion rights, 189
American dream, 218–220
automobile industry, 124
balanced reciprocity in, 125–126
baseball players, 274
beef industry, 109–111
capitalism in, 132, 134–136
class system, 224–228
colonial history, 305–307
diversity in, 14–15
elites, 14
English only campaign, 90
family system, 31
foreign born population, 258
gender relations in, 188–189
globalization and, 15
Hurricane Katrina, 226, 245
immigration policy, 212–213
immigration to, 256–260
income inequality in, 225
language pronunciation, 86
life changes, 334
middle class expansion, 235–236
middle class identity, 227
pollution and, 328
polygamy in, 164–165
racism in, 243–245
social hierarchy, 260
social relationships in, 84
women's status in, 188–189
United States Agency for International Development (USAID), 317
Universal grammar, 74*g*
Untouchables, 231
Urbanization
migration and, 322
population pressures, 324–327
social associations and, 323
USAID. *See* United States Agency for International Development

Vaisyas, 231
Valckenier, Adriaan, 296
Values
Chinese, 259
cultural context, 34–35
defined, 32*g*
political organization and, 194
Varna, 231
Venezuela, Yanomamo of, 183, 205
Violence. *See also* Warfare
band societies, 201
ethnic, 252–253
Vitalistic prophecies, 280–281
VOC. *See* Dutch East India Company
Vocabulary, 86–87, 88
Vodou doll, 274
Vogel, Craig M., 137
Voluntary minorities, 260

War, 201*g*
Warfare. *See also* Violence
function, 205
tribal, 204–206
Yanomamo, 205–206
Warner, W. Lloyd, 58
Water ownership, 120–121
Waters, Tony, 40
Wealth
accumulated, 225
Asante state, 194–195
colonial, 296
defined, 221*g*
European desire for, 290–291
gospel of, 235–236
nation-state, 316
population density and, 326–327
prestige and, 222
production of, 221–222
Weber, Max, 32, 223
Weiner, Annette, 184
Weinreich, Max, 80
Wesch, Michael, 7
Western Apache, 70, 78*m,* 79
White, Margaret Bourke, 6
Whorf, Benjamin Lee, 82
Widowhood, 1
Wilson, Charles, 194, 196, 211
Winthrop, John, 298–299
Witchcraft, 277*g*
Wodaabe of Niger, 151
Women
agriculture industrialism and, 186–187
American, 188–189
anthropologists, 55–56
in China, 325
child rearing obligations, 181
colonialism and, 184
in Congress, 189
descent through, 159
dress, 333
food contribution, 185–186
genital mutilation, 189–191
Hindi and, 77
in horticulture societies, 183–184
in India, 150, 153–154
infanticide by, 205–206
initiation rights, 190
labor and, 186–189
marriage responsibilities, 144
in matrilineal groups, 160
men's control over, 176
MNC employees, 321–322
Ndembu puberty rites, 29
Nukumanu, 184–185
in pastoral societies, 185–186
in patrilineal groups, 159
political power of, 196
rites of passage, 179, 190
sexuality, 174–177
social class and, 228
solidarity of, 205
subordination of, 180–181
Turkish, 133–134
wages paid to, 187
witchcraft and, 277
work requirements, 122–123
working outside home, 155
Word-Faith movement, 264–265
The World Is Flat (Friedman), 334
Workers. *See* Labor
World Bank, 255, 316
World War II
balance of power changes, 306–307
decolonization following, 306–307
political instability following, 330
Wovoka, 279–280

Xanith of Oman, 171

Yanomamo of Venezuela
gender relations, 183
portrayal of, 63
territory, 205*m*
warfare, 205–206
Yarahmadzai of Baluchistan, 101
Yoruba of Nigeria, 196
You Owe Yourself a Drink (Spradley), 57
Yugoslavia, ethnic violence in, 252–253
Yunus, Muhammad, 318

Zaloom, Caitlin, 7
Zedong, Mao, 229
Zinacantan, Mexico, 187